Using

T...orld
V...eb,
Se...ition

Using

The World Wide Web,

Second Edition

— David Wall —

with
Karen Cooper
Dave Gibbons
Gregory J. Hathaway
Jim Minatel
John Taschek

Using the World Wide Web, Second Edition

Library of Congress Catalog No.: 95-71753

ISBN: 0-7897-0645-8

98 97 96   6 5 4 3 2 1

Interpretation of the printing code: the rightmost double-digit number is the year of the book's printing; the rightmost single-digit number, the number of the book's printing. For example, a printing code of 96-1 shows that the first printing of the book occurred in 1996.

Screen reproductions in this book were created using Collage Plus from Inner Media, Inc., Hollis, NH.

Composed in *ITC Century*, *ITC Highlander*, and *MCPdigital* by Que Corporation.

Credits

President
Roland Elgey

Publisher, New Technologies
Stacy Hiquet

Title Manager
Jim Minatel

Editorial Services Director
Elizabeth Keaffaber

Managing Editor
Sandy Doell

Director of Marketing
Lynn E. Zingraf

Senior Series Editor
Chris Nelson

Acquisitions Manager
Cheryl D. Willoughby

Product Director
Benjamin Milstead

Production Editor
Danielle Bird

Copy Editors
Kelli M. Brooks
Noelle Gasco
Nanci Sears Perry
Heather Kaufman Urschel

Assistant Product Marketing Manager
Kim Margolius

Technical Editors
Alfonso Hermida
Chris Nelson
J. Michael Roach

Figure Specialist
Nadeem Muhammed

Acquisitions Coordinator
Ruth Slates

Operations Coordinator
Patricia J. Brooks

Editorial Assistant
Andrea Duvall

Book Designer
Ruth Harvey

Cover Designer
Dan Armstrong

Production Team
Steve Adams
Claudia Bell
Joan Evan
Bryan Flores
Jason Hand
Michelle Lee
Julie Quinn
Bobbi Satterfield
Chris VanCamp
Paul Wilson
Jody York
Karen York

Indexer
Mary Jane Frisby

For my family.

About the Authors

David Wall works as a freelance writer in Charlottesville, Virginia, where he writes mainly about Internet and World Wide Web issues. He's written for the *Wall Street Journal*, the *Washington Post*, the Bloomberg Business News global information service, and several book publishers. He now focuses his attention on the personalities of the people behind the Web's great publishing ventures. David also spends time bicycling and playing with hypertextual literary analysis.

with

Karen Cooper is a 1993 graduate of the University of Missouri-Columbia with degrees in Electrical and Computer Engineering. She started using the Internet while she was in college and continues to browse on a regular basis. She currently is a Staff Developer for a Communications software company. When not developing course work or teaching, she enjoys reading, running, and hanging out with her husband and/or their two cats.

Dave Gibbons is a former technical trainer and writer for DATASTORM TECHNOLOGIES in Columbia, Missouri, and LaserMaster Technologies in Eden Prairie, Minnesota. He began his professional writing career in chilly Cando, North Dakota, at age 16. Now a freelance writer and consultant, Dave spends much of his free time rock climbing on the Internet.

Gregory J. Hathaway is a computer analyst employed by Rockwell in Cedar Rapids, IA. He is Rockwell's Webmaster, responsible for selection, implementation, and training of Web tools on more than 4,000 computers. He has 15 years of experience which includes systems analysis, supercomputer programming, and product database management development.

Jim Minatel is a Title Manager working for Que. His areas of expertise include the Internet and new technologies. He is the author of Que's *Easy World Wide Web with Netscape* and has contributed to several other books. Before coming to Que, he developed college math texts, earned a MS in Mathematics from Chicago State University, and a BA in Mathematics and Physics from Wabash College.

John Taschek is currently Senior Analyst with *PC Week*, covering client/server database systems. He got his start in internetworking technologies at The Source, the first mainstream online service, which was acquired by CompuServe Inc. in 1989. He has held contractor positions at the Department of Housing and Urban Development, where he helped plan and implement its wide-area email system, and where he helped integrate the Windows version of its LAN-based email system. He has also been a technical reviewer for Ziff-Davis Press, most recently reviewing Frank Derfler and Les Freed's *Building the Information Highway*. Before coming to *PC Week*, he spent two and a half years at *PC/Computing* magazine as a technical editor and manager of the magazine's performance labs.

Acknowledgments

This book represents a collaboration of the sort that's bound to become more common as the Internet grows. As I worked here in Charlottesville, Karen Cooper, Dave Gibbons, Gregory Hathaway, Jim Minatel, and John Taschek each wrote their chapters in their own homes and offices—many of them far from me and our editors at Que. The Internet and other communications technologies render geography obsolete, and make it possible for Que to "assemble" the team of talented writers that wrote this book.

Jim Minatel and Cheryl Willoughby launched the project—approved an outline, acquired authors, and made sure the manuscript was written by deadline. The story doesn't end there. Once the chapter manuscripts found their ways to Que, a world-class group of editors and production experts went to work. Benjamin Milstead checked each chapter for coherence and logic. Noelle Gasco, Kelli Brooks, Nanci Sears Perry, and Heather Kaufman Urschel painstakingly examined grammar and style. Ruth Slates coordinated the technical edits: J. Michael Roach verified the technical accuracy of this book's contents—including every URL—and Alfonso Hermida and Chris Nelson pitched in their technical expertise. Danielle Bird guided each element of the book through the editorial process and gave the book its final read. Andrea Duvall assisted by performing a number of tasks for the team. Design, Layout, and Illustration performed magic on the text and illustrations, making this book visually stunning as well as content-rich. Proofreaders gave the book its final polish by scrutinizing its design, grammar, and spelling.

Additionally, I'd like to thank my family and friends for their help during the course of this project. The members of my family don't know the first thing about the Web (yet), but they've been completely behind my writing. Adam Bergman, Adam Bernstein, Beau Bonner and Ellen Marcus each offered their own isotope of friendship to me as my work on this book progressed.

I owe special thanks to Bryan and Suzanne Pfaffenberger and their family. Bryan, a seasoned author of all kinds of books, offered sage advice on many aspects of this book. His influence permeates my chapters. He and the members of his family are some of the kindest people I've met.

While you're browsing the Web, please stop by my home page (**http:// www.comet.net/personal/wall/home.htm**) or send me an email at **davidw@comet.net**.

David Wall
Charlottesville, Virginia
November 1, 1995

We'd Like To Hear from You!

As part of our continuing effort to produce books of the highest possible quality, Que would like to hear your comments. To stay competitive, we *really* want you, as a computer book reader and user, to let us know what you like or dislike most about this book or other Que products.

Our Internet site is at **http://www.mcp.com/que;** Macmillan Computer Publishing also has a forum on CompuServe (type **GO QUEBOOKS** at any prompt) through which our staff and authors are available for questions and comments. You can also snailmail your comments, ideas, or suggestions for improving future editions to the address below, or send us a fax at (317) 581-4663.

In addition to exploring our Web site and forum, please feel free to contact me personally to discuss your opinions of this book: I'm **bmilstead.que.mcp.com** on the Internet, and **102121,1324** on CompuServe.

Thanks in advance—your comments will help us to continue publishing the best books available on computer topics in today's market.

Benjamin Milstead
Product Director
Que Corporation
201 W. 103rd Street
Indianapolis, Indiana 46290
USA

Contents at a Glance

Contents

Introduction

You've no doubt heard of the World Wide Web. Maybe you've seen something about it on TV. Or maybe your boss or a consultant has decided that someone in your company needs to get on the Web and you are the chosen one. Or maybe your third grader came home from school and told you how her class is having fun exploring cyberspace on the Web. Whatever the case, the Web has become a part of our pop culture and now you need to learn the ins and outs.

The Web is huge, and growing fast. There are literally millions of pages on the Web (Chapter 1 explains the term "pages" and some other Web terms). There's no way that anyone could find his or her way around the Web without a little help. Consider this. Most people can make toast if given a loaf of bread and a toaster. And most adults can find their way to the local grocery to buy the loaf of bread or a department store to buy the toaster.

Imagine that instead of a local grocery, you need to do your shopping in a superstore the size of a few dozen football stadiums. The store carries five million items from aardvarks to zener diodes. There are over a hundred thousand aisles in the store and nothing is arranged in any logical way. You don't have a map to the store and there's no one to help you. All you have is a cart with a few strange buttons labeled URL (not to be confused with your Uncle Earl, but pronounced the same way), Home (I just got here, why would I go home?), Forward, and Back (one step forward and two steps back). On top of that, the grocery cart (with wheels that lock and point the wrong way for no apparent reason) comes with no directions.

Welcome to the Web. How do you find anything useful? With a little help and a lot of luck! You may find a few neat things along the way, but it will take much longer than it should and your finds will be random. If you're looking for something in particular, chances are you won't find it. And until you learn how to use the cart, there's not much you can do to gather a few items.

What makes this book different?

Many books about the Web exist. So why read this book instead of one of the other choices? Because of its approach. This book gives you a brief introduction on how to use your Web browser like a grocery cart. Pretty soon, you'll be strolling along the Web aisles and gathering the goodies you need. This book shows you all the basics that you need to know to get the essential Web software and to find some useful Web sites.

It doesn't matter which Web browser you use; like grocery carts, they are all mostly the same (we'll try to steer you clear of the ones with broken wheels). We're going to use the browser called Netscape Navigator for the examples in this book, but you can use any browser you want—you'll see that the Web looks almost the same no matter which browser you use.

This book guides you to the most popular and useful places on the Web. While there are millions of pages and hundreds of thousands of servers, this book focuses on places that should be of interest to most readers. Very few people have a need for aardvarks and zener diodes. But most people can think of something in arts, business, sports, entertainment, and even computers that they want or need. This book covers hundreds of the best and most popular sites on the Web.

This book concentrates on the software and Web pages that will be most useful to casual Web users. If you want to learn how to get started on the Web and see how it can be useful to you, this is the book to read. We'll leave out all the gory technical details of software and skip the Web pages that would only be of interest to specialists in aardvarkology and zener diodes.

Finding good pages that other people have put on the Web is one thing. But perhaps the most exciting thing about the Web is how easy it is to create your own Web pages. Creating Web pages isn't brain surgery. In fact, if you can use a word processor you can make Web pages. With this book, you'll learn just how easy it is.

How this book is put together

A guidebook isn't of much use if the reader being guided can't find a way through it. So, this book is split into two very easy to recognize parts. The first part explains what the Web is and how to use some simple Web browsing software. The second part lists the best places on the Web for you to start exploring and searching.

Here is a chapter-by-chapter breakdown of what to expect—along with a brief description of each chapter:

- Chapter 1, "What Is the World Wide Web?" gives you a no-nonsense, no-hype look at what the Web is and what you can do with it.

- Chapter 2, "Browsing the World Wide Web," shows how to use a Web browser, using the very popular Netscape program as an example.

- Chapter 3, "How To Create a Web Page with HTML," demonstrates how you can create your very own Web pages using a few simple commands. You can put these pages on the Web for others to see.

- Chapter 4, "Web Page Editors," looks at a few programs that simplify making Web pages of your own.

- Chapter 5, "Art and Music," lists and describes the best Web sites for many fields of artistic expression including painting, sculpture, photography, and performing arts such as theatre and music.

- Chapter 6, "Business and Employment," is a one-stop resource for finding major corporate resources on the Web. (If the company you're looking for does business in one of the categories covered in the other chapters of this book, look there first. For example, Microsoft is covered in Chapter 7 because it's a computer business and CBS is listed in Chapter 19 because its major business is television.) Look here for coverage of corporate giants like MasterCard, Ford Motor Company, and Wal-Mart. And if you're looking for a new job (or have a job to advertise), employment resources are covered here too.

- Chapter 7, "Computer Hardware and Software Resources," covers one of the biggest areas on the Web. Naturally, since Web users have access to computers, there are a lot of computer resources on the Web. We'll look at the best hardware sites, the best places to find software and software information for business and pleasure, and the best places to buy computer equipment. (Because there is so much computer information about the Internet and Web, we've made those topics into a separate chapter. See Chapter 11.)

- Chapter 8, "Education," lists and describes great resources for parents, teachers, and students.

- Chapter 9, "Government," looks at some of the most popular and useful government sites—mostly at the national level—and the branches of government.

- Chapter 10, "Health and Medicine," examines sites that healthcare professionals and people with a general interest in health and medicine will find interesting.

- Chapter 11, "Internet and Web Information," is the chapter to look at for all the best sites about the Internet and Web. We'll look at software for connecting to the Internet and Web, online services, Internet service providers, and other related Web pages.

- Chapter 12, "News, Politics, and Current Events," covers these popular topics. Because of the immediacy of the Web, you can always get up-to-the-minute information on news stories, events, and politics.

- Chapter 13, "Publishing: Books and Magazines," examines a new sort of publishing—the electronic medium of the Web. We'll also look at traditional print publishers that have set up shop on the Web as well as new publishers whose home is the Web.

- Chapter 14, "Religion," details sites where you can explore the many religions of the world. The emphasis here will be on a breadth of coverage that looks at mainstream, as well as lesser-known religions.

- Chapter 15, "Recreation and Hobbies," looks at sources for some of the most popular recreations and hobbies. While we can't cover every possible recreation and hobby, we'll look at broad categories including cooking, exercise, collecting, games, and more.

- Chapter 16, "Science," looks at some general interest science topics that most people can relate to. You'll find sources for NASA space photos, the environment, and the latest advances in engineering and transportation. You'll also discover sites on the Web that keep you informed of local and global weather conditions.

- Chapter 17, "Shopping," is a look at places to buy things directly on the Web. This chapter presents areas that are set up as shopping malls and department stores with a variety of sellers and products. You'll also find popular specialty stores that have a handful of unique services or goods.

- Chapter 18, "Sports," looks at all the major professional sports on the Web and popular collegiate and amateur sports sites. It lists sites that are major sources of information about any sport in addition to specialty sites that focus on one sport.

- Chapter 19, "Television and Movies," looks at the many major television networks and movie studios that have a presence on the Web. You'll also see some television shows and movies that have their own Web pages.

- Chapter 20, "Travel," wraps up the book with a look at sites that highlight travel destinations, how to get there, and what to do when you arrive. You'll also see geography sites listed here.

How do I use this book?

You can dip into this book at the point you need help—you don't have to read from page one to the end if you don't want to.

There are a number of ways for you to find information. There's a detailed Table Of Contents—in most cases you'll be able to skim through this and find exactly where to go. There's a thorough index at the back of course, to help you jump directly to a page.

It's a good idea to spend a few minutes just leafing through the book, finding out what's there. That way, when you find yourself stuck in the depths of the Web, you'll have an idea of where to go to find the directions you need.

Information that's easy to understand

This book uses a number of special elements and conventions to help you find information quickly—or to skip things you don't want to read.

Web addresses are all in **bold type,** like this: **http://www.mcp.que/que**. Information that you type also appears in **bold type**.

Throughout this book, we use a comma to separate the parts of a menu command. For example, to start a new document, you choose File, New. That means "Open the File menu, and choose New from the list."

If you see two keys separated by a plus sign, such as Ctrl+X, that means to press and hold the first key, press the second key, and then release both keys.

TIP   **Tips either point out information easily overlooked or help you** use your software more efficiently, such as through a shortcut. Tips may help you solve or avoid problems.

CAUTION   **Cautions warn you about potentially dangerous results. If you** don't heed them, you could unknowingly do something harmful.

Q&A   *What are Q&A notes?*

Q&A notes appear as questions and answers. We try to anticipate user questions that might come up and provide answers to you here.

 Plain English, please!

These notes define technical terms or computer jargon.

Sidebars are interesting related bits of information

Sidebars include information that's relevant to the topic at hand, but not essential. You might want to read them when you're not online.

Here you may find more technical details, or interesting background information.

1

What Is the World Wide Web?

● **In this chapter:**

- **What is the World Wide Web and what can it do?**

- **The Web can educate and entertain as well as give career assistance**

- **Learn how to gain access to the Web via online services like Prodigy and America Online, as well as by means of Internet Service Providers**

- **Get a taste of the Web's direction, and catch a glimpse of what the Web will be like in a year or so**

Imagine a single resource for multimedia information and high-quality entertainment. That's the World Wide Web. This globally acclaimed phenomenon is changing our culture as much as radio and television once did. . . . . ➤

Congratulations! You've taken an interest in the World Wide Web, an information resource that has already begun to take the world by storm. That's not surprising, since the Web offers professional, educational, commercial, and entertainment resources that rival—and, in many cases, exceed—those available in other media. Once you're on the Web, you can use and enjoy information from all over the world, without leaving the chair in front of your computer. For less than the cost of cable television each month, you can browse online museums in Paris, play games on computers in Chicago, learn Japanese from residents of Tokyo, and compare vacation spots in the Caribbean, all in the same evening!

How does the Web work?

On a literal level, the Web is a huge collection of computer files scattered across the Internet—more than two million of them, with more being added all the time. These files contain information of all sorts, including sounds, videos, and still graphics. The Web presents this huge collection of information in a way that makes it easy to access and use.

What's unique about the Web, though, is its use of **hypertext** and other hypermedia. In a hypertext system, certain highlighted words and phrases are connected to entirely different documents. The highlighted words may be underlined, or appear in a color different from that of the rest of the text, or both. These highlighted words and phrases are called **hypertext links**—or **hyperlinks** (or even just **links**) for short. You can choose to follow the hypertext links, or ignore them and continue reading the document in which they appear. If you follow a hyperlink, you'll see a new document, which may contain more hyperlinks.

A Web page put together by your employer, for instance, might have hyperlinks to Web resources of use to people in your line of work. Those resources, in turn, might have links to the personal pages (called **home pages**) of the people who maintain the resources, and the home pages might contain hyperlinks to sites related to the hobbies of their owners. Web's hypertext design makes it easy and fun to explore the available information resources. In the next chapter you'll learn more about exploring the Web—a process called **browsing**.

66 *Plain English, please!*

The Web is a **hypertext** system, that is, it's not organized in a linear way like a traditional book or other presentation. The Web has no "beginning" and no "end." It's a cloud of information through which you can make your way however you want.

If you've used a dictionary, you've used a hypertext system; the cross-references in definitions constitute hyperlinks (see *goat*, see *conundrum*). The Windows Help system also is a hypertext system, since clicking highlighted words and phrases brings up documents related to those passages.

On the Web, passages that lead to other Web pages are called **hyperlinks**. Hyperlinks can be words or pictures. When you click a hyperlink with your mouse, you "follow" that hyperlink; you call up the document to which it has been attached.

A **home page** is a Web page that serves as the main Web presence for an entity—a person or an organization. Sometimes, the term also applies to the main page in a collection of related Web documents. Personal home pages usually contain information about their owners, including occupation, interests, a photograph, and other information, such as the data on a resumé. Organizational home pages include links to the organization's other Web documents. 99

How is the Web different from the Net?

You've probably heard of, and maybe even used, the global system of computer networks called **the Internet**. Though the Web uses the Internet to store and transmit its pages, the Web and the Internet are not the same thing. The Web is one of several features of the Internet. Other systems that run on the Internet include UseNet (a collection of topical discussion groups called **newsgroups**), **FTP** (File Transfer Protocol—a means of sending and receiving files via the Internet), **Gopher** (an old-fashioned tool for exploring hyperlinked information that provided some of the groundwork for the Web), and **email** (which allows you to communicate with other Internet users).

One of the nice things about the Web is that it does a good job of integrating many of these other systems on the Internet. You can examine the contents of a newsgroup, send email, download a file, or browse a Gopher menu with the same tools you use to navigate the Web.

Regarding the Web as the Net's killer app

Experts say the Web is the Internet's killer app—the application that draws lots of people to the Internet and motivates them to learn how to use it. The experts compare the Web to the word-processing and spreadsheet software that inspired hundreds of thousands of people to acquire and learn how to use personal computers in the early 1980s.

Unlike the unadorned Internet, with its cryptic command prompts and arcane menus that you must navigate with a keyboard, the Web is user-friendly; it has an easy, graphical interface that you manipulate with a mouse. Figure 1.1 shows a screen from Gopher. Figure 1.2 shows a page from the Web.

Fig. 1.1
A Gopher interface like those used to navigate the Internet before the Web came along.

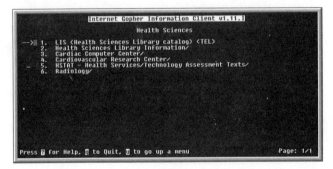

Fig. 1.2
A Web page—much friendlier and more visually appealing than the Gopher interface.

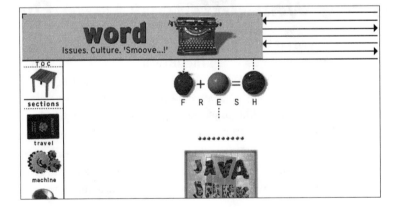

Experts also credit the Web's seamless integration of multimedia with its soaring popularity. Modern people, used to entertainment in the forms of shatteringly clear sound from compact disc players and extravagant television productions, aren't willing to put up with command prompts for long. The Web caters to this yearning for a multimedia presentation of information.

Great, but what can I do with it?

A more apt question is, "What can't I do with the Web?" Pretty much anything you can do with your computer alone, you can do five times better with the Web. The Web opens the information resources of the world to you, your family, your company, and your friends. Never again will you reach for the encyclopedia or the financial pages of the newspaper—or spend hundreds of dollars on educational CD-ROMs for the kids. Instead, you'll turn to the Web for the up-to-the-minute information you need.

Doing work on the Web

The Web is packed with resources for busy professionals who need current information about dozens of subjects. The Web community provides fantastic resources on virtually every subject, from equity quotes to the weather at your organization's branch office on another continent. Take a look at the Internal Revenue Service's Web site, shown in figure 1.3. Tax forms aren't fun, but they're at least easy to get on the Web. You'll be able to get precisely the forms you need without trekking all over town to three different post offices and a library. See Chapter 9 to learn more about government sites that can give you all the information you need this easily.

Additionally, many merchants have established shops on the Web. Usually, they display their wares, either in a searchable text-based catalog or in a series of graphical pages, and allow you to examine them. When you're ready to order, you either call a telephone number or send your credit-card number via a secure connection that prevents ne'er-do-wells from stealing it. See Chapter 17 to learn more about shopping on the Web.

Fig. 1.3
The Web page of the
U.S. Internal Revenue
Service makes tax forms
available online.

Uniform Resource
Locator (URL)

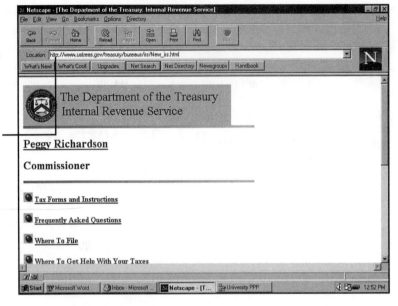

66 *Plain English, please!*

What is that ugly string of characters in the box at the top of the screen in
figure 1.3. It's a **Uniform Resource Locator (URL)**—the "address" Web
browsers use to find information on the Web. You're likely to see URL
spelled out as *Universal* Resource Locator in some publications. A URL
(pronounced you-are-ell, or, less frequently, "earl") describes the filename
of a resource, the machine on which it resides, the directory in which it's
kept, and the scheme used to transport it across the Internet. Let's examine
the IRS URL in figure 1.3.

The URL is **http://www.ustreas.gov/treasury/bureaus/irs/
New_irs.html**. That means the resource is a file called New_irs.html, which
is in a directory called /treasury/bureaus/irs/ on the machine called
www.ustreas.gov. The http://, which you'll see in front of most Web URLs,
means the file should be sent over the Internet with the HyperText Transport Protocol (HTTP).

How do you use URLs? You'll learn more about them in the next chapter,
but you should understand that you can enter them into your browser and
instruct your browser to find the resources they describe. Essentially, this
book is a directory of URLs: if you see a description of a resource you like,
enter its URL into your browser and see it for yourself. 99

CAUTION

Lots of Web merchants *don't* use secure servers, meaning they offer no means of preventing thieves from stealing your credit card number and committing fraud. Unless a merchant's site says it is secure—and you believe it—don't send your credit card number over the Web! Instead, phone in your order, or, as an incentive for the merchant to improve security, shop somewhere else.

That's just the beginning. Before long, the governments of the world will approve a secure online currency system that will allow you to buy and sell things on the Web much easier. Imagine posting a page that shows a picture of a car you want to sell and lists its features and price. With a mouse-click, a buyer could transfer electronic funds from his account to yours, and claim the title to the car. Some experts say the age of widespread electronic commerce is less than five years away.

Learning on the Web

The Web provides you with an electronic schoolhouse, with classrooms for learners of all levels. On the Web, you'll find everything from an introductory guide to jungle ecology to the searchable card catalog of the Library of Congress in Washington, D.C. Combined with other capabilities of the Internet—email, in particular—the Web can serve as the textbook and chalkboard for a variety of virtual courses.

Look at Nicolas Pioch's WebMuseum, an educational tool for people of all ages (see fig. 1.4). Its URL is **http://www.cnam.fr/louvre/**. An avid art fan, Pioch has collected hundreds of famous works of art and put them on the Web for all to enjoy. Furthermore, he's included a wonderful art-history tutorial that teaches the key points of various styles of art. His site is both content-rich and informative, qualities that rarely occur simultaneously in relatively expensive CD-ROMs. Check out Chapter 5; it lists many more sites for art-lovers.

Having fun on the Web

The Web isn't all work, by any means. It's a product of the academic and commercial computing community—a culture rife with pranksters, hams, and amateur comedians—and, therefore, it possesses a playful spirit that other media usually lack. Nowhere but on the Web will you find humor that ranges from the hilarious (the Shakespearean Insult Server) to the almost surreal (Joe's Couch Rating Page, on which Joe provides reviews of his friends' couches).

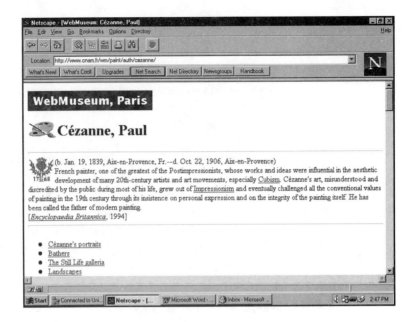

Take a look at the Riddler (see fig. 1.5). Its URL is **http://www.riddler.com/**. The Riddler is a game you play by solving word games, traversing the Web to find clues. You can spend hours trying to solve the problems, and if you're good, you can pick up a cool $500 cash. Also check out the Internet Underground Music Archive (IUMA). Its URL is **http://www.iuma.com/**. IUMA serves as a repository for the music of garage bands that haven't made the big time yet—you can actually download their songs and play them on your computer. Granted, lots of these bands haven't made it out of the garage for good reason, but browsing their work is a great way to blow an afternoon. See Chapter 5 to learn more about what music sites are out there.

Contributing to the Web

The Web isn't like television; it's a two-way medium. You can publish your own information on the Web almost as easily as you can examine other people's information. You may have heard about home pages, Web pages people and organizations create to tell the world about themselves and their interests (you'll learn more about home pages in the next chapter). Individuals also create and post pages about their hobbies and professions, making their knowledge available to people with similar interests. The ability for individuals with minimal time, money, and technical skill to publish information on the Web makes it a wonderful community of information-sharers. You'll learn how to contribute to the Web in Chapters 3 and 4.

Fig. 1.5
The Riddler, a Web
puzzle.

Okay, how do I sign up?

Convinced the Web is for you? Great! You have three basic options in deciding how to get access to the Web. Each has advantages and disadvantages.

- **Access via an organization's system**. If you work for a large company, college, university, or other organization with an elaborate
computer network, you may be in luck. If the organization's network
interfaces with the Internet—and if your organization does business
electronically with people at distant locations, it probably does—you
may be able to use its connection to browse the Web at no direct cost to
you. Talk to your organization's information systems experts and ask
how you can access the Web. If that doesn't work out, your city or town
may have a low-cost local-access network—called a **freenet**—through
which you may be able to access the Web. Not many freenets offer Web
access, but it's worth asking about. Try inquiring at your community
library for information about a local freenet.

- **Online services**. Commercial services, such as America Online and the
Microsoft Network, offer a collection of services that includes access to
the Web. Typically, online services charge a monthly fee of about $10,
plus an hourly fee for usage beyond a certain number of hours.

This route is much more expensive than using an Internet service provider or an organization's system. On the other hand, online services offer excellent user support and, often, the ability for parents to block their children from using certain Web features.

- **Internet Service Providers**. Companies, such as Netcom, offer Internet and Web access but rarely offer anything extra. These no-frills services allow you to spend lots of time on the Web for little money, relative to online services like CompuServe. Internet service providers typically charge a monthly fee of $10-$20, which gets you an account from which you can browse the Web via SLIP, CSLIP, or PPP (you'll learn about these later in this chapter).

Using Direct Net and Web access

If you decide to connect to the Web via an Internet Service Provider (ISP) or by means of an organizational network, you'll probably save some money and have greater flexibility in deciding how to work with the Web and other parts of the Internet. On the other hand, you may need to have quite a bit more computer prowess than users of online services, as many Internet Service Providers and organizational networks provide little hand-holding and often leave you to your own devices when problems arise. This is changing though, as more ISPs offer technical support services.

SLIP, CSLIP, and PPP

If you opt to gain access to the Web with an Internet Service Provider, you'll probably get what's called a **dialup IP account**. Dialup IP accounts allow you to actually establish your personal computer as part of the Internet by calling another Internet computer with your modem.

 Plain English, please!

Dialup IP is a means of connecting a computer to the Internet—and the Web—by using a standard telephone line and a modem. Dialup IP uses one of three techniques to communicate Internet information across a telephone line: the Serial Line Internet Protocol (SLIP), Compressed SLIP (CSLIP), or Point-to-Point Protocol (PPP). Since Dialup IP makes your computer a part of the Internet, at least temporarily, you can access Web pages and other Internet resources.

Your computer needs a way to talk to the other Internet computer, though. That's where SLIP, CSLIP, and PPP come in. These three communications schemes take information from your computer, package it in a form that can be transmitted over a telephone line, and decode it when it reaches the other Internet computer. Your service provider will tell you which of the three communications protocols to use, and provide you with software to manage the protocol. You may be able to use Microsoft Windows 95's Dialup Networking feature, which supports PPP and may work with your service provider's system.

Q&A *Which is best, SLIP, CSLIP, or PPP?*

Technically, PPP makes it easier for you and your modem to negotiate the technical details of an Internet connection. On the other hand, you rarely have a choice of which protocol to use. If you're considering two service providers, one of which uses SLIP and one of which uses PPP, go with the PPP provider. Usually, though, you're stuck with what you can get. Just grin and remember that the differences among the three aren't enormous, and that most Internet Service Providers are migrating from SLIP and CSLIP to PPP.

This book focuses on direct Internet and Web access, since it's the most popular and fastest growing means of reaching the Web. It also allows you great flexibility in choosing your browser. You'll most likely want to use Netscape Navigator (available from Netscape Communications' home page, **http://home.netscape.com/**) or Microsoft Internet Explorer (available from the Microsoft Network home page, **http://www.home.msn.com/**.)

Netscape Navigator, since it's the most popular browser, is used for all the examples in this book. You'll find that if you can use Netscape—and you'll learn how to use it in Chapter 2—you can use any browser, since they all have similar designs and commands. The latest version of Netscape Navigator (usually called simply "Netscape") features support for reading Usenet news-groups and embedded Java applets, which you'll learn about later in this chapter.

Network access

The best way to access the Web is via a network connection, such as those found in many offices and other places of work. If your Local Area Network (LAN) has a connection to the Internet, you may be able to browse the

Web—and at much higher speed than over a telephone line. Check with your organization's computer and network specialists to see if you can run Web software on your computer.

Using online services

Online services constitute the fastest-growing means of accessing the Web. In fact, while such services once were isolated information systems, they now market themselves as entry points to the Web—meaning they cater directly to your interests. Though they're not cheap—you'll quickly use up your monthly allotment of time and start paying the extra-time fee—online services boast user-friendly access to the Web and give you access to technical support if you encounter problems.

Four major online services exist: America Online, CompuServe, Prodigy, and the upstart Microsoft Network. America Online is the most popular service, but Prodigy—the first commercial service to offer Web access—recently revamped its interface and the Microsoft Network promises to attract tens of thousands of Microsoft Windows 95 users (Windows 95 makes it easy to join the Microsoft Network). You'll have to decide which of the online services best fits your needs, or if an Internet Service Provider is more in line with your Web plans.

America Online

America Online (AOL) has more members than any other national online service, and for good reason; its interface is good-looking, fast, and generally easy to use. AOL's Web interface is the best of the four major online services. On top of AOL's exemplary Web browser, the service offers other Internet features, including UseNet newsgroups and email.

To get access to AOL, you need a copy of the company's starter kit, which you can get for free by calling 800-827-6364 and asking that a copy be sent to you. When you get the kit, run the setup program on the disk. The setup program will step you through the process of installing the AOL software on your hard disk and finding a local service telephone number. To use the Web with AOL:

1 Log in to AOL (type your password in the Password text box and click the Connect button). You'll see America Online's welcome screen.

2 Click the Internet Connection button to gain access to AOL's Internet gateway.

3 When you see the Internet Connection screen (see fig. 1.6), click the World Wide Web button to gain access to the Web. If you've never used the Web on AOL before, the service will download its browser (the program you use to navigate the Web) to your computer—a process that takes a few minutes for which you are not billed. Your AOL software sets up the browser automatically. The AOL home page viewed with the AOL browser is your entry point to the Web on AOL.

Fig. 1.6
The America Online
Internet Connection
screen.

World Wide
Web button

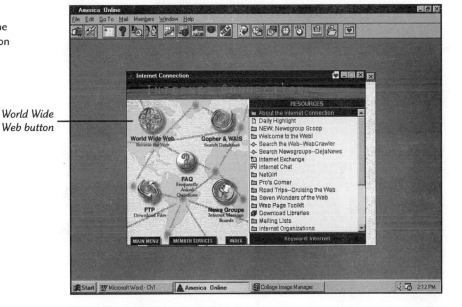

CompuServe

Once the belle of commercial online service users, CompuServe has fallen behind other services in popularity lately. It began to offer Web service only recently.

To acquire CompuServe software for free, call 800-848-8990 and request it. Your software will arrive in about a week and a half, if you're in the United States. Alternately, if you're in a hurry, go to your favorite software store and pay about $25 for a CompuServe Membership Kit, which includes some documentation for the service and the software.

Run the setup program that comes on the disk. This program will set up CompuServe's software on your computer, but will not sign you up to use the service. To do that, you must run the Membership Sign Up program that appears in your CompuServe program group after you run the setup program.

To use CompuServe, start the CompuServe Information Manager. This program won't connect you to CompuServe right away; you must first click the Connect button in the Connect to CompuServe dialog box. When your computer connects to CompuServe, you'll see the welcome screen.

To download CompuServe's Web software and access the Web:

1 Choose Services, Go and type **internet** in the dialog box. You'll see the Internet Services screen (see fig. 1.7). Here, you'll download the software you need to access the Web with CompuServe.

Fig. 1.7
The CompuServe Internet Services screen.

Direct Internet access (PPP)

2 Double-click the Direct Internet Access (Dial PPP) item in the menu.

3 In the Dial PPP dialog box, double-click the NetLauncher for Windows list item.

4 In the NetLauncher for Windows, double-click Download NetLauncher.

5 In the Download dialog box, select the Retrieve button. CompuServe's Web-access software will download to your computer.

6 Disconnect from CompuServe by choosing File, Disconnect from the menu bar.

7 Run the downloaded program CNL.EXE in your cserve\download directory. The program will decompress the CompuServe Web tools.

8 To browse the Web with CompuServe, start Spry Mosaic. A program called CompuServe Internet Dialer will start automatically, and dial in to your local CompuServe server. You'll see the CompuServe Web welcome page, as shown in figure 1.8.

Fig. 1.8
The CompuServe Web browser.

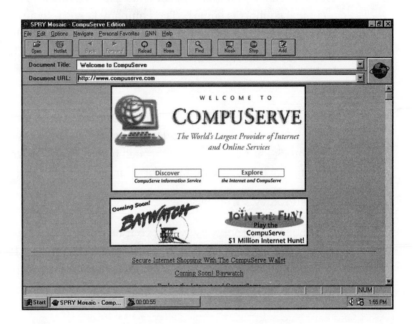

 TIP **If you've already installed Microsoft Windows 95, CNL.EXE will** replace a file called WINSOCK.DLL in your WINDOWS directory with its own version of the same file. This should not cause any problems, but if it does, download the CNLMOVE.EXE utility from the NetLauncher for Windows CompuServe screen—the same place you found NetLauncher—and run it. If you install NetLauncher before you install Windows 95, you'll have to download and run CNLMOVE.EXE before installing Windows 95 or you won't be able to use CompuServe's Web tools.

Note that you can't use the CompuServe Information Manager and Spry Mosaic at the same time. When running Spry Mosaic, you're using CompuServe as an Internet Service Provider running PPP.

Prodigy

Prodigy recently hired a lot of new programmers and instructed them to revamp this service into a Web-wise online powerhouse. The efforts of the new programming team are still underway, but already Prodigy has lost the archaic interface that characterized it for several years. Prodigy, like other online services, boasts email and UseNet newsgroups as well as Web access. Though some compatibility problems with Windows 95 exist, Prodigy's technical support is superb. The company keeps telephone hold times short. Prodigy's most attractive feature is that it allows subscribers some control over which users of a Prodigy account get Web access. That's an appealing feature for parents who want to keep their kids away from the Web's seamier side.

To acquire Prodigy software free of charge, call 800-776-3449 (800-PRODIGY) and ask for a membership kit. Run the setup program on the disk that comes with the kit—it will guide you through installing the program and getting a local access telephone number for your modem.

To use Prodigy's Web service:

1 Log in to Prodigy by typing your member ID and password (these came with your membership kit) into the marked boxes. Prodigy will prompt you for your credit card number and other information. When the service finishes collecting information, you'll see the Prodigy new member welcome screen.

2 Click the Web button at the bottom of the screen to access Prodigy's Web service.

   After clicking the Web button, you'll see the Web Browser screen. Be careful, this is something of a misnomer. You can't use the Web from this screen—you must establish that you want access to the Web and are willing to take responsibility for any unsettling material you find there.

3 Click the Browse the Web button. Prodigy will display a warning about the potentially offensive content of the Web.

4 Click the Choose Names button. Prodigy will display another warning.

5 Highlight your name and press Enter (if other people's names, such as those of your children, are listed, you can leave them unselected and your children will not be able to access the Web).

6 Highlight Go to World Wide Web and press Enter. You'll see the Web Browser page again. You won't have to deal with the name-selection process again.

7 Click the Browse the Web button again and you'll see Prodigy's Web browser (see fig. 1.9). That's your starting point for exploring the Web with Prodigy.

Fig. 1.9
The Prodigy Web browser.

The Microsoft Network

New on the online-service scene is The Microsoft Network (MSN), which is put together by the same folks who bring you Microsoft Windows 95 and Microsoft Word. Boasting almost seamless integration with the Windows 95 user interface and lots of appealing features, MSN suffers from a lack of **local servers** (the computers you dial in to with your modem to use the service). The servers that do exist, though, offer fast data-transfer rates (up to 28,800 bits per second). You may have to call a server 250 miles away to use MSN if you live in a rural area, but you'll swap data with it quickly. Microsoft is establishing more local servers all the time. In contrast, the other commercial services have mainly 14,400 bps modems. Rural towns often have still slower connections, making Web use a ponderous task.

Of the four major networks, MSN also is the easiest to join. Double-click the MSN icon on your Windows 95 desktop to run the setup program and join the network. In fact, other online services cried foul when they learned how easy it is for Windows 95 users to join MSN, claiming the desktop icon gave Microsoft an unfair competitive advantage. The U.S. Department of Justice investigated and found that Microsoft was within the law.

 TIP **MSN takes 24 hours to process your application, so you can't** access the service immediately after signing up. Run the setup program, and then try to access MSN the next day. Otherwise, you'll get an error message saying your computer can't connect to MSN.

To use MSN, double-click the same icon you double-clicked to join the network. When your modem connects to MSN, you'll see the welcome screen.

If you have installed Microsoft Plus! on your computer, you can double-click the icon labeled "The Internet" to start Microsoft Internet Explorer, the tool you'll use to browse the Web. Microsoft Internet Explorer appears in figure 1.10. Alternately, you can click the Categories button on the welcome screen, and then click the Internet Center button on the Categories screen. On the Internet Center screen, click the World Wide Web (WWW) button. Clicking the World Wide Web Button will start Microsoft Internet Explorer if it's on your computer, or install it otherwise.

Fig. 1.10
Microsoft Internet
Explorer, The Microsoft
Network's Web
browser.

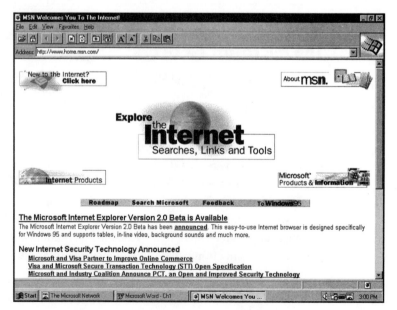

Microsoft Internet Explorer, now available in version 2.0, supports more fancy features than other services' browsers. Microsoft Internet Explorer supports tables, background sounds, video, and other attractive features. Still, Microsoft Internet Explorer is technologically behind Netscape Navigator, which you can use with a direct Internet connection such as that provided by CompuServe or an Internet Service Provider.

What will I be doing with the Web two years from now?

By no means is the Web a static medium. It's changing all the time. In fact, lots of Web users feel the Web today is where the personal computer was in 1984—pretty good, and very exciting, but not nearly realizing its potential. Within a couple of years, you'll be using the Web in an entirely different way—largely because of these emerging technologies.

Experiencing 3-D Virtual Reality

One faction in the Web community favors eliminating the two-dimensional Web page completely and replacing it with three-dimensional "rooms" or "worlds" you could navigate sort of like you navigate a real three-dimensional environment. Virtual reality hobbyists are developing a technology called **Virtual Reality Modeling Language (VRML)**, which may make three-dimensional Web browsing possible in the future. Figure 1.11 shows a typical VRML "world" viewed with a popular VRML browser called WorldView.

Using embedded applications

A team of programmers at Sun Microsystems, a respected designer of Internet computers and software, has introduced a scheme called **Java** that may soon allow Web page designers to include miniature programs in their pages. These mini-programs, called **applets**, will be able to handle such tasks as playing sounds or videos automatically when you access a Web page, or making a Web page perform like a spreadsheet, so the page can perform calculations automatically, without any assistance from you. Eolas is attempting to do much the same thing with their "Weblets" project, as is Ncompass with a project that takes advantage of Windows' Object Linking and Embedding (OLE) capabilities.

Fig. 1.11
A three-dimensional
VRML model of an
M.C. Escher structure,
viewed with
WorldView, a VRML
browser.

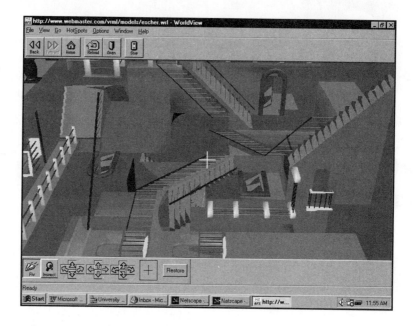

Java won't work without a browser with special features, but such browsers
are becoming more common all the time. The new version of Netscape
Navigator, version 2.0, supports Java. Additionally, Sun publishes its own
browser, called **HotJava**, that interprets Java instructions.

Browsing the World Wide Web

● **In this chapter:**

● **Acquire and learn to use a browser— the tool you'll use to explore the Web**

● **Learn to surf for both pleasure and business**

● **What else do you need to know about Uniform Resource Locators (URLs), the addresses browsers use to find Web resources?**

● **What are helper applications, and how do you use them?**

Access to the World Wide Web is your ticket to browse—to explore the global resources of the Web with your computer. Here is your first lesson in global information surfing . . . . ▶

O n the Web, browsing involves looking for information, not physical items like clothes, cars, or members of the opposite sex. You move from one bit of information to another, absorbing what you like and skipping the information you find irrelevant or boring. Note that "information" isn't just dry, functional data. It's entertaining material, too. On the Web, a sound file containing the theme song from "The Love Boat" qualifies as information as much as a breakdown of voting patterns. In any case, the Web lets you examine the information that's available and look deeper into subjects that appeal to you.

The Web's hypertext design makes browsing easy. If you're looking at someone's home page, and you read a sentence that says, "Click **here** to read about my vacation in Hawaii," with the word **here** highlighted as a hyperlink, you can click the highlighted word to read more about the page owner's vacation in Hawaii. On the Hawaiian vacation page, you might see links to other pages about Hawaiian fish or Hawaiian history. You can click those links to examine each of those topics further.

66 *Plain English, please!*

A **hyperlink** is any object, such as a word, phrase, or image, that calls another document (or another portion of the current document) to the screen. Hyperlinks are at the center of the Web's unique information-organization scheme. 99

In another situation, you might start a browsing session in Yahoo, a search tool you'll learn about in Chapter 11. Yahoo might show you two dozen links to sites related to soccer. After following a link to a site devoted to English soccer, you see a hyperlink to the Manchester United home page—a page for your favorite team! You might follow that link and discover game summaries, player biographies, and predictions, as well as links to other soccer-related resources. Since most Web pages have at least one hyperlink to another page, you can browse indefinitely.

The act of following hyperlinks from one page to another, either in search of specific information or for entertainment, often is called **surfing**. Some people think that moving from one bit of information to another simulates gliding around a wave on a surfboard. Don't think that surfing the Web is as much of a waste of time as channel surfing, though. You'll get much more out of the most aimless browsing session than from any time spent flipping through television channels.

What do Web browsers do?

The **Web** is a network that stores and distributes (shares) information in forms that all of its linked computers can use. A **Web browser** translates most of the information on the Web into a form that you, as a human being and not a computer, can interpret. It serves as an intermediary between you and the Web, translating your requests for information into commands the computers in the network can understand. You'll learn more about the various kinds of information on the Web in Part II, "Exploration and Discovery: The Best of the Web."

Note that the previous paragraph says that browsers translate most of the information on the Web. Though browsers can display several kinds of text and graphics easily, they need to work with other programs in order to interpret specialized kinds of information, such as sounds and video clips. These auxiliary programs are called, appropriately, **helper applications** or **helper programs**. Browsers send certain kinds of information to the helper apps for interpretation.

Before you begin to browse the Web with a browser, you have to do two things: acquire a browser and learn how to use it. This chapter teaches you to do both. You'll learn where to find the software and the basics of calling up Web documents with your browser. Though the interfaces and operating details of different companies' browsers vary, they're all basically the same. If you learn to use one, you'll be able to use any of the others. This chapter focuses on Netscape Navigator, the most popular browser by a wide margin.

How do I get a browser?

It's obvious that you'll have to get a browser and install it on your computer before you can use it. What's not so obvious is how you acquire it. You can buy some browsers at the store or by mail; others you can download for free on the Internet. Here's how and where to get the software, starting with Netscape Navigator.

Netscape Navigator

With more than 60 percent of the browser market to its credit, Netscape Navigator (usually called Netscape) boasts excellent technical features, good speed, and an intuitive user interface. Many Web sites take advantage of special Netscape capabilities by including elaborate tables, simple animations, and fancy formatting. The latest version of Netscape includes support for reading UseNet news, sending and receiving email, and supporting sites that contain Java applets.

Furthermore, Netscape Communications Corporation distributes Netscape free of charge on the Internet and Web—though you must pay to register the program if you use it for commercial purposes. Unless you have a really good reason to use another browser, you probably want to use Netscape.

The best way to acquire Netscape Navigator is to use File Transport Protocol (FTP). Windows 95 comes with a program that enables you to use FTP with a dial-in connection to the Internet. It's called FTP.EXE and it's in the WINDOWS folder.

FTP isn't much to look at. There's just a command line with an `ftp>` prompt. Here's how to use FTP to retrieve Netscape Navigator:

1 At the `ftp>` command line, type **open ftp.netscape.com**.

2 When prompted for your login ID, type **anonymous**.

3 Type your electronic mail address as your password.

4 Type **cd netscape**. Just as in DOS, this makes the Netscape directory the current directory.

5 Type **cd windows**.

6 Type **ls**. This is the UNIX equivalent of the DOS `DIR` command.

7 Look for a file called something like n32e20blj.exe (the exact file name probably will change by the time you read this as new versions come out). If you're not sure which file you need, download and read the readme.txt file (downloading instructions follow).

8 Type **get n32e20blj.exe**. Wait while the Netscape FTP site downloads the file to your computer. It will take several minutes.

 TIP **Netscape isn't just for Windows 95. Versions exist for Windows** 3.1, the Macintosh, and X Windows. You can get these versions at the Netscape FTP site, too.

Q&A ***This sounds like a Catch-22—I need to be in the Net to get these programs, but I need the programs to use the Net. What's up?***

You can get Netscape and other browsers with tools that come with Windows 95 if you have an Internet connection, which you'll need to browse the Web anyway. If you don't have an Internet connection yet, ask a friend to download the necessary programs for you, or go to a public terminal in a university computer lab or public library to download the programs you need.

If you already have Web access, or have a friend who does, you can download Netscape Navigator by clicking the Netscape Now! button on the Netscape home page (**http://home.netscape.com**).

The file n3212b6.exe is a self-extracting archive. All you have to do to install Netscape is run n3212b6.exe and follow the instructions that the setup program gives.

TIP **If you move n32e20blj.exe to its own temporary directory before** running it, you'll be able to easily delete the setup files after installation.

Microsoft Internet Explorer

The odds are excellent that you already have a Web browser installed on your computer. If you're one of the millions of people who bought the Microsoft Plus! Accessory kit for Microsoft Windows 95, you have a program called Microsoft Internet Explorer on your hard disk. It should be in the Programs/Accessories/Internet Tools folder on your Start menu. If you haven't seen the Internet Explorer icon (a globe with a magnifying glass over it) on any of your menus, try running a search for it. If that doesn't turn up anything, you didn't install Internet Explorer when you installed Microsoft Plus! Put your Microsoft Plus! floppy disk or CD-ROM disc in the appropriate drive on your computer, run the setup program, and make sure that you select the Internet Explorer check box.

If you don't have the Plus! Package, you can download Microsoft Internet Explorer via File Transport Protocol (FTP). Follow the directions in the Netscape Navigator section above for starting the Windows 95 FTP program, and then follow these steps:

1 At the `ftp>` command line, type **open ftp.microsoft.com**.

2 When prompted for your login ID, type **anonymous**.

3 Type your electronic mail address as your password.

4 Type **cd PerOpSys**. Just as in DOS, this makes the PerOpSys directory the current directory.

5 Type **cd Win_News**.

6 Type **ls**. This is the UNIX equivalent of the DOS `DIR` command.

7 Look for a file called `msie20.exe`.

8 Type **get msie20.exe**. Wait while the Netscape FTP site downloads the file to your computer. It will take several minutes.

If you already have Web access, or have a friend who does, you can download Microsoft Internet Explorer from a page on Microsoft's Web site (**http://www.microsoft.com/windows/software/iexplorer.htm**).

When you run msie10.exe on your computer, it will automatically unpack compressed files and set them up on your computer.

Other browsers

Netscape and Internet Explorer aren't your only browser options. Though the following browsers aren't as popular as the two you learned about before, they represent viable browser options.

- **NCSA Mosaic** is the browser that started it all. Developed by the National Center for Supercomputing Applications (NCSA) at the University of Illinois, Urbana-Champaign, the latest version of NCSA Mosaic offers support for hot formatting features, including tables. You can download NCSA Mosaic from **http://www.ncsa.uiuc.edu/SDG/Software/WinMosaic/General.htm#obtain**.

- **Quarterdeck Mosaic** is a commercial version of NCSA Mosaic. Developed by Quarterdeck Systems, the company famous for making the Desqview operating environment and the QEMM memory-management program, Quarterdeck Mosaic boasts a nifty object-oriented, drag-and-drop bookmark system. You have to buy this product in a store or by mail, though: it's not available as freeware or shareware. You'll pay about $30 for Quarterdeck Mosaic.

- **InterAp**, a new offering from California Software, has earned rave reviews from experts. Featuring a drag-and-drop bookmark system and a great deal of customization capability, InterAp may successfully challenge longer-standing Web browsers. InterAp (which comes with a UseNet newsreader, FTP client, and other Internet software) is a commercial product that retails for about $100.

- The Wollongong Group's **Emissary** browser boasts a highly integrated interface that includes a Web page editor, email, and newsgroups. Emissary also supports Object Linking and Embedding (OLE)— enabling you to easily share Web information with other applications— and has a highly customizable toolbar. You can get Emissary from Wollongong's Web site: **http://www.twg.com/emissary/eftp.html**.

Navigating with a browser

This section uses Netscape Navigator for purposes of illustration. Though other browsers have slight interface differences, you'll find that they all have similar ways of accomplishing various tasks related to navigating the Web. Figure 2.1 shows the Netscape Navigator interface.

Fig. 2.1
Netscape Navigator, the most popular Web browser. Most other browsers have similar interfaces.

Button bar─┐

Current URL─┘

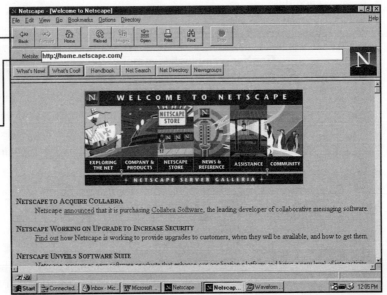

Duke of URL: More about Uniform Resource Locators (URLs)

Before you get too deeply involved in browsing the Web, you need to under-stand the addresses attached to every resource on the Web. The addresses, called **Uniform Resource Locators** (**URLs**, pronounced *you-are-ells* or, sometimes, *earls*) describe the file name of the resource, the directory and machine on which it's stored (every Internet machine has a name), and the method that should be used to transport the file across the Web to your browser. A typical URL looks like this:

http://www.rhodo.commcorp.com/web/html/salsa.html

That URL tells your browser to contact the machine www.rhodo.commcorp.com, look in the web/html/ directory, and retrieve the file salsa.html with the hypertext transport protocol (http). Other kinds of URLs tell your browser to send an electronic mail message, retrieve a story from a UseNet newsgroup, download a file via File Transfer Protocol (FTP), or browse information with Gopher, an obsolete Internet browsing tool. Figure 2.2 shows a Gopher site and Figure 2.3 shows an FTP site, both viewed with a Web browser. You'll encounter both of these kinds of sites in a typical browsing session, though Gopher sites are growing fewer in number each day.

 Plain English, please!

Gopher is an obsolete means of browsing the information on the Internet. Developed at the University of Minnesota (home of the Golden Gophers), Gopher relies upon nested subdirectories to organize information. Though Gopher is useful for organizing textual data, its capability to handle multi-media files is limited and it does not support hypertext. The Web has usurped Gopher as the dominant information-browsing tool on the Internet.

 Q&A *How do I access a particular URL?*

You can direct your browser to a URL in several ways. The most common way is to click a hyperlink, which tells your browser to display the resource at the URL contained in the hyperlink. If there's no handy hyperlink to the resource you want, most browsers let you enter URLs manually by typing them into a text box. This method is tedious—many URLs are quite long, and contain sequences of obscure characters. Usually, you can paste URLs copied from electronic mail messages or word-processing documents into the text box to save time and reduce the chance of error. Also, you can click the Open button and type or paste the URL into the dialog box—this method is rarely used because it's much easier to type or paste URLs into the box on the main screen.

Fig. 2.2
An FTP site viewed with a Web browser.

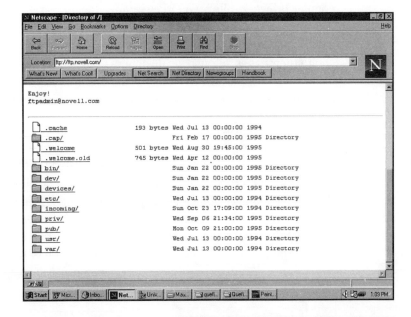

Fig. 2.3
A Gopher site viewed in a Web browser.

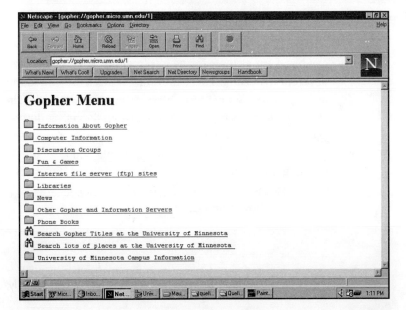

Following hyperlinks

The single most important thing to learn about your browser is the way it displays hyperlinks. Netscape Navigator and Microsoft Internet Explorer display their hyperlinks (both text and images) in blue, and underline hyperlinked text. NCSA Mosaic displays hyperlinks in green. All of the popular browsers allow you to customize the appearance of hyperlinks, so your browser may show them in an entirely different way. Additionally, new developments in HTML, the programming language Web publishers use to create their pages, allow page designers to designate the appearance of hyperlinked objects. Lately, many authors seem to be making their hyperlinks red, but another color may come into vogue in the future.

Following a hyperlink couldn't be simpler: just click it. Clicking a hyperlinked object will cause your browser to display the resource at the URL embedded in the hyperlink. Hyperlinks don't have to be words, either. Page authors— the people who create Web pages—can designate images as hyperlinks, too. Hyperlinked images appear as they would normally, but with a border the color of hyperlinked text around them. Figure 2.4 shows a hyperlinked image. You click a hyperlinked image—anywhere, not just on its border—to follow its hyperlink.

Fig. 2.4
A hyperlinked image. Note the border— which is optional, but which usually surrounds hyperlinked images.

A hyperlink doesn't have to be an entire image, either. Web page designers can break up a single image into regions, each of which is attached to a different hyperlink. These multilink images are called **imagemaps**, and they make possible some of the coolest pages on the Web. The White House Web site, for example, features an imagemap depicting downtown Washington, D.C. You can click different buildings on the map and see descriptions—on different Web pages—of the departments and bureaus that occupy each building. Imagemaps also make it possible for Web page authors to create Graphical User Interfaces (GUIs). Figure 2.5 shows the Microsoft home page, which uses imagemaps in this way.

Plain English, please!

An **imagemap** is an image that you can click in different places to follow different hyperlinks. Imagemaps enable Web page creators to develop intuitive graphical user interfaces for their pages—making them better looking, easier to use, and more accessible to people who speak languages other than that of the page creator.

Fig. 2.5
Imagemaps on the
Microsoft home page.

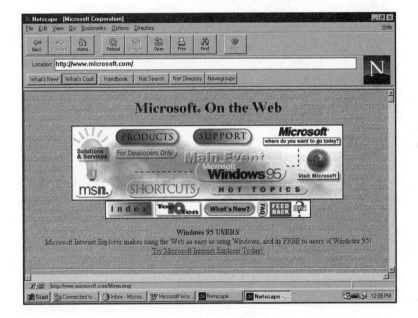

Hyperlinks don't have to lead to another document. They can lead to another point in the same document—a feature that's useful when navigating very long documents that would take many minutes to scroll through. Hyperlinks that lead to other points in the current document are called **local hyperlinks**; those that lead to other documents are called **remote hyperlinks**.

The Forward and Back Buttons

What happens when you click a hyperlink accidentally, or you click one intentionally and find that the new resource isn't what you wanted? You go back. Netscape makes this very easy; it has a Back button that returns you to the last URL you accessed. Netscape provides a Forward button, too. The Forward button undoes a click of the Back button, returning you to the resource that was displayed on your screen when you clicked the Back button.

If you want to go back or forward more than a step or two, you'll probably save time by using the history list. The history list, described in detail later in this chapter, allows you to choose from any of the URLs you've dealt with, either in the current browsing session or in the most recent browsing sessions.

Going Home

Sometimes, while browsing, you'll want to return to your home page (you'll read about home pages later in this chapter and in the next chapter). Instead of typing in your home page's URL or choosing it from a list of bookmarks or favorite places, you can click a special Home button in Netscape. Whenever you click the Home button, your browser will call up and display the page you've designated as your home page.

How do you make a page your home page? In Netscape, open the Options menu and choose Preferences. In the Options dialog box, choose Styles from the drop-down list at the top. Make sure the Home Page Location radio button is selected and enter the URL of your home page in the text box below that radio button.

 Plain English, please!

> A **home page** is a Web page designated as the main Web presence of a person, corporation, or other entity. Personal home pages typically contain a person's name, photograph, electronic mail address, and a list of hyperlinks the page's owner uses frequently or finds appealing.
>
> Corporate and organizational home pages serve both as a corporation's marketing presence on the Web and as a guide to the other Web pages associated with the corporation. The Microsoft Corporation home page, for example, includes links to Microsoft's software archives, Human Resources department, and technical support resources. Corporate home pages often also include links to directories of employees' personal home pages. 🙽🙽

Using other buttons

Netscape has other buttons that you won't use as frequently as the Forward, Back, and Home buttons, but which will be useful at different points in browsing sessions. Here's a brief summary of the function of each of the other buttons:

Button	Name	What it does
	Reload	Downloads the current page again. The Reload button comes in handy when a communications problem interrupts transmission of the page, or when a page—such as a stock-quote page—changes frequently.
	Images	Switches the display of images on and off. You may want to turn images off if you're on a modem connection slower than 14,400 bps.
	Open	Allows you to enter a URL in a dialog box instead of the Location box.
	Print	Sends the current document to your printer.
	Find	Searches for specific words in the current document. Use the Find button when you want to navigate large documents that do not include indexing—hyperlinks from one point in the document to another, as you'll learn later in this chapter.
	Stop	Interrupts the current transfer. Use the Stop button when you don't want to wait for all of the images on a Web page to download.

Using the history list

During a long browsing session, the odds are good you'll want to return to a site you visited earlier. There's a way to do that without clicking the Back button a dozen times.

Open the Go menu and pick the site you want from those listed. If you don't see the site you want:

1 Choose View History.

2 Highlight the resource you want.

3 Click Go To. The browser will call up that site. Remember that Netscape stores history only for the current browsing session. If you want Netscape to hold on to a URL longer, you'll need to make it a bookmark.

TIP   To save time, you can view your history list by clicking the down arrow at the right end of the Location box. Select the site you want from the list that drops down.

Bookmarks: Saving your place

Within minutes of beginning your first browsing session, you'll discover a resource you'll want to use again and again. Netscape allows you to add useful resources to lists so it's easy to visit them again later.

Let's say you're browsing and you happen across the Keirsey Temperament Sorter, a personality test that determines the kind of work you enjoy and the way you interact with other people. You take the test, and decide it would be fun to have your co-workers take it, too. They're not around, though (you were so engrossed in browsing, you missed the fact that they've all gone home for the day). You can make a bookmark for the site and call it up first thing in the morning.

Open the Bookmarks menu and choose Add Bookmark. This sequence will add the title of the current page to the list of bookmarks under the Bookmarks menu. To retrieve the marked resource again, all you need to do is open the Bookmarks menu and choose the title of the marked page from the drop-down menu.

Sometimes, a Web page creator will have attached a poor name to his or her page—one that won't mean much when it appears in you list of bookmarks. You can alter the name that appears in the bookmarks list.

1 Open the Bookmarks menu and choose View Bookmarks. Figure 2.6 shows the Bookmark List dialog box.

2 Select the name of the bookmark you want to change.

3 Click the Edit button. The Bookmark List dialog box will expand to the right, revealing more detail about the highlighted bookmark.

4 Modify the text in the Name field to suit you.

5 Click the Close button and Netscape will save the changes.

Fig. 2.6
The Bookmark List
dialog box.

To remove a bookmark from the list:

1 Open the <u>B</u>ookmarks menu and choose <u>V</u>iew Bookmarks.

2 Select the Edit button.

3 Highlight the title of the bookmark you want to eliminate.

4 Select the Remove Item button.

TIP **Whenever you see a site you like, add it to your bookmark list.**
You'll find that you can drive yourself crazy looking for a particular resource if you don't have its URL, so make life easy for yourself and add anything you find entertaining or useful to your bookmark list.

On the other hand, beware of adding too many sites. Having to wade through dozens of bookmarks defeats the purpose of the list—namely, making it easy to access sites.

Using internal navigation aids

Sometimes, browser navigation tools aren't enough. Many Web sites, particularly those that use more than one Web page to represent an organization or convey an idea, use internal navigation aids. These are hyperlinks (either words or icons) that lead to other pages on the same site. Typically, each page in a multi-page Web presentation will have links to the previous page, the next page, and the beginning of the presentation. Internal navigation aids help those browsing multi-page presentations keep track of what they're seeing and make it easy for them to backtrack if they get confused or to move ahead if they understand a point. Figure 2.7 shows internal navigation aids on a Sun Microsystems page.

Fig. 2.7
A Sun Microsystems page, with internal navigation aids.

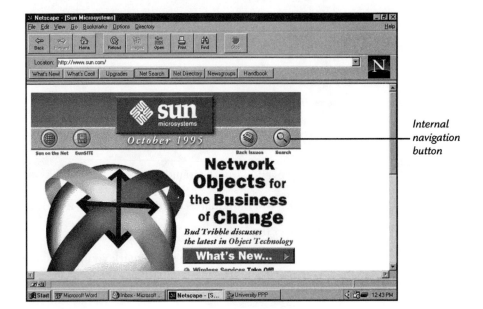

Internal navigation button

Helper applications

Quite frequently, a browser will encounter a file it can't process on its own. Instead of ignoring the file and preventing you from experiencing the information it contains, browsers will call on **helper applications**—also called **helper apps** or **helper programs**—to process the file. Typically, this happens with multimedia files—sounds, videos, and still images in certain file formats.

When Netscape encounters a file type it recognizes but can't display, it starts the appropriate helper application. The helper application runs simultaneously with Netscape. You can close the helper application whenever you want—usually after absorbing whatever information it handled for Netscape. Figure 2.8 shows Waveform Hold and Modify, a program used to play various sound files, running as a helper application with Netscape Navigator.

Fig. 2.8
Waveform Hold and
Modify acting as a
helper application by
playing a sound file.

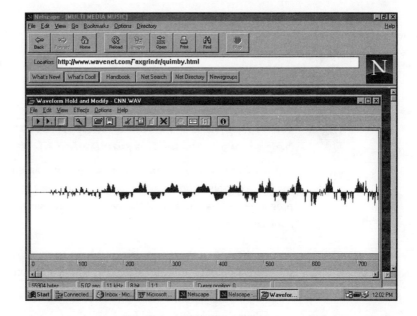

When Netscape comes across a file it doesn't recognize, it prompts you with
a dialog box that asks you what to do with the file. Figure 2.9 shows the
dialog box you'll see when Netscape gets confused.

Fig. 2.9
The Unknown File
Type dialog box in
Netscape Navigator.
This dialog box appears
when Netscape
encounters a file it
doesn't recognize.

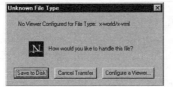

Choose Save to Disk if you don't have the proper helper application yet, but
want to save the file and acquire the helper application later. After selecting
the Save to Disk button, you'll see a standard Save dialog box; use it to name
and save the file as you would save a file in any other Windows program.

Choose Cancel Transfer if you made a mistake in calling up the file or don't
want to find a helper application that can handle the file you accessed.

Choose Configure a Viewer if you want to designate a program on your hard
disk as the helper application for all files of the kind you've started to download. When you select the button, you'll see a dialog box with a place for you
to enter the path to the appropriate helper application (see fig. 2.10). If you
don't know the path, select the Browse button and find the helper application
in your directory structure, just like you'd find a file to open in any other
application.

Fig. 2.10

The Configure External Viewer dialog box in Netscape Navigator.

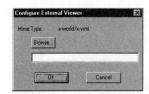

Q&A

What happens if I accidentally associate the wrong helper program with a particular file type?

First, you'll know you've done this when you get an error message from the helper application—a dialog box or other alert that tells you the program can't handle files of the type your browser has sent to the helper application.

It's not the end of the world—you just have to re-assign the file extension to the correct helper application. Do that with the Preferences dialog box.

1 Open the Options menu and choose Preferences. The Preferences dialog box appears (see fig. 2.11).

2 Click the Helper Apps tab.

3 In the list box, highlight the line for the file type that's assigned to the wrong helper application. Look at the third column for file extensions.

4 Make sure the Launch the Application radio button is selected.

5 In the text box at the bottom of the dialog box, enter the path to the correct helper application, or click the Browse button and select the application from the directory tree.

6 Click the OK button.

Fig. 2.11
The Preferences dialog box, with the Helper Apps tab selected. Use this part of the dialog box to reconfigure helper applications.

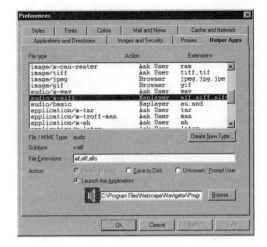

Starting out

Now, you're ready to go. You have a browser, you know how to use it, and you understand the concept of browsing as a resource-discovery tool and a type of entertainment. But you don't yet know where to begin. That's where this section comes in. Here, you'll learn where to start browsing. Where you go from there is up to you.

Don't forget, this is just an introduction to starting points. Any Web page can serve as an entry point. I selected these pages because they have lots of links to other sites. Feel free to start your own browsing sessions wherever you want. Perhaps your company, university, or other organization has a page with links of interest to you and your co-workers.

Using this book's directories

The majority of this book consists of references to places at which you might start browsing sessions. Take a look at chapters 5-20. Each one deals with a particular subject, and contains dozens of URLs. Plug the URL of an appealing resource into your browser and follow hyperlinks from there. You'll find that many of the resources in each chapter have links to the other resources in the chapter. Web page maintainers tend to know what other resources will be of interest to their visitors.

Using special-interest pages

Chances are, there are several people using the Web who have the same interests as you. It's also quite likely that at least one of these people has taken the time to build a Web page containing hyperlinks to all the resources he or she could find that related to a particular subject. These pages sometimes are called **trailblazer pages**, because the builder of the page did the hard work of finding all the resources and linking them all to a single page, much like an explorer cutting a path through thick brush from a town to a frontier outpost.

You'll find special-interest pages containing links to resources dedicated to everything from foxes to figure skating. For example, the Journalist's Toolbox contains hyperlinks to dozens of resources of use to journalists (see fig. 2.12). This page contains no information of its own, just links to other places that keep information.

How do you find special-interest pages? Well, you might hear about them via electronic correspondence with colleagues or by word of mouth among people with interests that match yours. More likely, you'll find trailblazer pages as a result of using one of the Web search tools you'll learn about later in this book.

Fig. 2.12
The Journalist's Toolbox, a special-interest page.

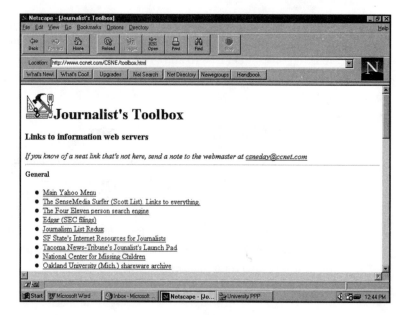

Using general-interest What's Cool and What's New pages

What's Cool pages are online compilations of links to sites that one person or a group of people think comprise the neatest stuff on the Web. You may not agree with them, but their picks generally have some merit and these pages are great places to start browsing sessions. There are also **What's New? pages** that list newly available resources without attesting to the quality of the resources.

- The Netscape What's Cool? page (**http://home.netscape.com/ home/whats-cool.html**) lists sites that appeal to the Netscape Communications site maintainers. Usually, these are sites that take advantage of special Netscape capabilities and may not work as well when viewed with other browsers. You can reach the Netscape What's Cool? page by clicking the What's Cool! button in your Netscape Navigator browser.

- The Netscape What's New? page (**http://home.netscape.com/ home/whats-new.html**) lists sites brought to the attention of the Netscape site maintainers by electronic mail. These sites work with all browsers, not just Netscape. You can reach the Netscape What's New? page by clicking the What's New! button in your Netscape Navigator browser.

- What's New on Yahoo (**http://www.yahoo.com/new**) lists sites newly added to the Yahoo subject tree. The descriptions here are kind of spare, so you may have to use your Back button a lot.

- The Coolness Page (**http://www.iaehv.nl/users/lucien/**) lists sites that appeal to Lucien Stam, a Web user in the Netherlands. Lucien's page focuses on music and television, but it has lots of general-interest links, too.

- What's New with NCSA Mosaic (**http://www.ncsa.uiuc.edu/SDG/ Software/Mosaic/Docs/whats-new.html**) includes links to sites that Web users have sent to the maintainers of the NCSA site. These sites work with all browsers, not just NCSA Mosaic.

Home again, home again

On the Web, you need a place to hang your electronic hat—your home page. Not only does your home page serve as your presence on the Web, it provides you with a convenient place to start browsing. In the next chapter, you'll learn how to design a good home page. For now, remember that your home page should play a big role in your browsing activities. Figure 2.13 shows the home page of Meng Weng Wong, a student at the University of Pennsylvania. Meng probably uses her home page as a starting point for browsing sessions because it's loaded with links to resources that interest her—keeping her bookmarks list small and reducing the load she puts on search tools.

Fig. 2.13
Meng Weng Wong's exemplary home page.

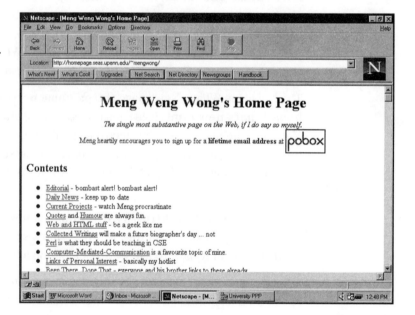

How To Create a Web Page with HTML

● **In this chapter:**

- ● **Create a World Wide Web page, complete with headings, graphics, hyperlinks, and lists**

- ● **Open your page with your Web browser**

- ● **Learn about advanced HTML techniques, such as forms, imagemaps, and tables**

- ● **Get a glimpse of where new ideas like VRML and Java will take the Web**

You can participate in the Web community as a publisher of information almost as easily as you can browse. Here's your guide to publishing on the Web with a language called HTML. . . . . ●>

Y ou know how to browse the Web, but that's only the beginning of the Web experience. The beauty of the Web is that it's a two-way, participatory medium. Unlike television, radio, or print media, you can easily participate in the Web as a publisher as well as a consumer of information. This chapter teaches you how to create your own Web pages and make them available for other Web users to see.

What's HTML?

You can use HTML to create pages for the Web. Technically, that makes HTML a computer programming language, but don't let that frighten you. You'll find HTML easy to learn and extremely forgiving of mistakes. Unlike other programming languages, which are fraught with complex syntax rules and obscure commands, HTML employs a logical structure and generally simple commands. If you can read and understand the function of parentheses in standard English grammar, you can learn to create Web pages with HTML in no time at all.

Understanding the basics of HTML

HTML and other **markup languages** make up a subset of a basic class of computer languages called **declarative languages**. Declarative languages differ from other computer languages (called **procedural languages**) in that they usually don't unequivocally tell a computer what to do. Procedural languages, like C++ and Visual Basic, give a computer instructions, such as:

> Add these two numbers, then take the result, store it in memory, and ask the user for a third number. Divide the stored number by the number the user provides and display the quotient in the center of the screen in 12-point bold Helvetica characters.

❝ *Plain English, please!*

Markup Language is a computer language in which codes that the computer interprets are scattered throughout a text document that you and I can read. The text of a document written in a markup language, then, is "marked up" with the computer instructions. ❞

In contrast, declarative languages—including markup languages like HTML—state the way things are. HTML declares the functions of various portions of your document—designating one group of words as a title, for instance, and another group of words as body text. HTML does this with **tags**. Tags are sequences of characters that bracket marked text. Typically, tags consist of an opening tag, which has the form *<TAG>*, and a closing tag, which has the form *</TAG>*. Text appears between the opening and closing tags, as in the following example (you'll see these tags again later):

<TITLE>Larry's World of Acoustics</TITLE>

Together, the opening and closing tags define an **element**—a portion of a document. In this example, the <TITLE> tag and the </TITLE> tag define the title element.

Understanding how browsers work with HTML

You use a **Web browser** to interpret HTML documents. Web browsers evaluate the tags in HTML documents, and display the text surrounded by the tags in a particular way. Because HTML doesn't give absolute instructions to the computer about displaying text, browsers have a great deal of latitude in deciding how to interpret tags—some say too much. One browser might display text surrounded by heading tags in 36-point bold Arial type, while another browser might display the same text in 24-point italic Times New Roman.

Q&A *How do you know how your Web documents will appear on someone's browser?*

You can't know for sure, and great debates rage in the Web community about this subject. The best you can do is test your Web pages on a variety of browsers to be sure they look okay on all of them. Even this doesn't protect you from people who alter their browsers' factory settings or who use an oddball browser you've never heard of.

How do I get started?

Remember Notepad, that little applet on your Windows desktop you thought you had outgrown long ago? It's about to become important to you once more. Because HTML is ASCII text with some special character strings sprinkled throughout it and Notepad saves its files in ASCII format, you can use Notepad to create pages for the Web.

You can use your regular word-processing program if you want, as long as it can save files in ASCII format (all major word-processing programs—including Microsoft Word, WordPerfect, and Lotus Word Pro—and the WordPad applet that comes with Windows 95 can save text in ASCII format). In the next chapter, you'll learn about programs designed especially for editing Web pages.

 TIP **You'll probably find it best to use a full-featured word-processing** program for at least some editing of your Web pages, since even the Web page editors you'll see in the next chapter lack the advanced editing tools found in typical word-processing programs. For example, you'd be hard-pressed to replace all the level-one headings that follow bulleted lists in Notepad or a Web page editor, but a program like Microsoft Word makes such a task easy. You'll find that you use different programs at various stages of the page-creation process.

Creating your first Web page

This section teaches you how to create a Web page. For purposes of illustration, we'll assume you're a fancier of exotic mustards and want to put a page on the Web that advertises your hobby. Follow along and you'll create your first Web page within half an hour.

To begin:

1 Open Notepad or your word-processing program.

2 Create a new document.

3 Save the document as MUSTARD.HTM

HTML documents usually get the extension HTML. On DOS machines that can't handle four-letter extensions, they get the HTM extension.

Framework elements

If you were building a house, you wouldn't start by standing sheets of drywall on edge and hanging paintings on them. Neither would you attempt to install a jacuzzi before running plumbing through the walls or lay carpet directly on the bare earth. In building a house, the framework and other infrastructure items must come first, even if they won't be visible when construction is complete. The same holds true for HTML. You must include certain elements that won't affect the ultimate appearance of your page, or your page won't work properly with the browsers that attempt to interpret it. It's easiest to insert these elements in the document at the beginning of the page-creation process.

TIP **Web browsers ignore returns and extra spaces. They won't format** text unless tags tell them to do so. You can take advantage of this fact by widely spacing the components of your documents, by putting a space or two after each paragraph, for example. Doing so makes documents easier to read and, if there is a problem, easier to repair and modify. Liberal spacing also makes pages easier for someone else to modify—an important consideration if you're part of a workgroup putting material on the Web.

The <HTML> element defines the language used to encode your document. Though modern browsers usually can figure out when a document is in HTML and when it's in another form, older browsers can't. Web experts consider it good style to bracket HTML documents in <HTML>...</HTML> tags. Put an <HTML> tag at the beginning of your document, press Enter a few times, and type an </HTML> tag at the end. These tags define your document as a file encoded in HTML. All the other tags and text you type go between the <HTML> tag and the </HTML> tag.

Q&A *Why do I have to use the **<HTML>** and **</HTML>** tags to tell browsers that my pages are in HTML? Is there another Web language?*

No, there isn't another Web language that can handle hypertext. Some documents on the Web are encoded in ASCII text and other formats, though. The <HTML> and </HTML> tags are holdovers from the language from which HTML grew: **Standard Generalized Markup Language (SGML)**. Originally developed as a way for academics and scientists to share documents electronically, SGML required lots of extra tags that modern versions of HTML don't need.

All HTML documents have **head sections** and **body sections**. The head section contains information *about* the document—the title, for our purposes—while the body contains the text, tags, and other information that make up the bulk of the Web page. HTML uses the <HEAD> and <BODY> elements to define the two portions of a document. The head region usually goes above the body region, though it doesn't absolutely have to go there.

1 In your document, type **<HEAD>** on the line below the <HTML> tag.

2 Press Enter twice, and type **</HEAD>**.

   You've just defined the head region of your document. The title of your document, which you'll learn about soon, goes between the <HEAD> tag and the </HEAD> tag.

3 Type **<BODY>** on the line below the </HEAD> tag (if there isn't a blank line after the </HEAD> tag, press Enter to create one).

4 Press Enter several times, and type **</BODY>**. Make sure the </BODY> tag appears before the </HTML> tag. Most of the information in your Web page appears between the <BODY> tag and the </BODY> tag.

Figure 3.1 shows how your document should appear after you insert the framework elements.

Fig. 3.1
Your Web document's
framework elements.

```
mustard - Notepad                                              _ 8 X
File  Edit  Search  Help
<HTML>
<HEAD>

</HEAD>
<BODY>

</BODY>
</HTML>
```

CAUTION **Don't forget to save your document frequently as you create your**
Web page. Though most full-featured word processing programs have
automatic saving features that will protect you in the event of a power
failure or other unexpected computer shutdown, Notepad and many other
word processing programs do not. Choose File, Save from your program's
menu bar, or press Ctrl+S.

The title

When a browser looks at an HTML document and interprets it for display, it takes the title text and prints it in the title bar of the browser window. The title bar of a browser displaying a Web page might say something like "Microsoft Internet Explorer—Ted's Taco Barn" or "Netscape Navigator—The Isuzu Trooper Page."

You may confuse the title of a Web document with the first heading in the document (you'll learn about headings next). Often they include the same text, and frequently the title gets overlooked in favor of the larger, bolder first heading. The title, however, has special significance in that some of the **spiders** (automated Web-exploring programs) that add to the databases of certain Web search tools pay attention only to the titles of Web documents. You need to have a descriptive title in order for the search tools to lead interested Web users to your page.

You define the title with—what else?—the <TITLE> and </TITLE> elements, which fit inside the <HEAD>...</HEAD> tags. In your document, position the cursor on the line below the <HEAD> tag. Type the following:

<TITLE>Exotic Mustard Central</TITLE>

Figure 3.2 shows how your document should look now.

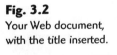

Fig. 3.2
Your Web document, with the title inserted.

Title

Headings

People find it hard to read long passages of text on computer screens, so you'll want to break up long documents you post to the Web into smaller parts. Small parts make it easy for readers to find and read only the portions of your document that they need, and encourage them to take periodic breaks to rest their eyes. HTML provides six sets of header tags that enable you to label the portions of your documents hierarchically:

- <H1>...</H1>

- <H2>...</H2>

- <H3>...</H3>

- <H4>...</H4>

- <H5>...</H5>

- <H6>...</H6>

These tags designate text as **headings**. H1 headings are emphasized the most (they're usually largest) and H6 heads are emphasized least. In the Exotic Mustard Central example, you'll use H1 and H2 headers.

On the line after the <BODY> tag in your document, type the following:

<H1>Welcome to Exotic Mustard Central!</H1>

Then, press Enter several times to make a few blank lines and type this:

<H2>Mustards of the World</H2>

<H2>Mail-Order Mustard Dealers</H2>

<H2>Mustard Trivia</H2>

You've added four headings to your document: one H1 heading, which browsers will interpret as more important and deserving more emphasis than other headings, and three H2 headings, which are interpreted as less important than H1 headings. Figure 3.3 shows how your document should look now.

Fig. 3.3
Your Web document, with headings added.

Level 1 heading

Level 2 headings

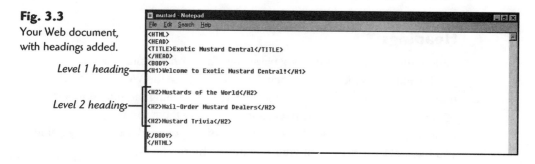

Body text

Headings exist to organize body text. Adding body text under your headers couldn't be easier. All you do is put a <P> tag at the beginning of each paragraph. You can put a </P> tag at the end of each paragraph if you want, but you don't have to. The <P> tag (or heading tag) that marks the beginning of one paragraph also defines the end of the previous paragraph.

1 In your Web document, make a blank line after your H1 heading, the one that says `Welcome to Exotic Mustard Central!`

2 Starting on the blank line, type the following:

> **<P>Thanks for stopping by my mustard page. I've been a mustard aficionado for years, and I've collected or sampled mustards from locales as exotic as rural Germany and Amarillo, Texas. This page should serve as a gathering point for the on-line community of mustard lovers. I've assembled here some reviews of my favorite mustards, as well as a guide to mail-order mustard dealers so you can expand your collection.**

You've added a paragraph of text below the first heading on your page. You can add more paragraphs of text, if you want, as long as you start each additional paragraph with the <P> tag. Otherwise, the paragraphs will run together.

TIP **Remember, Web browsers don't pay any attention to extra spaces** and line breaks. Use this to your advantage, if your word-processing program doesn't feature word-wrapping, by pressing Enter at the end of each line. The extra line breaks will make it easier for you to see your HTML code—no need to scroll left and right—and will have no effect on your document's appearance.

Figure 3.4 shows how your Web document should look now.

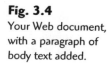

Fig. 3.4

Your Web document, with a paragraph of body text added.

Body text —

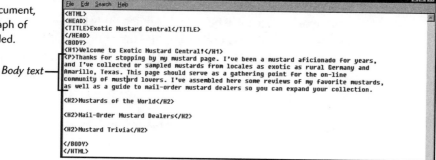

Lists

Odds are, you'll want to list something in your Web page. You may want to list sequential things, such as the steps involved in a recipe, or nonsequential things, such as the contents of a toolbox. HTML provides an easy way to perform each task, without resorting to lots of <P> tags and numbering or bulleting by hand.

HTML supports two basic kinds of lists: **ordered** (numbered) and **unordered** (bulleted). When confronted with lists tagged as ordered lists, Web browsers automatically numbers the list items sequentially. Web browsers also place bullets before each item in an unordered list.

Let's say you want an unordered list in your Exotic Mustards page. Put your word-processing program's cursor on the line below the Mustards of the World heading (press Enter to make this line blank, if needed). Type the following:

> **<UL>**
>
> **<LI>German Mustards**
>
> **<LI>French Mustards**
>
> **<LI>English Mustards**
>
> **<LI>North American Mustards**
>
> **<LI>South American Mustards**
>
> **</UL>**

Note that the <UL>...</UL> tags frame the entire list, while the <LI> tags mark the beginning of each item in the list. You don't have to put </LI> tags at the end of each line, but you can if doing so makes your HTML document easier to understand. When a Web browser interprets this code, it arranges the list items with a bullet (a round, black dot, usually) before each one.

You may find it helpful to remember that **LI** stands for List Item, **OL** stands for Ordered List, and **UL** stands for Unordered List. Not all HTML tags are intuitive, but fortunately these basic ones are.

TIP **If you replaced the <UL> tag in this example with an <OL> tag and** the </UL> tag with a </OL> tag, this would become an ordered list. In place of bullets, Web browsers automatically attach sequential numbers to the items in ordered lists.

Figure 3.5 shows how your Web document should appear now.

Fig. 3.5
Your Web document, with an unordered list added.

Unordered (bulleted) list

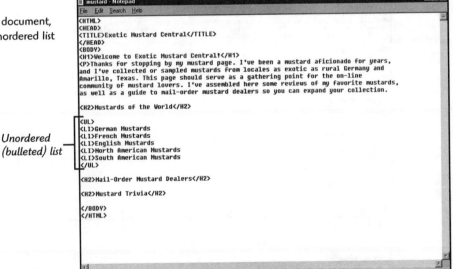

Rules

Anyone who's scanned a box score page in a printed newspaper knows that even the simplest graphical elements can make text easier to understand. HTML provides several means of inserting simple graphics into text—notably bullets, about which you learned in the last section, and tables, which are too complex to be covered in this chapter in depth. Simple horizontal lines can add a lot to the appearance of a page, too, and HTML has an ultra-simple means of inserting them.

Imagine you want a horizontal line (called a **rule** in typographers' jargon) on your page right below the paragraph of body text. Create a blank line below the paragraph of body text, and put an <HR> tag on a line by itself. That's all there is to it.

Note that there is no </HR> tag. You couldn't insert one if you wanted to. The <HR> element is called an **empty tag**, meaning it's there by itself and does not surround a passage of text. The <IMG> element, which you will learn about next, also is an empty tag.

Figure 3.6 shows how your Web document should look now.

Fig. 3.6
Your Web document, with a horizontal rule added.

Horizontal line
<HR> tag

```
HTML mustard - Notepad                                        _ |8|X
File  Edit  Search  Help
<HTML>
<HEAD>
<TITLE>Exotic Mustard Central</TITLE>
</HEAD>
<BODY>
<H1>Welcome to Exotic Mustard Central</H1>
<P>Thanks for stopping by my mustard page. I've been a mustard aficionado for years,
and I've collected or sampled mustards from locales as exotic as rural Germany and
Amarillo, Texas. This page should serve as a gathering point for the on-line
community of mustard lovers. I've assembled here some reviews of my favorite mustards,
as well as a guide to mail-order mustard dealers so you can expand your collection.

<HR>

<H2>Mustards of the World</H2>

<UL>
<LI>German Mustards
<LI>French Mustards
<LI>English Mustards
<LI>North American Mustards
<LI>South American Mustards
</UL>

<H2>Mail-Order Mustard Dealers</H2>

<H2>Mustard Trivia</H2>

</BODY>
</HTML>
```

Images

The day before Netscape Communications Corp.'s record-breaking initial public stock offering, someone called the company's main desk and, having heard that Netscape was involved in cutting-edge Web research, asked the receptionist, "Do you have a home page with a picture on it?" Indeed, among the basic HTML capabilities, nothing gets as much attention as inline images.

Surprisingly, such images aren't hard to include in Web pages. There's just one element involved—the <IMG> element—and it's an empty tag, so you don't even have to worry about surrounding text with tags. If you have a graphics file, you can attach it to your page in just a few seconds.

Q&A *How do I acquire a graphics file?*

The easiest way is to look around in archives on the Web. Tens of thousands of images reside in Web archives, often freely available for your use. Just download one of these images to the directory in which you keep your Web page files and it's there for your use. You can also buy libraries (on CD-ROM or floppy disk) of image files at software stores and mail-order outlets. If you want a specific image, such as a photo of you or your cat, you'll have to find a scanner. Scanning techniques fall outside the scope of this book, but remember to save your scanned image in the JPEG graphics file format. You also can use the Graphics Interchange Format (GIF), but Web experts prefer the JPEG format for most applications, especially large illustrations. They prefer JPEG because they use a clever compression scheme that allows these illustrations to be transmitted quickly across the Internet.

CAUTION **Not all images on the Web are available for your use. Some, such** as corporate logos and copyrighted symbols, may not be used without the permission of the copyright holder. You may use other images only after paying a fee to their creator. Be sure to look around in image archives for information about copyright rules.

In this example, you'll learn how to insert a file called MUSTARD.JPG. If you don't happen to have such a file on your computer, substitute the name of whatever file you want to use. Make sure the image file appears in the same directory as your Web page.

In your HTML document, type the following on the line after the first heading:

<IMG SRC="*MUSTARD.JPG*">

The <IMG> element also illustrates the concept of the **attribute**: a piece of information that modifies the function of the basic tag. In the case of the <IMG> element, the SRC attribute is mandatory because it describes the location of the image file. Many HTML tags have attributes, and several tags have more than one. SRC is easy to remember, since it denotes the SouRCe of an image.

Figure 3.7 shows how your HTML document should look now, with the <IMG> tag inserted.

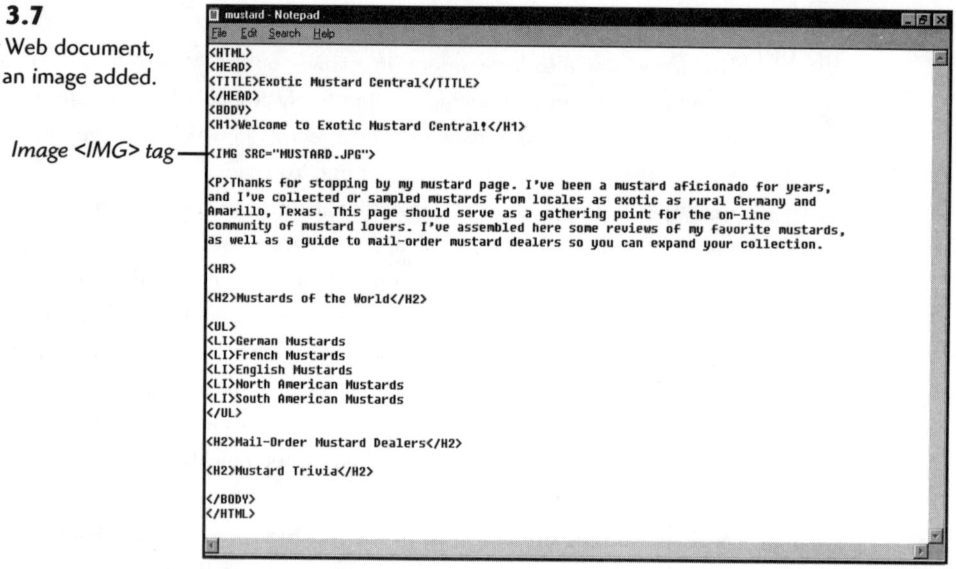

Fig. 3.7
Your Web document,
with an image added.

Image <IMG> tag ——

```
mustard - Notepad
File  Edit  Search  Help
<HTML>
<HEAD>
<TITLE>Exotic Mustard Central</TITLE>
</HEAD>
<BODY>
<H1>Welcome to Exotic Mustard Central!</H1>

<IMG SRC="MUSTARD.JPG">

<P>Thanks for stopping by my mustard page. I've been a mustard aficionado for years,
and I've collected or sampled mustards from locales as exotic as rural Germany and
Amarillo, Texas. This page should serve as a gathering point for the on-line
community of mustard lovers. I've assembled here some reviews of my favorite mustards,
as well as a guide to mail-order mustard dealers so you can expand your collection.

<HR>

<H2>Mustards of the World</H2>

<UL>
<LI>German Mustards
<LI>French Mustards
<LI>English Mustards
<LI>North American Mustards
<LI>South American Mustards
</UL>

<H2>Mail-Order Mustard Dealers</H2>

<H2>Mustard Trivia</H2>

</BODY>
</HTML>
```

Hyperlinks

Hyperlinks constitute the real appeal of the Web; your page shouldn't be
without them. Fortunately, inserting a hyperlink into your document is as
easy as adding an image. You establish hyperlinks with the <A> element. The
<A> element isn't as easy to remember as some of the other elements (it's
supposed to stand for "anchor"), but you'll use it so much, you'll soon find
you have it memorized.

The <A> element has an attribute, like the IMG element: HREF. The HREF
attribute describes the URL to which the hyperlink leads. Think of HREF as
an abbreviation for Hypertext REFerence—the Web page to which the link
refers.

In your document, under the Mail-Order Mustard Dealers heading, type
the following:

> **<A HREF="http://www.gov.pe.ca/homepage/preserve/
> antipast.html">PEI Preserves</A>**

That string of characters establishes a hyperlink to the page of PEI Preserves,
a vendor of mustards, antipastos, and chutneys based in Prince Edward
Island, Canada. When a Web browser interprets that line, it will show the

words PEI Preserves as a hyperlink. When clicked, those words will lead to the PEI preserves page (**http://www.gov.pe.ca/homepage/preserve/ antipast.html**).

Figure 3.8 shows how your page should look now.

Fig. 3.8
Your Web document, with a hyperlink added.

A hyperlink

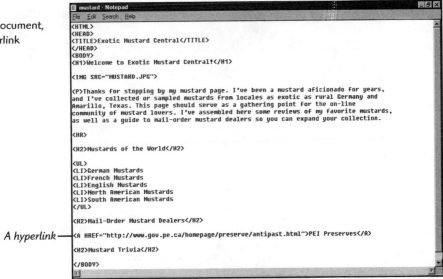

```
mustard - Notepad
File  Edit  Search  Help
<HTML>
<HEAD>
<TITLE>Exotic Mustard Central</TITLE>
</HEAD>
<BODY>
<H1>Welcome to Exotic Mustard Central</H1>

<IMG SRC="MUSTARD.JPG">

<P>Thanks for stopping by my mustard page. I've been a mustard aficionado for years,
and I've collected or sampled mustards from locales as exotic as rural Germany and
Amarillo, Texas. This page should serve as a gathering point for the on-line
community of mustard lovers. I've assembled here some reviews of my favorite mustards,
as well as a guide to mail-order mustard dealers so you can expand your collection.

<HR>

<H2>Mustards of the World</H2>

<UL>
<LI>German Mustards
<LI>French Mustards
<LI>English Mustards
<LI>North American Mustards
<LI>South American Mustards
</UL>

<H2>Mail-Order Mustard Dealers</H2>

<A HREF="http://www.gov.pe.ca/homepage/preserve/antipast.html">PEI Preserves</A>

<H2>Mustard Trivia</H2>

</BODY>
```

Viewing your first Web page

Now comes the test: opening your Web page with a Web browser and seeing if it looks the way you want. This section shows you only how to open your page on your computer; unless you happen to be working on a Web server, no one else can access your page. Your service provider can tell you how to post your page for the world to see.

Opening your page in your browser

To open your new Web page:

1 Save your Web page and close it.

2 Start your Web browser.

3 Open the File menu and choose Open File.

> **4** Look through the directories until you find MUSTARD.HTM, and open that file. Your browser will interpret your HTML code and display the results.

Figure 3.9 shows how your page should look.

Fig. 3.9
Your Web document, interpreted by a Web browser.

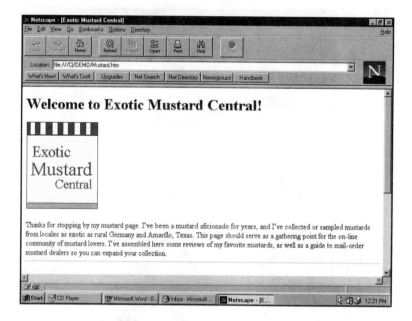

Fixing mistakes

If you see a mistake, don't panic. Just open the file in Notepad or your word-processing program again, and make the necessary adjustments. Then save the file, close it, and open it in the browser again. Repeat this process until the page looks right.

Is there more to HTML?

By all means, there is more to HTML than we've explored here. This chapter represents just a taste of what you can do with this very powerful and flexible language. HTML is a living language—it's changing all the time. Standards-setting bodies constantly revise the HTML specification to make the language more useful. This section tells you a little bit about the special capabilities of the current version of HTML and describes some features future HTML versions may include.

Learning about advanced HTML techniques

The people who really know their way around HTML are called **Webmasters**. This section, while it doesn't attempt to make you a Webmaster, shows you some of the experts' tricks. You'll soon be using the Web with an understanding of how HTML programmers do some of their slickest tricks. See Que's *Special Edition Using HTML* to learn more about advanced HTML techniques.

Forms

If you've used a search engine, you've used a **form**. Forms simulate a graphical User Interface, such as Windows, on the Web, enabling Web users to enter data via familiar tools such as radio buttons, drop-down lists, check boxes, and text boxes. Figure 3.10 shows a Lycos search form—a fine example of forms in use on the Web.

What happens when you enter information into a form? That's what makes forms complex. A special program has to take the data, do something with it, and return it in a form Web browsers can handle. These programs are called **Common Gateway Interface (CGI) scripts** (programming them falls far outside the scope of this book).

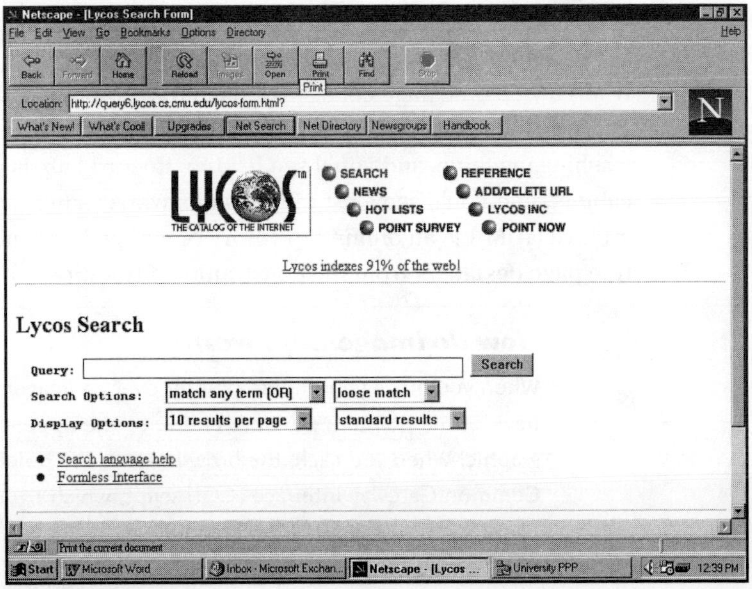

Fig. 3.10
A Lycos search form.

Imagemaps

Imagemaps take the graphical-user-interface concept one step further. By enabling Web users to click different portions of a single graphic to accomplish different things, imagemaps let Web page creators develop wild and beautiful interfaces to their pages. The welcome page for the Internet Underground Music Archive is a good example (see fig. 3.11).

Fig. 3.11
The Internet Underground Music Archive welcome page.

IUMA's welcome page consists of one large graphic. Different parts of that graphic are hyperlinked to different pages at the IUMA site. Click the washing machine, and you'll see IUMA's Record Labels page. Click the hi-fi cabinet, and you'll see a list of the bands whose songs appear in the IUMA archive (IUMA is an online repository of garage-band music). Imagemaps free page designers from the constraints of traditional hyperlinks.

Q&A *How do imagemaps work?*

When you move your mouse pointer over an imagemap, the browser keeps track of the pointer's position relative to the upper-left corner of the graphic. When you click, the browser sends the pointers coordinates to a Common Gateway Interface (CGI) script, which figures out what action corresponds to a click at those coordinates (different coordinates on a single graphic may correspond to different actions).

Tables

Tables allow HTML programmers to organize text and numbers in grids, making the information easier to understand. Table tags take care of the creation of the grid itself, leaving the programmer free to manipulate the information that fits inside the grid. Figure 3.12 shows some sample tables.

Fig. 3.12
Sample tables.

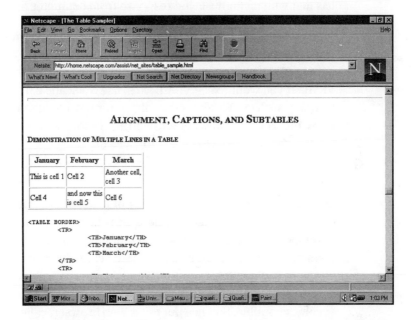

Early versions of HTML didn't support multicolumn text layout—and neither does the latest version, except as a sort of trick. By putting text and graphics into the cells of tables, HTML programmers can organize their text and graphics into multicolumn layouts. You'll see evidence of this use of tables all over the Web, particularly in online newspapers and newsletters.

Understanding the future of HTML

The Web is young yet, and it changes all the time. Though forms, tables, and imagemaps are difficult for the average Web user to create, they don't represent much of a challenge to a skilled Web publisher. The real cutting-edge stuff hasn't even come close to being standardized yet, and it will dramatically change the way you use the Web.

VRML

Virtual Reality Modeling Language (**VRML**) has the potential to make the Web into a three-dimensional space that you can navigate in somewhat the same way you navigate a city. With provisions for modeling solid surfaces, such as tabletops and walls, VRML (pronounced to rhyme with "thermal") has met with an enthusiastic response from computer hobbyists.

VRML got a big boost when Netscape Communications announced that Netscape Navigator 2.0 would support VRML. Microsoft also recently announced that a future version of Microsoft Internet Explorer would support VRML. If you want to see VRML sites, use Netscape 2.0 or get a special VRML browser, such as Worldview (available for download at **http:// www.intervista.com/worldview.html**) or VRWeb (available for download at **http://hgiicm.tu-graz.ac.at:80/Cvrweb**).

Java

Sun Microsystems, the manufacturer of many of the workstations that comprise the Internet, has developed a scheme under which Web page developers can embed executable computer code in their Web pages. The potential of **Java** (as the language of the embedded programs is called) is huge—everything from sounds that play automatically when you access a page to application programs and operating systems that upgrade themselves becomes possible. Sun has put out a Web browser, called **HotJava**, that can process embedded applications.

66 *Plain English, please!*

Java is unique among computer languages because programs written in it can run on any computer for which there is a Java interpreter. When Java development progresses beyond the testing phase, you'll be able to run the same Java programs on a Windows 95 system, a Windows NT system, a Macintosh, and a Sun Solaris workstation. This means Java developers will be able to devote their time and money to coming up with new ideas rather than to writing multiple versions of the same program.

Web page designers will embed Java programs into their pages with the <APP> tag, a new tag that will direct the browser to the URL of the Java program. 99

Isn't there an easier way to do this?

Typing all those tags and hard-to-remember URLs is hard, isn't it? Remembering and entering obscure tags gets even harder as you begin to use more advanced HTML features, such as forms and tables. Fortunately, there are ways to save yourself the tedium of entering tags in Notepad or your word-processing program. This section describes some of the tools that can help save time—and prevent your angle bracket keys from wearing out prematurely.

Hiring HTML consultants

If you have the budget, you may want to hire an HTML expert. Like the work of most experts, the labor of HTML consultants doesn't come cheap. Furthermore, the field of HTML consulting is so new, there's no generally accepted rate of compensation for HTML programming work.

How do you find an HTML consultant? Bear in mind that no college or university yet offers a degree in hypertext design, and most computer science programs give HTML only passing coverage, if any at all. There's no professional certification for HTML experts.

The best way is to look around the Web until you see a page you like, and then approach that page's creator—his or her electronic mail address usually appears on the page somewhere. Many HTML experts happen also to be students or low-paid computer experts and will jump at the chance to gain exposure and income as a consultant. You can also look at the HTML Consultants Directory at **http://www.holonet.net/holonet/consultants.html**.

Using converters

If you have a large archive of documents you want to put on the Web, consider using a **converter**. Converters take files in a word-processing or page-layout program's file format (such as Microsoft Word DOC files, or Aldus PageMaker PM5 files) and change them into HTML format. Converters make it easy to translate large numbers of files into HTML, but they work with varying degrees of accuracy. The chances are good you'll have to edit the output of a converter to make sure it appears the way you want.

Looking for a converter for a specific type of file? Joe Walker, a scientist at North Carolina State University, has compiled a page that has links to many converters. You'll find his page at **http://www2.ncsu.edu/bae/people/ faculty/walker/hotlist/htmlconv.html**.

Using Web page editors

Web page editors, also called **HTML editors**, insert tags into text automatically, freeing you from the need to remember and type them. Typically, you'll highlight a passage of text—a heading, say—and click a button that attaches heading tags to that passage. Many Web page editors work as add-ons to word-processing programs. The next chapter deals with acquiring and using Web page editors, particularly Sausage Software's stand-alone **HotDog** and **Microsoft Internet Assistant**.

Web Page Editors

● **In this chapter:**

- **Learn the differences between stand-alone Web page editors, and programs that allow you to more easily create Web pages with your word-processing program**

- **Where do you acquire a Web page editor?**

- **Learn to use your Web page editor to speed the creation of Web pages**

- **Test Web pages you create with your Web page editor**

Creating Web pages with a word-processing program is a good educational experience, but so is starting a fire with flint and steel. Using a Web page editor to create a Web page is like using a bucket of gasoline and a blowtorch to start a fire. . ▶

Once you've mastered the tedious art of creating Web pages in a word-processing program by typing all the tags manually, you're ready to move into the world of efficient Web page creation. With **Web page editors** (also called **HTML editors**), you'll be able to save yourself the time and frustration of typing arcane HTML tags by hand. You'll be able to focus your attention on the large-scale issues of page planning and content instead of the small-scale issues of syntax and typing.

Why use a Web page editor?

Web page editors have two main attractions: the speed with which they allow you to write HTML, and the assurance they provide that your tags will be syntactically correct. With a Web page editor, you'll be able to generate technically correct code much faster than the fastest typist could generate it on a word processor.

Arguments against using Web page editors exist, too. They isolate you from the tags that make browsers interpret your pages the way they do, making it harder for you to identify and solve problems. Web page editors also discourage you from using any HTML tags or attributes that the editor's creators weren't familiar with. You can type them in by hand, but doing so defeats the advantages of Web page editors.

Additionally, Web page editors lack many of the advanced editing features that high-end word-processing programs have. At this writing, no stand-alone HTML editor has the capability to sort lines alphabetically, or to replace each occurrence of the word "ocelot" in large boldface type with the word "marmot" in small italics. Many word-processing programs have these capabilities. In practice, you'll find that you use both your word-processing program and your HTML editor to create Web pages. This is one advantage of using an HTML editing package, like Microsoft Internet Assistant, that extends the capabilities of a word-processing program.

Save time

When you're using a Web page editor to create Web pages, you'll do a lot of highlighting and clicking. You'll highlight a group of words—a heading, say—and then click a toolbar button. When you click the button, the program will insert the <H1> tag before the group of words you highlighted and the </H1>

tag after the group. By using an HTML editor, you exchanged at least eight keystrokes for one mouse drag and a mouse click (and remember, H1 is one of the shortest tags). That means you'll save a significant amount of time, especially if your planned Web site will involve hundreds of tags.

Make sure that your code is right

Clicking a button to insert HTML tags in text has another advantage; you can't make a careless typing or syntax mistake. Thanks to the programmers of HTML editors, each time you click a toolbar button to insert a tag, you can be sure it will have the proper spelling and syntax, and that all the attributes will appear in their proper places. When you use a word-processing program, the quality and accuracy of your code depends upon your typing ability and knowledge of HTML syntax.

Web page editors provide no protection, however, against what programmers call **logical errors**—errors in the design of HTML documents. An HTML document with a logical error may have perfectly functional HTML tags, but accomplish the wrong task. You can tell your Web page editor to make a passage of text a hyperlink to a particular URL, but if you give the editor the wrong URL, your page won't do what you want. Web page editors don't eliminate the need for careful planning on your part.

How do I get a Web page editor?

Before you set out to obtain a Web page editor, you'll have to decide which of the two basic kinds you want. The two kinds are:

- Stand-alone Web page editors, which are independent programs that work like word processors dedicated specifically to writing and editing HTML documents.

- Add-in programs, which expand the capabilities of a word-processing program such as Microsoft Word or WordPerfect.

This chapter concentrates on one product from each category. You'll learn about HotDog, a shareware stand-alone HTML editor distributed by Sausage Software, and Microsoft Internet Assistant, which adds HTML editing and Web browsing capabilities to Microsoft Word. Though there's much more variation in the interfaces and capabilities of Web page editors than in those of Web browsers, you'll find that if you master a program of one type, you'll be able to figure out other programs of that type without too much trouble.

Acquiring HotDog

The easiest way to acquire HotDog is to point your Web browser at Sausage Software's Web site (**http://www.sausage.com/**). There, you can get the scoop on the newest version of HotDog, and get a look at Sausage's other offerings.

To download the demonstration version of HotDog (which is fully functional for 30 days, and then stops working):

1 Click the link to the HotDog page.

2 Scroll to the bottom of the HotDog page.

3 Click the Demonstration Version link. Your browser will download a file called hdgsetup.exe to your computer; be sure to save it in its own directory.

4 Run hdgsetup.exe, which will install HotDog on your machine.

Remember, the version you download from HotDog's site works for only 30 days. To get it to work beyond that deadline, you must register your copy with Sausage Software—and pay $29.95. When you register and pay, the company will give you a code number that lets you defeat the timer protecting HotDog. Also, you'll get a year of email technical support when you register HotDog.

Q&A ***If I can download HotDog for free, why don't I just download it every 29 days and save the registration fee?***

First of all, that's dishonest. Second, it's a real pain—especially since HotDog alters a setting in your configuration files to foil this sort of ploy.

HotDog is **shareware**—software that you can acquire and use for a while without paying, but that you eventually must pay for. The shareware distribution scheme allows small software houses, like Sausage Software, to compete with software giants like Microsoft. Since the innovations of small entrepreneurs created the personal computer industry and continue to play a big part today, you probably want to encourage their continued competitiveness by registering and paying for your shareware.

Acquiring Microsoft Internet Assistant

To use Microsoft Internet Assistant, you must own Microsoft Word. Microsoft offers one version of Microsoft Internet Assistant that works with Microsoft Word 6.0, and another version for Microsoft Word for Windows 95. There is no version of Microsoft Internet Assistant for Word 2.0.

You can download the Word 6.0 version of Microsoft Internet Assistant (contained in a file called wordia.zip from the Virtual Software Library (**http://vsl.cnet.com/**). Unlike the Windows 95 version of Microsoft Internet Assistant, you'll have to use a program like WinZip to decompress Microsoft Internet Assistant for Word 6.0.

You can download the Windows 95 version of Microsoft Internet Assistant from Microsoft's Web site at **http://www.microsoft.com/msoffice/freestuf/ msword/download/ia/ia95/default.htm**. From that page, you can download a file called wordia2.exe. Save wordia2.exe in its own directory, and then run it. Its setup program will install Microsoft Internet Assistant so it works with your copy of Microsoft Word.

How do I write HTML with a Web page editor?

Now that you have a Web page editor installed on your computer, you're ready to put it to use. You're ready to learn how a Web page editor can make it easier to use the tags you typed by hand in the last chapter.

One of the biggest differences between HotDog and Microsoft Internet Assistant is that Microsoft Internet Assistant is a what-you-see-is-what-you-get (WYSIWYG) editor; you see the effects of your tags on-screen rather than the tags themselves (you can see the tags by choosing View, HTML Source from the menu bar). HotDog, in contrast, shows the tags, but does not show their effects, though it does provide an easy way to export Web pages to a Web browser for viewing.

Inserting framework elements

Every time you start a new Web page, you have to insert <HTML>, <HEAD>, <TITLE>, and <BODY> tags, as well as their corresponding closing tags. Web page editors make this part of the page-creation process extremely easy.

CAUTION   **Remember, HTML tags do not format text absolutely. Web browsers** have a lot of latitude in determining what individual tags mean. As a result, a level-one heading may look one way in Netscape, another way in Emissary, and still a third way in the Microsoft Internet Assistant editing screen. What you see in Microsoft Internet Assistant may or may not be what you get when you view a document created with Microsoft Internet Assistant with a Web browser.

HotDog

When you start HotDog, or open a new document, you'll see that all the framework elements already are in place. To insert your document's title, highlight the words `Type_document_title_here` between the <TITLE> and </TITLE> tags, delete them, and type the title you want. Figure 4.1 shows a HotDog Web page with its framework elements in place and a title inserted.

Fig. 4.1
Framework elements in a HotDog Web page. HotDog inserts these elements each time you create a new document.

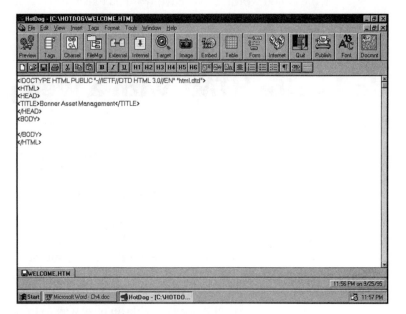

Microsoft Internet Assistant

Microsoft Internet Assistant inserts framework elements automatically, too, but since it hides HTML tags unless you instruct it otherwise, you can't see the tags. How do you change the document's title? By clicking the Title button on the toolbar (it's the one that looks like an "i" on a sheet of paper). When you click the Title button, the HTML Document Head Information dialog box pops up, and you can enter the title you want into that box in place of the words, HTML document for the World Wide Web. Figure 4.2 shows the dialog box and the location of the Title button.

Fig. 4.2
The HTML Document Head Information dialog box. Use this box to define your document's title.

Title button

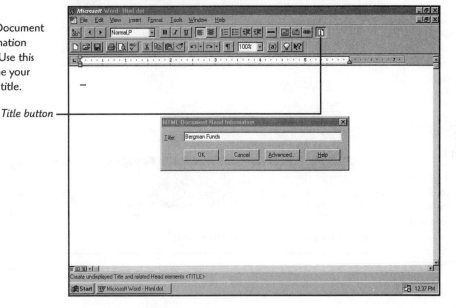

Making headings

Web page editors also make it easy to insert headings. With a click of the mouse in HotDog and a quick selection procedure in Microsoft Internet Assistant, you can designate text as any kind of heading you wish.

HotDog

Designate a heading in HotDog by selecting the heading text with your mouse and clicking the appropriate heading button on the toolbar; there are buttons for each of the six heading levels. Figure 4.3 shows some text tagged as a level 1 heading, and also shows the location of the six heading buttons.

Microsoft Internet Assistant

In Microsoft Internet Assistant, you designate headings in the same way you apply a style to text in a regular Microsoft Word document. Select the heading text with your mouse, and then choose Heading 1, H1 from the Style drop-down list box. Microsoft Internet Assistant won't show the tags, but it will reformat the text. Figure 4.4 shows text formatted as a level 1 heading in Microsoft Internet Assistant, and also points out the Style drop-down list box.

Heading buttons

Fig. 4.3
Text tagged as <H1> in HotDog. This text will appear as a large heading when interpreted by a browser.

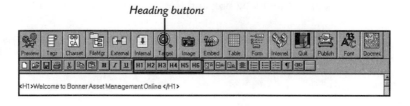

Style drop-down list box

Fig. 4.4
Text tagged as <H1> in Microsoft Internet Assistant. Note that the text appears large immediately since Microsoft Internet Assistant is a WYSIWYG editor.

Adding Body Text

Regardless of how many graphics you include in your page, you'll probably have some body text. In most pages, the body text is where the bulk of the page's information resides. Both Web page editors make inserting the <P> tag extremely easy.

HotDog

Designate body text in HotDog by selecting the body text with your mouse and clicking the Paragraph button on the toolbar (it's the one with a paragraph symbol on it). Figure 4.5 shows some text tagged as body text, and also shows the location of the Paragraph button.

Microsoft Internet Assistant

You use the Style drop-down list box to designate text as body text in Microsoft Internet Assistant. Select the body text with your mouse, and then choose Normal, P from the Style drop-down list box. Microsoft Internet Assistant won't show the tags, but it will reformat the text. Figure 4.6 shows text formatted as body text in Microsoft Internet Assistant.

Fig. 4.5
Text tagged as <P> in HotDog.

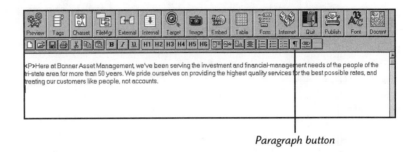

Paragraph button

Fig. 4.6
Text tagged as <P> in Microsoft Internet Assistant.

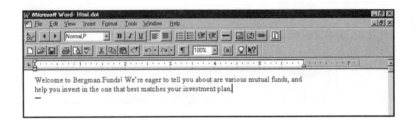

Creating lists

Without help, many Web page designers find creating lists a tedious and confusing task. Not only do you have to tag each line with a special tag, but you must surround the entire list with tags—and those tags vary, depending upon whether you want the list items to be numbered or bulleted. Web page editors, however, make it as easy to create lists of many items as it is to define a heading.

HotDog

In HotDog, you create an ordered list by highlighting all the list items and clicking the Ordered List button (the one that looks like a numbered list). You create an unordered list in the same way, except you click the Unordered List button (the one that looks like a bulleted list) instead of the Ordered List button. Figure 4.7 shows ordered and unordered lists in HotDog, and shows the locations of the Ordered List and Unordered List buttons.

Fig. 4.7
Ordered and unordered lists in HotDog. To add new list elements, you must type in the <LI> tag.

Unordered List button

Ordered List button

Ordered list

Unordered list

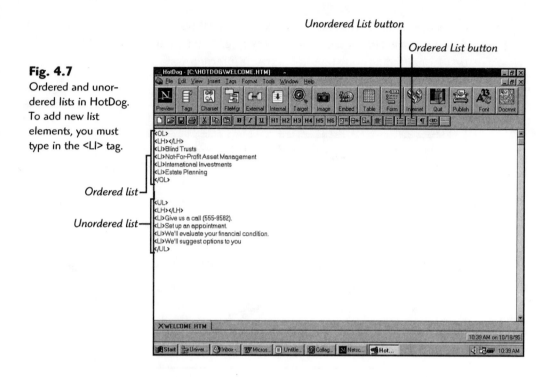

Microsoft Internet Assistant

Surprise! You don't have to use the Style drop-down list box to designate text as an ordered or unordered list in Microsoft Internet Assistant. Though that method will work, you also can use buttons on the toolbar to accomplish the same task.

If you want to use the Style drop-down list box, highlight your list with your mouse and choose List Number, OL (for an ordered list) or List Bullet, UL (for an unordered list) from the list. Microsoft Internet Assistant will format your selection appropriately.

If you want to use the buttons on the toolbar—and you probably do if you're used to working with Word—you should highlight the list with your mouse and click either the Numbered List button or the Bulleted List button. Figure 4.8 shows the locations of these buttons, as well as text formatted as ordered and unordered lists in Microsoft Internet Assistant.

One of the nice things about WYSIWYG HTML editors like Word is that you can add list items to ordered and unordered lists very easily: you just insert the new list items where you want them, and the program takes care of inserting tags. Text-based HTML editors like HotDog require you to manually type in tags for new list items.

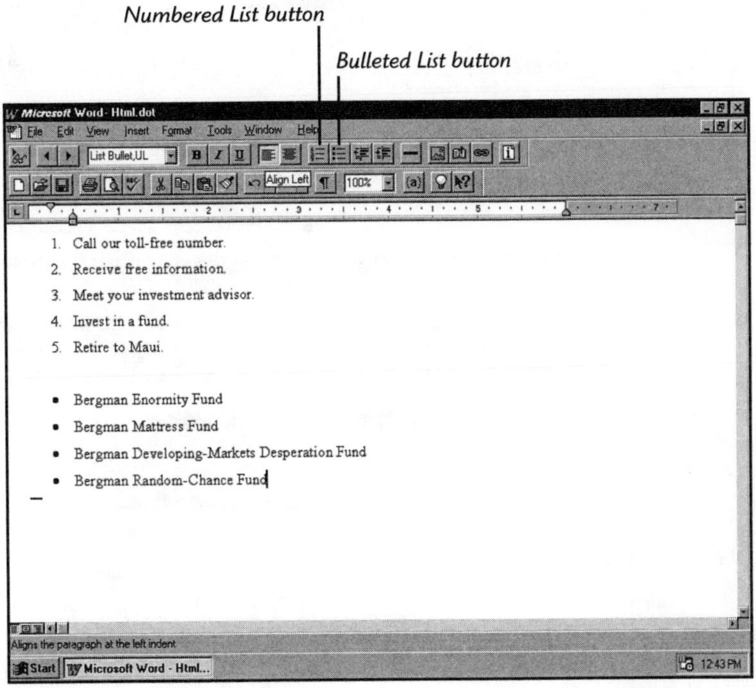

Numbered List button

Bulleted List button

Fig. 4.8
Ordered and unordered lists in Microsoft Internet Assistant. You can add list elements with ease.

Inserting images

The <IMG> tag can be one of the thorniest for beginning HTML programmers because it involves at least one attribute and some fairly obscure syntax. Again, Web page editors come to the rescue with easy ways to insert graphical elements.

HotDog

To insert an image in a Web page with HotDog:

1 Click—what else?—the Image button. When you click the Image button, the Insert Image dialog box appears.

2 In the Image File text box, enter the URL of the image file you want to use (or, if the file is in the same directory as your HTML file—and your life will be easier if it is—just put the file name).

3 In the same dialog box, HotDog lets you attach a hyperlink to the image. By typing a URL in the Document To Launch text box, you can make browsers load the resource at that URL when a user clicks the image. Hyperlinked images add new dimensions of complexity to Web page designs, but HotDog makes hyperlinked images simple.

4 Click the OK button to close the dialog box and insert the <IMG> tag. Figure 4.9 shows the Insert Image dialog box and the Image button.

Fig. 4.9
The Insert Image dialog box in HotDog. Use this dialog box to specify the path to an image file, or to attach a hyperlink to an image.

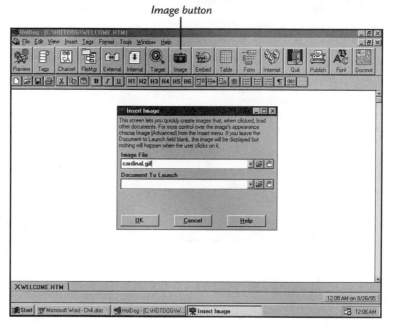

Image button

TIP **If you're creating a Web page on a machine other than the one on** which it will reside when it's made accessible to the rest of the Web community, you should keep all your documents—HTML and images—in the same directory. That way, you can just give the image's file name in the Insert Image dialog box, and not have to worry about keeping directory structures the same on both machines.

Microsoft Internet Assistant

Inserting images in Microsoft Internet Assistant is easy, but Microsoft Internet Assistant does not make provisions for attaching hyperlinks to images when you insert the image (you can, however, attach images to hyperlinks when you insert the hyperlinks).

To insert an image:

1 Click the Picture button (the one with the mountains and sun on it) on the toolbar.

2 Choose the image you want to include from the directory tree.

3 Click OK.

Unlike HotDog, Microsoft Internet Assistant shows the image in your document right away. You may find this feature useful if you're designing your page without much of a plan.

Figure 4.10 shows the Picture button and the Insert Picture dialog box.

Fig. 4.10
The Insert Picture dialog box in Microsoft Internet Assistant.

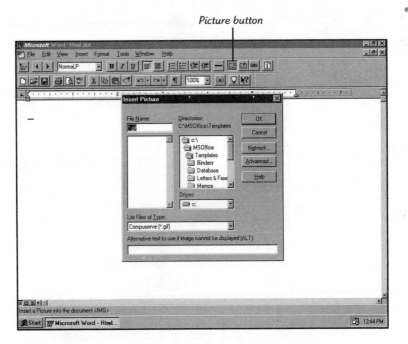

Picture button

Establishing hyperlinks

Both HotDog and Microsoft Internet Assistant make inserting hyperlinks extremely easy, which means you can use lots of them without spending hours typing long URLs and tags.

HotDog

To establish a hyperlink to an external document in HotDog, click the External button on the toolbar. The Build External Hypertext Link dialog box will appear. You can either enter the URL of the target resource in the URL drop-down list at the bottom of the dialog box, or you can enter the URL bit-by-bit in the text boxes labeled Machine, Path, File Name, and so on. Enter the words you want to be hyperlinked in the Description of Link text box at the bottom of the dialog box. The words you type there will appear in your document as a hyperlink; if a user clicks them, his or her browser will load the resource at the URL you typed.

TIP **When entering a URL, try to avoid typing it character-by-**
character. Instead, use your computer's cut-and-paste capability to copy the URL from an electronic mail document or the location box of your Web browser and paste it into the hyperlink dialog box in your Web page editor. This way, you save time and avoid typographical mistakes.

Figure 4.11 shows the Build External Hypertext Link dialog box and the External button.

External button

Fig. 4.11
The Build External Hypertext Link dialog box in HotDog. You can enter URL portions individually, or enter the entire URL in the URL text box.

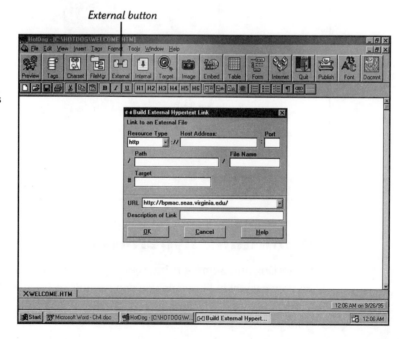

Microsoft Internet Assistant

In Microsoft Internet Assistant, you create a hyperlink by clicking the Hyperlink button (the one with chain links on it). Clicking the Hyperlink button calls up the Hyperlink dialog box, in which you can establish a link to any URL you wish. The Hyperlink dialog box has three tabs:

- Use the To Local Document tab to establish a link to another Web page on the same machine.

- Use the To URL tab to establish a link to a remote URL.

- Use the To Bookmark tab to create a link to another point in the same document.

This example assumes you want to create a link to a remote URL.

Q&A ***What are the differences among the kinds of hyperlinks?***

There are three basic kinds of hyperlinks.

- **Hyperlinks to other points in the same document**. Hyperlinks of this kind rely on special capabilities of the <A> tag and are used to provide indices to the material in a single document. The URLs in these hyperlinks need only include the name of the target index point in the same document. Use the Microsoft Internet Assistant Bookmark tab to create this kind of hyperlink.

- **Hyperlinks to other documents on the same machine**. The URLs in these hyperlinks need only specify the transport protocol, directory, and file name of the target document, not its machine name. Use the Microsoft Internet Assistant Local Document tab to create this kind of hyperlink.

- **Hyperlinks to documents on different machines**. The URLs in these hyperlinks must be complete, including transport protocol, machine name, directory, and file name. Use the Microsoft Internet Assistant URL tab to create this kind of hyperlink.

In the Text to Display text box, type the text you want to appear as a hyperlink in your document. If you want to attach a hyperlink to an image, you can click the Image button and select an image file. Then put the URL to which you want the hyperlink to lead in the URL text box. Figure 4.12 shows the Hyperlink dialog box and the Hyperlink button.

Fig. 4.12
The Hyperlink dialog
box in Microsoft
Internet Assistant. You
can attach an image to
a hyperlink with this
dialog box.

Hyperlink button

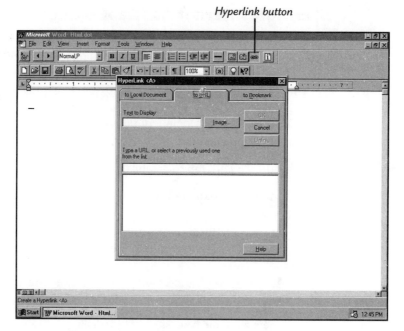

Testing your page

Before you release your page to your audience, you'll want to view it yourself to catch any mistakes. Both HotDog and Microsoft Internet Assistant make it simple to do this.

HotDog

Before you preview a HotDog document, you need to tell HotDog where to find your browser.

1 Choose Tools, Options from the menu bar. The Options dialog box appears (see fig. 4.13).

2 Select the File Locations tab.

3 Enter the path to your browser in the Preview Browser text box, or click the button to the right of that box to browse your directories in search of your Web browser files. After you tell HotDog where to find your browser, your browser's icon (instead of a movie projector) will appear on the Preview button.

4 Click the Preview button to load the current document into your browser for viewing.

Fig. 4.13
The Options dialog
box in HotDog.

Preview button

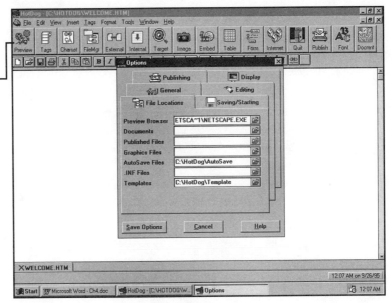

Microsoft Internet Assistant

Microsoft Internet Assistant is a WYSIWYG HTML editor, but as you have learned, browsers have a lot of freedom in deciding how to display tagged text. Microsoft Internet Assistant's display is just one way the tags can be interpreted—Netscape and NCSA Mosaic might have two other interpretations. You'd be well-served to see how other browsers interpret your document.

You have to do that manually. Start your browser, and open your HTML file with it. In Netscape, you do that by Choosing File, Open File from the menu bar and selecting your document from those listed in the Open dialog box.

TIP **Want to keep abreast of the latest Web page editor develop-**
ments, including editors designed to work with the new capabilities of Netscape Navigator 2.0 and Microsoft Internet Assistant 2.0? Point your browser at Forrest Stroud's Consummate Winsock Apps page (**http:// cwsapps.texas.net/**). Stroud's page, which he updates frequently, directs you to the newest and best Web page editors (and other Web programs, too).

Art and Music

● **In this chapter:**

- **Stroll through virtual galleries around the world**

- **Find enough art to build a private gallery—including posters for your walls and graphics for your computer**

- **Hear the latest music from your favorite recording artists—and ones you've never heard**

- **Make music, with help from major instrument manufacturers and dealers**

- **Shop for CDs online**

Has the new wave of high technology washed out the arts community? Not even close. Whether you're an artist or an art-lover, you'll find a few hundred friendly enclaves on the Web. . . . . >

There's no question that the Web is a *technical* marvel, brimming with enough programming and engineering information to keep even the most obstinate propeller-head giggling. But what about those of us who lean more to the artsy side of the spectrum?

Thankfully, the art and music community has elbowed its way into a place on the Web.

Vatican Online wires the Sistine Chapel

http://www.christusrex.org/www1/vaticano/0-Musei.html

The Sistine Chapel frescoes, Vatican City, and over 500 other images from the Vatican and its vicinity are at this site. The URL is in Italian, but the text is in English. Vatican Online truly is an amazing site with fantastic graphics and clear organization.

Fig. 5.1
Michelangelo's Sistine Chapel ceiling on the Vatican site.

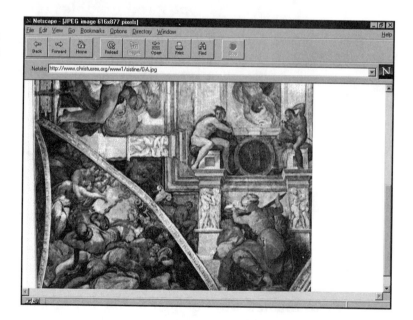

Start your tour of Vatican Online on the welcome page, where you'll find links to transcripts of the Pope's recent speeches, and position statements of the Roman Catholic Church. To access the art collection, click one of the links near the bottom of the welcome page—the ones with images to their left. These links will take you to such exhibits as:

- The Gallery of Tapestries
- Five different parts of the Gallery of Paintings
- The Treasury of Saint Peter's Cathedral
- Various parts of the Apostolic Library

Music to the extreme: the Internet Underground Music Archive

Regarded by practically every site-rating service as one of the best sites on the Web, the Internet Underground Music Archive (IUMA) maintains an archive of garage-band music and makes it available for download to anyone who's interested. This way, garage bands—including such outfits as the Japanese band Platinum Kiss Kiss and the Connecticut-based Sons of the Corporate Dog—get exposure, and music lovers can explore the bleeding edge in artistic creation. You'll discover why some of these bands remain without record contracts. Sometimes you'll find a treasure—a band or performer who's really good, but hasn't been commercially published for some reason or other.

IUMA lets you download samples of each band's music, in both .au and .mpeg format. The .mpeg files are of higher fidelity than the .au files, but they're much larger and therefore take longer to download.

Q&A **What's this about audio files of different formats?**

Just like music from the record store coming on both LPs and CDs, music on the Web comes in different forms, too. Also like different recording media from the record store, you'll need special equipment—helper applications—to play each one. Some common audio file formats include:

- **.au** Originally developed for Sun workstations, files in the .au format can be handled with the Naplayer applet that comes with Netscape.

- **.aiff** A hold-over from the now-defunct Amiga personal computer, .aiff files also work with Naplayer.

- **.mpeg** Generally thought of as a video specification, many people forget that an MPEG specification for high-fidelity sound files exists, too. You can play .mpeg files with MPEGplay, an applet that comes with Microsoft Windows 95.

- **.ra** One of the most exciting audio file formats on the Web, the RealAudio standard lets you start hearing a sound file—a radio news broadcast or a stand-up comedy routine, say—before the file downloads completely. The sound quality isn't very good, though—RealAudio files sound a lot like AM radio. Learn more about RealAudio, acquire a RealAudio player, and locate some sites that use RealAudio at the Progressive Networks RealAudio page (**http://www.RealAudio.com/**).

- **.wav** Microsoft Windows native sound file format, .wav files are large but have quite good sound quality. Play .wav files with Sound Recorder, an applet that comes with Windows 95.

Fig. 5.2
The Internet Underground Music archive has all the garage-band music you could want.

Fig. 5.3
IUMA organizes its bands in several ways, making it easy for you to find the one you want.

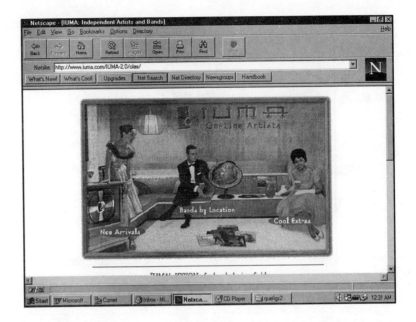

Download Leonardo da Vinci's greatest works

http://www.leonardo.net/museum/main.html

This online tribute to the original Renaissance Man has been voted one of the top ten sites on the Web. This site is about as close to an educational CD-ROM as you'll find on the Web.

The museum includes four main exhibits, each highlighting a different aspect of the man—painting, engineering, drawings, and his life. Each exhibit includes a great deal of informative text, as well as pictures available for download. Yes, you can get the *Mona Lisa* and the *Last Supper*, but some of the more interesting displays are of the great thinker's visionary ideas—a machine gun, several flying machines, and others.

Fig. 5.4

Leonardo da Vinci's design for the helicopter.

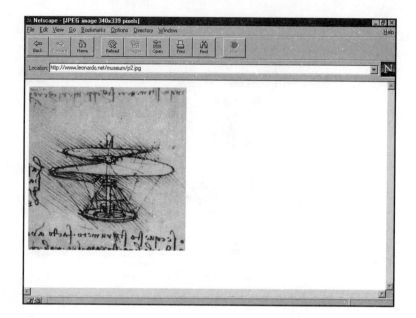

The text on the site is a pleasure to read because it neither pretends to be authoritative or reverential. In the flying machines display, for example, the author says "Never mind that they were fundamentally unworkable, or that…modern hang gliders could easily have been built with materials available at that time."

The Rock & Roll Hall of Fame

http://www.rockhall.com

Alan Freed started it all in Cleveland, introducing rock-and-roll music to a generation that cut its teeth on hot jazz and the patriotic pop of wartime. Generations later, the rock-and-roll community has brought it all back to Cleveland in the form of the Rock & Roll Hall of Fame.

The inductees exhibit includes audio clips from and about everyone from Paul Ackerman to Frank Zappa. You can also join the debate about which songs belong on the list of the top 500 rock songs of all time. If you've had a brush with greatness, you could win free stuff (that's the icon's title—"Win Free Stuff") for your story.

Be sure to check out the "Inductees Live" link from the welcome page. This link leads to an index of all Hall of Fame members, and each index entry leads to a page about that band or performer, complete with links to clips of their music. These pages aren't to be missed by any fan.

Fig. 5.5

Why go to Cleveland when you can tour the Rock & Roll Hall of Fame through the Web?

The Rock & Roll Hall of Fame is hardly a one-visit site. Rock News helps you keep up with the rock world, and the "Today in Rock" section gives you daily reasons to celebrate (and maybe take the day off from work—James Brown's birthday is a national holiday, isn't it?).

Art on the Web

If you're a connoisseur of fine visual arts, or an eager art student, you'll get a lot out of the sites in this chapter. How else can you visit the Sistine Chapel, the finest New York art dealers, and the Berkeley Art Museum and Motion Picture Film Archive in one afternoon?

Q&A   *Why are there so many visual arts sites on the Web, and relatively few dance, music, and motion picture arts sites?*

As is often the case on the Web, it's a matter of bandwidth—the amount of information the Web's physical infrastructure can handle quickly. Music, and especially dance, require enormous amounts of bandwidth (audio files, and the video files required to record dance, are very large). Still images require relatively little bandwidth, and are therefore easier to include in Web sites.

On the Web, the images you'll see most often are in either GIF or JPEG format, both of which modern browsers can display without helper applications. GIF images have the advantage of enabling the artist to use a transparent "color" that allows the background to show through. GIF images generally appear as small images, such as icons.

JPEG images, on the other hand, take advantage of the human eye's inability to perceive tiny variations in color. By ignoring such tiny variations, JPEG files can be significantly smaller than GIF files containing the same image. JPEG images generally show up as large images that fill a significant part of your screen.

Online art presentations tend to fall into a few general categories:

- **Galleries**, which display some of the works they sell. These sources are great for the art lover who can afford to spend hundreds to thousands of dollars to cover up a wrinkle in the wallpaper.

- **Museums**, public and private. Many of the world's great collections are available online, either as downloadable pictures or full-fledged virtual tours. Some Web museums are little more than electronic versions of the little guidebooks they give out at the entrance, but some are positively breathtaking.

- **Poster companies**. The pictures are often the same as those you find in galleries and museums, but you don't feel so bad about putting them up with masking tape.

 TIP **Like everything else on the Web, the visual arts offerings are** always changing. If you don't find what you're looking for, check out Worldwide Art Resources (reviewed below).

The Web is also a perfect place for artists whose work is outside of the standard "commercial appeal" realm. Individual exhibits pop up now and then, but sadly, most disappear after a few weeks.

Galleries Online: Worldwide art resources

http://www.concourse.com/wwar/

Worldwide Art Resources is *the* visual arts home page for the Web. Not only is it very comprehensive, with links to hundreds of museums, art resources, and galleries, it's also very easy to use.

Some of the resources you'll find include online magazines, contests, newsgroups, and (naturally) artists. The site's designer (Markus Kruse) appears to be open to listing any resource that could benefit the arts community, even if some of the resources are only tangentially related to art. In the magazine list, for example, you'll find almost as many pop culture magazines as arts-only mags.

For those involved in the professional end of the arts, WWAR includes an exhaustive listing of colleges, universities, and other institutions with Web resources—everything from exhibits to classes to job opportunities.

Bring the world's largest university museum home from Berkeley

http://www.uampfa.berkeley.edu/

The Berkeley University Art Museum and Pacific Film Archive (the largest university museum in the world) is also one of the finest museums on the Web. The real thing includes 11 galleries, a sculpture garden, and over 7,000 films. The online version isn't quite as extensive, but it does include an impressive MPEG-based tour of the site.

In true Berkeley fashion, the exhibitions are often based on social themes rather than art trends or specific artists. One recent exhibition covers the changing roles and views of children in art from the 17th to the 19th century, including thought-provoking text on the development of primary education.

Fig. 5.6
18th century painting from a recent exhibition at Berkeley's University Art Museum.

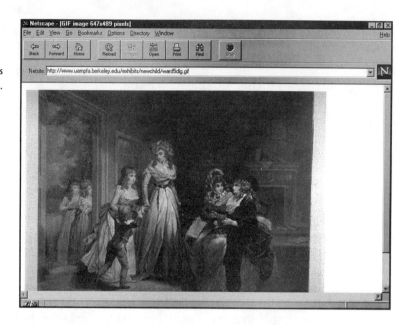

Virtual galleries and museums

You won't get the free coffee and the pretentious guide, but touring a Web museum promises to be the most comfortable art experience you've ever had. You don't have to dress up, and nobody cares if you touch the art or bring food.

Most virtual museums are more flexible than their real-world counterparts, with database searches and quick transport to other sites. Some, however, take the "virtual tour" concept very seriously and give you pictures of everything from the entryway to the stairs (kind of like Myst). Regardless of the format, all the virtual galleries and museums listed here include first-rate works of art, usually with educational text included.

The LAVA Museum of Architecture

http://www.bwk.tue.nl/lava/galleries/museums/musea_ix.html

If architecture is your thing, the LAVA Museum of Architecture is the place. It offers links to over 25 pictorials from museums in Europe and America, including Frank Lloyd Wright's Guggenheim designs.

Fig. 5.7
Frank Lloyd Wright's Guggenheim Museum designs are featured prominently on the LAVA Museum of Architecture.

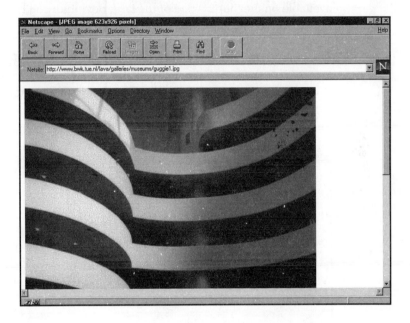

The MPEG Movie Archive

http://www.eeb.ele.tue.nl/mpeg/movies/music/index.html

Moving pictures, for many people, hold more appeal than stills. This site, maintained by Heini Withagen in the Netherlands, has MPEG movies of all kinds—from astronauts repairing the Hubble Space Telescope to model Cindy Crawford jumping rope. Use the MPEGplay applet included in Windows 95 as a helper application to play these video clips.

Bayly Art Museum at the University of Virginia

http://viva.lib.Virginia.EDU/dic/exhib/exhibitions.html

Though it's not as far-reaching as some of the other sites, the Bayly Art Museum is a good-quality site with a great deal of potential. Currently, the "African Art: Aesthetics and Meaning" exhibit is the only complete exhibit available online, but it's one of the larger exhibits you'll find—by itself, it outclasses most multi-exhibit sites.

The pictures are available for download, and the accompanying text is insightful and informative. For example, the text with the twin wooden statues (shown in figure 5.8) describes the symbolic importance of twins in certain African cultures, and how statues were often carved to commemorate the loss of one.

Fig. 5.8
These wooden statues from Africa commemorate the loss of a twin.

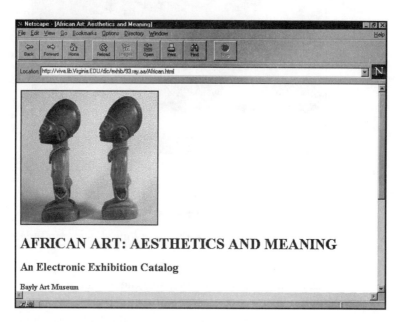

The Teyler Museum in the Netherlands

http://www.nedpunt.nl/teylersmuseum/

The oldest museum in the Netherlands, the Teyler Museum has a huge collection—unfortunately, there isn't much of it online yet. What *is* available is a schedule of upcoming exhibitions, a few high-quality photos, and an extensive history of the museum. A tip: Make sure you click "English" in the home page's language selection, or you'll have a pretty confusing ride.

Entourage

http://entourage.com/

Entourage is a searchable database of antiques, fine art, and Native American art. The surprisingly easy search engine isn't the only thing to rave about, though—the photo quality is (usually) very good, and available for download. While Entourage includes several galleries' collections, the display format is fairly standardized, so you'll immediately be able to tell the date, artist, and price of every piece.

Das Staatliche Museum Schwerin

http://hamburg.bda.de:800/bda/nat/hn/sms/welcome.html

Bring a German translator with you for the words, but the pictures are great. At the first screen, click "Die Schlösser und Gärten" (castles and gardens); "Die Gallerie am Alten Garten" followed by "Spaziergang durch die Gallerie" ("Strolling through the Gallery"); "1000 Jahre" (exhibitions of art and history for the past 1,000 years); or "Die Aktuelle Austellung" (the current exhibition).

The Andy Warhol Museum

http://www.warhol.org/warhol/

Pittsburgh's Andy Warhol Museum showcases the entire life of pop art's greatest spokesperson. Exhibits range from his beginnings in the 50s through (arguably) his "15 minutes of fame" in the 60s to his impressive later works in the 70s. Currently, only a few dozen of his hundreds of works are available online, but most are downloadable.

Online art shopping: posters and prints

Online exhibitions are great, but they don't do much to spruce up your personal living area (unless you can afford to buy rare art from galleries). The Web does offer some options for the art lover on a less Trump-ian budget, however. Poster and print dealers now sell their wares through virtual space, with electronic catalogs and advertisements on the Web.

TIP

You can improve the appearance of your Windows desktop easily, and at no charge, with art Web sites and your browser. With a modern browser like Netscape Navigator 2.0, just right-click an image you like, choose the Save This Image As option from the pop-up menu, select the directory you want, and enter a file name.

You'll have to convert the JPEG and GIF images that populate most of the Web to BMP format before you can use them as wallpaper. The best way to do this is with Paint Shop Pro, a shareware program published by JASC, Inc., and available at **http://www.winternet.com/~jasc/index.html**.

Global Innovations

http://www.icw.com/global/global.html

Available on Access Market Square, Global Innovations is a specialty products company. One of its specialties is a wide assortment of 3D stereogram posters that you can purchase by mail order. The posters aren't really *viewable* online, but GI's approximation of each image is good enough to give you a fair idea of what you're buying.

If you're an artist, you might want to try Global Innovations' 3D stereogram software, SIRDS for NIRDS (Single Image Random Dot Stereograms for Normal Individuals, Radical Dudes, and Scientists).

Novagraphics Space Art Gallery

http://www.novaspace.com/

Photorealistic images of "places we'll never be able to photograph" are the specialty of Novagraphics Space Art Gallery. It sells posters and stationary with amazing images like Saturn looming over another planet's horizon. But invention isn't the only strong suit for Novagraphics—it's also got the real thing. The catalog includes autographed works from astronaut-turned artist Alan Bean, and photographs from several U.S. and Russian space missions (most autographed by the astronaut-photographers).

Beyond the Wall

http://www.beyondthewall.com/

Art is, above all else, in the eye of the beholder. In the eyes of Beyond the Wall, art can be found in the magazine ads of Joop Jeans, Wonderbra, VISA, Sprint, and other companies. Beyond the Wall sells oversized prints of interesting ads, and apparently business is booming. The site is divided into eight "rooms" of advertising art, each with an interactive ordering feature.

Iconographics

http://www.newmexico.com/icon/

Iconographics calls itself the "Largest traveling movie poster show on the planet." It specializes in original movie posters from the 70s to the present, but you can also find classics such as Casablanca in the electronic catalog. The online pictures are available for download, and most of the catalog should qualify as "art" in anyone's book. You can order movie posters at this site, too.

Fig. 5.9
Current movie posters are a specialty at Iconographics, but you'll find classics as well.

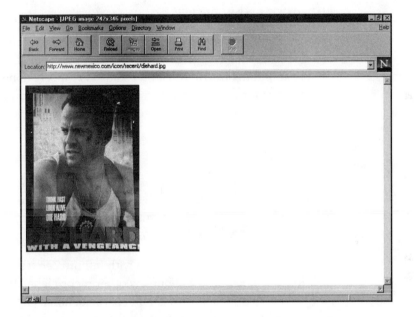

Dancing Dragon

http://www.northcoast.com/unlimited/product_directory/ dancing_dragon/

Dragons are big—not just in (mythical?) stature, but in popularity. At Dancing Dragon, you can fill just about any dragon craving, from posters, puzzles, and stationary to jewelry, masks, and virtually every other form of media.

Artdirect

http://www.artdirect.com/home.html

Artdirect is one of the few online publications that really goes beyond acting like a magazine. Its site has something for every taste, from national arts guides to interviews with artists. Check out the Permanent Collection for articles and photos on pottery, film, performance, and many other arts.

ArtWhere

http://www.artwhere.com/

Though ArtWhere is primarily surrealistically-designed clothing, it's not much of a stretch to include it in the Art section of this book. In addition to clothing from beautiful to bizarre, you'll find some very nicely-done posters and cards. The enhanced fractals from Snakebite are phenomenal, and many of the clothing selections could easily qualify as pop art.

Music on the Web

Whether you're a struggling musician, a fan, or an instrument collector, the Web has plenty to offer. Maybe you'd like to take a virtual tour of the Rock and Roll Hall of Fame, or The World of Classical Music.

Perhaps you'd like to see what's up with Infinite Zero (Henry Rollins and Rick Rubin's label) or just about any other record label. If you're a fan, you may be able to find their own genuine, official home pages. Their record label is probably the best place to look.

For music makers, the Web offers links to most instrument manufacturers, many recording studios, and professional associations for songwriters, musicians, and recording professionals. You can even find a new manager and hook up with other players in your area.

Even if you just want to fill up a few more empty notches in your CD rack, you'll be very welcome on the Web.

The World of Classical Music

http://classicalmus.com/

The World of Classical Music is a mecca for those who prefer Stravinsky to Slash's Snakepit. It's one of the best-designed sites on the Web, with ray-traced graphics and a very easy interface. This extensive and entertaining site has a huge collection of audio clips, CDs for sale, and information about classical composers and performers.

The musical clips are all 44.1kHz 16-bit (CD-quality) in MPEG format. Just in case you don't have an MPEG audio player, you can download one on TWCM's home page. Count on waiting a while for your clip of "Wenn ich in deine Augen seh'," though—the average audio file size is about 500K.

Geffen

http://geffen.com/

Music magician David Geffen shows off his stable of chart-toppers on this well-done site. If you want to keep tabs on Nirvana, Peter Gabriel, Sonic Youth, Hole, Beck, Weezer, White Zombie, or just about any other big name in cutting-edge pop, this is the place. Artists have their own pages (some, like Sonic Youth, have several), and each appears to get free reign on what appears there. Common elements include lots of photos and audio clips, but you'll also find the odd dose of band history, politics, and road stories.

A nice touch for true tech-heads: in a section dedicated to Geffen's 80s retrospective CDs, the first page is done in plain ASCII "in keeping with the spirit."

Total Guitar Magazine

http://www.futurenet.co.uk/music/totalguitar.html

The most far-reaching guitar magazine on either side of the Atlantic is also one of the best publications on the Web. The online version of *Total Guitar* has a design that improves on its paper cousin (rather than mirroring it). The back issues bin represents a valuable resource that will draw many guitarists to this site. The site also has an extensive list of guitar resources on the Web.

The folks at *Total Guitar* probably aren't too worried about the Web surfers wiping out their sales—the real newsstand version includes a CD.

Guitar World

http://www.guitarworld.com/

Guitar World is one of America's biggest contributions to the guitar magazine rack (online and off). The Web site has a slick design, but much of the printed version is left out, presumably for sales reasons. At least you can download sound clips and software from the magazine's columns.

Fig. 5.10

Guitar World's online version.

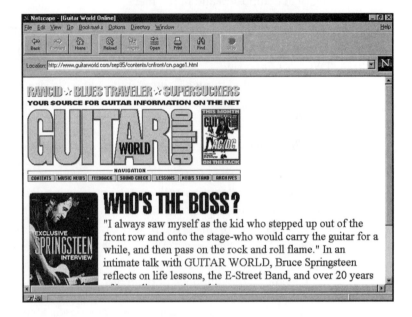

American Recordings

http://american.recordings.com/

Named one of the top Web sites, American Recordings' home page includes games, only a smattering of promotional fluff, and a nice database of band pages. One of the highlights has to be an interview with Rick Rubin and Henry Rollins about the formation of their music preservation label, Infinite Zero, which breathes new life into all-but-forgotten vinyl records that haven't yet been released on CD.

Keeping up with the stars

If you look up your favorite little-known musician in a WWW search program, you're likely to be in for a shock. No matter how obscure the person or group is, somebody out there has at least *part* of a page dedicated to them. Sometimes, you'll find genuinely interesting information on these sites, other times just a photo or a bootleg recording. These sites, like most other noncorporate Web sites, usually don't last forever, but they're fun while they're around.

There are, however, some fan-oriented sites that don't come and go like independent Presidential candidates. One of the best is Geffen's (reviewed earlier in the chapter). Some of the others are highlighted in this section.

ArtRock

http://www.shopping2000.com/shopping2000/artrock/

For posters and shirts of your favorite musician or group, check out ArtRock's catalog. The interface is easy (it's part of Shopping 2000), and prices aren't bad.

The Nashville Collection

http://www.nashville-collection.com/

If twang is your thang, check out The Nashville Collection. It's got music clips, interviews, tour schedules, and photos from Nashville's top artists. As the site is quick to point out, the Nashville music scene is more than just country—it's also jazz, rock, and more.

Rock Online

http://www.rockonline.com/

This site is not only home to EMI's rising stars (Queensrÿche, Milla, and many, many more), but also several independent bands. It includes several downloadable pictures and some good fanzine-type information.

Making music—and industry contacts

So how can the Web help you if you happen to be the next Leon Redbone? Check out the following sites, designed to help you make music and sell it once it's made.

Harmony Central

http://harmony-central.mit.edu/

MIT's Harmony Central is the probably the best place for musicians to start their Web voyage. It's a list of links to every sort of musical resource on the Net. Don't worry—this isn't just another page of fan sites; it's for real, working musicians.

Fig. 5.11
Harmony Central is a great resource for music lovers—it points to dozens of useful sites.

The WholeArts Music Mall

http://www.wholarts.com/music/

The WholeArts Music Mall is a list of links to many industry/sales sites. You can find music lessons, instruments, and agents in its catalog. The site is very graphics-intensive (sometimes for no good reason); if you're using a slower modem, turn the graphics off before you go in.

Vintage Instruments

http://expert-sys.com/vinstruments/vinstruments.html

While Vintage Instruments isn't a very visual site, it's positively a jewel for collectors of stringed instruments. The company sells, repairs, and appraises the finest stringed instruments in the world, from worthless, unplayable old things to priceless, unplayable antiques. A $14,500 Martin guitar was the most expensive piece I came across, with most instruments closer to the $1000-$5000 range.

Edinburgh University Collection of Historical Musical Instruments

http://www.music.ed.ac.uk/euchmi/index.html

Maybe this should be in the art section, but if you want to learn more about your musical instruments, the Edinburgh University Collection of Historical Musical Instruments is a great place to start. Every category of instrument is represented with downloadable pictures and historical text.

Fig. 5.12
A French bagpipe? Well, the site's in Scotland, so they'd know.

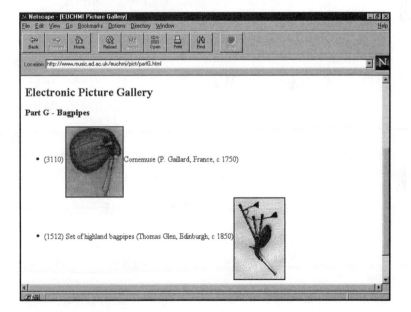

FenderWorld

http://www.fender.com

FenderWorld is a very visual site, with the main controls in the shape of (what else?) a Fender amplifier. Check out the real history of the near-mythical Stratocaster, along with photos of Fender players through history.

Fig. 5.13
Fender's site includes pictures, players, and histories of some of the best-selling guitars in the world.

Drummer's Web

http://valley.interact.nl/AV/MUSWEB/DRUMWEB/home.html

The best part of Musician's Web, Drummer's Web features interviews, equipment reviews, and just about anything else that could interest the modern beater. The percussion resource list is positively indispensable.

Dr. Bob: Friend of electronic musicians

http://www.zeelandnet.nl/people/rsm/

Dr. Bob Muller has done a great service for the community of musicians who use MIDI and other electronic media to express themselves. Dr. Bob's MIDI and Sequencing Website offer links to MIDI samples, as well as to sites that offer MIDI and sequencing tools for downloading.

Other guitar manufacturers

To be fair, I should point out that Fender is hardly the only guitar manufacturer on the Web. Also check out:

http://www.gibson.com/

http://www.washburn.com/

If you're in a band, put I-Site on your hot list

http://www.i-site.com/

I-Site is home to several independent companies and music organizations. It's mostly for independent bands, but professionals at any level will find interesting contacts here. The main areas are management, recording studios, and NAS (the National Academy of Songwriters). Unfortunately, NAS publications aren't currently available online.

Online music shopping

With the catalog of available compact discs growing so fast, most real-world stores can't even hope to keep up. If you've looked for a slightly obscure title, you know the drill: they'll order it for you and it'll be at the store in a week. Online music stores, however, can get just about anything right away, and have it sent directly to you. With the major online music stores charging competitive prices and boasting catalogs of 100,000 to 150,000 titles, how can you go wrong?

Besides, why would you slog through the mall crowds to get your next bunch of CDs when you can stay home in your robe and have them sent directly to you?

CD Connection

http://ftp.cdconnection.com/

One of the original online music stores, CD Connection isn't really a Web site—it's a BBS and Telnet site. It does, however, offer over 100,000 CD titles in every category, so it's worth checking out.

CD World

http://cdworld.com/

CDworld also boasts an online catalog of over 100,000 titles, but it's a full-fledged Web service with a relatively simple interface. Prices are fairly competitive, with $13.77 being a commonly-used base point.

Emusic

http://www.emusic.com

Emusic's catalog also features 100,000+ CDs. Its prices are slightly cheaper than CDworld's (a comparison of several disks showed Emusic consistently 10 cents per disk lower), plus it scores over all the other music stores with a *very* easy interface. It's well worth a visit.

Interrogative Music Media

http://www.icw.com/cd/imm1.html

Interrogative Music Media's site has a few more bells and whistles (more artist information, for example), but the prices are not pretty. In a comparison with Emusic and CDWorld, IMM came up $2-3 higher on most discs.

There's more to music than CDs

http://www.musicsales.co.uk/

If making music means more to you than pressing a Play button, check out The Internet Music Shop. It has over 20,000 items, including sheet music and MIDI files. One of the more convenient features is a sheet music fax service, but since they're in the UK, you could run up a pretty hefty credit card bill in phone charges alone.

Fig. 5.14
The Internet Music Shop is an amazing resource for sheet music and MIDI files.

Business and Employment

● **In this chapter:**

● **Where can you get information about financial markets and personal finance on the Web?**

● **Help yourself find a new job, change careers, or advertise a job opening you need to fill**

● **Use the World Wide Web to establish worldwide business contacts**

● **Find expert advice and resources for small businesses and entrepreneurs**

● **Get involved in a labor organization or be a more educated consumer**

From corporate giants like Ford Motor Company to the smallest home office, businesses are staking their claims in the virtual office space on the Web. . . . . ●

Two major factors have fueled the growth of the Internet and the Web in the last few years: the development of slick software like Netscape and Mosaic and the rush of businesses to join the Web. In this chapter, we're going to take a look at the types of businesses and the sources of business information on the Web.

When it absolutely, positively has to be there overnight: Federal Express

http://www.fedex.com/

This site is one of the most truly useful ones yet. When your boss asks you how the Internet has improved your job performance, tell her "Why, just this morning I used it to track a FedEx package."

That's right, now you don't even have to call FedEx or use their special tracking software (although you can download Windows and Mac versions of the software). All you have to do is enter the tracking number for your package and instantly you'll know whether it has been delivered.

Fig. 6.1
Track a package at the FedEx Web site.

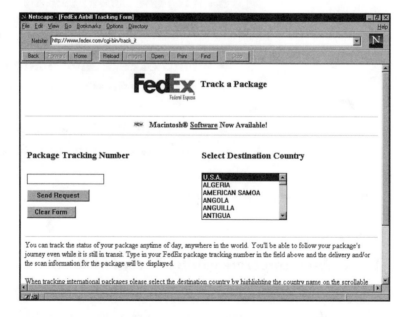

On top of that, if you need to send a package by FedEx, there's also a similar page here at the FedEx site that gives you information on availability of FedEx services. The information is based on the date and time you shipped it, where it left, and where it's going.

Plan your investment strategy at Fidelity Investments

http://www.fid-inv.com

Financial planning is something that most of us aren't very good at. Sure, you may put a few dollars into CDs, and IRA, or a 401K plan, but are you really planning? Are you looking at your investment goals and determining how to get there? In order to do this right, most people need to turn to the advice of a professional investment planner.

The Fidelity Investment site doesn't take the place of a personal investment advisor. But if you don't know where you're headed in the investment world, this site is a good place to assess your needs and current situation. Current or potential investors will get good use from this site. You can view summary information on various Fidelity mutual funds, download prospectuses for some, and request mailed prospectuses and applications for others. If you're planning for retirement, you'll find valuable information here about Fidelity retirement services.

There's an online questionnaire that you fill out so that your investing attitudes can be assessed and so that an investment strategy can be recommended. You'll also find descriptions of various brokerage services, worksheets for planning 401K investments, and even a couple of contests. With all the online forms you can fill out to assess your investing and retirement options, you'll find that spending some time at this site is well worth it.

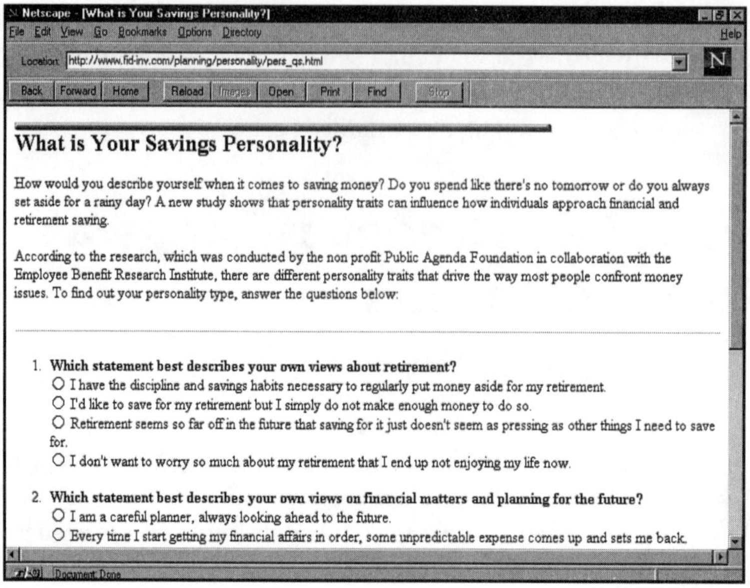

Fig. 6.2
Fill out an online questionnaire and assess your investment personality. Find out what types of invest-ments are best-suited to your tolerance for risk and need for reward.

Netscape - [What is Your Savings Personality?]
File Edit View Go Bookmarks Options Directory   Help
Location: http://www.fid-inv.com/planning/personality/pers_qs.html

Back | Forward | Home | Reload | Images | Open | Print | Find | Stop

What is Your Savings Personality?

How would you describe yourself when it comes to saving money? Do you spend like there's no tomorrow or do you always set aside for a rainy day? A new study shows that personality traits can influence how individuals approach financial and retirement saving.

According to the research, which was conducted by the non profit Public Agenda Foundation in collaboration with the Employee Benefit Research Institute, there are different personality traits that drive the way most people confront money issues. To find out your personality type, answer the questions below:

1. **Which statement best describes your own views about retirement?**
   ○ I have the discipline and savings habits necessary to regularly put money aside for my retirement.
   ○ I'd like to save for my retirement but I simply do not make enough money to do so.
   ○ Retirement seems so far off in the future that saving for it just doesn't seem as pressing as other things I need to save for.
   ○ I don't want to worry so much about my retirement that I end up not enjoying my life now.

2. **Which statement best describes your own views on financial matters and planning for the future?**
   ○ I am a careful planner, always looking ahead to the future.
   ○ Every time I start getting my financial affairs in order, some unpredictable expense comes up and sets me back.

Document Done

CareerMosaic

http://www.careermosaic.com/cm/

CareerMosaic is a large clearinghouse for job seekers. Many major compa-nies including high-tech companies like 3M, AT&T, Novell, Rockwell, and Unisys post company profiles and job openings to CareerMosaic's database. The database is fully searchable by company name, location, job description, and title. CareerMosaic also indexes thousands of job postings from UseNet newsgroups in a searchable format. There are also special links for recent or upcoming college grads, online job fairs, and other career-related Web sites.

Fig. 6.3
Get your Career on the
right track with the
online resources at
CareerMosaic.

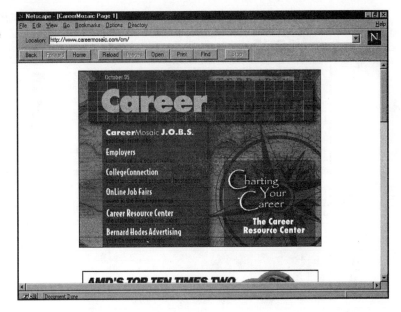

Spend Real Money Safely Online with First Virtual Holdings

http://www.firstvirtual.com

First Virtual is an Internet electronic banking system. Many major companies on the Web allow payment through a First Virtual account. To get a First Virtual account, provide information about yourself (name, address, email address). First Virtual will send you an email confirmation. You'll then need to call the 800 number and provide a credit card account number. Once you provide a credit card number, you get a First Virtual account number and password.

In order to buy something from a company that accepts payments from First Virtual account members, use your First Virtual account number. This way valuable credit card numbers are never sent over the Internet. After making a purchase, you'll get an email confirmation and a chance to let First Virtual know if you didn't make the purchase.

Fig. 6.4
With a First Virtual account you can buy goods and services on the Web and not have to worry that someone might steal your credit card number.

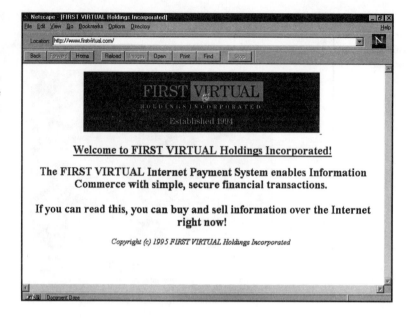

Finance, Investment, and Banking

The Web is a fantastic source of information for investors. Whether your investment interests are for personal use (saving for retirement, college, or a new house) or you're investing for a business, you can keep up-to-date with financial markets, and find companies to help you with your investment decisions.

TIP **Due to government and stock market restrictions, all financial** data on all of these Internet services are time delayed by a minimum of 15 minutes.

Quote.Com

http://www.quote.com

This service offers up-to-date information on and about financial markets. You can get current stock quotes, historical stock data and trend analysis, and portfolio tracking. Users can get a free account that gives access to a small sample of services. A paid account opens up a wider range of features.

Fig. 6.5
Quote.Com provides information on individual stocks, markets, bonds, commodities options, and much more to its subscribers.

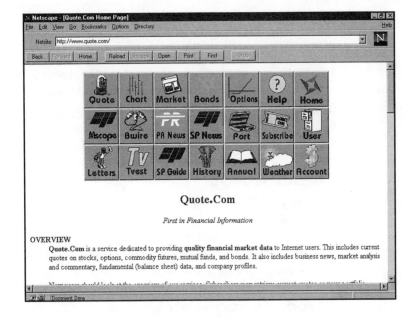

BankAmerica

http://www.bankamerica.com

Whether you need information about personal or business banking, this site has it all. You can get background on checking and savings accounts, various types of loans, credit cards, and other services. One interactive feature here is a home loan calculator. To use it, input your monthly income, down payment, and interest rate and the Web site calculates the maximum price home you should look for, the total mortgage payment, and other payment information.

Wells Fargo Bank

http://www.wellsfargo.com

This site has abundant background information available for various banking services Wells Fargo offers to individuals and businesses. Information ranges from simple checking and savings accounts to investment planning for individuals, to commercial banking services. Wells Fargo also offers online banking. To take advantage of this feature, you'll need to use Netscape 1.22 or later (the versions that incorporate a security fix).

U.S. Bank

http://www.usbanksl.com

This Web site provides information about U.S. Bank student loan and financial aid programs. You will find why you would want to apply for financial aid (that seemed rather obvious to me), how to apply, and a long list of answers to commonly asked questions about the financial aid form (FAF). This site should be valuable to parents and students planning a college education.

Charles Schwab

http://www.schwab.com

You can download demo versions of the popular StreetSmart and FundMap software from this site. There's also extensive online information about mutual funds and various accounts and services.

Corporate Financials Online

http://www.cfonews.com/

This company posts financial information from publicly traded companies. Information includes recent news, earnings, dividends, and shareholder information.

Ernst and Young

http://www.ey.com/

This site provides information about accounting, auditing, tax services, and management consulting at Ernst and Young. It also has information about the services offered by Ernst and Young member firms in countries worldwide.

PAWWS Online

http://pawws.secapl.com/top.html

This service offers real-time stock quotes for a fee. PAWWs Online also offers portfolio accounting, brokerage services, and online discount brokerage.

Chicago Board Options Exchange

http://www.cboe.com/

Look here for market statistics, research, and news releases from the Chicago Board Options Exchange. There's an educational and information section that explains what options are, how options trading works, and answers frequently asked questions about options trading.

Fig. 6.6
The CBOE is one of five U.S. exchanges that trade options. If you don't understand options trading, learn all about it at this site.

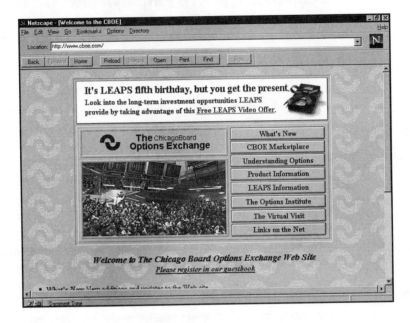

Employment

Wouldn't it be nice to have an electronic help wanted section? Rather than read every ad in the Sunday paper looking for your dream job, you could perform a simple computer search and have a short list of jobs to read about. The Web can be your link to many of these job databases. You'll also find Web sites where you can post your resumé, get resumé-writing tips, find upcoming career events in your area, and read about prospective employers.

CareerWeb

http://www.cweb.com/

Employers, franchisers, and other career-related companies (like placement services and search agencies) post job openings and information about their companies here. All the information here is fully searchable.

E-Span Interactive Employment Network

http://www.espan.com

E-Span has an online job database with over 1,700 employers. In addition to searching for jobs in the database, you can take a more proactive approach and post a resumé. E-Span's career guide includes a salary guide with current salary survey data by region and occupation, career fair calendars, resumé tips, and more.

America's Job Bank

http://www.ajb.dni.us/

This site lists job openings known to the over 1,800 state Employment Services offices. There are over 100,000 jobs in the nationwide database, most of which are in the private sector. You can search on a nationwide basis or by specific state—if that state has its job database online. (Currently, about 20 states have put Employment Services offices online.)

Fig. 6.7
America's Job Bank is a gateway to searching a database of over 100,000 jobs online.

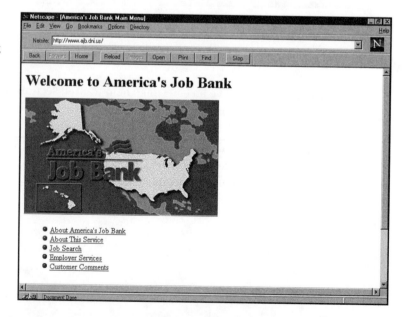

The Riley Guide

http://www.wpi.edu/mfriley/jobguide.html

This guide discusses issues for job seekers who are using the Internet as part of their search. Topics include how to use the Internet in your search and how to post job listings. This site also has many links to sites with job postings.

Automobiles

If you want to explore examples of what big businesses are doing on the Web, you don't have to look further than the automotive industry. Check out what some of these corporate giants are using the Web for, and see which related businesses are setting up shop.

Chrysler

http://www.chryslercorp.com

This car maker's site focuses on a technology tour. Browse information about concept cars (including pictures and video clips), alternative and flexible fuel vehicles, recycling, and environmental programs.

Goodyear

http://www.goodyear.com

This site features tire care information, driving tips, a blimp and motor racing schedule, and news about the tire industry.

Ford Motor Co.

http://www.ford.com

This automobile giant's Web page delivers information about the many lines of automobiles the produce and affiliated goods and services. You'll find features and specifications for Fords, Lincolns, Mercurys, and Jaguars. Other information relates to Ford financial services, which include auto loans and lease programs.

BMW

http://www.bmw.de/HOMHOME.html

There are some great pictures here of current BMW models. Besides these pictures, the pickings are slim at this site. There is some information on sales figures and some new technology developments (like round reduction and on-board navigation systems), but the site does leave you wanting more.

Fig. 6.8
You can download a picture of a BMW for free, but the real thing will still cost you a bundle.

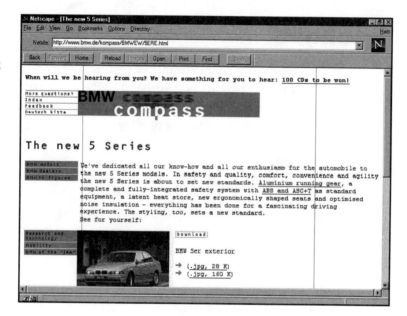

Saturn

http://www.saturncars.com/

This site is mostly centered around providing information about the 1996 line of Saturns. You can get rather detailed descriptions of the features of each car and photographs from a couple of different angles. (Kudos to the Webmaster here for keeping the file size small on the photos so they download fast, while not sacrificing much in image quality or size.) You can find your nearest Saturn dealer and browse the Saturn magazine, which has news about the company and letters from readers.

If you're a Saturn owner, you can add your name to the database of Saturn owners (they call this their Extended Family Database) or search the database to find other Saturn owners.

DealerNet

http://www.dealernet.com/

DealerNet has over 4,500 pages of information from 48 different car companies. The information on new cars is searchable by manufacturer and price range. The search returns a list of models in your price range. You can then get more information (a sales pitch) about any of the models listed. There's also a list of used cars and some information on boating and recreational vehicle resources. Finally, you'll find a small selection of MPEG videos of some of these cars. Another service here connects you to a credit check form where you can (for a fee) get a copy of your current credit report.

Doing business on the Internet

Seeing what other companies are doing on the Web is one thing. Actually figuring out how to set up your own business on the Web, or make the most of business resources on the Web, is a totally different proposition. In this section, we've listed some sites that help you determine what your business can do on the Web and how to make the best use of Web resources no matter what business you are in.

Internet Business Center

http://tig.com/IBC/index.html

This site is a collection of information designed for business people using the Web. There's a listing of the best companies on the Web and a listing of other good sources of business information on the Web. You can jump to mailing lists that feature discussions of business issues in Internet use. The concise timeline of the Internet's history at this site could be useful for preparing a business presentation about the Internet.

CommerceNet

http://www.commerce.net

CommerceNet is a consortium of businesses working to explore the use of the Internet and new technologies for business. Unless your company is interested in joining CommerceNet (a fairly pricey venture), the most useful information to you here will be the CommerceNet Directories. These are a collection of business resources such as databases, catalogs, business services, and other directories.

Fig. 6.9
CommerceNet was one of the first major groups of businesses to exploit the Web for business use.

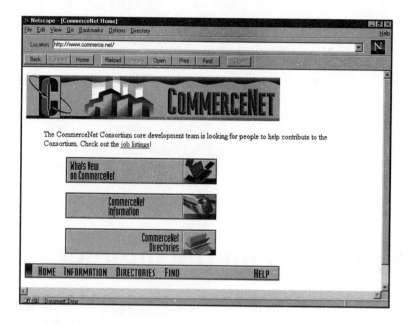

Internet Ad Source

http://www.primenet.com/mkropp/interad.html

If you want to advertise on popular Web pages or if you want to sell advertising space on your Web page, this site can help match you up with a buyer or seller. The listing of ad space for rent includes background on the sites, some demographics, and costs.

Global Trade Center

http://www.tradezone.com/tz/

This site contains an index of links useful to businesses doing international trade. You'll find links to international banks, importers and exporters, distributors, conventions and meetings, trade law, and more. There are descriptions of companies that are looking for contacts with other international trading partners. You can place a trade lead of your own here, too.

International Import Export Business Exchange

http://www.imex.com

This site is designed to help promote international trade through the Internet. Large and small business alike use this site to locate customers and suppliers for international trade, get answers to questions about international trade, and add their products and services to the list of international trading partners.

Market Link

http://nwlink.com/marketlink

Any company involved in any aspect of international trade will benefit from Market Link. You can search Market Link's large database of suppliers, distributors, importers and exporters, and other international trading categories based on industry, location, or company name. You can also add your company's information to the database, called the "World Wide Business Card File." There are also links to world market data, international language references, embassies, trade organizations, international commerce guides, and other information applicable to international trading.

Small Business and Entrepreneur Resources

People who run small businesses know that many of the issues and challenges faced are much different than what major corporations deal with. From finding financing to start or grow your business to getting your products or services sold and marketed, you'll find not just information, but contacts, customers, and suppliers on the Web. The sites listed in this chapter are all good places for small business owners and entrepreneurs to get a start with a new business, or expand an existing business on the Web.

CONNECTnet

http://darwin1.ucsd.edu/connect/

This site is part of a university project to connect entrepreneurs in the high-tech and bio-tech industries to investors, markets, and other resources they need to build their businesses. Here, there's a technology directory with an index of member companies by type (for example, banks, marketing, patent, software, stockbrokers), weekly and quarterly newsletters, and a calendar of events and meetings.

SoHo Central

http://www.hoaa.com/

As the name of this page suggests, it is of interest to Small Office/Home Office (SOHO) business people. This site is run by the Home Office Association of America (which advertises memberships in their organization on the site). There are articles here about raising capital for a new venture, home office startup ideas, and more.

Ideas Digest

http://www.ideas.wis.net/

Ideas Digest bills itself as an "Online Innovation Center." This site feature articles for inventors and entrepreneurs who are creating and marketing new products. Features range from how to measure quality service to how to buy patent insurance. There's a question and answer section where you can get advice from an experienced pro and a classified section where inventors advertise their products in search of manufacturers, dealers, and other partners.

Small Business Administration

http://www.sbaonline.sba.gov/

This site is another fine one brought to you by your tax dollars. Seriously, the Small Business Administration has done a lot of good work in encouraging development of small business in the U.S. This Web site has information on small business events (conferences), how the SBA helps people start businesses, and how to expand and finance your business. For example, one way the SBA helps people start businesses is through a program of retired business executives who volunteer to help others start a business. This program and others are described in detail.

Labor Organizations

Labor organizations of all sizes are increasing their exposure worldwide through the use of the Web. If you're a member of one of these groups or just interested in labor activities, you'll want to explore these sites.

AFL-CIO

http://www.aflcio.org/

The AFL-CIO is not one union, but a conglomerate of more than 80 labor organizations. This site presents news of interest to union members and labor organizers, lists of products the AFL-CIO is boycotting, and links to other labor organizations.

LaborNet

http://www.igc.apc.org/labornet/

Labor unions and activists organize this site. The information here includes a long list of labor and activist groups, with links to those that have Web sites. You'll find pages listing current strikes, news affecting labor groups, a calendar of labor organization conferences and events, and appeals for help in labor situations.

Consumer Resources

If all these businesses are doing business on the Web, someone has to be consuming these goods and services, right? If you're a Web consumer, you'll want to look at these sites to find the businesses of interest to you and to help you become a more savvy consumer.

Consumer Information

http://www.usps.gov/websites/depart/inspect/consmenu.htm

This group of pages is a part of the United States Postal Service's Web site. Consumers can find a variety of information about protecting themselves from fraud and other crimes that the postal inspection services works to fight. While the information here is primarily about mail and telephone fraud schemes, much of what is said here also applies to online and Internet schemes. Read up and beware because many people run pyramid schemes, fraudulent lotteries, and other scams on the Internet, particularly in UseNet newsgroups.

Consumer World

http://www.consumerworld.org/

This site is an extensive collection of links of interest to consumers. Categories listed here include news, consumer agencies, directories of 800 numbers and manufacturers, travel, entertainment, money, and shopping.

Fig. 6.10
Consumers can find 100s of useful Web sites through Consumer World.

Other Major Businesses

This chapter wraps up with a look at some other major businesses and sources of business information on the Web.

3M

http://WWW.MMM.COM/

The real name of this company is Minnesota Mining and Manufacturing, which explains why they go by the more elegant 3M. This Web site is a gold mine of product information. It includes feature articles about new and innovative products like a thin film strong enough to support a person standing on it and a portable multimedia projector that is bright enough to use with the room lights on. The product information pages include an alphabetical listing of 3M products, a list of acronyms and abbreviations, and a keyword search option for products ("Honey, have you seen the Scotch Tape?" "Was that the drafting tape, cellophane fiber tape, or cloth duct tape?") Wow. With over 60,000 products, don't get lost!

General Electric

http://www.ge.com/

This site has information about the many divisions that make up General Electric as well as GE as a whole. GE's divisions range from aircraft engines to television broadcasting.

REFER.com Real Estate

http://refer.com/real/realestate.htm

This online real estate service page has searchable listings for residential, commercial, and vacation properties. The residential offerings can be searched by number of bedrooms and baths, price range, and state. The listings are primarily in the U.S., but there are also some Caribbean properties.

Zima

http://www.zima.com

This site is purely for fun. (If you're thinking of some off-the-wall advertising and promotion on the Web, this might be an example to study.) Read about Zima's malt beverage (who knows exactly what this stuff really is), see their bar and restaurant guide, or explore the 'fridge.

Wal-Mart Stores Inc.

http://sam.wal-mart.com

At the Wal-Mart site you can search for the nearest Wal-Mart (or Sam's Club) by city, state, area code, or zip code. You can also get a listing of some jobs available at Wal-Mart. The Sams Club portion of the site describes the Sam's credit options and an online gift ordering service.

MasterCard International

http://www.mastercard.com

The Web seems like an unlikely place to apply for a credit card, but that's one of the things you can do at this site. You can also find out about a new secure transaction method MasterCard is helping develop. This method will enable you to exchange financial information (including credit card numbers) on the Web without fear of someone intercepting your card number. You'll also find a wide variety of background information about MasterCard and an eclectic collection of links to other sites.

Chiat/Day

http://www.chiatday.com/web

This agency was one of the first major advertising agencies to really get involved in the Web as an advertising medium. Chiat/Day now says that it is "in the business of creating and promoting brands" rather than an "advertising agency." You'll find a lot of information here about this company's philosophy, creativity, and invention. There's also some cute but silly stuff like quotes from the boss and a catalog of Valentine's Day presents the boss has given them.

Thomas Register

http://www.thomasregister.com

If you've ever researched a type of product or service at your local library, you've probably browsed through the printed versions of the Thomas Register in the library's reference section. (With 29 volumes, this is a major publication.) A free registration entitles you to search the 52,000 categories in this database online. The database is searchable by product or service and company name. There's also information here about a CD-ROM version of the Thomas Register, how to get your company listed in the register, and tutorials on how to buy some high-tech hardware and software.

Dun & Bradstreet

http://www.dnb.com

Dun & Bradstreet is a massive publishing and information services company. Its divisions include Neilson Media Research (the company that does TV ratings), Donnelley (the Yellow Pages company), and several software and data groups. Dun & Bradstreet is best known in the business community for its business information publications. Online you'll find snapshot predictions of U.S. business growth and failure trends, a weekly newsletter, and links to divisions that have their own Web sites.

Interactive Age Hot 1,000 Businesses

http://techweb.cmp.com/techweb/ia/hot1000/hot1.html

This table lists the top 1,000 North American companies based on U.S. sales in dollars. For each company, the company name is linked to the company Web site if it has one. U.S. sales revenue (in dollars) and a contact telephone number are also listed.

Computer Hardware and Software Resources

● **In this chapter:**

- Where are the computer hardware manufacturers on the Web?

- Get help with the software you use and find out about new versions or improvements

- Find a cool new computer game or learn how to master a game you've been playing

- Shop for computer hardware and software on the Web without going to the store or picking up the phone.

Is it any surprise that the Web, part of a global computer network, is a huge resource for information about computers? . . . .

f you're reading this book, you use a computer to cruise the World Wide Web. And when you use a computer, there's going to come a time when you want a new computer or some new gadget or software for it. And it's inevitable that at some point you'll have a problem with your computer hardware or software that you need help with.

In the past, if you wanted to buy some new computer software or hardware, you would go to the local computer store. There you would find a slick salesman trying to sell you something you didn't need or a high school kid that didn't know a mouse from a mouse trap. Getting help with hardware or software problems meant hours on the phone listening to elevator muzak (and sales pitches) while waiting on hold, impatient technical support representatives, and often no help on evenings or weekends.

So along comes the Web and all your problems are solved, right? Well, maybe not all of them are solved. But if you're willing to do a little digging, you can often find information about any new product you might buy online. You can then go to the store (or call a mail-order reseller) armed with all the facts you need to buy exactly what you want. Some of the sites listed here even take online orders for their products. (Check out Chapter 17 for a discussion of online shopping.)

If you know a little bit about the hardware or software that's giving you trouble, you can often find updated versions of software that fix (or work around) bugs. You can even read directions for completing some task that is stumping you.

Keep in mind, this approach isn't for everyone. If you like to help yourself, the Web is a great resource for computer information. But if you'd rather still have the comfort of talking to someone and having them help you get what you need, the Web may not be the best source for you.

 TIP In this chapter, we look at general-interest computer products. If you need information about companies that specialize in Internet and Web products and services, look at Chapter 11, "Internet and Web Information." Because there are so many Internet- and Web-related software and hardware products, we've devoted all of Chapter 11 to that niche.

The granddaddy of them all: IBM

http://www.ibm.com

It seems appropriate to begin a discussion about computer resources on the Web with IBM. After all, IBM's products dominated the world of mainframe computers in the early days of computers. And its personal computers helped usher in the whole personal computer trend. So this is where we start our look at Web resources for computer aficionados.

The IBM Web site includes news about IBM and the computer industry, information and news about the many computer systems IBM sells, and a searchable software library with many software files for IBM products. The software includes utilities and diagnostics for IBM hardware, upgrades and fixes for IBM software, and even some free software.

Fig. 7.1
Here you can find news and information about PCs from IBM as well as about the rest of the PC industry.

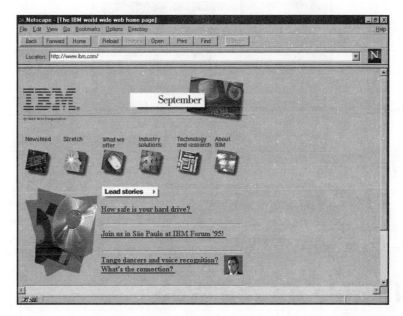

Compare apples to apples (or Windows) at Apple Computer

http://www.apple.com

Apple thinks Macintosh computers are better than PCs running Windows 95, and this home page tries to prove it by showing comparisons of the Mac and

PCs running Windows. You can also get product descriptions and support for Apple hardware and software (with press releases and special information for the newest products) and specialized information for various user groups such as educators, publishers, and multimedia users. Apple also includes links to many other Web sites that have information about products for Apple computers.

Fig. 7.2
Apple emphasizes how Macs are different than PCs running Windows 95.

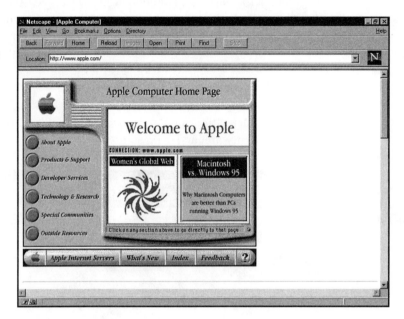

 TIP **Have you been looking for Apple's QuickTime viewer so you can** view all the great QuickTime movies on the Web? The place to look is **http:// quicktime.apple.com**. Mac and Windows versions are available.

Intel inside on the Web

http://www.intel.com

Here's Intel's home page—Intel makes the processors that power most of the personal computers in use today. This Web site offers easy-to-read information about the many types of processors available (486s, Pentiums, and the new Pentium Pro). Depending on the technical level of information you need, you can get simple comparisons of the speeds and features of the various processors or detailed specifications for how the processor is built and how it works. (A lot of the technical documentation here is in either Adobe Acrobat's Portable Document Format or PostScript. To view the documents in your Web browser, you may need to install a helper application. Chapter 2 covers helper installation.)

Fig. 7.3

Intel's site focuses on their processors, especially the newer Pentiums and Pentium Pros.

If you've been considering upgrading the processor in your PC, Intel makes upgrade processors (called OverDrive) that you can use. Figuring out which OverDrive processor is right for your computer and your needs can be difficult, but you can read all about them here. With the information you get here, you should be able to walk right in to your local computer retailer (or go to one of the Web-based computer stores listed later in this chapter) and buy the OverDrive chip that's right for you.

Intel makes more than just processors, like modems, network cards, and video-conferencing hardware. Information about all these products is available here, too.

Does Bill Gates want to rule the world with Microsoft?

http://www.microsoft.com

You have heard of Microsoft, right? The Internet community has been the source of endless humor at the expense of the world's largest software company, but don't expect to find Microsoft's plans to buy the Catholic Church or the Justice Department here.

So, what can you find at Microsoft's Web site? It has descriptions and sales pitches for all its desktop application products, such as Word, Excel, and PowerPoint. Windows (NT, 95, 3.1) gets the coverage it deserves here, too. You can also find out about Microsoft's new online service, The Microsoft Network. (Microsoft Network is covered more in Chapter 11.) There's a massive file download area where you can get some of Microsoft's free products and upgrades, including the Microsoft Internet Explorer, Microsoft Internet Assistant for Word, and Microsoft Word viewer. Updated Windows 3.1 and NT files are there now and as soon as updates for Windows 95 are available, I'm sure they'll be posted on the site.

Fig 7.4
The world's largest software company tells you about its products and services.

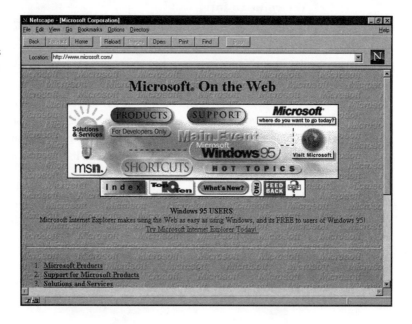

TIP **If you're having problems saving documents from Word 6, check** out the information here about the Prank macro virus. The Web site tells how to determine if Word is infected and includes a small program to fix it.

Computer Systems

So you want to buy a new computer, but you really aren't that into computer terminology and you don't know kilobytes from gigabytes. You went to the local computer store and the sales rep intimidated you with technobabble. You tried the department store but the salesperson was too busy selling washer/dryer combos to help you.

Well, the Web is an excellent resource to help you prepare for your shopping trip. Comparison shop to see what models and features all these companies offer. Read the product descriptions to acquaint yourself with the terminology. Once you have all this information, you'll be ready to buy the right system, with or without the help of the retail sales world.

After you buy your new computer, how can you get the inevitable product support questions answered? Using the Web to get tech support sure beats waiting on hold on the phone. And the Web is always there, 24 hours a day, seven days a week, unlike most tech support phone staffs. It's true; you can get personalized answers to your questions from a tech support staff, but you can quickly solve most common problems with the tech support available on the Web.

This section covers Web sites for some of the more popular brands of computers on the market today.

Acer America

http://www.acer.com

Acer makes low-cost computers that are popular sellers in many of the leading discount retailers. Its Web site offers information for U.S. customers as well as for customers living in the many other countries Acer serves. There's a typical mix here of product information, support (such as a special section with information Acer users need to update their computers for Windows 95), and downloadable files.

Compaq Computer Corp.

http://www.compaq.com

Compaq is one of the leading manufacturers of PCs for Windows and DOS; it's also Microsoft's leading "systems partner" for Windows 95. Compaq's Web site describes its efforts in this role to work with Microsoft on Plug and Play, Hot Dockable Notebooks, and some other technology advances. Additional areas of information at the Web site include product descriptions, a separate area for the new Compaq Presario, and special ordering and pricing information for government, education, and medical customers.

Fig. 7.5
Compaq delivers information about its popular hardware with special sections for customers in the government, educational, and medical communities.

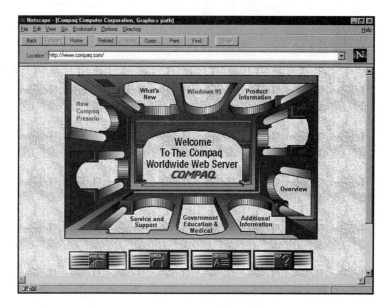

Dell Computer Corp.

http://www.dell.com

Dell was one of the first major computer manufacturers in the mail order business. Its Web site includes information about its products (mainly desktop and laptop PCs), employment opportunities, and a user survey.

Power Computing

http://www.powercc.com

Are you looking for a Macintosh computer but you don't want to buy one made by Apple? Power Computing is one of the first companies other than

Apple to build Macintosh-compatible computers. Its Web site includes the usual product information and support areas. It also has a neat form for helping you determine the cost of a new system. You specify things like the case type, monitor size, hard drive size, and how many megabytes of RAM you want. After you submit the form, the Power Computing Web site quotes a price for the system. Once you determine the system you want (and can afford to pay for it), give them a call. (Dell is planning to add an online ordering option soon, too.)

Packard Bell

http://www.packardbell.com

This basic support page has file updates and product information for Packard Bell's popular line of low-cost computers.

Add-ons and extra hardware

Many computer users buy computers that they can take out of the box and use as is. They never need to add new hardware, upgrade existing equipment, or replace anything when it breaks down.

For the rest of us, there's always a faster CD-ROM drive, a bigger hard drive, a better video card, or a new toy such as a scanner to add. For those of you who enjoy a couple of hours of browsing at the computer store, browsing at hardware manufacturers' Web sites listed here provides a similar thrill.

And, like the computer systems sites listed earlier in this chapter, most of these sites offer more than just information about products. You can get technical support, fixes, driver updates, and more.

 Plain English, please!

> A **driver** is a small piece of software that your applications and operating system use to communicate with your hardware. **"**

Ascend Communications

http://www.ascend.com/

There comes a time in every Web surfer's life when the modem is just too slow. If you decide it's time to replace your modem with a high-speed, state-of-the-art ISDN device, Ascend is one of the leading manufacturers. Ascend's

Web site includes information about its ISDN products as well as links to information you need to know to order ISDN service from your phone company.

 Plain English, please!

ISDN stands for **Integrated Services Digital Network**. This high-speed telephone service makes using a computer online much faster, and allows you to use a fax machine, an ISDN connection to your computer, a phone, or even video conferencing all on the same ISDN telephone line. **,,**

Diamond Multimedia

http://www.diamondmm.com

Diamond makes a variety of multimedia products, including video cards, CD-ROM drives, and even some modem and telephony products. The Web site contains product announcements and descriptions, links to software fixes for video drivers, and information about support for Windows 95 with Diamond products.

U.S. Robotics

http://www.usr.com

U.S. Robotics is a leader in the modem industry. It manufactures a variety of modems for PCs and Macs, including the well-known brands Courier and Sportster. (I use a Sportster in one of my PCs and it's great!) Look at this Web site to get product specifications on each of these brands. You can also download support files.

Hayes

http://www.hayes.com/

This modem manufacturer makes a variety of products for PCs and servers. In addition to standard information about its products and technical support at the Web site, Hayes has a nice section called "Tech Tips." Tech Tips answer commonly asked questions the Hayes tech support team answers about its products and about modems in general, such as how to install a modem on a PC, how to select the right comm port or IRQ, or how to troubleshoot lost data. Also available for download are technical documents such as the Hayes Technical Reference Manual. This manual includes a list of the entire Hayes AT command set, which is the industry standard that programmers use to enable software to communicate with modems.

Fig. 7.6
Here you'll find information about Hayes modems and about modems in general.

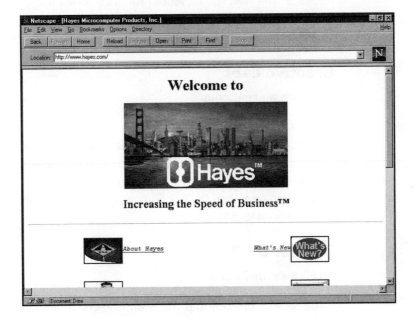

NEC Corp.

http://www.nec.com

NEC makes so many computers and peripherals (including a very popular line of high-quality, high-speed CD-ROM drives) that it's difficult to decide where to list them. When you look closely at NEC's product information at the Web site, you'll see that most of the links there describe its many peripherals. You can get information on a wide variety of products, some of which aren't tied to PCs (such as PBX phone systems and Satellite Earth Station Systems).

Radius Inc.

http://www.radius.com/

Radius is known mainly for its high-speed video accelerators and monitors for Macs. The Web site includes product information, current price lists, and technical support documents for these products as well as for Radius' digital video editors and its new line of Macintosh-compatible computers.

Creative Labs

http://www.creaf.com/

Creative Labs makes the industry's leading line of sound cards, the Sound Blaster. Other related products include CD-ROM drives, video capture and playback cards, multimedia kits, and new sound cards that include a modem. In addition to product information and support, there are links to background information on Sound Blaster compatibility. There's also a Web interface to all the files on its FTP site.

DayStar Digital

http://www.daystar.com/

If you have an old Mac and you want to speed it up, take a look at the DayStar site. DayStar makes accelerator products that upgrade your Mac to a faster processor, including upgrades that turn your Mac into a PowerMac. The Web site includes documents that explain which upgrades are compatible with various Mac models as well as a price list. DayStar also now sells a new Mac-compatible computer, the Genesis MP.

Hewlett Packard

http://www.hp.com/

Hewlett Packard makes many computer products including systems, scanners, and specialized components, but you're probably most familiar with its printers. The Web site has scores of documents with product information and specifications for all HP printers. You can download new versions of printer drivers and find out what HP products are Windows 95 compatible. HP is also making a push to sell itself in the Internet community; it's adding Internet information such as an Internet primer, case studies, and links to Internet business partners.

Fig. 7.7
HP printers are the
most familiar products
you will see here.

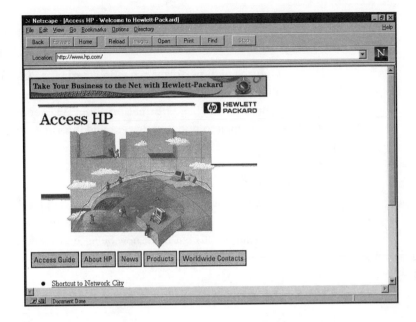

Western Digital

http://www.wdc.com

If you've ever bought a new hard drive for a PC, there's a good chance you've
seen a Western Digital drive, probably one of the respected Caviar models.
Western Digital drives are very popular in mail order, as well as in retail
computer and electronics outlets. (I use Western Digital drives in my PCs at
home and at work.) The Web site contains detailed specifications for all its
current drives, including a nice table that compares all the drives feature by
feature. There's also information about Western Digital multimedia and input/
output cards.

Conner Peripherals

http://www.conner.com/

Conner is well known for its hard drives and tape drives. The drives are
included as standard equipment in many brands of PCs and are sold as add-
ons in retail outlets. Conner's site includes information about its products as
well as links for service and support. If you're considering moving to Windows 95, you can download a free program called Storage Detective that
will advise you on you hard drive needs when you move to Win 95. It also
includes information about the data back ups you need to make before
you upgrade to Windows 95.

ATI Technologies

http://www.atitech.ca

ATI manufactures high-performance video cards for PCs, and it recently began manufacturing video cards for the new Macintosh models that include a PCI bus. The Web site has information about ATI's relationship with Apple as well as many links to updated drivers and information for ATI PC video products.

 Plain English, please!

> The **PCI Bus** is a new high-speed standard for plugging in new adapter cards such as video cards and network cards. This standard has been used for a few years on PCs but is just now being implemented in Macs to replace the Nubus slots.

STB Systems

http://www.stb.com

STB makes a variety of fast video accelerators for PCs. Its Web site includes information about STB Systems products, but unfortunately, there are no links to technical support or updated driver software. Maybe the site will have these links in the future.

Thrustmaster

http://www.thrustmaster.com/

This company makes realistic flight simulator joysticks (and a few other types of joysticks) for PCs and Macs. The Web site includes product information and support.

Computer productivity software

The real reason you invest a couple of thousand dollars (or more) in your computer is usually to do something productive. It might be to type a memo, to calculate the profit for your company's yearly widget sales, or to create a graphic logo for a new company.

Whatever it is that you do with your computer, you probably have a substantial investment in software. You spent several hundred dollars on the operating system and applications you use every day, and you spent weeks or even months perfecting the use of them.

So, take a few minutes to investigate the Web sites for the major applications you use most. You may find some new information about how to use your software that will make your job easier. Or maybe you're considering switching word processors. The Web is a great source for comparing the features of the software. And of course, it's a great place to find answers to common questions and to learn about patches or fixes for many bugs.

Lotus

http://www.lotus.com

A pioneer in the PC software industry, Lotus continues to make popular software for business applications. Although Lotus was recently acquired by IBM, it still maintains its own Web site. This site offers extensive information about 1-2-3 and the other SmartSuite products.

Macromedia

http://www.macromedia.com

Many game and edutainment software developers use Macromedia software to create multimedia products for both Macs and PCs. Macromedia's Web page has information about these products as well as about its new products that deliver better multimedia and video on the Web.

Fig. 7.8
Macromedia products can bring new pizzazz to your PC with multimedia and video.

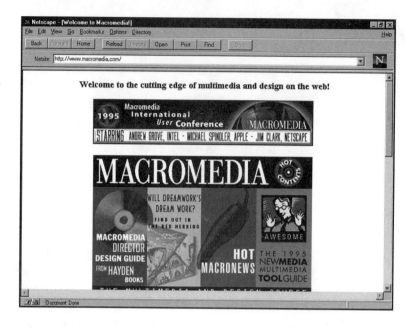

Quarterdeck

http://www.qdeck.com

Quarterdeck made its name in the PC business by making software that makes DOS and Windows run better, such as memory managers. This Web site describes these products as well as its new Web and Internet software, which you can currently download for free and use on a trial basis.

Fig. 7.9
Quarterdeck's products can make your PC run faster and better.

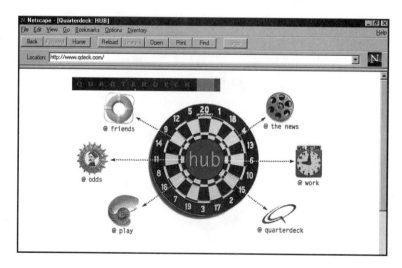

Novell Inc.

http://www.novell.com

Novell was probably better known among "power users" until its acquisition of WordPerfect a few years ago. This Web site has information about the Novell Perfect Office products and about the many Novell networking products. There are neat virtual "tours" here, too.

Borland

http://www.borland.com

This is the Web site for the maker of the popular dBASE database software and compilers such as the Delphi programming environment.

Corel Corp.

http://www.corel.ca/

Corel is the maker of the popular CorelDRAW! program for Windows. Corel's home page links to information about the latest, greatest version of the software. Product support is linked here too.

Adobe

http://www.adobe.com

In addition to many other products, Adobe makes Acrobat. Acrobat files (in a format called PDF) are being used by many Web sites to create Web pages that have complicated layout that HTML can't produce. The Adobe site includes directions for downloading and using the free Acrobat reader, which lets you view these Acrobat files on the Web. Also look for information here about products that were once made by Aldus. Now that Adobe and Aldus have merged, Pagemaker and other Aldus products are supported here.

WinZip

http://www.winzip.com

WinZip is a popular software used for file compression on PCs. WinZip is shareware and you can download and try versions for both Windows 3.1 and Windows 95 from this Web site.

 TIP **You can configure your Web browser to use WinZip as a helper** application to unzip files when it encounters zipped files on the Web.

Aladdin Systems

http://www.aladdinsys.com

Aladdin makes several commercial and shareware/freeware file compression products for Macs. If you've ever run across a "stuffed" file, Aladdin's software is the standard for dealing with it. You can get information about and download its software here.

Mcafee Antivirus

http://www.mcafee.com

If you cruise the Internet and the Web, you're taking some risk if you don't protect yourself from computer viruses. Mcafee is best known for its antivirus software, which you can download from this site.

Symantec Corporation

http://www.symantec.com/

Symantec makes a popular line of utilities software, including the Norton utilities. Its Web site contains plenty of product information about these products for both Windows and Macs. As a public service, Symantec also includes a Virus Information Center. Here you can learn about any new computer viruses that may be running rampant, and download new signature updates for Central Point AntiVirus, Norton AntiVirus, and other anti-virus products.

Plain English, please!

Every virus has a **signature**, which is a collection of information about the code that makes up the virus program. By searching for this signature, anti-virus software can find and destroy viruses. You need signature updates for your virus software to protect you from any new viruses that have been unleashed since the virus software you use was programmed. **99**

PC Software Links

http://alfred.uib.no/People/wolf/daniel/pc-eng.html

This site isn't a software site but rather a page with links to many major software vendors' pages and to pages related to vendor software.

Fun and games

You justify dropping a few hundred dollars on a new video card or CD-ROM drive by explaining how much time it will save you and how much more productive you'll be. But, if it happens to make your favorite computer game run faster or better, you won't complain.

Computer game makers have made really good use of the Web. Some of the sites listed in this section are the most interesting ones in the chapter. Most of the sites offer demos of games, hints and tips, information on new games, and tech support. Many of the sites hold frequent contests and give away all sorts of cool or useful stuff.

FX Fighter

http://www.im.gte.com/

Use this Web page to learn about this popular PC game. You can see screen shots of the action, see how the PC game relates to the comic book (and download pages from the comic), and download images, movies, and even a demo of the game.

Burn:Cycle

http://www.burncycle.com/

This ever-changing Web site makes good use of animation. New "episodes" of *Burn:Cycle* are added on a weekly basis. The site itself is rather surreal because you're introduced to the Windows and Mac game through parts of the game itself. You can also download screen shots and movie clips that are scattered throughout the Web pages.

Maxis

http://www.maxis.com/

Maxis is best known for its *SimCity* game. You can get hints and tips on software (avoid diagonal roads and rail lines in *SimCity*), download free software and demos, or visit the Teacher's Lounge. The Teacher's Lounge is a collection of Web resources for teachers using simulation in education. Finally, don't miss the links to online user groups.

7th Level

http://www.7thlevel.com

This game maker is one of the first companies I've seen to use the Internet Relay Chat (IRC) on the Web to host Web conference rooms. Here, you can discuss a variety of topics in real time with other users that share an interest in gaming and 7th Level games. In addition, you'll find a good assortment of free demo software (I got a demo of *Monty Python's Complete Waste of Time* the last time I visited), product support, information, and chances to enter contests.

Electronic Arts

http://www.ea.com

Electronic Arts makes games for video-game systems such as 3D0 as well as for PCs and Macs. Check out its Web pages to see demos of hot new games and get product support for existing games. You can even submit an application to test new games. Some of the popular EA games you may be familiar with are *BioForge* and *College Football USA*.

Fig. 7.10

Electronic Arts gives you demos of hot action and sports games.

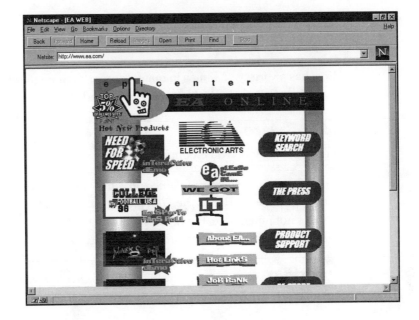

Simon and Schuster Interactive

http://www.mcp.com/musoft/ssint/

This Web site has links to popular interactive multimedia Star Trek products including the *Star Trek Omnipedia* and *Star Trek Next Generation Interactive Technical Manual*. Other non-Trek products featured here include educational products such as *Total Amazon* and *American Heritage History of the Civil War*.

Berkeley Systems

http://www.berksys.com

Who hasn't seen the Flying Toaster screen saver? Often imitated and spoofed, Berkely is a leader in this not-so-necessary-but-still-fun category of software. The Web site includes samples of its screen savers and other goodies.

Activision

http://www.activision.com

Cool games from these folks include *MechWarrior 2* and *Pitfall*. You can download sample video clips or images from these popular games, and even participate in on-going contests for little prizes such as hats and T-shirts.

Epic MegaGames

http://www.epicgames.com/

Epic has a variety of games in many genres. Its more popular titles include *One Must Fall*, *Epic Pinball*, and *Jill of the Jungle*.

Id Software

http://www.idsoftware.com/

No discussion of computer game software would be complete without a mention of *Doom*. Here's the Web page for the company that started it all. There's not much here, but if you don't already have a copy, this site is the place where you can download various shareware versions.

InterPlay

http://www.interplay.com

InterPlay is one of the bigger and better known game publishers in the computer software world. At its Web site, you find information on many of its titles, including *Star Trek: 25 Anniversary* and *Star Trek: Judgement Rites*, *Virtual Pool*, *Descent*, *Cyberia*, and dozens of others. InterPlay takes a very

Doomed to Death

If you can't get enough of *Doom*, here are a few more sites (not affiliated with Id) where you can get additional levels, *Doom* editors, lists of people to play against over a modem, and much more.

Doomgate: **http:// doomgate.cs. buffalo.edu/**

Dwango MultiPlayer Network: **http:// www.hti.net/dwango/**

Mac Doom: **http://www.nauticom.net/ users/mccollum/doom.htm**

"Official" Doom FAQ: **http:// www.portal.com/~hleukart/**

List of *Doom* Sites: **http:// www.msilink.com/~solso/doom.html**

For even more sites than this, see Yahoo's *Doom* index at **http://www.yahoo.com/Recreation/ Games/Computer_Games/Doom/**.

thorough approach to technical support on the Web; its entire customer support database is online, organized by game. So if you are having a problem with a game, *Cyberia* for example, choose Cyberia from the list and then search for your particular problem. There's also a good variety of product announcements, downloadable upgrades and patches, and hints for gameplaying.

LucasArts Entertainment Company

http://www.lucasarts.com

From the same creative genius that brought us the *Star Wars* and *Indiana Jones* movies, LucasArts now offers a great collection of entertainment CD-ROMs, including several based on the *Star Wars* and *Indiana Jones* movies. The Web site has demos and screen shots from popular games such as *Dark Forces* and *The DIG*, an online magazine called *The Adventurer*, and special online offers.

Sierra Online

http://www.sierra.com

Sierra is a major game developer with titles including *King's Quest, Space Quest,* and *Ultra Pinball*. Online they have a stock market challenge where you pit your stock trading skills against other online players. You need to register to use this (registering is free); doing so gives you access to your own customizable Web page on the Sierra site.

Where to buy computer stuff online

Many of the software, hardware, and game sites listed throughout the rest of this chapter have online stores where you can order products. That's one way to shop, but what if you're looking for several products from different vendors?

In that case, you need to go to one of the big online retail sites that functions like a computer superstore. These sites usually carry the same wide selection you find in a "real" store or a major mail-order outlet. Many of these sites offer special offers for online shoppers. You can get prices that are more up-to-date than magazine ads and search the products at your leisure.

Egghead Software

http://www.egghead.com/

If you're not familiar with Egghead, you may not know that this software retailer has some of the best deals around on selected hardware. The Web site has special sections for corporate, government, and business users. Most of the site is arranged around a "store" theme. You can browse the store by product category or use a search field to search for products by name. You can order products online (with a discount if you join the CUE club) or use another search page to find the store closest to you.

ElekTek, Inc.

http://www.elektek.com/

This hardware and software reseller carries a variety of PC and Mac systems, as well as peripherals and software. To help you find products you may like, ElekTek includes lists of best-selling products in several categories on the premise that the best sellers have more and better features, are easier to use, and are more reliable.

Ingram Micro

http://www.ingram.com/

Ingram Micro is a large computer products distributor that sells software and hardware to retail outlets. Its Web site includes best-seller lists (although they were several months out-of-date when I visited last), lots of industry news, and information about the products it carries and the vendors who make them. You can't order anything here, but you can get a lot of product information on over 30,000 products from hundreds of companies.

Insight Direct

http://www.insight.com/

You can order online from this large mail-order vendor, but you have to set up an account first. Insight carries hardware and software for the PC, and its Web site offers the latest pricing information, including specials for Web customers. The Tech Talk section includes answers to frequently asked questions, driver updates and documentation, and links to manufacturers' Web pages.

Computer Recycler

http://www.coolsville.com/recycler/

This company specializes in buying, selling, and trading used Macintosh equipment. It also sells new Mac products. Check out a list of its inventory and prices at the Web site.

Computer Price Cruncher

http://www.killerapp.com

Here's a useful page if you're looking for a new computer or new parts for an existing computer. Through this page, you can comparison shop online. You narrow your search to the type of equipment you're looking for (such as sound card or CD-ROM drive), or you can narrow it further to just a particular vendor; the Cruncher returns a table with specifications for all matching products. From this table, you can proceed to a list of resellers selling each product. This list is complete with the selling price, address, phone number, and a link to the seller's Web site if *it* has one. The number of sellers was still small when I looked at this, but it will certainly grow and get even better over time.

Fig. 7.11
Comparison shop for the best deals on PCs and peripherals with the Price Cruncher.

NECX Direct

https://necxdirect.necx.com/docroot/index.html

This online superstore boasts an inventory of over 20,000 computer items. NECX encourages you to buy a membership, which entitles you to discount prices, but you can still browse the site and shop as a guest without a membership. This site offers daily "Super Deals" and it does have some very good prices. The site is organized by product category with categories such as notebooks, multimedia hardware, RAM, modems, printers, and a Mac Headquarters.

 TIP   **The "s" at the end of *https* in this Web address indicates that this** server is secure.

Lots of free (or really inexpensive) software

The Internet and the Web just wouldn't be what they are today without the hundreds of thousands of programs you can download and try for free. It's hard to find a Web site that doesn't have at least one link to some software that you can download for free.

But there are a few major sites whose sole reason for being here is as a storehouse for shareware, freeware, and public domain software. These are usually divided into several categories such as word processing, utilities, or Internet tools. (Chapter 11, "Internet and Web Information," looks at some sites devoted exclusively to free software for use with the Internet.) Some of these sites have links to tens of thousands of files with gigabytes of drive space. It's a sure thing that you'll find something of interest at one of these sites.

Software Creations BBS

http://www.swcbbs.com

This site is a new type of Web site, a BBS on the Web. All the usual BBS features are here, including a large file area (it claims to get 70–100 new files every day), message areas, and reviews of software. In addition to software that you can download for free, several companies and authors have software that you can purchase and download from the site. To use this site, you have to fill in a rather lengthy registration, but registration is free. However, parts of the site aren't free, including many of the file areas. You have to pay to get access to those.

Cica

http://www.cica.indiana.edu/cgi-bin/checkftp/

This Web page links you to the FTP site for one of the biggest and best-known sites for Windows software. The Web page does a quick check to see if there's a space available to log on to the FTP site, tells you how many users are on, and gives you a list of mirror sites. The files here are grouped in directories for Windows 3.x, Windows 95, and Windows NT. Within these groupings, you'll find directories for applications (such as Access, Word, and Excel), games, network utilities, drivers, and Internet software. There are about two dozen categories in all.

So what's the difference?

I get this question a lot, even from experienced computer users: What's the difference between shareware, freeware, and public domain software?

Shareware is essentially software that you can try before you buy. You can download a copy, use it for a few weeks, and if you continue to use it, you're supposed to pay the author. The time you can use it and how much you should pay vary a lot from program to program, but the basic principal is the same. With shareware, the author usually includes a licensing document (a "readme" file or something similar) explaining the conditions for the use of the software, stating the copyright, and telling you whether or not you can copy and distribute the software.

Freeware takes this concept a step further. You can download the software and use it all you want

for free. You never have to pay. Again, the author usually includes an online document stating the copyright and any usage or distribution restrictions.

The final category is **public domain software**. In this case, the author or developer has voluntarily given up the copyright on the software. Anyone can do anything they want with it, including modify it and sell it.

If you're in the software business, understanding these differences is important. Selling a disk full of shareware or freeware can get you in trouble if you don't follow the restrictions placed on distribution. For most users, however, the only real difference ends up being whether or not you need to pay for continued use.

❝ *Plain English, please!*

A **mirror site** is an FTP site that carries all the same files as another site. Using a mirror helps give more people access to popular files. **❞**

California State University Windows World

http://coyote.csusm.edu:80/cwis/winworld/winworld.html

This Web server keeps a list of the top 50 most popular downloads and lists of all new software with descriptions. There is also a good search page to help you find the software you are looking for. The site is divided into more than 50 categories from address books to image-morphing software to Word macros and add-ons.

Jumbo

http://www.jumbo.com/

This Jumbo site has more than 23,000 programs available for download. Windows, DOS, Mac, OS/2, and UNIX platforms are all represented here. The site is searchable and divided into about half a dozen categories.

SimTel

http://www.coast.net/SimTel/

This site gained fame for being one of the best places to find DOS software available on the Net. It has added extensive collections of Windows 3.x and Windows 95 software as well, and it has an OS/2 repository.

Windows 95 shareware

While many of the shareware sites listed in this section contain some Windows 95 software, it can be difficult to find them among the thousands of Windows and DOS programs. Here are a few sites that specialize in software for Windows 95. You'll also find information about Windows 95 and links to other, non-software items here.

The Windows 95 Page: **http://biology.queensu.ca/~jonesp/**

Windows 95 Resource Center: **http://www.cris.com/~randybrg/win95.html**

One Stop Windws 95 Site: **http://www.win95.com/**

Fig. 7.12
This DOS and Windows software site is one of the major collections on the Net. Many shareware and freeware authors post software here first.

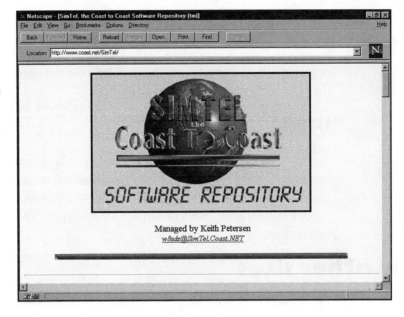

PGP

http://web.mit.edu/network/pgp.html

PGP (Pretty Good Privacy) is a program for encrypting messages on the Internet. It's free, it works on a variety of programs, and it's the standard that most people use. So, if you need to send private e-mail that you don't want to be read by anyone except the intended recipient, see this Web page for some background, downloading, and configuration directions. If you need PGP for commercial purposes, you need to contact ViaCrypt at **http://gn2.getnet.com:80/viacrypt/**.

Harris Semiconductor

http://mtmis1.mis.semi.harris.com/ftp.html

This Web page is an index of links to FTP sites with software for DOS, Windows, UNIX, Mac, OS/2, and X Windows.

InfoMac HyperArchive

http://hyperarchive.lcs.mit.edu/HyperArchive.html

InfoMac is one of two very well-known FTP sites for comprehensive collections of Mac software. This Web page is a front end to the FTP site, and it includes a search box that searches the entire archive (something you can't do from FTP) and finds software regardless of the category. You can access roughly two dozen categories, including anti-virus, user interface, and communication, can be accessed directly from the page as well as look at a list of recently submitted files.

UMich

http://www.umich.edu/~archive/mac/

In addition to the InfoMac HyperArchive site, the other FTP site that Mac users all know about is this site at the University of Michigan. There's no fancy interface here, just a dozen or so categories with thousands of files.

A few other sites

I hate to refer to these as miscellaneous, but that's what these sites are. The last few sites in this chapter don't really fit in the major categories listed, but they're still worth mentioning.

The Well Connected Mac

http://www.macfaq.com/

There's more information at this site about Macs than most Mac users will ever care to read. If you're looking for a little tidbit of information about how to make your Mac do just about anything, check out one of the dozens of FAQs. If you need to find Mac hardware or software companies, try the vendor directory. These are just two of the many Mac resources here.

Allegro New Media

http://www.allegronm.com

Interactive business reference and instruction titles are Allegro's specialty. Some of its products that you may be familiar with are the Berlitz Travel Guide series, a "Learn to Do" series on topics like word processing and Windows, and some libraries of clip art and graphics. The Web pages include descriptions, support, and an order form.

Compton's New Media

http://www.comptons.com/

Compton's specializes in interactive multimedia; its most widely recognized package is the Interactive Encyclopedia. You can see a demo of the encyclopedia (it's set up as Web pages that run online), get product information on many other titles, and connect to technical support.

Walnut Creek CD-ROM

http://www.cdrom.com/

Walnut Creek makes a wide variety of low-cost CD-ROMs. Most of its products are compilations of software or information that is freely available. The value to you is the convenience of having it all together on one CD and not having to spend hours (or days) downloading it all. The Web site tells you about all its current and new CD-ROM titles, as well as upcoming new products, all of which can be ordered online. Sample files from CDs and multilingual catalogs are available. You can also find information about getting your own CD-ROM projects published.

Education

● **In this chapter:**

● See what exciting educational resources are on the Web and who provides them

● Find out how schools get into the swing of Web publishing and show off their wares

● Dig into Web sites for financial aid, rather than into your own pockets!

The Web opens a door to a limitless set of educational information banks. Imagine having the ability to go to any library or school and extract practically anything that is available to the public. . . . . ▶

Out there, a wonderful well is bubbling over with information; all you have to do is know where to look. This chapter walks you down several avenues of information: schools, educational resources, and financial assistance.

How many times have you gone to the library only to find out that a book you wanted is checked out or wished you could have reserved the book over the phone but no one answered. The Web is here to save you time and money.

For science teachers looking for help on your next science project, the Web can be an excellent resource for reference materials. If you're a teacher and haven't had the time to prepare a lesson plan, the Web offers a pool of lesson plans.

When you're looking for college information, especially alternative funding choices, make sure to investigate the section on financial aid. You'll be surprised at how much free information is available!

Getting educated by the U.S. Department of Education

http://www.ed.gov/

"Where are my tax dollars going?" How many times have you asked yourself that question? Here is one place where your tax dollars are being used wisely. You no longer need to wait for monthly publications to find out what the government is doing in education. You can read about it online.

The U.S. Department of Education is hard at work providing you with easy access to educational information. Daily, they post new information about current educational events that affect parents and educators. If you have concerns about educational legislation and what the Secretary of Education is doing, you can find information here.

If you're a teacher and you need to know the National educational goals or how to get a grant, you should look here first. For parents concerned about education, there are monthly newsletters, educational materials, and access to an educational list server. The U.S. Dept. of Education broadcasts town hall meetings monthly live via satellite all across the country; these broadcasts can keep you up-to-date on educational changes.

Fig. 8.1
The U.S. Department of Education provides many educational services and publications on the Web.

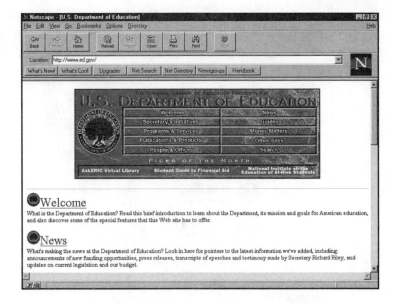

When you're looking for government educational information for your state, click the imagemap of the United States. This map takes you right to your state's programs and services. For anyone interested in education, don't pass up the Pick of the Month, which contains the U.S. Government's top three choices of educational resources.

Putting your classroom on the Web is easy with Classroom Connect

http://www.wentworth.com/

Here's a business that provides free Internet services and sells Internet products. If you're an educational administrator looking to connect or extend your Web capabilities, this site is for you. Classroom Connect's goal is to help you use the Internet to its fullest potential.

What Classroom Connect has created is a one-stop shop for Internet activities. Like any store, the window keeps changing. Each week you will want to look in the "What's New" section to find out which schools have been added to the Internet and to learn what other new Internet tools are available. One of the best attractions is the Jump Station. The Jump Station can take you to a wealth of Internet Resources.

Fig. 8.2
Classroom Connect gets your classroom on the Net.

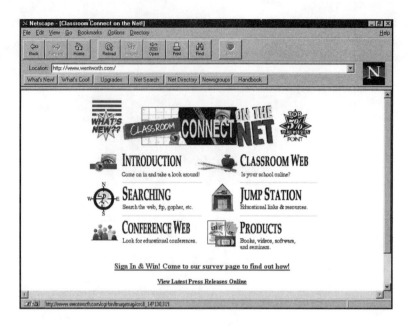

If you're looking for educational software, don't miss out on the Showcase link. There's access to over 7,000 software packages for grades K-12. You will also want to check out the NetSchool. NetSchool is organized to minimize the time you spend trying to find schools on the Web. The schools are broken down by subject and alphabetically by state.

If you're still searching for more Internet assistance, Classroom Connect offers offline seminars nationwide. Not only does Classroom Connect promote its own seminars, it keeps track of other national educational seminars.

NASA K-12 Internet Initiative brings outerspace to the classroom

http://quest.arc.nasa.gov/

NASA doesn't just send rockets to outerspace; the administration provides key resources and makes them available. NASA is actively bringing science and Internet knowledge to the classroom.

Fig. 8.3
NASA's K-12 Internet
Initiative links kids with
scientists.

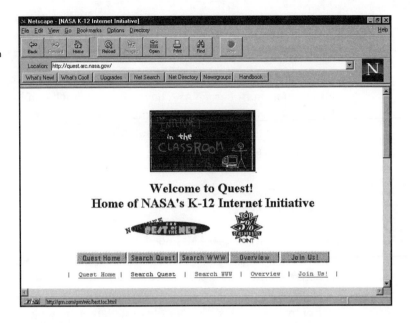

NASA's site includes information that can help your school plan, install, and maintain an Internet classroom. The level of planning information is for the novice to the expert. If you don't have the funding to start an Internet classroom, NASA provides a full range of resources that can assist you in your funding requests. In addition to identifying funding resources, NASA also provides funding for projects during the year. At this site, you can read about current projects and learn how to submit a NASA project funding proposal.

One of NASA's outstanding efforts is how they're bringing the Internet classroom together with projects. Two or three times a year NASA conducts a project that involves the Internet classroom. All you need to do is fill out the online volunteer form. In addition to active projects, NASA also provides an archive of past projects.

Governmental and corporate resources on the Internet

Thousands of electronic resources are at your fingertips. Many of them are provided by your Federal, State, and Local governments. The Web relieves you of the need to trudge down to your local government office to obtain information. Let's learn how to find information after 5:00 on a Friday night.

Educational Resources

http://www.nas.nasa.gov/HPCC/K12/edures.html

Help! I'm lost in cyberspace! If you don't know where to turn for educational information, start here. NASA has put together a list of lists in Internet Education. Their lists are quite exhaustive and information is available to all age groups. Of course, if you're looking for outerspace information, this is the best place to start your search.

AskERIC

http://ericir.syr.edu/

"I'm a teacher; it's 2:00 AM; I need an answer to a teaching question." No problem, AskERIC. AskERIC is an online question answering service for teachers on the Internet. The site has an extensive library that you can search. If all you need is a little help in preparing a lesson plan, AskERIC has it. For instance, AskERIC has a lesson plan on making change for a dollar. This lesson plan is just one of over 700 available. Another exciting resource is PBS's Newton's Apple. AskERIC contains information on current shows and has archives to past seasons.

Peterson's Education Center

http://www.petersons.com:8080

Peterson's provides online catalogs of schools that provide you with the unique ability to select a school using multiple indices. You can find a school either alphabetically or geographically. Once you choose a school, the guide describes the school or instructs you on how to order information about the school. Remember, you're never too old to learn!

Fig. 8.4
Peterson's Education
Center provides the
consumer with an
educational reference
catalog

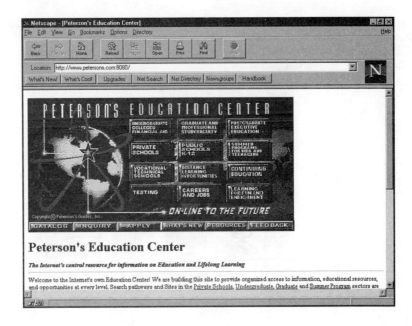

Cisco Educational Archive and Resources Catalog

http://sunsite.unc.edu/cisco/cisco-home.html

Cisco provides a simple and fast educational search. Cisco is made possible
by a joint venture between Cisco and MCI Telecommunications Corporation.
In addition to Cisco's search feature, check out its choice of the Internet
School of the Month.

Global SchoolNet Foundation (GSN)

http://gsn.org/

Here's a great site if you're looking for interactive projects on the Internet.
The Global SchoolNet Foundation allows children to become actively
involved within a project. Project registration is a simple email form that
takes only a matter of minutes to complete. The children will love this
method of teaching because they experience the adventure of the project and
can receive answers to their questions. Another great link on this site is to
the Global Schoolhouse, which links K-12 classrooms within communities
and around the world.

Fig. 8.5

The Global SchoolNet Foundation allows kids to interact on projects across the Web.

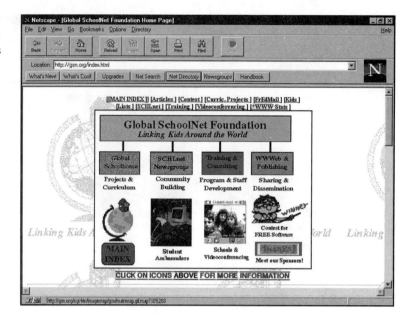

EdWeb Home Page

http://k12.cnidr.org:90/

Are you wondering if the Web can keep growing like it is and still be educational? This site is sponsored by the Corporation for Public Broadcasting. It's attempting to answer how education fits in with the Internet. What you will find are answers to questions on how the Web is being used in education. In addition to getting answers to your questions, you can learn how this group is trying to create the K-12 Internet Test Bed.

IDEAnet Home Page

http://ideanet.doe.state.in.us/

Indiana's Department of Education is using the Internet to tie its 294 school districts together. This resource sharing is unique because no other state has taken on this great of a commitment. Besides tying the school districts together, IDEAnet is advertising many of the state's attractions, such as the Indiana State Fair and the Indianapolis Zoo.

IPL—The Internet Public Library

http://ipl.sils.umich.edu/

The IPL offers access to gigabytes of information in electronic format. The virtual library has information for all age groups. The youth section really gets the children involved; one place that kids love is the story hour. For adults, the ready reference section is very good; you can look up references by subject. Each item within the subject goes into enough depth to give you a top-level overview. If you would like further information on the subject, there's a hyperlink to the full Internet material.

Elementary schools on the Web

The Web is a great place to show your school's pride. Thousands of schools are on the Web and the number is increasing daily. If your school is not on the Web, you're really missing out on a great way to advertise your school district.

Arbor Heights Elementary in Seattle, Washington

http://www.halcyon.com/arborhts/arborhts.html

Arbor Heights has everyone in the school actively participating in providing information. You can read about aspiring authors or gumshoe reporters. For the parents who lost their monthly calendar of school events, no sweat—that information is online. Besides reading what is available at this school, parents can get actively involved by posting information to the online parents section. If you want to know how this site was set up, you can read a brief Web history when you access it.

In addition to school information, this site provides community and world-wide information. For instance, you can quickly learn about Seattle's current news and weather forecast.

 TIP   If you're looking for schools organized by country or state go to Web 66 at **http://www.web66.coled.umn.edu/**.

Fig. 8.6
Arbor Heights
Elementary School
fosters future authors
via the Web.

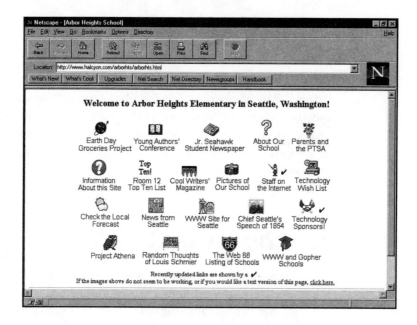

Highland Park Elementary School

http://www.hipark.austin.isd.tenet.edu/home/main.html

Highland Park Elementary School (K-5) offers exciting places to learn about the school and places that are stimulating to students, teachers, and parents. This school does a good job of displaying its commitment to excellence. You will enjoy walking down the site and meeting the teachers and seeing the students work. If you need a simple diversion, you can go on one of the museum tours this site offers.

Highland Park Elementary has worked with many companies to achieve this informative Web site. You can find information on school and technology plans. If you're simply looking for educational fun, click "Resources by Subject" and pick math brain teasers. I'll leave you with one: Find the missing numbers: 0, 6, 24, 60, 120, 210, ___, ___, ___.

 TIP **Many major corporations within each school district provide** hardware, software, and training at no cost. All you need to do is contact Human Resources in whatever corporation you're interested in.

Riverdale School

http://www.riverdale.k12.or.us/

What school is in the Northwest corner of the United States and has something fishy going on? Riverdale School and its Web salmon page. This school uses the Web to provide information about itself and the Northwest. You can read almost anything about salmon, learn about the local forecast, or gain insight on Mount St. Helens. If you decide to stay on campus, you will really enjoy how the students are involved at this school. The student press section covers many subjects, including movie reviews.

The Rice School

http://riceinfo.rice.edu/armadillo/Rice/Rice_home.html

Rice School is one of the few schools on the Web that offers bilingual pages in either Spanish or English. Rice was built in 1994 and prides itself in being a high-technology school. The Web benefits Rice offers is within its technology overview and school background. Within the overview, you can find out how the school is equipping itself to be one of Houston's best educational institutions. Teachers from all over the world will find this school very interesting.

Saint Paul's School

http://www.st.pauls.edu/

Saint Paul's School, located in Clearwater, Florida, is a private school for preschool through eighth grade students. What makes its home page stand out is the effort put forth to form an easy-to-use knowledge base. You can quickly jump to almost any major topic within a few mouse clicks.

Walker Upper Elementary School

http://pen.k12.va.us/Anthology/Div/Charlottesville/SCHOOLS/
WALKER/Walker.HTML

Here is a simple model for your school's Web page. Walker school offers a good example of how to lay out a Web page. Using this as a baseline, you should be able to create an informative site using approximately six HTML pages. Walker's pages provide school, community, and Web resources without a lot of navigating.

Homespun Web

http://www.ICtheWeb.com/hs-web/

Homespun Web is a site that answers questions on home schooling and links home-schooling families together. You'll find answers to frequently asked questions, learn which newsgroups are available, identify local and state support organizations, and learn where you can find printed material.

High schools on the Web

The Web has thousands of schools and the number increases daily. This section lists a few high schools out there as well as the University of Chicago Laboratory Schools, which is an institution for nursery through high school students.

The University of Chicago Laboratory Schools

http://www.ucls.uchicago.edu/

This site is one of the many private educational institutions on the Web. The University of Chicago Laboratory Schools provides education from nursery school through twelfth grade. As you click pages on the site, you will feel as if you're looking at a high-quality brochure. Information at this site covers a very broad range of educational interests. You can find information on student government, foreign language clubs, or learn about specific departments. The resource section provides access to many Internet providers, including access to Merriam Webster's Collegiate Dictionary and Roget's Thesaurus.

Brownell-Talbot College

http://www.brownell.edu/

This private school ties the students, faculty, and alumni onto their Web server. You can read about what is going on within the school or easily obtain a stock quote. The College Options section is one of the best places to visit at this site. The College Options pages provide you with resources for college exploration and planning.

St. Mary's School

http://www.stmarys.medford.or.us/

If you're looking for college preparatory schools, the Web provides an easy way for you to learn about a school's mission, policies, and course work. While visiting St. Mary's Web site you can learn all about the school. A section that you don't want to miss is the course catalog. It's very complete in that it breaks down each subject area by grade level.

The Blake School

http://www.blake.pvt.k12.mn.us/

The Blake School is a college preparatory school in Minneapolis, Minnesota. This school offers information on school publications, school resources, class art work, and administrative information. What makes this site stand out is how the school has organized its Class Pages. Rather than find out about class information located at this school, you jump to places that are specific to a subject. These place could be anywhere is the world. For example, you might jump to Russia to learn Russian.

Higher education on the Web

The Web is a great place to show school pride. Also, you can shop around for a college and learn about how universities differ. It's also just plain fun to roam through the many impressive university pages.

University of Arizona

http://www.arizona.edu/

Wow, what an impressive university! If you're trying to select a university, don't pass up the free information that University of Arizona has online. It provides extensive admissions information which includes semester catalogs and course availability. An impressive feature is how this university has integrated an online version of the bookstore tied directly to each course's required books. The book information includes the ISBN number and cost. Another slick feature is the electronic office supply store, which again ties in with each course's required supplies. If you need a side diversion, take a walk down the student information area and you will find excellent information about ongoing activities at this school and other major universities.

The University of Michigan

http://www.umich.edu/

The University of Michigan is one of the country's leading academic institutions. I hope that you're as impressed as I am at this outstanding Web site. You'll find that this site offers deep pockets of information about the main campus at Ann Arbor plus information about other campuses. One of the extra features are the links to the University radio stations. The radio station pages contain information about programming material and listener commentaries from past broadcasts. If you happen to get lost at anytime while at this site, try using its search engine; it's quite extensive.

Fig. 8.7
The University of Michigan promotes excellence in education both on and off the WWW.

Cambridge Center for Adult Education

http://www.ccae.org/CCAE/index.html

Are you looking for adult education? Cambridge Center offers a wide range of courses for adults over 50 years old. Their course catalog takes you to a detailed list of all courses offered at the school. Subjects include, but aren't limited to literature, writing, religion, music, wine making, cooking, and travel. Almost classes are at the school. However, they are starting to offer Virtual Classroom courses over the Internet. You can find a list of virtual courses within the Virtual Classroom project. If you have an idea for a class to be taught in the Virtual Classroom, fill out the form this site provides.

Need money for school?

If you've looked at the cost of college over the past few years, I'm sure you noticed that it has not gotten any cheaper. The following sites are a few of the good places to investigate when you're trying to find financial aid or grants.

The Student Guide 1995-96

http://www.ed.gov/prog_info/SFA/StudentGuide/

Uncle Sam provides several alternatives for you to stretch your hard-earned dollar towards higher education. The site contains in-depth information on how financial aid works and on the different types of financial aid that are available. This site also offers excellent guidelines for your investigation of financial aid from various organizations, including pitfalls to avoid when selecting financial aid. Online instructions are available on how to obtain financial aid publications. For your convenience, this site allows you to download all its information in one single file.

Signet Bank Student Loan Home Page: College Financing, Financial Aid, Student Loans

http://www.infi.net/collegemoney/

Signet Bank is out to do you a favor and potentially do itself a favor. This bank offers detailed financial aid information online. A key feature of this site is the electronic version of *A Student's Guide to Financial Aid*. The guide covers six major aspects of financial aid. If you would rather read the guide offline, you can visit the online bookstore and order a copy. The bookstore also offers electronic ordering forms for other books and brochures. In addition to the financial aid information, you can order a government financial aid form or a Signet Bank loan application.

Financial Aid Information

http://www.cs.cmu.edu/afs/cs/user/mkant/Public/FinAid/finaid.html

This site is a good starting point when you're looking for financial aid. The site is primarily a list of lists on financial aid and grants. If you don't want to look for financial aid by topic, there is a lengthy alphabetical list of everything that the site offers.

Foundation Center

http://FDNCENTER.ORG/

If you want to learn about the foundation field, the Foundation Center provides good reference information. The center offers information on 200 agencies around the country that can aid you in obtaining grants. If you need help in grant proposal writing, you can use the online training or learn about offline training seminars. The center also has access to databases on grantmakers and grants, information on how to research a foundation, and links to charities on the Internet.

 Q&A *I have read everything that is in this chapter and still want more. Where can I get a top-level list of educational links?*

That's easy, go to Yahoo at **http://www.yahoo.com/Education/** and browse their index or use their search feature.

Government

● **In this chapter:**

- ● Would you like to see the Oval Office or read the President's biography?

- ● Don't get lost in the nation's largest library

- ● What are the Republicans and Democrats planning for the 1996 elections?

- ● Learn the goals and structures of current government agencies

The World Wide Web makes Abraham Lincoln's government "of the people, by the people, for the people" more accessible to the people. . . . . ▶

Thanks to the Internet and the World Wide Web, you have little reason not to know what's going on in the U.S. government. You'll be amazed at how much you can learn about its inner workings. You may expect to find information on the President, Congress, and such, but you'll also find lists of current bills, press releases from government agencies, directories of government resources, and so much more.

You'll also find lots of fun information. I found pictures of President Clinton's cat, political cartoons, speeches from all sorts of government officials, scripts from political programs, and even a theme song or two. Some of the pictures are incredible. I found a picture of the Air Force's newest fighter, and others of my representative, the Pentagon, and most of the rooms in the White House. I also enjoyed the political editorials that I found not only at party headquarters, but at judicial sites, agency sites, and many others.

Thanks to the World Wide Web, I am now a better-informed citizen. I know what's going on in our nation's capital and I know who to contact and what to do to have my voice heard.

Meet the first family and other Executive Branch members

http://www.whitehouse.gov

The White House home page is a great place to visit whether you want interesting tidbits about the leading families or detailed reports about their activities. You can get information about the Executive Branch families, take virtual tours, and discover pertinent information about Executive Branch views, history, and initiatives. Don't forget to listen to the welcome messages from the President and Vice President or to sign the guest book.

TIP   **Whitehouse.gov is graphic intensive. If you watch your online** time, as I do, I suggest you set your Web browser so it won't load images automatically. I prefer this to selecting a text representation of the page (which is an option) because I can choose whether I view any particular graphic. Choosing the text-only option will make many of the graphics unavailable.

If you explore the Executive branch and look in the White House, you can drop by President Clinton's office and find more audible messages, his current initiatives, and a biography. You really should stop by Vice President Gore's office and take a tour of his cartoon gallery. I personally like the cartoon of Gore and Clinton on a train by Jeff MacNelly. Visit the first family; besides interesting tidbits, you can find that picture of Socks, the family cat.

Fig. 9.1
From the White House Welcome page, you can even find a picture of Socks!

 TIP

http://www.cuhk.hk/rthk/helper.html

If you don't know how to play audio files or view videos, you should visit the helper site at RTHK. From this site, you can download the appropriate "helper" application and learn how to configure both Netscape and Mosaic.

http://www.delosmus.com/audplay.html

Another great place for help is the site by Delos. You'll find some great information and links to other helpful sites.

You should also delve into the White House Publications. These are updated daily and include all the current press releases, the proposed budget, topical releases, and a plethora of other documents.

Finally, you shouldn't forget to tour the Executive Branch hot spots. You can virtually walk through the White house, the Oval Office, the Old Executive Building, and the First Ladies' Garden of the White House.

Roam the vast halls of the Library of Congress

http://lcweb.loc.gov

Established nearly 200 years ago, the Library of Congress houses one of the largest collections of printed materials in the world. Even if you aren't looking for government information, the Internet version of the Library of Congress is a great place to visit. Besides being able to search through tons of titles and publications at its location, you can search the World Wide Web. The Library of Congress can even help you search for soldiers that have been reported as Missing in Action or Prisoners of War.

Fig. 9.2
You can search through the Library of Congress digital libraries, check out up-coming events, and find government information all at this one site!

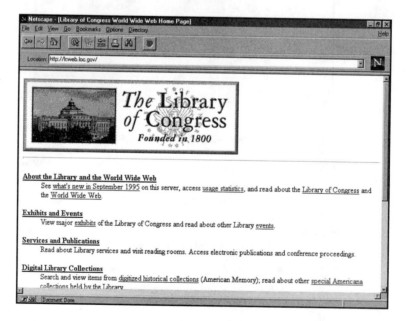

From the Library of Congress, you can gather information about the government at the federal and state levels. You can also take advantage of **Thomas** (**http://www.thomas.gov**). Thomas, named after Thomas Jefferson, is an Internet service provided by Congress that gives you access to all bills being considered, "hot" bill updates, and congressional records. The Constitution and an explanation of how laws are made are also provided through Thomas.

From the Library of Congress, you can also jump onto the White House site, U.S. House of Representatives page, all the agency pages discussed later in this chapter, and many other government pages.

Fig. 9.3
Review a current bill, check the congressional records, or check the status of hot bills with Thomas.

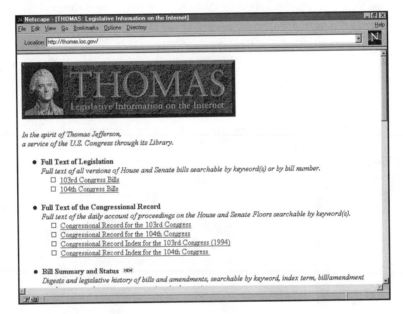

Welcome to FedWorld

http://www.fedworld.gov

Developed by the National Technical Information Service (NTIS), FedWorld is a comprehensive listing of government-related information. FedWorld is sorted into different categories to make finding the information you want easier. For example, if you want to know where to find Internet resources that deal with the government and energy, just scroll down to the list of Subject Categories and click Energy.

FedWorld also provides links to Government reports and services and even hosts its own site for the U.S. Treasury department. You can also order free catalogs that list hundreds of documents you can get from NTIS.

Pachyderms galore

http://www.rnc.org

The Republican National Committee, the RNC, may not have the presidency, but it does have an interesting Web site. I found the Café to be especially interesting. You can actually try to balance the budget online! In addition, the Café also has some live chat rooms where you can converse in real time, although the rooms aren't very active. Even if you can't find an active chat room, you can still post your thoughts on the HyperNews Discussion Board. But, be glad the Café can't offer real food because the continually updating debt clock could ruin anyone's lunch.

Fig. 9.4
You'll find current events, news, campaign strategies, and more at the Republicans National Committee.

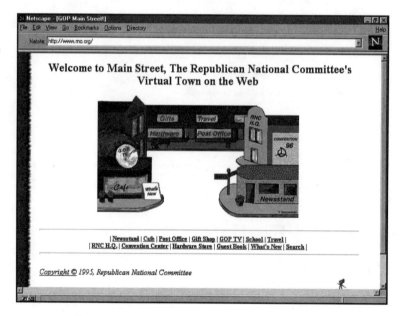

You'll also find current RNC news, events, and commentaries at the News-stand and of course on GOP TV. If you don't have the applications that you need to view or listen to the messages at the GOP TV, you can stop by Hardware and get the latest. (I know it's really software, but I didn't design the site.)

If you're after some humor, you'll surprisingly find it at school. Check out the background material on the Economy and you'll find loving titles such as "Democrats and the Big Lie," or "Clinton's FY '95 'Missing In Action' Budget."

You can locate other local Republicans at the Post Office. While you're there, you may also want to look up your senator's or representative's email address.

If you're interested in joining the RNC, you need to visit the Headquarters. If you're already a member and are interested in becoming a delegate at the 1996 convention, stop by Convention '96.

If you're interested in other Republican Web sites, you need to travel a bit. The little airplane that moves across your screen makes stopping by the travel page worth the time. You'll find links to the different government branches, 1996 Presidential candidate home pages, and other interesting sites.

Democrats online

http://www.democrats.org

The Democrats also have an entertaining and informative site. I really like the Top Ten ways to mispronounce Newt Gingrich under the What's Cool link. This site also includes a search engine to help you find information.

Fig. 9.5
Visit this site to uncover the happenings at the DNC and other Democratic issues.

Under Organizations, you can find the addresses of your local Democratic party headquarters, as well as the names and addresses of all the Democratic congresspeople in your state. This page also provides links to Democrats on the Internet broken down into useful groups such as national sites, state sites, county sites, and even student Democrats.

What's Hot at the Democratic National Committee? Press releases and briefings are what's hot. Don't forget to browse through copies of NewtGrams, Democrat criticisms of the House Speaker. Oh, and the Democrats do have a few clever titles like, "How To Renounce Your U.S. Citizenship: The GOP Way."

TIP **http://bingen.cs.csbsju.edu:80/letterman**

The Newt Gingrich Top Ten is a link to the collection of David Letterman's Top Ten lists. For more lists pop on over to the Letterman Top Ten archive.

Click "Connecting with America" if you would like to join the DNC. You'll find the membership information as well as organization facts, DNC history, and how to be a delegate in 1996. You can also jump to the Declaration of Independence and the United States Constitution.

Fig. 9.6

The Democrats really connect with America by offering a state-by-state look at President Clinton's accomplishments.

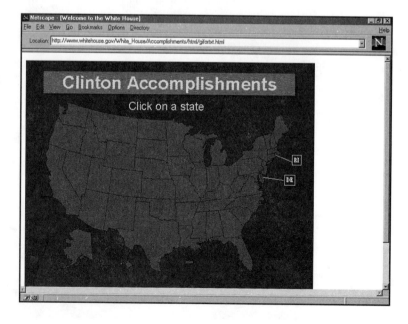

What's Cool at this site? Spoofs on Newt Gingrich seem to be a lively topic. In addition, you can also listen to and watch a speech by Ted Kennedy and expect similar clips from Martin Luther King Jr. to be added soon. You can also listen to a hilarious rendition of capitol life as produced by The Capitol Steps, a group of congressional staffers gone Broadway.

Capitol Hill

Congress represents the broad base of opinions, cultures, and backgrounds needed to equally represent the interests of a vastly diverse country. The World Wide Web provides information on both the House of Representatives and the Senate.

The House of Representatives

http://www.house.gov

You won't find any cute stories or pictures at the House of Representatives, but you can find comprehensive information about events taking place in our nation's capital. The server displays the Legislative process in depth with lists of current house actions, the status of current bills and amendments, and committee activities.

 TIP **Although the site is still under construction, from house.gov you** will soon be able to find out how your representative voted on all recorded votes. This will provide individuals with a nearly effortless means to review a representative's performance. In the meantime, to find out how your congressperson voted, hop over to **http://world.std.com/~voteinfo.** The document is updated regularly.

If you're curious about what Congress is doing today, you should check out the Weekly House Floor schedule and Today's committee meetings. If you want to get in touch with your local representatives, you need to know who's who, **http://www.house.gov/Whoswho.html**. You can find your representative by name or state. The server will provide a representative's Washington office address, email address, service information, and the representative's committees.

The Senate

http://www.senate.gov

When this chapter was written, the Senate site was not complete. In fact, it was simply a Gopher site that usually produced errors when I tried to access information. Judging by its brother URLs, I would think this site will soon be a complete graphic Web site just as the other "www.sitename.gov" pages are. You may want to test the site above and see if it has improved.

Even though senate.gov isn't complete, you can still locate your senator and tell him/her that the Senate Web site needs some work (just kidding). Check out Policy.net's senate listing at **http://policy.net/capweb/Senate/Senate.html**. The list sorts the senators by name, state, and political party.

Study the Judicial Branch

http://www.uscourts.gov

The weighty task of deciding what is legal versus illegal or unconstitutional versus constitutional falls to the Judicial Branch. The Judicial server uscourts.gov is not a very colorful or aesthetically pleasing site, but as noted on its home page, it is under construction. Despite the construction, you can still gain some insight into the court system.

Finding all the info you need

You can find many listings of congresspeople, but it's hard to find a listing that has all the information you want. I was able to use the following two sites to get all the information about my representative that I thought I would need.

http://www-mcb.ucdavis.edu/info/congress.html

Jump to Contacting the 104th Congress for Washington phone and fax numbers, email addresses, and home district phone numbers. This site will also link each representative to the respective page on the House server. Senators don't have a server that lists all the individuals, but many senators have created their own home pages and this site provides links to these pages as well.

http://policy.net/capweb/congress.html

Jump to Policy Net's CapWeb for another listing of congresspeople. Besides providing the same information as Contacting the 104th Congress, CapWeb provides a picture for most members and a list of the committee the congressperson belongs to. So if you forget what your representative looks like, this is the site to see.

The section on Understanding the Federal Court takes a comprehensive look at the court structure. You can read detailed information about each level including the Supreme Court, Appeals Court, and even the U.S. Tax Court. There's also a diagram of the court structure, but, at the time of this publication, it was very hard to read.

Back issues of a judicial publication, "The Third Branch," are also online and contain many interesting articles discussing current judicial issues, interviews with judicial heads, and the current judicial state of affairs. For example, in the April issue, there's an article discussing the merits of video conferencing court sessions. In the February issue, there's an article detailing Chief Judge Gilbert S. Merritt's (6th Circuit) speech to Congress, explaining why the Judicial Branch should be excluded from Line-Item Veto.

The Federal Judicial Center

http://www.fjc.gov

The Federal Judicial Center provides additional information on judicial issues. In its list of publications, you can find a reference manual for scientific evidence, a summary of the results of mandatory minimum prison terms, a sentencing guideline, and much more. I found many of these articles to be enlightening and certainly thought-provoking.

Fig. 9.7
The Federal Judicial Center provides access to many intriguing documents.

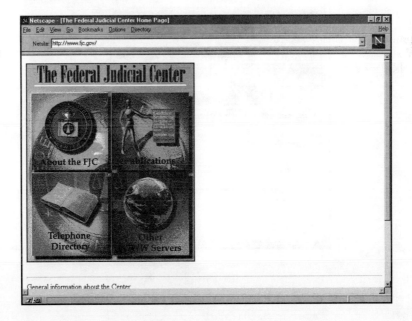

The Federal Judicial Center also provides the best list I could find of links to other Judicial World Wide Web servers. From this site, you can jump to the Supreme Court of Circuit Court Opinions. It also provides links to many other useful government documents such as Commerce Business Daily, the House of Representative's home page discussed previously, and many others.

National security

http://www.dtic.dla.mil/defenselink

You can't deny that the Department of Defense is one of the largest and most visible Government agencies. It also has a cool Web site from which you access lots of defense information. You can visit all the defense heads starting with the President, then working down through the Secretary and Joint Chiefs. You can also visit each of the military branches, the reserves, the National Guard, and the Coast Guard. Don't forget to read about Defense agencies like the Defense Intelligence Agency. I also found an intriguing list and associated documents on the Combatant commands.

Fig. 9.8
Visit the Department of Defense heads, find out how to join the Coast Guard, or locate all the Combatant commands at DefenseLINK.

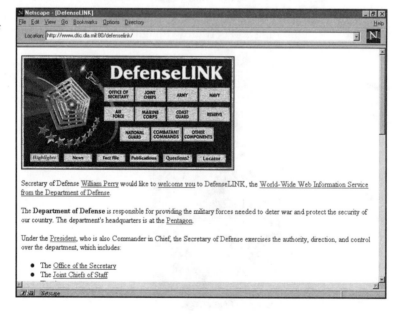

United States Army

http://www.army.mil

Although the opening picture made me laugh, the Army has some interesting data at its Web site. If you're interested in joining, it's definitely the place to go for recruiting information. You can also read through *Soldier's Magazine*, other publications, and news releases. It's also the place to stop if you are trying to locate personnel, retirees, or veteran and alumni associations.

The United States Navy

http://www.navy.mil

If you're trying to decide between joining the Army or the Navy, I can tell you I like the Navy's Web site better. It includes FAQs (Frequently Asked Questions) and a search engine to assist in finding information. If you like watching F-18's maneuver, you might want to look at the Blue Angel's schedule to see if they'll be near you sometime. You can also find recruiting information and a long list of resources about all sorts of Navy topics.

The United States Marine Corps

http://www.hqmc.usmc.mil

The Marine Web page also includes FAQs and a large list of resources and general information about the Corps. You can even listen to the Marine hymn. If you're a Marine, a section about mail, news, and other topics of interest has been created for you.

The United States Air Force

http://www.dtic.dla.mil/airforcelink

The Air Force has my favorite military home page. It starts with current hot topics and new, rather than recruiting, information. You can also access its library and look at some awesome pictures, including the new F-22.

TIP If you're interested in the Reserves, you can jump to information about the three branches, Army, Navy, or Air Force, from **http://www.dtic.dla.mil:80/defenselink/reserve.html**.

If you're interested in the National Guard, you can jump to information about the two sections, Army or Air Force, from **http//www.dtic.dla.mil:80/defenselink/natguard.html**.

Fig. 9.9
Take a look at the F-22, the newest advanced fighter plane at the Air Force Web site.

Coast Guard

http://www.webcom.com/~d13www/welcome.html

The Coast Guard has an eye-pleasing page with lots of useful information. You can view a clickable map to locate the different Coast Guard districts, discover how to join the Coast Guard, and gather navigation information. There's also a section on the Coast Guard flags, logos, miscellaneous images, and audio that is fun to explore.

Government agencies

Although there are three governing branches, a lot of work, research, and policy enforcement is done through various government agencies.

Department of Agriculture

http://www.usda.gov

The U.S. Department of Agriculture has one of the better agency Web sites. You can evaluate the current Farm Bill, read about current events, and review previous milestones and major events. You can also investigate all the different programs and missions being implemented by the USDA. Another nice feature is a list of Internet sites including the White House and Congress. There's also an "awesome" list of WWW sites and the WWW Virtual Library.

Department of Commerce

http://www.doc.gov

Everyone concerned about the economic future should visit the Department of Commerce on the World Wide Web. You can find out what's happening, read current press releases, and connect to the home pages of commerce agencies. This site also provides you access to CILS (Commerce Information Locator Service) and other online commerce services. You can even examine the Federal budget for 1996.

Department of Defense

http://www.dtic.dla.mil/defenselink

You can familiarize yourself with the Joint Chiefs of Staff, nose around the Pentagon, and investigate all the military branches from the Defense link. This site is discussed in detail earlier in this chapter under "National Security."

Department of Education

http://www.ed.gov

The Department of Education is another great agency Web site. It's chock full of reports and documents that should interest just about anyone. Besides the department's mission, goals, and programs, you can also get information about obtaining a grant or financial aid. If you're a teacher or researcher, this site will provide you with guides to resources. Soon, a parent's guide to resources will be added.

Department of Energy

http://www.doe.gov

I really enjoy browsing the site provided by the Department of Energy. Like all agency sites, you can find information about the department, press releases, and current events. You can also search through declassified information with a feature dubbed Opennet. If you think the Department of Energy is just about power and lights, you should explore the documents on the Electronic Exchange Initiative. By the year 2000, the Department of Energy hopes that the primary means to exchange scientific and technical documents is an electronic format.

Department of Health and Human Services

http://www.os.dhhs.gov

A good portion of the 1992 presidential race centered on health care reform and the issue is still a hot topic of debate. To find out exactly what is happening, stop by the Department of Health and Human Services home page on the World Wide Web. You can easily find all the current press releases and health care information. In addition, you can also gather grant information and find out what research projects are currently underway. Invaluable data and facts for consumers are also readily available.

Department of Housing and Urban Development

http://www.hud.gov

Hud.gov is a good place for home buyers to visit. You can find out about special loans and funding or look through the lists of available HUD housing. You can also electronically file mortgage insurance claims, load default reports, and record changes or terminations. This greatly speeds claim processing. You can grab information about HUD programs, projects, and plans.

Department of Interior

http://www.usgs.gov/doi

What exactly does the Department of Interior do? Find the answer to this and many other conservation questions at the Department of Interior.

If you dig around at this site, you will probably be surprised at the topics it covers. You can learn about the mining industry, our national parks and resources, and you can even access the FECA (Federal Employee's Compensation Act) from the Department of Interior. (I guess people are a natural resource.) This page contains jumps to many places on the Net with weekly updates.

Department of Justice

http://www.usdoj.gov

The largest Law Firm in the Nation is also present on the World Wide Web. I enjoyed this view of the complex judicial system. This site contains many interesting judicial documents from the reward for information on the Oklahoma bombing to President Clinton's speech on affirmative action. If you're an attorney looking for a federal position, you should go through the listing of attorney vacancies.

Department of Labor

http://www.dol.gov

If you're job hunting, you should visit the Department of Labor. Through the America Job Bank you can search for jobs across the nation. If you're an employer, you may want to check into listing your open positions with the American Job Bank. Even if you are currently employed, this site should still spark some interest. You can evaluate your workplace on its implementation of OSHA (Occupational Safety and Health Administration) standards, read current media releases, and review the rules enforced by the department. Make sure you visit the DOL department agencies including the Bureau of Labor Statistics to check the current economic indicators and analyze other labor statistics.

 TIP   **If you're job hunting, you will want to take advantage of the** employment sites listed in Chapter 6.

Fig. 9.10
If you're job hunting, you should stop by the American Job Bank and see if your dream job is waiting.

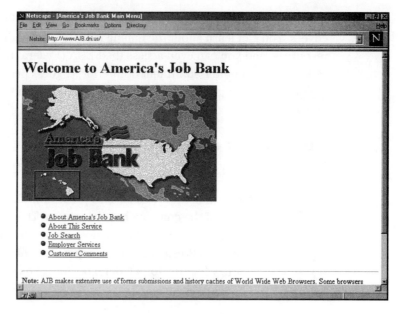

The Department of State

http://www.whitehouse.gov/White_House/Cabinet/html/
Department_of_State.html

The Department of State isn't a very interesting site, but the emblem at the top is pretty cool. It's also a well-written document that provides insight into this department's function, vision, and duties.

Department of Transportation

http://www.dot.gov

Do you fly a lot? If so, you'll want to cruise by the Department of Transportation Web site and see how often specific flights were late in the last month. The Department of Transportation has a well-organized, in-depth, and cool-looking site. I could spend hours browsing the DOT news and information including the data, like flight times, from the Bureau of Transportation Services. There are also plenty of other interesting spots under news and information like the Federal Aviation Administration, National Highway and

Traffic Administration, and the list continues. In addition, the Department of Transportation has a great list of other enjoyable sites as well as back copies of the newsletter *DOT Talk*.

TIP **Www.dot.gov is graphic intensive. If you want to save online time,** see the tip given earlier in the chapter.

The Department of the Treasury

If April 14 gives you nightmares about your dollars flying out the window or Treasury agents arresting you for evasion, you need to visit the IRS on the World Wide Web. The Department of Treasury provides tax form instructions, a list of commonly asked questions and their respective answers, a guide on where to file, and a listing of free tax help services. Besides the IRS facts, you can get information about all Department of Treasury agencies. I like the United States Secret Service page. It is so blunt, and it provides a list of all the people the Secret Service protects (I wasn't on the list). A complete list of all treasury services, current events, and issues is also accessible through this site.

Fig. 9.11
Drop by this site for a list of free tax help.

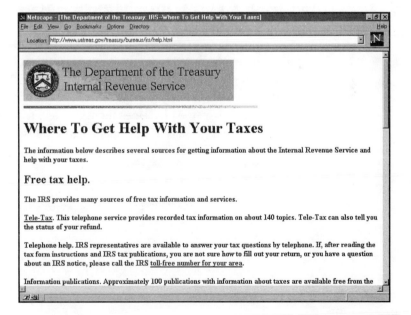

Department of Veteran Affairs

Veterans should visit the Department of Veteran Affairs. It provides information about benefits, special programs, where to get additional help, and a complete list of VA facilities. You can also read about current appeals, legislation, publications, and research.

Independent Agencies

Many independent agencies make a large contribution to national and world politics. Unfortunately, there are simply too many independent Federal agencies to list, but I will list my favorite ones. You can find larger lists at the following two sites:

- http://www.whitehouse.gov/White_House/Independent_Agencies/ html/independent_links-plain.html

- http://lcweb.loc.gov/global/executive/executive.html

The CIA or Central Intelligence Agency

http://www.odci.gov/cia

Everything you ever wanted to know about the Central Intelligence Agency is yours with a simple mouse click. Well, maybe not everything, but the FAQ (Frequently Asked Questions) document does cover a lot of the questions most people have, even the old "Does the CIA really assassinate people?" You can also read current press releases, speeches, and testimony.

Fig. 9.12
Does the CIA assassinate people? Does the CIA spy on Americans? You can find the answer to these and other common questions at the CIA Web site.

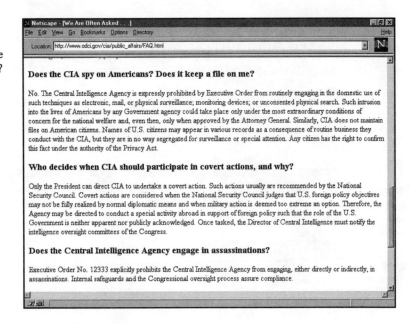

The EPA, Environmental Protection Agency

http://www.epa.gov

The EPA Web site provides access to bunches of documents, reports, and other resources concerning environmental issues. If you're looking for information on recycling, clean water, or chemical waste, you've found the right place. The site is not too exciting because most of it is search engines, but it is a bountiful resource of environmental data.

The FDIC, Federal Deposit Insurance Corporation

http://www.fdic.gov

Just what does it mean if a bank is a member of the FDIC? Where can I find a list of banks that are members of the FDIC? Find these answers and more at fdic.gov. You can also get information on bank performance, press releases, and other interesting tidbits. Investors, you can also get a list of assets being sold by the FDIC.

NASA, National Aeronautics and Space Administration

http://www.gsfc.nasa.gov/NASA_homepage.html

I could spend days at the NASA site. It contains NASA's history and plans, logs of previous space flights, such as Apollo 13, launch schedules, and much more. This site is covered in detail in Chapter 16, "Science."

Fig. 9.13

Find out what really happened on the Apollo 13 space mission at the NASA Web site. For a detailed discussion of this site's features, see Chapter 16.

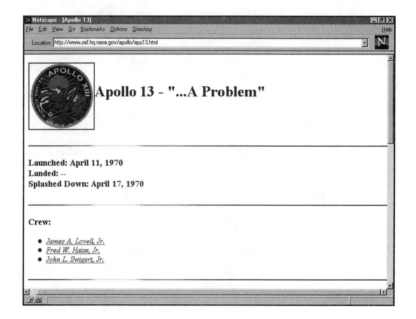

Peace Corps

http://www.clark.net/pub/peace/PeaceCorps.html

Over 6,000 Peace Corps volunteers are currently feeding the hungry, comforting the sick, and uplifting the hopeless around the world and right here in our own country. The Peace Corps Web site explains how to become a volunteer and highlights the worldwide and domestic projects it sponsors. I was astounded by the accomplishments of this organization.

Small Business Administration (SBA)

http://www.sbaonline.sba.gov

For anyone who owns a small business or would like to open a small business, the SBA Web site is going to be a favorite resource. Get tips on how to start a small business and finance the expense. You'll also find reports on current regulations and reforms. In addition, this site has a lot of cute graphics.

The United States Postal Service (USPS)

http://www.usps.gov

Finally, an easy online function to locate that pesky zip code you can't remember. This feature is just one of the things you can do at usps.gov. You can check on postal rates, consumer information, and a package location. If you collect stamps, the USPS site lists upcoming stamps and furnishes details for ordering.

10

Health and Medicine

● **In this chapter:**

- **Locate health resources from public and private institutions**

- **Learn about cancer and the fight against it**

- **Are there other alternatives to traditional medicine? Yes, the Web offers information on both traditional and alternative medicines**

- **Check out what's happening in the fight against Alzheimer's Disease**

Need information on a prescription? Want to know what vaccinations are needed for a trip to North Africa? The Web can answer these and many more health-related questions . . . . ▶

The Web has brought the knowledge of medicine right to your fingertips. When you're seeking information regarding the U.S. government's role in medicine, you no longer need to go down to your local library. The government brings you health and medicine information online. The government's health information covers the latest policies on flu vaccinations to modifications to the Medicare budget.

In addition to the government providing health and medicine information, there are thousands of Web sites bringing you information about medical treatments and methods toward a healthy lifestyle. The health information on the Web is quite broad; you can get information about traditional medicine and alternative medicine.

If you're seeking health knowledge or advice, there are plenty of choices on the Web; all you need to know is where to look. This chapter explores many Web sites pertaining to health and medicine information and provides you with resources where your questions can be answered.

WHO's got worldwide health on the Web

http://www.who.org/

World Health Organization (WHO) is an amazing international organization dedicated to providing the world with the best health information. WHO has seven international locations, each running its own Web server. The information included here is from WHO's main Web site.

WHO is involved in the prevention and documentation of major diseases and illnesses worldwide. AIDS is one of the world's most deadly diseases. WHO's site has AIDS information covering many facets of the disease. The AIDS information includes Frequently Asked Questions (FAQs), Women and AIDS, general news, and AIDS newsletters. WHO provides statistics on the disease that might shock you, for instance, from July 1994 until June of 1995, AIDS increased worldwide by 19 percent. If you're interested in AIDS statistics by countries, you can find excellent statistics at WHO's Web site.

Fig. 10.1
The United Nations
approved The World
Health Organization
on April 7, 1948.

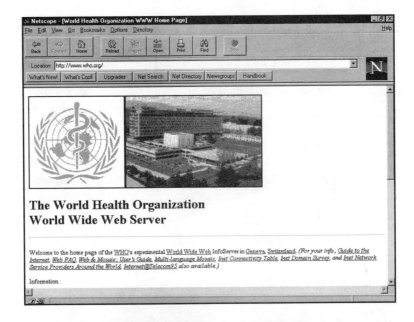

Fig. 10.2
Distribution of the
world's AIDS cases
within 1994–1995 and
from the late 1970s
until present.

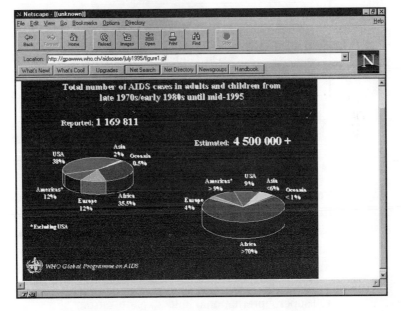

WHO offers numerous links to many health organizations and provides up-to-
date information on major health issues. If you're looking for health publications or bulletins, WHO has it. The publication information covers a complete
preface, an outline, ISBN numbers, and suggested pricing.

The Global Health Network

http://www.pitt.edu/HOME/GHNet/GHNet.html

Our social and business environment has changed dramatically over the past 50 years. Every day we have opportunities that can take us anywhere in the world. The Global Health Network is an organization that combines health care and telecommunications.

Fig. 10.3
The Global Health Network links telecommunications with health information.

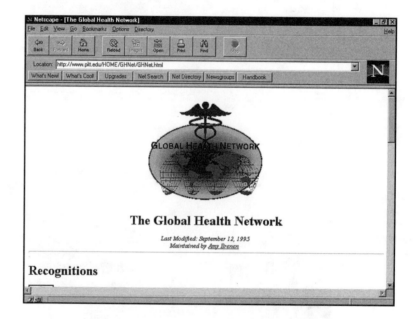

The resources that are available at this site cover many major health areas. The Global Health Network provides the information in several broad categories, such as by disease or by subject (e.g. nutrition, Rural Health, or Vaccination). Selecting one of these categories links you to a Web site that contains the full information. If you're not looking for a specific disease but want a summary of on-going major diseases, this page has that too. When you're trying to find other major public health organizations, you have over 100 superb international links to choose from.

The next time you travel abroad, make sure you look into the travel section. It provides common-sense advice on travel medications and information on clinics and vaccinations.

The Department of Health and Human Services

http://www.os.dhhs.gov/

The Department of Health and Human Services (DHHS) is committed to protecting America's health. The U.S. government has created this and many more health-related sites, such as the National Institute of Health. There's an entire section within this site dedicated to you, the consumer. If you're looking for information on AIDS, cancer, or possibly consumer guidelines, this site provides it. For those who are interested in the current health news, the DHHS posts all of its press releases online. Better yet, you can go to the DHHS press release section and have your email address added to its press-release email server.

Fig. 10.4
The Department of Health and Human Services provides Americans with the best possible health care.

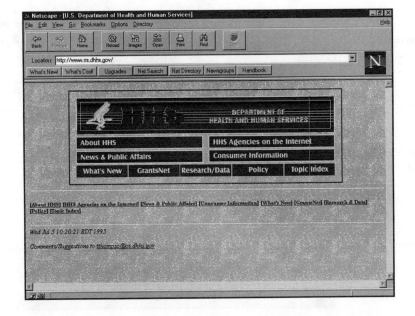

If you need facts on health, DHHS has a complete list. DHHS has the facts organized by subject area (such as AIDS, Women's Health, and Aging). For each fact, DHHS presents its position on the subject and what its goals and objectives are. If you're looking for a specific fact sheet, use the search engine DHHS included.

TIP You can find a list of federal government WWW servers at
http://www.sbaonline.sba.gov/world/federal-servers.html

The Good Health Web

http://www.social.com/health/

The Good Health Web has done an outstanding job at bringing you a fast way to locate government health providers. This site has an index to all government health locations, which consists of over 1,000 locations. For each government location, this site provides you with the location's address, phone number, and a summary of the location's services. The locations are organized alphabetically and by major geographic regions. Using this index, you can find a location quickly anywhere in the United States.

Fig. 10.5
The Good Health Web is your link to health news and discussion forums.

When you're looking for general health information try the general health library. The information in this easy-to-use library is provided by the Consumer Information Center and International Food Information Council Foundation. If you're not quite sure where the information is located in the library, try the search engine; it's quite fast.

If you're interested in health forums, the Good Health Web provides several. The forums include: general health, allergies, Chronic Fatigue Syndrome, and fitness. If you would rather have health information mailed to you electronically, the Good Health Web lists over 50 electronic mailing groups that you can join. In addition to the forums and mailing lists, this site has included lists of health newsgroups and frequently asked questions.

Cancer

Did you know that three out of ten Americans will get cancer some time in their life? That is a startling fact! Within this section, you will find Web sites that inform you about all aspects of cancer and what's being done to cure this deadly disease.

National Cancer Institute (NCI)

http://wwwicic.nci.nih.gov/

National Cancer Institute should be your first resource when looking for information on cancer. NCI provides an informative site. This site is quite comprehensive for both physicians and patients. It offers CancerNet in both Gopher and an HTTP format. Using CancerNet, you can look up topics either by name or search vast archives of information. If you're looking for bibliographic abstracts on cancer cases, you can access a database that contains more than one million cases. If you know a child or have a child that is dealing with cancer, don't miss the "Kid's Home" section.

OncoLink, The University of Pennsylvania Cancer Resource

http://cancer.med.upenn.edu/

OncoLink has done its homework when it comes to using the Web to distribute information about cancer. OncoLink has taken all its cancer information and packaged it in a manner that is intuitive for the reader. Whether you're looking for breaking news on cancer or online medical journals, OncoLink has both. As you dig into this site, you may be impressed with how it presents the cancer information. Not only does OncoLink discuss pediatric and adult cancer, it also talks about drug treatments and new information on each cancer type.

Fig. 10.6
Oncolink provides
direct access to
Oncology education
and news.

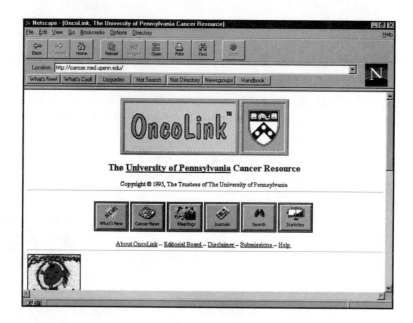

General Cancer Information

http://www.cancer.org/cancinfo.html

This site, sponsored by the American Cancer Society, provides facts on cancer and answers many questions. Did you know that there are over two million cancer cases a year? If you would like to know more about what you can do to prevent cancer, take a look at this site.

Breast Cancer Information Clearinghouse

http://nysernet.org/bcic/

Breast Cancer Information Clearinghouse is a great starting point for obtaining information on breast cancer. You can gain information on how to do a self exam or how mammography works. In addition to all the information it offers, this site also provides you with links to other Internet cancer databases and national support groups.

The Prostate Cancer InfoLink

http://www.comed.com/Prostate/

The Prostate Cancer InfoLink Web site presents cancer information in layman's terms. At this site, you can see pictures of where the prostate is located, learn about symptoms of the disease, find out what treatments are available, read answers to frequently asked questions, and send in questions.

Medicine on the Web

The government and private organizations are using the Web as an explosive device to inform you about medicine and its progress. This section covers information that is available on the Web from the FDA, pharmaceutical companies, and organizations concerned with your child's well-being.

Food and Drug Administration (FDA)

http://www.fda.gov/

Have you ever wondered what monosodium glutamate is? If you want to find out, all you need to do is ask the FDA. The FDA is responsible for many of the items we eat, drink, and apply to our bodies. This site has vast amounts of information available for you to browse, or you can quickly locate information using the site's search tools. Check out this site if you're looking for information on new drugs or drug testing, need food advice, or want to look at the electronic journals that span the past five years. If you have specific questions for the FDA, you can ask through an electronic feedback form.

Fig. 10.7
The Food and Drug Administration protects our health by overseeing the safety of foods and drugs.

Pharmaceutical Information Network

http://pharminfo.com/

When you're looking for information on a particular drug, PharmInfoNet can help you find your answer. This site is for pharmacists and consumers. Pharmacists will enjoy the ease of digging into electronic publications or the latest drug reviews. For consumers, there are answers to common questions and references to newsgroups on medicine. If you're wondering about a specific drug and its side effects, the drug database will quickly point you in the right direction.

The Virtual Hospital

http://vh.radiology.uiowa.edu/

The Virtual Hospital in Iowa City, Iowa is your 24-hour medical information center. The hospital offers information for patients, physicians, and health care providers. Included is a full set of online maps starting from the state of Iowa and including the floorplans of the hospital and clinics. You can easily find the information you're looking for because it's broken down by title, organ, and department. You can find thorough information on many areas— for instance, dieting tips, overviews on particular diseases, or information on women's health. When you first visit the Virtual Hospital, take a look at the demonstration that is in the help section.

Fig. 10.8
The Virtual Hospital is a medical reference library that never closes.

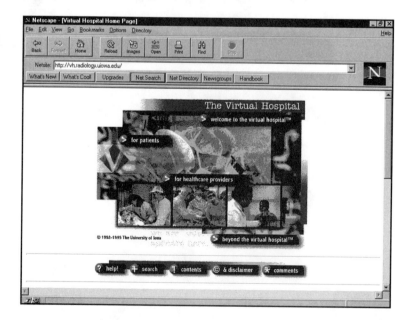

Mayo Clinic

http://www.mayo.edu/

When I hear "Mayo Clinic," I think world-class medicine. Mayo's Web site is just as good as its medicine. This site provides great online directions to each of Mayo's five locations. Information about the Rochester, Minnesota facility is extensive; the site provides information about the entire city, including lodging information.

Mayo's Web site is very complete and includes patient and medical professional information. For patients, they have provided appointment information, billing information, and local weather facts (it gets chilly in Minnesota). Medical professionals and want-to-be's can read about Mayo's residency programs and learn how to apply to the medical school.

Stanford University Medical Center

http://med-www.stanford.edu/

Stanford is the oldest medical school in the Western United States. Its site includes information on Stanford's medical school, research facilities, hospitals, and clinics. Stanford provides a rich array of information for those seeking admission to the research facilities plus offers online information to research results. If you're interested in the medical school, take a look at the admission requirements and course catalogs online. While browsing this site, you'll enjoy "Desktop Tools"; these tools have a dictionary online, postal information, weather, and access to five San Francisco Bay area newspapers. One fantastic concept that Stanford included was to provide the health care information in seven different languages.

Go Ask Alice

http://www.columbia.edu/cu/healthwise/

Here's a unique site that offers information similar to Ann Landers' newspaper column. Alice is a question-and-answer Web site sponsored by the Health Education division of Columbia University. The site is informative and fun. For example, do you know what the number one cause of stress is? The lack of time to get everything accomplished according to our schedules.

PEDINFO

http://www.lhl.uab.edu/pedinfo/

PEDINFO provides a broad range of pediatric information for parents. The site provides multiple pediatric links to HTTP, Gopher, and newsgroup servers. If you're looking for a particular pediatric specialist or are trying to find information related to a child's condition, this site can help. Along with medical information, PEDINFO contains helpful parenting information.

Health Issues and Your Children

http://www.parentsplace.com/readroom/health.html

Do you have a question for your child's doctor but the office is closed? This site may be your answer. This site contains answers to common health questions relating to children's health. If you're in no rush and want to ask a question, you can post a question to the Web doctor. The site also contains information on a variety of parenting topics, online mini-books, electronic newsletters, and access to a kids' shopping mall.

Alternative medicine

Many forms of alternative medicine have information available on the Web. The following list covers some general alternatives to traditional medicine.

Chiropractic OnLine Today

http://www.panix.com/~tonto1/dc.html

Many people suffer from back pain and often turn to chiropractors after they've given up with their own doctors. Chiropractic OnLine Today provides you with a wealth of resources where you can learn more about chiropractic. The site keeps track of chiropractic news, journals, newsgroups, and offers teaching advice. If you need the location of a chiropractor, you can find one in the online referral directory.

Fig. 10.9
Chiropractic OnLine Today is an electronic chiropractic journal for consumers and health professionals.

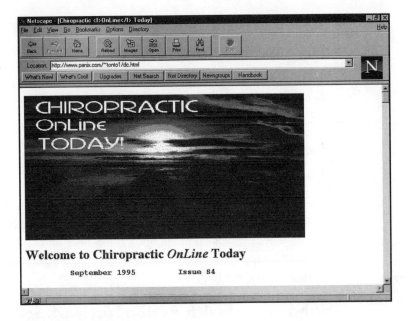

Herb'n Outfitters

http://204.213.234.53/

Herb'n Outfitters offers herbal information and direct mail ordering of herbal products. The site's information provides you with an overview of selected herbs and how the herbs interact with your body. Each herb group affects different parts of our body; for instance, one group affects our bones and another affects our cardiovascular system. In addition to learning about herbal products, you can also learn about Herb'n Outfitters' herbal supplier.

The World Wide Web Virtual Library: Sumeria

http://lablinks.com/sumeria/

Sumeria is a unique site that takes a very different perspective on many topics, including health and medicine. This site offers information on what Sumeria classifies as alternative health and medicine. Topics discussed include oxygen therapies, rejuvenation, and the role of light in health.

Gerson Institute Action Network Society

http://www.homepage.com/mall/gerson/gerson.html

Gerson is a method used to treat all sorts of ailments; learn all about it at this site. You'll find newsletters, patient testimonials, and information giving the costs associated with the therapy.

Healing Ways

http://zeta.cs.adfa.oz.au/Spirit/healing.html

Do you feel that some days you're just not yourself? Healing Ways focuses on healing your soul first and then your body. The spiritual healing resources Healing Ways provides include book references and online lectures. If you're looking for support groups, Healing Ways offers links to support services and Internet Relay Chat (IRC).

HANS: The Health Action Network Society

http://www.hans.org/

HANS provides alternative health news and commentaries. This site is organized by major topics. These topics include information on fluorides, pesticides, and vitamins. Within a selected topic you can read book reviews or highlights from an author's lecture. If you're seeking the full lecture or a book from the author, HANS provides information on how to order them. HANS also offers health video tapes for sale.

Alzheimer's disease

Alzheimer's is a disease that you hear more about each day. The following sites provide good overviews of the disease and what actions are being taken to fight the disease.

Alzheimer's Association

http://www.alz.org/

Did you know that 10 percent of people over 65 are affected by Alzheimer's? The information presented at this site answers many of your basic questions about Alzheimer's disease and what is being done to combat it. You will find other helpful information regarding family stress, where Alzheimer caregivers are located, financial aid information, and what support groups are available in your area.

Fig. 10.10
The Alzheimer's Association provides research grants in the battle against Alzheimer's.

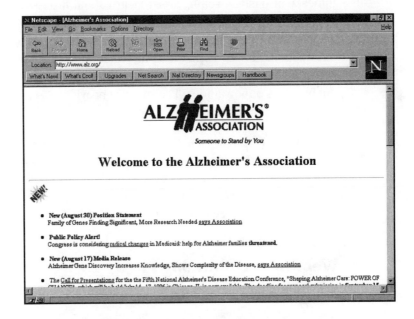

Institute for Brain Aging and Dementia

http://www.alz.uci.edu/

Alzheimer's is the fourth major cause of death. This site is dedicated to studying Alzheimer's disease and dementia. It walks you down several paths of the disease and provides clinical information, such as pictures of DNA structures from brains afflicted with it. At this site you'll be able to learn about the causes of dementia, what you can do to prevent it, learn which newsgroups are available, and how you can help.

Internet fitness

The Internet is making it easier for you to get together with your fitness peers to learn about new equipment and share experiences. The next two sites offer free fitness advice and allow you to purchase fitness training materials.

FitnessWorld Home Page

http://www.fitnessworld.com/

FitnessWorld is an exciting area to learn about fitness trends for both fitness providers and enthusiasts. Health clubs and exercise equipment manufacturers will find FitnessWorld's professional area to be an excellent resource for information. FitnessWorld offers information for upcoming trade shows, news and events in the health field, and forums to discuss issues and carry out business opportunities. The site also provides a searchable database of equipment manufacturers and supplies.

FitnessWorld offers tips on the latest fitness techniques and forums for discussions of training methods. It also publishes an online monthly fitness magazine, which has archives that go back until 1993. The online database can be useful if you're seeking work in the fitness field or trying to hire someone for a fitness position. This site also includes a cartoon section that is updated daily.

WebRunner© Running Page

http://www.webrunner.com/webrun/running/running.html/

WebRunner's a site for running enthusiasts. This site has information about races held all over the Eastern United States. If you need to know about specific race dates, entrance fees, age groups, or how to register, you can find it at WebRunner. The site includes links to other running clubs on the East coast and other Web sites that provide running information. The site also provides downloadable software specifically for runners. The software can keep track of your progress or serve as your personal trainer. The cost of the software is between $15-$30.

Q&A *Where can I find a list of Web sites that organize medicine by category?*

There are several Web indexing sites:

Galaxy: **http://galaxy.einet.net/galaxy/Medicine.html**

McKinley Group, Inc: **http://www.mckinley.com/**

Yahoo: **http:/.www.yahoo.com/Health/**

How come when I use a search form, each returned result does not contain all the keywords I entered?

When you use a site's specific search form, you must check its rules for matching keywords. The rules are generally posted right above or below the search field. If you want to find documents that only contain your keywords, you usually need to place a Boolean "and" operator between each keyword. For example to find "brain, cancer, and research" in the same document, you would enter "brain and cancer and research" in the search field.

Why do some Uniform Resource Locators (URL's) end in a slash? For instance: http://www.os.dhhs.gov/

All Web sites have a default document that they serve you if the URL ends in a slash. At most sites the document is actually named index.html or Welcome.html. For example: **http://www.os.dhhs.gov/index.html** is the same as **http://www.os.dhhs.gov/**.

11

Internet and Web Information

● **In this chapter:**

● You want Web browsers? We've got Web browsers. Look at what's hot and see how to keep up with this ever-changing arena

● Discover the latest in Web technology with Java, VRML, interactive chatting, radio broadcasts, and more

● Explore software for connecting to the Internet, reading email, and other online activities

● See how you can find new Web pages

The Web is your one-stop source for free software for connecting to the Internet, information about the hottest Web technologies, and comprehensive lists of Web pages . .

A couple of years back, there was a terrible catch-22 situation for personal computer users wanting to get onto the Internet. At that time, the best way to connect to the Internet was to download the necessary software from the Internet. But, of course, you couldn't get that software without already being connected!

Things have changed a lot in the past couple of years. Now, you can go into any retail computer store or bookstore and buy inexpensive software or a book to get connected. Problem solved! In fact, some of this software is so cheap, you'll even see *free* starter disks in magazines.

But even with all of this software you can buy, the Internet itself is still a great place to get new software once you get connected. Are you looking for a better Web browser? You can download dozens of browsers and go for a spin. If you bought software that doesn't come with an email program, just go to the Web for one.

And the Internet is not just a place to find software. You can find endless volumes of information about how to use the Web and the Internet. All the major companies that connect people to the Internet have Internet sites. Online services (companies such as CompuServe and America Online) have Web pages.

Oh no, Mozilla! Netscape Communications

http://www.netscape.com

If there's one company whose name has become synonymous with the Internet and the Web, it's Netscape. Netscape has been the darling of the media, Madison Avenue, and Wall Street and it is known as the leading company in the development of the Web.

 TIP **Mozilla was the name given to the Netscape Navigator browser** during the early days of development. Some users still refer to it affectionately by that name, the name of the big green monster that adorns some Netscape pages.

This site is, without a doubt, one of the most frequently visited on the Web. Netscape makes the most widely used Web browsing software, which is called simply **Netscape Navigator**. Netscape also makes other related products including Web server software, an Internet Relay Chat client program, and software for developing online applications. A new version of Netscape Navigator called Netscape Navigator Gold has added features for creating Web pages.

 Plain English, please!

Internet Relay Chat is a service that lets you communicate with several other users at the same time over the Internet. They see everything you type and you see what they type, all in real time. A **client** is the program you use to participate in these chat sessions.

Fig. 11.1
Read about Netscape's market leading products and innovative technologies.

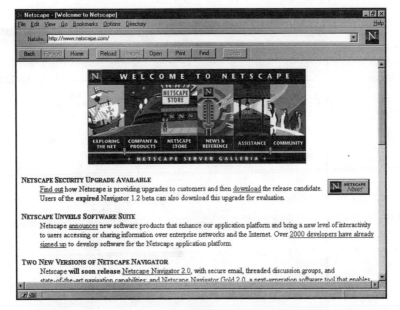

Netscape's large Web site includes links to download their software (that you can try for free), helpful information for learning your way around the Web, and links to many directories and search pages. You'll also find press releases and information about the many companies involved in developing products in conjunction with Netscape.

 TIP **If you follow the links from the main Netscape page to download** Netscape software, you'll come to a page with a list of many links. All these links will download a copy of the software. The reason for the multiple links is that Netscape is so popular, more than one server is needed to handle all the downloads. If you can't get connected, try clicking a different link.

All the URLs that are fit to print: Lycos

http://www.lycos.com/

Lycos has the biggest database of Web pages that I've seen on the Web. From the search page, you can initiate a search of over seven million Web pages. (The section "Searches and Directories" later in this chapter shows how to use these types of pages.) The good news is, if what you're looking for is on the Web, chances are you can find it with Lycos. I've never found a topic that existed on the Web that I couldn't find with Lycos. Lycos recently upgraded the hardware that runs this search engine and now you can get results very quickly.

Fig. 11.2

If it's on the Web, Lycos will find it.

One downside of this search engine is the number of **hits** returned. (Hits are pages that match your search criteria.) I searched for "Macmillan" and got over 1,400 matches. Luckily, the first one was the one I wanted (Macmillan Information SuperLibrary, Home of Que on the Web). Hits are ranked in order with the ones most likely to be what you're looking for first. Ordering is determined by the number of occurrences of the search words in each document, where the words are in the documents, and other criteria.

Another downside is the repetition of pages. For example, the Macmillan search lists the Macmillan Information SuperLibrary no less than six different times with six different (but equally functional) addresses (**http://www.mcp.com**, **http://mcp.com**, **http://www.mcp.com:80**, and so on.) To make the best use of this resource, try to make your search specific by using more than one keyword, go to the search page with options by clicking the "Search Options" link and then choose "match all terms (AND)" in the Search Options box. Still, even with this method, be prepared to wade through long lists of results.

Protecting the freedom of the Net: Electronic Frontier Foundation

http://www.eff.org

I consider this site to be one of the most important ones on the Web. This group is actively involved with protecting the constitutional rights of "Netizens." It works to protect freedom of the electronic press. It encourages thought and debate on the proper role of government involvement in the Net and looks for solutions that balance freedom and responsibility.

The Alerts link at EFF takes you to current events that affect online freedom. You can find out about pending legislation as well as court decisions and proceedings. When the matter is legislation, there's usually information explaining who you can contact to voice your opinion.

You'll also find links to a newsletter (the current issue as well as an archive of back issues) and other sites with related content. Whatever your opinion on the state of the Net, I'd encourage you to get involved here.

Fig. 11.3
The EFF works to protect freedoms of the press and speech in online and electronic media.

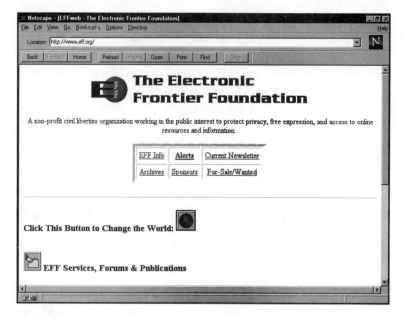

Get your Winsocks here: The Consummate Winsock Apps list

http://cwsapps.texas.net/

Where do you go when you want to find software on the Internet? What do you do when a colleague tells you about a new email program but doesn't tell you where to get it? Or maybe you need a newsreader but don't know which one to try. Forrest Stroud has devised the biggest and baddest site for this. Yes, it's the *Consummate* Winsock Apps list.

Stroud's list lists and rates hundreds of programs related to using the Internet. The site has lists categorized by type of application such as Web browsers, email clients, newsreaders, and so on. There are also categories devoted to lists of top-rated software, starter kits recommended for new users, and links to new programs.

The links for each program include descriptions of the software, the maker's Web page if available, a description, and a link to a download site if the software can be downloaded. The download links connect to the main site for each program so the copy you get will always be up-to-date.

Fig. 11.4
The Consummate Winsock Apps page lists hundreds of programs for Windows users on the Internet.

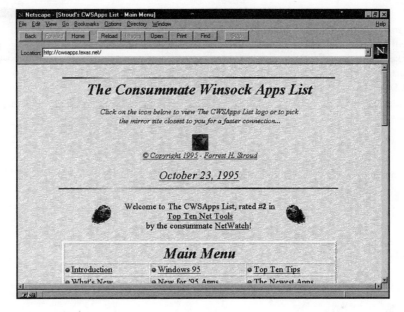

Web browsers

Do you really need more than one Web browser? For most people the answer is "No." But, that doesn't mean that we don't all occasionally like to try a new browser and see what it can do. There are so many browser options, it's nice to try a new one and compare its features to what you're using.

The Web is also an excellent source of information about browsers, including extensive online help, FAQs, installation instructions, and troubleshooting advice.

NCSA Mosaic

http://www.ncsa.uiuc.edu

This site is the home of the original "killer app" Web browser—Mosaic. However, there's much more here than just Mosaic. The NCSA (that's the National Center for Supercomputing Applications) has multimedia exhibits, information about high-performance computing systems, and links to some of the technical publications (not light reading by any means). Other software NCSA develops relates to scientific modeling, data analysis, and file transfer and sharing.

Fig. 11.5
Interest in and
development of the
Web skyrocketed with
the introduction of
Mosaic, NCSA's
original graphical Web
browser.

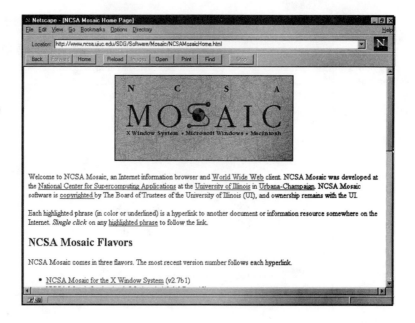

If you follow the Mosaic link, you can read about and download Mosaic for
Windows, Mac, and X Windows. NCSA maintains a popular What's New page,
tutorials about the Internet and the Web, and links to information about
VRML and SGML.

Microsoft Internet Explorer

http://www.microsoft.com/windows/ie/iexplorer.htm

TIP   **Microsoft's site is infamous for changing addresses of individual**
pages frequently. If this address doesn't work, try starting at **http://
www.microsoft.com** and following the links to Internet Explorer.

This popular Web browser is distributed as part of Microsoft Plus for Windows 95. You can also download it free. Check this Web site for the most
recent version of the browser and for announcements about new features.
Watch for Microsoft to update and improve this browser regularly to keep up
with and to keep ahead of competing browser products. Version 2 supports
neat new features like background audio clips and inline videos. Download
the browser and try the example pages to see these features in action.

SlipKnot

http://plaza.interport.net/slipknot/slipknot.html

Many people think that if you only have a shell (command line) account with your Internet service provider, you have to suffer through a text-based Web interface. SlipKnot is a clever product that gets around this limitation for Windows users. It gives you a Windows-based graphical Web browser that you can use without having a SLIP or PPP account.

Framing the Web

The Browserwatch page was one of the first ones I saw that uses a new Web feature called **frames** that was introduced in Netscape 2.0. With frames, the Web page is divided into several parts, each of which is sent to your browser separately. You can scroll through these parts independently. The top section is a frame, the middle has a left and a right frame, and the bottom section is a frame. You can use all these frames independently of the others.

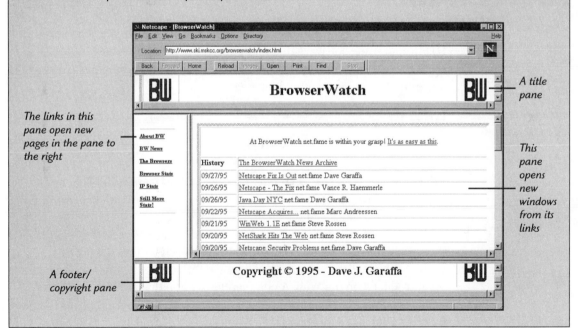

The links in this pane open new pages in the pane to the right

A footer/ copyright pane

A title pane

This pane opens new windows from its links

NCompass

http://www.excite.sfu.ca/NCompass

This Web browser for Windows 95 and NT is especially designed to make the most of inline movies and interactive 3D.

BrowserWatch

http://www.ski.mskcc.org/browserwatch/index.html

With the dozens of Web browsers available, most people don't have the time it takes to keep up with the constant flood of new versions, new features, and new products. BrowserWatch collects all that information in one place so that you only need to check one Web page. It also keeps track of what browsers people use to access its page, in case you're interested in which browsers are most popular.

HTML Creation

In Chapters 3 and 4, we looked at the language used to create Web pages, HTML, and some software that makes creating Web pages easier. In this section, we'll explore some Web sites where you can find the best software and information for creating Web pages.

Web Weaver

http://137.143.111.3/Web.weaver/about.html

 TIP   **Yuck! Who wants to type in a terrible address with all of these** numbers? If you think this is a pain but you use a site with this type of address often, add the site to your bookmarks.

Web Weaver is a shareware HTML editor for Macintoshes. It's highly customizable and allows you to add new HTML codes as new HTML elements are introduced on the Web. A commercial version that's under development includes additional editing features, advanced tools for scripting, and support for importing and exporting DOS, Windows, UNIX, and Mac text files.

Internet Assistant for Word

http://www.microsoft.com/msoffice/freestuf/msword/download/ia/
default.htm

This HTML editor from Microsoft works in Microsoft Word for Windows and
comes in versions for Word 6 and Word for Windows 95. Anyone familiar
with using Word will find this editor easy to use.

HTML Assistant

http://fox.nstn.ca/~harawitz/index.html

This HTML editor for Windows has earned lavish praise from some of the
leading computer magazines. You can download a free version from this site
or order the Pro version. Other related products you can download here
include a utility for "grabbing" (automatically selecting and copying) Web
addresses from any document and a graphics editor designed especially for
creating backgrounds for Web pages.

WebEdit

http://wwwnt.thegroup.net/Webedit/Webedit.htm

This site is the home page for the popular WebEdit HTML editor. You can
download and use WebEdit for free. If you register it, you get additional
features, such as a table editor and toolbar.

Sausage Software

http://www.sausage.com

Sausage Software has a uniquely named HTML editor—HotDog—for Windows. Download a free copy or read about the differences in the new professional version. See Chapter 4 for a more in-depth look at HotDog.

SoftQuad

http://www.sq.com

SoftQuad is a leading maker of software for creating Web pages. HoTMetaL,
which is used to create Web pages in HTML, has won prestigious awards.
SoftQuad also has products for creating more complex Web pages in SGML.

NaviSoft

http://www.navisoft.com

NaviSoft makes Web server software (NaviServer) and an HTML editing program (NaviPress). You can download free trial versions of both of these from this Web site. NaviSoft also has a Web page hosting service. This service lets you put your Web pages on NaviSoft's server for a small fee. The charge varies depending on whether the Web pages are personal or commercial, their size, and the number of visitors the pages get.

Excel to HTML Converter

http://rs712b.gsfc.nasa.gov/704/dgd/xl2html.html

Here's a special purpose macro for converting a range of cells in an Excel spreadsheet into an HTML table. Sure, there's not a lot of general need for this feature, but it's neat. This macro works for Windows and Mac Excel. (There's also a version for Mac Excel versions 4.01 and 5.0 at **http://www.rhodes.edu/software/readme.html**.)

HTML

http://www.w3.org/pub/WWW/MarkUp/MarkUp.html

If you're looking for information about HTML straight from the horse's mouth, look no further. This site is the official home of all the official specifications for HTML.

Java, VRML, and RealAudio heat up the Net

It's easy to get lost in all the new technology on the Web. Just when you think you're doing well because your computer is set up to play movies from the Web, along comes VRML and Java, and you feel lost again. What are the new technologies? What do they do? Are they something you need to look at and learn to use? This section looks at all the latest ways to exchange information and add value to the Web.

Java

http://java.sun.com

There's a picture of a steaming cup of Joe on this page but the site has nothing to do with beans, cappuccino, espresso, or any other variation of this all-purpose beverage.

Java is a new Web technology that allows for greater integration of application software on the Web. What does that mean to you? It means that, in addition to viewing text, pictures, and even multimedia on the Web, you can get little application programs (called **applets**) on the Web that automatically install themselves and run for special purposes, such as animation, interactive games, or interactive books. With a Web browser that has support for Java, the Web can be much more interactive and easy to use. You can use applets designed in Java without any additional steps or effort beyond clicking the links to go to the pages.

Fig. 11.6

This hot cup of Joe is your introduction to the hot worlds of Java and Hot Java (who would want it cold?).

The Java site has more information about Java (including technical information for developers who want to create Java applications) and links to browsers that support Java (Sun has a browser named Hot Java that demonstrates the technology and Netscape has built Java support into Netscape 2).

You can also click several links to see many sample pages that include Java applications.

VRML

http://vrml.wired.com

Wired Magazine runs this site and has become the "official" home of **VRML** information on the Web. Mostly what you find here are transcripts and papers from the folks who designed and shaped VRML.

 Plain English, please!

> **VRML** is the Virtual Reality Modeling Language. It adds virtual reality to Web pages through interactive graphics.

This VRML site isn't the only one around. You may also want to see **http://sdsc.edu/vrml/**.

 CAUTION Don't confuse VRML with plain old vanilla VR. Apple makes a product called QuickTime VR which is neat in and of itself and used on the Web, but not at all related to VRML. See the tip about QuickTime in the review of Apple's site in Chapter 7.

WebSpace

http://www.sgi.com/Products/WebFORCE/WebSpace/

Silicon Graphics has developed this VRML browser and several related VRML tools. The browser is available for several different platforms including Windows 95. A Macintosh PowerPC version is being developed as well.

Worlds Inc.

http://www.worlds.net

Worlds Inc. makes what they call "social computing" applications. You can use the Worlds Chat software to communicate and interact with other users in a 3D virtual world on the Web. Download the chat software from this site, visit the Internet World's Fair (a "theme park" online), and get information about the technology behind Worlds Chat.

Fig. 11.7
Visit virtual worlds with
WebSpace software
from SGI.

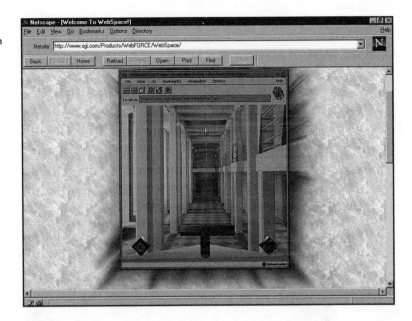

TIP **Worlds Inc. has also begun Alphaworld, which is similar to Worlds** Chat but much larger in scope. This new world allows users to "stake out" space in cyberspace, and build 3D buildings, trees, roads, and more on their "land." Point your browser to **http://www.worlds.net/alphaworld** for more information and free software.

WebChat

http://www.irsociety.com/webchat.html

WebChat is a multimedia chatting system that runs in most popular Web browsers. What's multimedia about it is that as you are "chatting" by exchanging thoughts via types text, you can also exchange audio, pictures, and video. You don't need any additional software to use this system. Simply enter your comments in a form and watch the comments of others appear on-screen. You'll see links to many different servers that run "channels" for hundreds of different chat topics.

Prospero Systems

http://www.prospero.com/globalstage

Prospero Systems is a Web-based chatting system that uses a small separate chat program in addition to your Web browser. You can download the software for free. The software connects to IRC chat channels as well as to new GlobalStage chat servers.

WorldView

http://www.intervista.com

This VRML Web browser is available for Windows 95 and NT as well as for the Mac. The WorldView browser runs either by itself or in conjunction with another browser such as Netscape. Use WorldView to go to **http://www.webmaster.com/vrml/model/reliant.wrl** to see the site shown in the next figure.

Fig. 11.8
Fly *Star Trek's* USS Reliant.

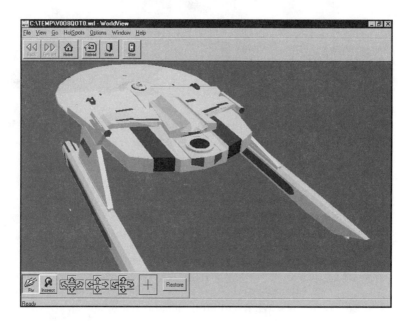

The Cost of VRML

VRML is neat but it may cost you if you have an older computer. The minimum recommendations are a PC with a 486DX2/50 and 8 megabytes of RAM. To really use it for anything other than toying with simple VRML worlds, you'll want a Pentium and 16 megabytes of RAM. On the Mac side, a PowerMac is recommended with 16 megabytes of RAM. In either case, don't try to use VRML with anything less than a 28.8 modem. It will just be too slow to appreciate.

PaperSoftware

http://www.paperinc.com

Here's one final VRML site that's worth a look. This company makes a VRML browser called WebFX that works directly within Netscape.

RealAudio

http://www.RealAudio.com

This program enables your Web browser to play radio-like audio in real time on your Windows PC or Mac. Several of the early uses of RealAudio broadcasts have included live sporting events, OJ Simpson trial updates, music clips, and talk shows. The RealAudio software you use to listen to these broadcasts is available for free download. Also, if you want to broadcast RealAudio events on your Web server, you can download a free trial version of the server software.

Internet Phone

http://www.vocaltec.com

The Internet Phone is an inventive application that lets you use your computer and the Internet to simulate telephone calls. The person you talk to also has to be using this software. You'll both need sound cards that function properly, speakers, and microphones. The person you call can be anywhere on the Internet and you don't pay the telephone company anything. Visit this site to learn more and download a free trial version.

RealAudio Sampler

Santa Monica Bank	http://hkbank.com/smbank
WSKU	http://www.wksu.kent.edu
Batman Forever	http://batmanforever.com
A little bit of everything	http://town.hall.org/radio

CU-SeeMe

http://www.wpine.com/cu-seeme.html

CU-SeeMe (pronounced "See You See Me") is a video and audio conferencing program for the Internet. Using this program, you can transmit and receive audio and video with your computer over the Internet. The software comes in versions for Windows and Macs. This site offers a free trial version that you can download. You can also visit a list of sites that use CU-SeeMe. Be fore-warned though, the video will be too slow to watch over a modem and if you use this on your computer on a LAN at work, the network administrator may come knocking to see why you're using so much bandwidth.

Xing

http://www.xingtech.com

This company makes a product called Streamworks that is used to broadcast audio or video on the Net. Several major companies broadcast including NBC and some large radio stations. (I'm watching NBC's NBC Pro, an Internet broadcast of the NBC Evening News as I write this.)

Q&A ***Why is the audio and video quality so poor with all of these Internet audio and video programs? Will a hardware upgrade or a faster connection help?***

If you're used to the beautiful picture on your 31" color TV and the sound quality of a top-of-the-line CD player, this will be a major disappointment. Moving from a modem to an ISDN connection improves matters somewhat, but not much. This technology is young; it isn't ready to replace your TV or stereo just yet.

Combo deals: Web browsers, email readers, and the kitchen sink

If you're looking for a suite of Internet programs that includes all the soft-ware you need for any Internet tasks, several companies make all-in-one combos. You can find these combos at retail software stores; you can also find free trial versions on the Net.

InterCon Systems

http://www.intercon.com

InterCon makes Internet software for Windows and Macs. You can connect to the Internet using NetShark and/or use the server software InterServer Publisher. From this site, download trial versions of the software, get technical support, and join InterCon's email mailing list.

NetManage

http://www.netmanage.com

NetManage makes two of the most popular software packages for connecting to the Internet. Chameleon Sampler was used for several years by many publishers and by service providers as a starter kit. Many people still use Chameleon Sampler; it's a smaller version of the full-retail Chameleon product that comes in different varieties for dial-up and network use. Read all about the different versions of the product to see which one is right for your needs. You can download trial versions of some products and order online. Special information about configuring Windows 95 and the Chameleon software to work well together is also available along with technical support.

Fig. 11.9
NetManage's Chameleon software has long been popular in wide area networks. That popularity served to launch NetManage in the Internet market.

Internet in a Box

http://www.compuserve.com/prod_services/consumer/consumer.html

CompuServe bought Spry in 1995; Spry's the company that makes *Internet in a Box*. CompuServe has done a good job upgrading this software, but it's next to impossible to find the Web pages that describe the software. However, now that you know where to go, you can read all about this Internet suite. *Internet in a Box* is a real leader in retail sales. Spry also has a related product, *Mosaic in a Box*, with fewer features but a real discount price.

California Software Inc.

http://www.calsoft.com

If you want more than just a Web browser and basic connectivity software, California Software makes a powerful Internet software package—InterAp. This software includes all the usual clients (Web browser, email, news, FTP, and so on) but it also includes a scripting tool and scheduler. With these, you can automate Internet tasks that you perform frequently and schedule them to run at any convenient time. These "Intelligent Agents" gather and sort information for you from the Web, newsgroups, email, or any other Internet source.

InterAp also is OLE 2 compliant; it works well with Windows applications such as Microsoft Office. Some of the sample scripts that come with InterAp show how to automatically publish Internet information in Word and Excel. Use this Web page to learn more about the features and to download a free trial copy.

Frontier Technologies

http://wwwfrontiertech.com

Frontier's SuperHighway Access and SuperTCP are two of the most comprehensive Internet access packages available. SuperHighway Access is geared toward individuals (or businesses) that just need to connect to the Net. SuperTCP has many additional tools for networking and connecting to mainframes in a corporate network setting. Frontier also has a CD-ROM product that includes the Lycos search database (there's a description of Lycos later in this chapter) along with the Frontier browser. With this browser and search database, you can search for sites of interest offline, and when you find a page you want to load, the Web browser fires up and off you go.

Emissary

http://www.twg.com

Emmissary is another all-in-one package for Windows. Check this site for the availability of a free trial version. The strength of this package is that all the services are integrated.

Other Internet software

There's more to the Net than just the Web. And while Web browsers are perfect for viewing Web pages, they aren't always the best at other Internet tasks. For example, some Web browsers include the capability to read email and news, but programs designed specifically for email and news do a much better job. Here we'll take a quick look at the cream of the crop.

Qualcomm

http://www.qualcomm.com

Qualcomm created Eudora, the popular email software for Windows and Macs. At this site, read all about the free and retail versions of Eudora, download the free version, and download other related software.

NewsXpress

http://www.malch.com/nxfaq.html

NewsXpress is still my favorite newsreader. I may be out of sync with the times; many people tell me Forte's Agent (and Free Agent) is the best. But, I find NewsXpress easier to use. This site includes a FAQ and a link to the latest version of NewsXpress. (You can find Agent at **http://www.forteinc.com/forte**).

SurfWatch Software

http://www.surfwatch.com

You've heard all about the amount of explicit material on the Web. If you're looking for a way to block access (maybe your kids use the Internet and there are certain things you don't want them to learn), this software allows you to screen out objectionable material. Read about all SurfWatch's features, how you can get it, and what online services are integrating it.

NetNanny

http://www.netnanny.com/netnanny

NetNanny is another program that prevents access to objectionable material on the Net. Parents can decide which words, phrases, and sites they want NetNanny to watch for and configure it to monitor activity and keep track of what happens—or to shut down when one of the screen sites or phrases is detected.

Fig. 11.10
While there is no real substitute for parental involvement and supervision on the Net, NetNanny helps you protect your kids when you can't.

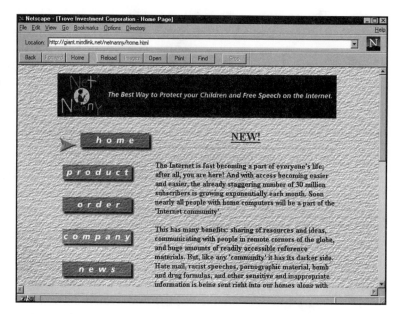

TUCOWS

http://www.tucows.com

The Ultimate Collection of Winsock Software is a must-visit site for any Windows user who likes to tinker with all the latest Internet software. If this describes you, here you can find links to every category of Internet software and helper applications.

Internet Service Providers

Unless you're connecting to the Internet through a LAN connection at work or at a university, you need to have an Internet account. This section looks at companies that specialize in Internet access. (The next section looks at online services that also offer access to the Internet.)

MCI

http://www.mci.com

If you didn't discover this from the InternetMCI commercials on television, MCI sells Internet access. You can also find out about their other telecommunication services here.

UUNET Technologies

http://www.uu.net

UUNET is one of the largest Internet Service Providers. Many other service providers connect to the Internet through UUNET. UUNET offers many types of connections—from dial-up service for individuals through its AlterDial service to T1 and T3 lines. Corporations and other service providers use these high-speed T1 and T3 connections. See this Web page to find out more about these services including pricing, availability, and options.

PSI

http://www.psi.net

This company is a large national Internet Service Provider. For new customers, they offer a complete startup kit including software.

IQuest

http://www.iquest.net

I have to mention this company because I get my Internet service through them. IQuest is a small provider in Indianapolis with local numbers throughout Indiana.

Portal

http://www.portal.com

Portal is an Internet service provider that boasts connections in over 1,000 cities with 200,000 modems. They have services for individuals as well as for corporations that want to connect.

Demon Internet

http://www.demon.co.uk

Demon Internet is the home of the UK's largest service provider. They offer low priced, one-fee dial-up accounts and leased-line accounts.

WinNet Communications

http://www.win.net/

WinNet uses a unique software program for connecting to its service. With it, any mail and news is transferred while you are connected. You then read the mail or news offline, saving on charges for online connections. If you find that you spend only a little time browsing the Web and more time with email and news, this service may be of interest. WinNet also offers 800-line access (for an extra fee). So, if you can't find a provider in your area, you can still get Internet and Web access without making a long-distance call.

NetCom

http://www.netcom.com/

NetCom is another major national service provider. It specializes in dial-up accounts for individual users and also offers high-speed connections for businesses. The dial-up service includes the NetCruiser software. NetCom has local numbers in over 200 cities.

Online Services

These services all offer a way to get connected to the Internet. In addition, they all have special services for subscribers. These include special forums for discussion of common topics, chat areas, up-to-date news and weather services, travel planning, and financial management services.

CompuServe

http://www.compuserve.com

Read about CompuServe's products and services from this major online service provider. CompuServe has a typical mix of services, but it's best known among experienced computer users for its good technical support areas sponsored by hundreds of computer hardware and software companies. Business users are also apt to find the mix of services here to be of interest.

Prodigy

http://www.prodigy.com

Once the ugly duckling of online services, Prodigy has blossomed and is rapidly gaining in popularity. Prodigy was the first of the major online services to offer a Web browser and has made a real effort to make a better interface to its whole service. This provider offers the usual mix of services such as news, sports, chat, and file areas with an emphasis toward nontechnical- and nonbusiness-related use.

Fig. 11.11
The bad news is the $1,000,000 Internet hunt will probably be over when you read this. The good news is maybe Baywatch will be too.

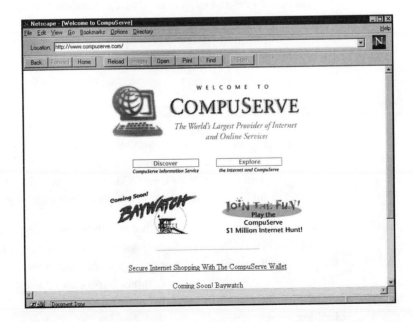

The Microsoft Network

http://www.msn.com

The Microsoft Network is still in its infancy so it's hard to say much about it. Microsoft plans to use this service extensively to provide support for Microsoft software products. Microsoft is also lining up many major content providers to fill the services with news, entertainment, and more.

America Online

http://www.aol.com

America Online appeals mostly to users connecting from the home or from a small business. It has a very large and growing subscriber base and easy-to-use software for Windows and Mac.

E-World

http://www.eworld.com

This home page says E-World's been waiting for you. Really, it isn't kidding; several Apple employees may be waiting. This service really is a good, but small, online service for Mac users. You'll find a high concentration of Mac-related information because this is Apple's service. But, E-World has never gained much mass appeal.

Searches and directories

There's going to come a time when you want to find something on the Web that isn't listed in this book. As great as this book is, we haven't tried to make it all things to all people at all times. So, what do you do when you want a site not listed in this book? Luckily, you can find listings of pages online.

Some online directories are searchable databases. Using a searchable database is like calling directory assistance to get a telephone number. You tell the operator whose number you want, and the operator searches and gets it for you. To use a searchable database, you enter a search word (or several words) in a box in a form and the search page finds the word(s) you're looking for.

After you do a search, notice the new page that appears in your Web browser. This page has a list of Web pages that match your search word(s). Just like any other Web page, these words are linked; click the name of the page you want to load.

Besides searchable-database-type directories, you can find directories that are like the yellow pages. To find something in the yellow pages, you look up a category, such as *plumbers* and then look for a certain plumber in the listings. On the Web, a category might be something general such as *art* or something very specific such as *velvet Elvis paintings*. Some directories of this type are arranged in hierarchies of categories:

> Art
> > Painting
> > > Velvet Elvis

To find something in an index like this, look for a category of interest and then look for a Web page on the topic you want in that category's list. (You may have to work down through a hierarchy of subcategories to get a list of pages.) A directory like this looks something like the one shown in the next figure.

Finally, some of the directories are combining these two approaches. These combo directories have a listing of categories you can browse to find a page, and a search function you can use to retrieve a list of related pages.

Get Linked Online with *Using the World Wide Web*, Second Edition

Wouldn't it be great if all the pages listed in this book were listed on a Web page online? This way you could just click the link and go there instead of typing in the addresses.

Well, the fine folks at Que have done this for you. There's only one Web address you need to know to get to every Web page listed in this book. It is **http://www.mcp.com/que/???**

This gives you the best of the printed and electronic worlds. And, if you want even more convenience, you can download the whole list in bookmark form and install it directly into Netscape.

A sample search and results

Here's an example of how to use a searchable database to find Web pages. The first figure shows the information you provide. The second figure shows the results that are sent to your Web browser.

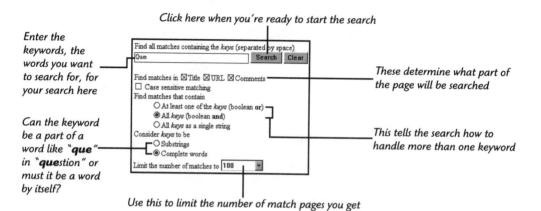

Click here when you're ready to start the search

Enter the keywords, the words you want to search for, for your search here

Can the keyword be a part of a word like "que" in "question" or must it be a word by itself?

These determine what part of the page will be searched

This tells the search how to handle more than one keyword

Use this to limit the number of match pages you get

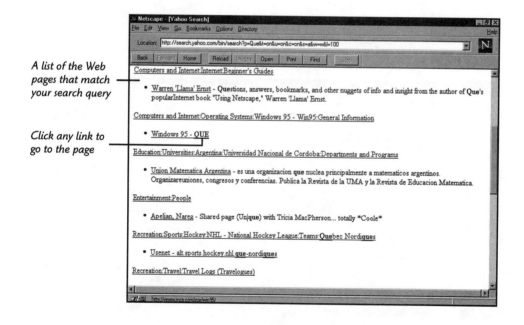

A list of the Web pages that match your search query

Click any link to go to the page

Many of these directories encourage users to submit the addresses of pages they like. The list maintainers then check the page out and add it if they like it.

Yahoo

http://www.yahoo.com

Yahoo is one of the most popular directory services on the Web. It has over 40,000 sites indexed into 14 top level categories. These categories include Art, Computers and Internet, News, and Recreation to name just a few. There's also a simple search feature. A couple of popular items here are the listings of new and cool pages and the random link that takes you to a randomly selected page.

Fig. 11.12
Yahoo! Whoopee! Eureka! You'll be excited too when you find what you're looking for.

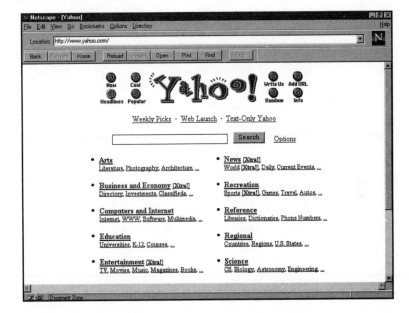

WebCrawler

http://Webcrawler.com/

This searcher was recently bought by America Online but it remains available and free to all Internet users. This was one of the first major Web search pages and is very well-known. The WebCrawler database has about 200,000 visited and indexed Web pages. The database includes another two million documents that WebCrawler has addresses for but hasn't visited and indexed yet. So, the database is big enough to give you some lengthy results but still small enough that it shouldn't overwhelm you. Here, you'll also find a list of the 25 most popular pages on the Web.

World Wide Web Worm

http://www.cs.colorado.edu/home/mcbryan/WWWW.html

World Wide Web Worm is a powerful but simple-to-use search index. You can set all the typically used options here by choosing them from menus on the search form. Be prepared to wait as this page is busy and can be slow.

World Wide Web Yellow Pages

http://www.mcp.com/nrp/wwwyp

The World Wide Web Yellow Pages is the online version of New Rider's best-selling book by the same title. You can search these pages by keyword or by category. If you submit a page to be added and it's added to the index, it will also be added in the next printed edition of the book.

InfoSeek Corp.

http://www.infoseek.com

This commercial Web search service allows users to sample the search database for free. In addition to this search database, you can find categorized lists of cool sites. If you become a paying customer, you can extend your searches to UseNet newsgroup articles and to special electronic publications for business, health, and other industries on the Net.

CUI Search Catalog

http://cuiwww.unige.ch/w3catalog

CUI Search Catalog is a small searchable database of Web pages. (This catalog is small when compared to the other catalogs but still includes more sites than you'll ever visit in a lifetime.)

EINet Galaxy

http://galaxy.einet.net/search.html

EINET Galaxy is a combined search page and index. The index is divided into about 12 major categories. The search page (at the main address) allows you to search on all links in the "Galaxy" (the database of entries), just Web pages, just the Web links, and other subparts of the list. The index is at **http:/ /galaxy.einet.net/galaxy.html**.

NCSA What's New

http://www.ncsa.uiuc.edu/SDG/Software/Mosaic/Docs/archive-whats- new.html

NCSA What's New was one of the earliest attempts to keep track of new additions to the Web. This page was started by the same fine folks that developed Mosaic. When it started, it was a good place to keep track of the few dozen new Web page announcements each month. At this point, the site gets hundreds of new entries every day. There's no real organization to this except by day (and old announcements are archived by month). This site might be useful if you're looking specifically for new sites or if you have the time to scan the entire update on a daily basis.

World Wide Web Virtual Library

http://www.w3.org/hypertext/DataSources/bySubject/Overview.html

The World Wide Web Virtual Library is a large directory organized by subject area. The top-level topics in the directory are very specific, such as Aborigi- nal Studies and Vision Science. This directory includes over 100 top-level categories.

McKinley Internet Directory

http://www.mckinley.com/

The McKinley Internet Directory is another combination of a directory-style index and a search engine. The real draw of this site is that many of the Web pages in the directory are rated. In fact, over 30,000 sites are rated with a four-star rating system. The more stars there are, the better the site is. Sites are graded on the basis of completeness, "up-to-datedness," organization, and ease of access.

In addition to the database of graded sites, another 500,000 sites are in a separate searchable database waiting to be graded.

Another interesting feature here is what's called a **concept search**. This type of search takes the keyword(s) that you enter and generates a list of similar or related words and searches for them as well. So, a search for *books* might turn up a publisher's Web site, even if the Web site didn't specifically use the word *book* as a keyword.

Point Communication's Best of the Web

http://www.pointcom.com/

This site is another one that isn't interested in indexing and cataloging every page on the Web. Instead, the focus is on just the best sites. They have reviews of the sites they see as best divided into 15 categories. You can browse by category or search the database. Sites are judged on content, presentation, and "experience" (a very subjective measure of whether or not the site is fun and worth going to). All three categories are scored from 0–49, with higher scores being better.

NetFind

http://www.nova.edu/Inter-Links/netfind.html

You can use this search page to find email addresses. You'll need to read the directions at this site to get a handle on how to use it.

Four11 White Page Directory

http://www.four11.com/

You can use the Four11 White Page Directory to find email addresses. In order to use this directory, you have to fill in a form giving your name and email address. This registration builds the database; everyone who does a search is added to the database.

Submit It

http://submit-it.permalink.com/submit-it/

Wouldn't it be nice if you could submit an announcement about your new Web page to all the major directories at once rather than fill out a form for each directory? Submit It does exactly that. Simply select the check boxes for each directory that you want your page submitted to, fill in all the requested information in the form, and sooner than you know it, you'll have more visitors at your Web page than you can handle.

The Best of the Rest

It's time for that final catch-all category. The sites listed in this last section don't really fit in anywhere else, but they're all worth mentioning.

Windows 95 Internetworking Headquarters

http://www.windows95.com/

The Windows 95 Internetworking Headquarters is a great place to get answers about networking, especially networking through the Internet with Windows 95. You'll also find a large collection of related software.

Fig. 11.13

Explore your Internet connectivity tools and options in Windows 95 at the Windows 95 InterNetworking Headquarters.

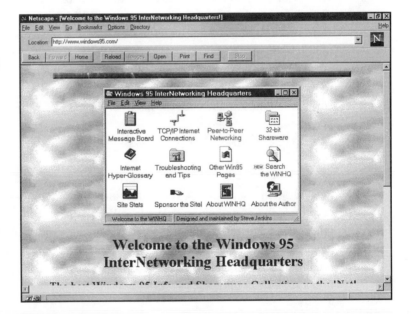

Intergraph

http://www.intergraph.com

If your company needs an Internet server but you have no interest in the technical details of installing and configuring one, you may be interested in one of Intergraph's complete Web server configurations. The complete server packages come with all the hardware and software you need for your Web site preinstalled and ready to run. See the Web page for more information and about this and related products and services.

StarNine Technologies

http://www.starnine.com

Do you want to turn your Mac into a server on the Internet? If so, look at StarNine Technologies' software. From this Web page, you can download trial versions of StarNine's Web server and email server software, and see examples of StarNine products in action—with links to some customer sites.

The WELL

http://www.well.com

The WELL (Whole Earth 'Lectronic Link) was one of the first Internet service providers. In addition to Internet service, WELL has a number of special conferences and information sources for customers, much like a commercial online service such as CompuServe or AOL would provide through forums or special interest groups. At the home page, you can check out a sampling of the services available to customers, register for the service, and download a software toolkit to use with the service.

MecklerWeb

http://www.mecklerWeb.com

MecklerMedia publishes several print and Web magazines about the Internet and the Web (Its site name is MecklerWeb). It also sponsors Internet World, one of the largest conventions for Internet users and vendors. You can get highlights from the printed magazines, as well as updates and extras that aren't in the magazine. The Net Day page gives you a daily update on late breaking Internet news.

12

News, Politics, and Current Events

● **In this chapter:**

● **Browse through the biggest news services on the Web for up-to-the-minute global news coverage**

● **Read the nation's newspapers complete with photographs**

● **Get political and learn about the big-name activist groups without leaving your chair**

● **Get in-depth information and opinion on current events shaping the world**

The Web's news services can put many national newspapers to shame. Not only can you get global news from sources stationed all around the world, you can get local coverage that extends right to your own backyard . . . . ▶

Are you stockpiling your newspapers until you have some free time to catch up on your reading? We've got news for you. The nation's best news services have their own Web pages that give you access to full news stories, pictures, and opinion articles. In other words, you get everything a newspaper gives you, but you get it when you want it, and you won't have to stumble outside in your pajamas.

The best part about news on the Web is that you're not limited to a single source for all your news. You can just as easily tap into a foreign country's news services as you can see what's up on CNN. News on the Web is also updated often, so you don't have to wait until tomorrow to read about what happened today.

The Web also has in-depth coverage of the issues that all of us are facing—from health-care reform to high-profile criminal trials. Along with comprehensive reporting, you'll also be able to read what the pundits have to say and see whether you agree with them or not.

Nowhere is there more controversy than in the nation's politics. With 1996 being a presidential election year, you'll want to keep track of what the politicians are saying. The Web is the place to do it. In this chapter, I'll show you how to access the Web sites for the major political parties so you can learn about what the candidates stand for. If you don't like what they have to say, jump on one of the many activists' bandwagons to get an entirely different point of view. The point is that the Web is your one-stop source for up-to-the-minute coverage of news, politics, and current events.

USA Today—The nation's (Electronic) newspaper

http://www.usatoday.com

Rich with colors and a larger-than-life logo, *USA Today* is arguably the most easily recognized newspaper in the nation. The paper, billed as "the nation's newspaper," breaks up news into bite-size chunks that are easily digestible even when you're on a tight time budget. It's a perfect fit for the digital world, and the *USA Today* Web site is just what you'd expect, and more.

Fig. 12.1

Snazzy colors and accessible news make *USA Today* a favorite site on the Web.

One thing that makes *USA Today* so readable is the way it is presented. Day after day, each section is always formatted in the exact same way. It gives everyone a reference point so they can find the kinds of news they want without having to look too far.

It's even easier to find the news you want on *USA Today*'s Web page. With one click, the Index located on *USA Today*'s home page opens a list of all available news topics. The Index is divided into five categories, starting with a what's new list from which you can browse the most recent additions to the site, access an electronic cross-word puzzle, or even download Web browser software.

TIP   **You'll need to download a special crossword puzzle reader** program in order to view the *USA Today* puzzles. The program should only take about five to ten minutes to download—and it's easy to set up.

Next in line is *USA Today*'s news section. Click Nationline, and you'll be whisked to breaking national news. For a more global perspective, click World for in-depth coverage of important news from other countries. If you just want to see what's happening at home, be sure to access "News from every State."

Once you've caught up on the news, check out *USA Today*'s excellent sports page. Since the sports page is updated every two minutes throughout the day, you'll never be at loss for a score. You'll also have instant access to your favorite teams' schedules, and analyses of their last game. If you want to increase your chances of winning the local football pool, nowhere else can you get the latest line, plus team-by-team match-ups.

If you're an investor, and you want to stack the odds in your favor, browse on over to *USA Today*'s Money page. You'll be able to get a graphical snapshot of the Dow Jones industrial average, and you can get the latest stock prices—updated every 15 minutes. Although some Web sites have more in-depth business stories and statistics, none of them can match the way *USA Today* provides so much information with so little work. You'll definitely want to add this site to your list of favorites.

TIP **You don't have to scroll down to the bottom to find what you're** looking for. The main graphic actually is made up of several hypertext links. For example, click the Life button to access the entertainment section.

Leave the graphics behind

Some sites, including the *USA Today* site, are full of graphics, which you may come to despise if you're using a slow modem. Unfortunately, many sites don't include an obvious way to skip the graphics to let you get directly to the information you want to see. But using the capabilities of your Internet browser, you can turn off the graphics and pump up your performance. Almost every Web browser has the capability to skip the downloading of inline images. In Netscape for example, select Options, and make sure Autoload Images is unchecked.

These images are really what add pizzazz to the Web, so you'll be sacrificing looks for performance. Once you turn off the graphics, you'll see small icons called **placeholders** for the undisplayed images. If you want to see what you're missing, go back and select Autoload images, and then click Reload to redisplay the Web page.

Some Web sites, no doubt run by those who have once used a modem, include an option to view the page in text-only mode. I really appreciate these sites because I can download the things I want from the Web and I don't have to configure any options to do it.

In the mood for something lighter? Click the Life button, and you'll find yourself in USA Today's Lifestyles section. There you'll find out what's hot and what's not at the movies and on television, articles on health and fitness, and a special section devoted just to children. Of special interest is the Entertainment link, where you'll find comprehensive and archived reviews of movies, videos, music, and even CD-ROM software.

As a last stop, make sure you check out the weather page, where you'll find *USA Today*'s unique weather map of the United States. You'll be able to be your own weatherperson without going back to school for a climatology degree. For more accurate information, be sure to click the Cities button to get the forecast for each major city.

CNN World Report provides global news at a glance

http://www.cnn.com/

Cable News Network's (CNN) objective and continuous coverage of the events that shape the nation and the globe make it one of the most dependable sources of news in the world. When people think of news, CNN is always at the top of the list.

Fig. 12.2
CNN Interactive provides a wealth of topical information.

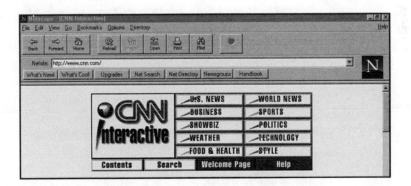

But CNN embodies more than just news programming. It began over 15 years ago as the first round-the-clock news show on cable TV. Satellite technology enabled it to be broadcast almost anywhere in the world. Nowadays, with its scope broadened to cover entertainment, sports, fashions, and discussion,

CNN can be heard or seen by millions of people on radio, television, and the major online services. Because of its web of worldwide coverage, it makes sense that CNN has a first-class WWW site.

The first thing you'll notice on CNN's site is its simplicity. Centered on the CNN home page is a map of CNN's contents. Before clicking any of the individual topics, scroll down the page for a look at the top news summaries of the day—with links to full version of each story and its related articles. CNN always places its lead story first, usually with a photo. Click the photo, and you'll be taken directly to the full story.

 TIP **Want to find an older article? CNN has a special agreement with** electronic news database magnate Lexis–Nexis to provide months worth of searchable news articles. Click the Search button to start it.

Notice that the CNN also has several "movies," actually video clips of major news events. These movies are in a special format called QuickTime that requires a special viewer. If you're a Macintosh user, you're in luck because a QuickTime viewer is built into the Macintosh operating system. Versions of the QuickTime viewer for Windows are also available.

 TIP **To download the latest version of QuickTime for Windows, click** the Help button on CNN's home page, and then click "Movie Help for Windows" on the new Web page. To go directly to the site, type in **http://quicktime.apple.com/form-qt2win.html** as the URL.

After perusing CNN's front page, you'll probably want to check out topical news. From the home page, click any topic you're interested in, such as World News, Style, or Technology. You'll be taken to a brand new page featuring the top stories of that category. Sports nuts, take note! CNN features a complete and up-to-date scoreboard, odds, feature stories, team-by-team analyses, and a special "Satellite sports guide" that features a month's worth of listings for televised sporting events.

Finally, if you're a CNN enthusiast, you'll want to check out "Today on CNN." Though this is an unabashed plug for itself, there's not a better place for finding out exactly what's on CNN at any given time.

Feeling a little lost on the CNN page? Click Help and get to the site map, or open **http://www2.cnn.com/feedback/sitemap.html**, for a graphical representation of CNN's world.

Fig. 12.3
CNN's home page gives you the topic areas at a glance.

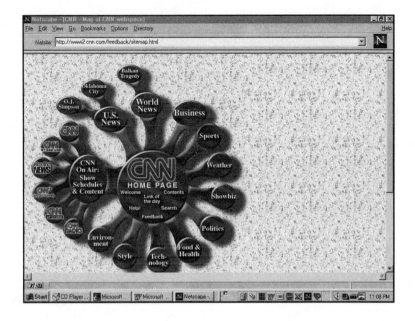

Access the major news feeds with WWW WorldNews

http://www.fwi.com/wnt/wnt.html

So far, the sites we've covered are electronic versions of news sources that already exist—either in the printer world or on television. WWW WorldNews, on the other hand, is one of the only news sources that's only available on the Web.

Fig. 12.4
WWW WorldNews is one of the few Web-only news services.

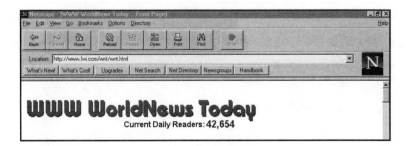

In its current form, WWW WorldNews doesn't have the glitter and panache of the news of CNN and *USA Today*. WWW WorldNews is plain and simply straight news, and lots of it. Since you won't be waiting for obtrusive (and unnecessary) graphics to download it's the ideal site for you to catch up on world events when you don't have a lot of time.

Following the format of a typical newspaper, WWW WorldNews puts its main stories on the "front page." Scroll down the page, however, and you'll see that it's unlike any newspaper you've ever read. News items are formatted for quick reading, with paragraphs taking no more than one or two sentences.

 TIP **For a roadmap of WWW WorldNews, all you need to do is click** "Turn the Page." A panel of buttons that contain links to each news section will appear.

Want to skip the world beat and head for the sports section? Click the Sports link, and the next thing you know, you'll be reading about your favorite college team. Just remember this is world news, so you might have to skip over coverage of rugby before you get to the football statistics of your choice.

Now that you've read all the news, you can have WWW WorldNews deliver your own personal paper. You get to pick the kinds of stories you want to see so you won't have to deal with any extraneous riffraff. For only $10.00 a month, you get to choose two topics. They can be as specific as "news regarding Macmillan publishing," or they can be as general as "Football." WWW WorldNews will then scour thousands of magazines, periodicals, and television sources to find the all the news that you think is fit to print and deliver it to you via email every morning. How's that for service? To access the service, open **http://www.fwi.com/wnt/wntserv.html**, or find the link that says "Daily News Service." You get 30 days free, and you won't have to send your credit card number over the Internet.

Subscribe to an interactive newspaper— The *San Jose Mercury News*

http://www.sjmercury.com

The *San Jose Mercury News* is the first newspaper to publish its entire contents on the Internet. Trivia aside, "the Merc" as it's called is one of the best places to get news on the Net. Although it's located in central California in the heart of Silicon Valley, there's an abundance of international and national news. You'll never feel like you're reading a small town paper. Of course, if you live in San Jose, you can also keep the locals as well.

The Merc is a perfect blending of a continuously updated news service and a national newspaper. Since the site is updated throughout the day, you'll always be on top of breaking stories. Likewise, if you want to read the complete stories from headline to the last line, access the site later in the day. You can also find the final text of each day's final edition.

Since the Merc is located in Silicon Valley, its coverage of computer technologies, news, and business is first rate. If you're a computer buff or own computer stocks, you should be checking this site every morning. It's that good.

Two cool things I love about the Merc are its classified ads and its comics. Granted, you'll probably not want to fly out from Scranton to pick up a scooter in San Jose even if you did fall in love with its four-line classified description. But the technology behind these classified ads is absolutely amazing. Using a Web form, you can search for any word that might fit what you're looking for. It's the equivalent of reading every single ad in the newspaper, but it only takes a second or two. Try doing that with a newspaper!

One thing that will appeal to everyone with an interest in working on the West coast is the Merc's classified employment section. You'll be amazed at how many companies post their ads here. This goes doubly for computer professionals. Nowhere else will you find as many big and small computer companies looking to recruit qualified candidates.

For lighter fare, click the Comics icon. The Merc carries the best syndicated comics, including Doonesbury, Sally Forth, Calvin and Hobbes, and many more. All the comics are in full color. It will be just like reading the Sunday funnies every day. The Merc even has a way for you to post your own comic strips.

Fig. 12.5
To lighten up your day, read the comics on *San Jose Mercury News'* Comics page.

Unfortunately, not everything here is free, comics included. While news summaries, classified ads, and special features are all available at no charge, comics, archived news articles, and full length articles cost $4.95 per month, a small price to pay for so much good information. If you're already a subscriber to the newspaper, it's only an extra buck a month. You get your own account and a password, so you can access it with most major Web browsers (they recommend Netscape) from any location.

Greenpeace

http://www.greenpeace.org/

So far, I've covered electronic newspapers and online services designed to keep you up-to-date. Access any of these services and you'll always know what's going on. But these news services are somewhat passive, meaning that the only interaction you'll have with them is a mouse click here and a page down there. If you want to be a real participant and create some news for your own, Greenpeace is for you.

Fig. 12.6

Learn about environmental activism on Greenpeace's home page.

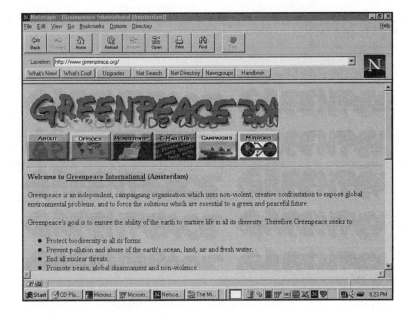

Greenpeace is perhaps the best-known environmental activist group in the world. Founded in 1971 when members changed the name of the Don't Make A Wave Committee of Vancouver to more accurately denote its mission—to make the world green and peaceful. The mission hasn't changed and the controversy hasn't stopped since.

The Greenpeace Web site is first and foremost an electronic mission statement. You'll find a list of Greenpeace's worldwide offices, learn about the projects Greenpeace is currently working on, and discover who is running the organization. Whether you believe in Greenpeace's policies or not, it's an excellent way of finding out where the political and human rights hot spots are.

One hotlink that everyone should get to is Ships. Click it, and you'll be taken to listings of all the ships and aircraft Greenpeace owns. The site includes photos and descriptions, so you'll know what these ships look like and where they're located today. You'll also learn about ships seized by national governments all over the world. It's a brief but eerie look at our troubling times.

No doubt that Greenpeace is controversial. Not everyone believes in its practices, and you'll have a hard time convincing doubters that Greenpeace's ways are right. Still, its cause is valid. You can sign up to become a contributor (and thus a member) right on this Web page.

Newspapers

If you're a newspaper nut who can't get through the day without reading at least one major paper, you'll be right at home on the Web. On the Net, you can get the same information that you can from reading a newspaper, down to the comics, with three exceptions: you don't get that "I've just killed a tree" feeling when you flip from one page to the next; you don't get newspaper ink all over your pressed white shirts; and you get access to dozens of globally recognized newspapers instead of just one or two.

If you think I'm a newspaper nut, you're right. I read at least three traditionally delivered newspapers a day. And when I want more, I head straight to the Net.

The Gate opens the Web to the City by the Bay

http://www.sfgate.com

You get two national newspapers in one when you access the Gate. Open this Gate, and you'll be reading the left coast version of the nation's news, sports, and lifestyles. A special Silicon Valley Report should not be missed by anyone in the computer industry—hackers and professionals alike. But The Gate is more than just reprinted news text, it's geared for the wired. Take, for example, the Gate Digital Gallery, a link to an audio-visual art extravaganza that's like no other gallery in the world.

Wall Street Journal Financial News

http://update.wsj.com

The *Wall Street Journal* is perhaps the most widely read business journal in the world. You can find all the information available in the daily newspaper right online. Some of the services require a subscription, but most of them are free for a trial period. Once you subscribe, you get access to a special Money and Investing section, the online version of the *Wall Street Journal*, and *Personal Journal*, which is a customizable edition of the Journal that's delivered to you via email. If you're wary of subscribing and don't want to bother with a free trial, you'll only be able to access story headlines.

Wall Street Journal Technical Update

http://ptech.wsj.com/

One thing that's free on the *Wall Street Journal* is Walter Mossberg's technology column, and it's a gem. Read about Mr. Mossberg's reviews of incredible (and sometimes mundane) software and hardware. All the reviews are more than just simple product reviews. Each one is interwoven with a full-fledged analysis of the impact of the technology. The column is well-crafted and approachable, making it a favorite of *Wall Street Journal* readers. Although there are no graphics nor is there much else besides the column, it's one of my favorite sites as well.

New York Times

http://nytimesfax.com/

Imagine getting a subscription to one of the best newspapers in the world—for free! Well, not exactly. Access this Web site and you'll be able to receive *TimesFax*, an eight-page facsimile version of the *New York Times*. All you need to do is register to receive it, and at no cost, you can read today the news stories that will appear in tomorrow's paper. You even get the famous *New York Times* crossword puzzle. *TimesFax* is stored as an Adobe Acrobat file, and you'll need the Acrobat reader in order to view the fax. If you don't already have the viewer, you can download it from the *TimesFax* site.

Point Reyes Light

http://www.ptreyeslight.com/prl/

Okay, so this isn't a national newspaper, and you won't be able to find out what bands are playing nearby your town next month. But the *Point Reyes Light* is a marvelous newspaper that captures the essence of this small coastal town in northern California and publishes it for all the world to see. The newspaper, which is one of the few to have won a Pulitzer prize, also has a unique angle on current events. Take for instance its coverage of the people of Croatia who have moved to northern California. The *Light* interviewed people in northern California and in Croatia. The result is a fascinating story that you won't find anywhere else.

Detroit Free Press

http://gopher.det-freepress.com:9002/

The *Detroit Free Press*, the ninth largest newspaper in the nation, was founded in 1831 as a four-page weekly to combat newspapers controlled by the "city aristocracy." Over 150 years later, the *Free Press* is available on the Web. Unfortunately, the *Free Press* Web site is merely a gateway to other sites on the Net. You'll be able to get local weather and learn about Michigan politics, but you won't be able to read the *Free Press*'s crack reporting and biting editorials. On a positive note, phone numbers and email addresses are published on this Web site, so you can tell the people who count how you feel about this site.

Investor's Business Daily

http://ibd.ensemble.com/

Investor's Business Daily is a newspaper for business people that also has the knack for publishing winning stock market tips. The online version of IBD is available through subscription only. Fortunately, it's free for a two-week trial. Once you subscribe, you'll have access to the IBD news summary of the most important business news, a look at the business reports that will be printed in the weeks ahead, profiles of industry leaders, and the all important investor's corner. Though *Investor's Business Daily* won't replace your local paper, its investment information and editorials are first-rate.

The Electronic Telegraph

http://www.telegraph.co.uk/

The Electronic Telegraph is a graphical Web-based newspaper with a twist. It's located in London. If you have business in Britain, if you are traveling abroad, or if you simply want to read another country's perspective on the things we usually take for granted, *The Electronic Telegraph* is a welcome site. Accessing "ET," as it's called, requires a subscription. Registration is free, and it doesn't take long. Once you've registered, be sure to check out the sports page. There you'll find that the football fantasy game is really about soccer and that coverage of cricket can make the headlines.

Maui News

http://www.maui.net/~mauinews/news.html

Every time I want to take a tropical vacation during the course of my busy day, I turn to *The Maui News*. This newspaper, which has been around since 1900, offers a glimpse into this island paradise brought to you by the people who live there. The Web version includes news, weather, a calendar of events, and even the classified ads for those of us thinking about relocating.

Fig. 12.7
The Maui News gives you a slice of tropical life.

Seattle Times

http://www.seatimes.com/

The *Seattle Times* Web site was brand new as this book went to press. But from the looks of it, it will be a winner. Although it had no news, no current events, and no weather maps, its fabulous feature entitled "50 Years from Trinity," is an amazing account of the impact of the atomic bomb. The site is aimed at teachers and students, but everyone will find it well worth checking out.

Taxi's Newspaper List

http://www.deltanet.com/users/taxicat/e_papers.html

Long URL aside, Taxi's newspaper list is the preeminent index of the international newspapers available on the Internet. Click the flag of the appropriate country, and Taxi's will list off the electronic newspapers published there.

World news on the wire

The Web isn't called "World Wide" for no reason. Since the Internet connects computers all around the globe, you can read news from all over the world. All the sites listed here are in English, but the news is usually filed by reports on-location.

CNN World News

http://www.cnn.com/WORLD/index.html

Although I covered CNN's home page earlier in this chapter, CNN's world news page is compelling enough that it deserves its own mention. Tap into this site and you'll see summaries of the top news stories and their related thumbnail-size pictures. Directly below each story is a link to the in-depth version of the story with several more pictures. Scroll down below the summaries, and you'll see additional news and even a search button, from which you can search CNN's archives.

Reuters

http://www.reuters.com/

When this book was published, the Reuters Web site was still in its pilot phase, and it had only a handful of links to other sites within the Reuters organization. But Reuters is an internationally recognized news source—by all estimates this will be a good site. A preview of what lies ahead in the future may be found in Money Net, a Reuters affiliate that's located at **http://www.moneynet.com**.

USA Today World Update

http://www.usatoday.com/news/world/nw1.htm

Like CNN's World news, *USA Today*'s World Update puts its best news forward. Within just a few minutes of reading, you'll know what's going on in the world, and if you want to read the complete article, it's just a click away. *USA Today* has fewer pictures than CNN's world site, and more links to related stories.

Yahoo International News

http://www.yahoo.com/News/International

Yahoo's International News articles are culled from the various wire services. Only the headlines appear on this page, and there's not a picture in sight. For the story, just click on the headline link.

Associated Press

http://www.trib.com/NEWS/APwire.html

Did you ever wonder how an individual newspaper can cover events happening around the world? Although all newspapers have highly trained reporters camped out in the world's hot spots, they also rely on the Associated Press news services. The AP is the largest pool of news writers, photographers, and editors in the world. With this Web site, you too can access the same news sources that the newspapers do—and it's free! Access to the AP requires signing up to the service to gain a user ID and password.

Clarinet

http://www.clarinet.com

Clarinet is the Internet's first comprehensive electronic news service. Keeping UseNet news crawlers satisfied years before the World Wide Web wave, Clarinet is now one of the largest electronic news services available on the Internet. Clarinet's news, called *e.News*, is available through subscription only, but if you're a true news hound, this site is worth the additional cost. But all this information comes at a cost. *e-News* will run $40 per month for individual users. Discounts are available for corporations, school systems, and religious organizations.

Fig. 12.8
Access the largest
electronic news services
in the Internet through
e.News.

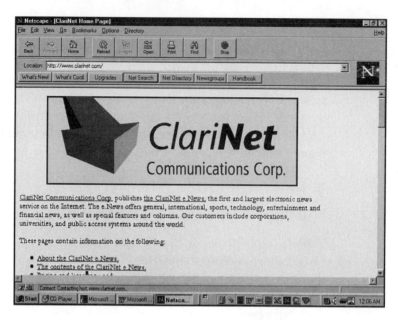

Current events

Keeping track of current events can be a major chore. Keeping an eye on current events is essential in the business world. An event that might once have passed unnoticed in a foreign country may now have major implications in the new global economy.

Right now, the best ways of learning about current events are to watch the news and read the weekly news magazines. But, I'm finding these media woefully inadequate because they often don't put events in context. The Web, however, through hypertext links, is made to put things in context. That's why I turn to the Web every time I need to update myself on the happenings in the world.

The Nando Times

http://www2.nando.net/nt/nando.cgi

The Nando Times is one of the best news pages on the Net. Although most of its news is culled from wire services, such as the Associated Press, the design of this page makes it easy to get to the news you want. A subscription is required, but it's free, and it will open up access the full text of news, sports, entertainment, and business stories.

Fig. 12.9

The Nando Times' easy interface makes surfing the Web for news a breeze.

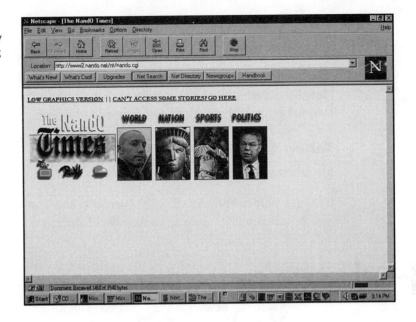

The War in Bosnia

http://www.yahoo.com/Regional/Countries/Bosnia/

The war in Bosnia has dominated world news for over a year. For news and historical information about this conflict, visit this Yahoo page. The site doesn't contain news itself; instead, it includes a comprehensive set of links to the sites that do.

OJ Simpson

http://www.yahoo.com/Government/Law/Legal_Research/Cases/
OJ_Simpson_Case/

Although the OJ Simpson trial is over, students, scholars, and people around the world will be discussing this case for some time to come. The most comprehensive set of links to sources about the OJ trial can be found on this page.

Time Magazine

http://www.pathfinder.com

Time Magazine has become synonymous with current events. Located on Time Inc.'s Pathfinder page, simply click the *Time* link to keep abreast of national and world events, and maybe read an opinion or two.

Yahoo Current Events

http://www.yahoo.com/News/Current_Events

It's impossible to list here all of the current events that might be important to you. Access this site for an up-to-date list of current events.

Political issues

You can watch the news, read the campaign literature, and listen to candidates' speeches, and still not be completely sure of how you'll vote. The problem isn't a lack of information. It's too much information that's not delivered in a digestible manner. But 1996 will mark the first year in which all major campaign materials will be available on the Web. Since you're actively looking for information, it automatically becomes more interesting, and you'll be able to sort out the issues, the candidates, and (hopefully) how you'll vote.

Amnesty International

http://www.io.org/amnesty/

Amnesty International is devoted to human rights issues. On this Web page, you'll learn about the campaigns in which this organization is currently involved. Especially disheartening is Amnesty International's country reports, which lists countries that the organization alleges have committed human rights violations. You'll be surprised at the countries listed, especially when you see the United States.

Animal Rights Resource Site

http://envirolink.org/arrs/index.html

The Animal Rights Resource Site tracks down abuses to domestic and wild animals. You'll be able to read news and investigative reports online. Especially awakening is this site's photo gallery that shows what happens to animals during testing, movie filming, and hunting.

Cyberporn Debate

http://www.yahoo.com/Government/Politics/Censorship/
Censorship_and_the_Net/Cyberporn_Debate__The/

The belief of some that the Internet is merely a way to transport pornography should cause concern for all. Not because the belief is true, but because these people vote too. Get the facts on the debate. This Yahoo site includes links to sites that fall on both sides of the debate.

Pro-Choice

http://www.cais.com/agm/nafline.htm

There's no debate raging more in America than that of pro-choice and pro-life. For the pro-choice point of view, this Web site is a good place to start.

National Right to Life

http://www.clark.net/nrlc/

For the pro-life point of view, the National Right to Life home page includes its mission statement, news, and links to other sites that share the same vision.

The National Review

http://www.townhall.com/nationalreview/

The National Review is the conservative magazine of William F. Buckley. If you think having a Democratic president in the White House proves that history has a sense of humor (really—the magazine alleges this in its mission statement), you'll want to add this site to your hot list.

Fig. 12.10

For an ultra-conservative viewpoint, visit *The National Review.*

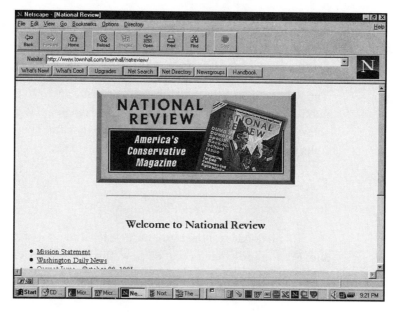

The Utne Reader

http://www.utne.com

Pulling its stories from the "best of alternative media," the *Utne Reader* site is a tour de force. Although its focus is not on politics, there are enough politically edged articles here to a merit a mention.

Presidential Election and Party Politics

http://www.yahoo.com/Government/Politics/Elections/
1996_U_S__Elections/Presidential_Election/

With a presidential election is coming up in 1996, this site includes links to the most popular political sites. This is a good place to start if you're not sure where to begin when forming your political opinions.

Election '96

http://dodo.crown.net/~mpg/election/96.html

Another place to sift through the quagmire often associated with Presidential elections is Election '96. Forget about the reference to an extinct bird in this site's URL. You'll find hot links to the major parties, candidates, issues, and opinion stories.

Fig. 12.11
There's no better place to catch up on the nation's politics than the Election '96 Web page.

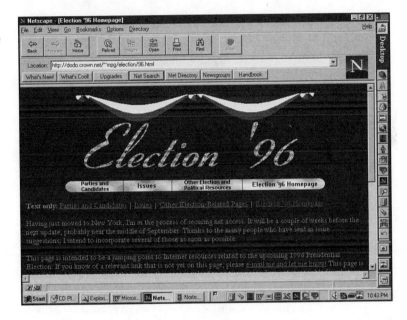

Democratic National Committee

Learn about upcoming Democratic Party events on Capitol Hill, find out what the party stands for, and even register to become a member of the DNC on this well-designed site. Even if you're not a Democrat, you'll like the What's Hot link. Click it, and you'll be able to download audio files that contain the voices of the politicians.

Fig. 12.12
Democratic campaign issues can now all be found in one place on the Democratic National Committee site.

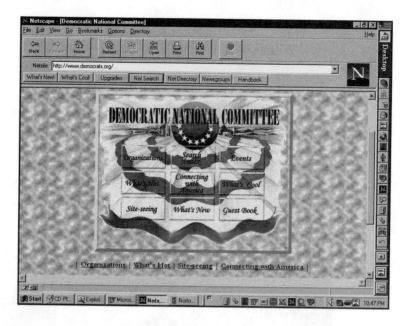

Republican Web Central

http://republicans.vt.com/

The Republican WEB Central is the home page of the Grand Old Party. View pictures of the 1996 Presidential hopefuls, access their biographies, and learn their positions. It's a fascinating way to educate yourself about candidates so you can make a voting decision you're confident of. This site also contains information about state and local elections.

Environmental activism

One of the problems with learning the issues about environmental activism is where to start. You don't want to commit yourself to one organization without knowing something about another that has somewhat similar goals. The Web brings the major environmental groups directly to your computer to allow you to learn the facts about their respective organizations. You'll find out what they stand for, where they operate, and in some cases you can even sign up to become a member right on the Web page.

The Ecological Society of America

http://www.sdsc.edu/1/SDSC/Research/Comp_Bio/ESA/ESA.html

Now over 70 years old, the Ecological Society of America has spent its entire history promoting the responsible application of ecological data and principles to the solution of environmental problems. This site provides access to the organization's newsletters and links to other environmental sites and scientific reports.

Econet

http://www.econet.apc.org/endangered/

This is one of the best places to learn about endangered species and the environment. Access this site and you'll immediately know where the trouble zones are. You'll also be able to get background information and even read the related federal laws in their entirety.

ANWR—Arctic National Wildlife Refuge

http://www.alaskan.com/anwr/

Alaska contains some of the most pristine lands in the world. But it's becoming endangered as people and businesses move in. Open this Web page to learn about the Arctic National Wildlife Refuge, a huge 19-million acre reserve that has become a national issue in the debate of jobs versus the environment.

Wolf Haven International

http://www.teleport.com/wnorton/wolf.html

Once thought to be fierce and predatory, wolves were nearly wiped off the face of North America. Through this Web page, Wolf Haven International's goal is to protect the remaining wild wolves and their habitat, educate the public on the value of wildlife, and provide sanctuaries or protected natural ranges so that wolves will not become extinct.

Chesapeake Bay Trust

http://www2.ari.net/home/cbt/

Stretching 200 miles from Annapolis, MD to the Virginia coast, the Chesapeake Bay is one of the largest bays in the world. An increase in recreational activities in the bay, combined with the over harvesting of seafood have taken its toll. The Chesapeake Bay Trust provides grants to individuals and organizations for restoration of the bay.

Sierra Club

http://www.sierraclub.org/

One of the most popular conservation organizations in the nation is the Sierra Club. Online, you can read its newsletter and special reports, join a local club, learn the history of the organization, and open a calendar of its outing events.

Companion Animal Rescue Effort

http://www.thesphere.com/CARE/

Everyone interested in protecting domestic animals should browse through the C.A.R.E. Web site. You can even view a poster of homeless pets ready for adoption!

Kiwi Conservation Club

http://www.chch.planet.org.nz/kcc.html

Although the Kiwi Conservation Club is based in New Zealand, it's one of the few conservation clubs for children. This page is oriented toward signing up members. You can also click the Info button for a list of additional conservation links.

Publishing: Books and Magazines

● In this chapter:

● **Find online bookstores with huge selections and special features for online users**

● **See what's up with your favorite authors and publishers at their Web sites**

● **Read classic works of literature online, as well as new never-before published manuscripts**

● **Get previews of your favorite magazines and enjoy features not available in the printed versions**

The World Wide Web is changing publishing as much as Gutenberg's press and movable type did. This chapter is your library card for tapping into this electronic publishing revolution . . . . ▶

Would you like to be able to order a new book from a catalog of more than one million books without even leaving your house? Or maybe you want to see what's up with your favorite author, but have no idea where to find the latest scoop. With the Web, publishers, bookstores, and book lovers alike have found a new way to distribute and promote their wares.

Most of the sites highlighted in this chapter are in commercial domains. Publishers and booksellers have sites that provide information about books and magazines, online ordering services, and special online events. Special events can include author "signings" (you don't get to meet the author, but if you buy the book, you get a signed copy) and author conferences in which authors answer questions and discuss writings online. Magazine publishers often include special items such as daily updates (for weekly magazines), extra photos not included in the printed versions, and a chance to provide feedback.

The Web is also a printing press for thousands of authors whose work you would never see printed. With this powerful new publishing medium, anyone can write anything and make it instantly available to millions of readers around the world. While a lucky few of these authors may find the Web is a springboard to commercial publishing success, most make their work available simply so that someone else can read it.

One of the best uses of the Web for publishing is the large effort that several groups are making to publish classic literary works online. Thousands of works of fiction, poetry, essays, philosophy and religion, history, and more are available from sites that take the time to convert these to online formats for the public interest.

Buying books online is easy at Amazon.com

http://www.amazon.com

Wow! I can't even imagine one million books, but this site claims to have a catalog of more than that. I didn't take the time to count the titles to verify the claim, but I'll take their word for it. You can do all of your book shopping using the online ordering form and never leave the comfort of your computer chair. And this site sells books at a discount too. Best sellers are currently 30 percent off the publisher's prices and other books are 10 percent off every day. There are other periodic discounts and special offers, so you'll want to check in to see what offers are available when you're shopping. (Okay, you do pay back some of the discount in shipping and handling fees, which are clearly explained at the site, but you probably still end up saving money because you aren't paying for local sales taxes, gas to drive to the bookstore, and a cup of espresso.)

In addition to the massive catalog of titles, features at this site include lists of selected titles in 20 categories. This organization makes it easier for you to find common titles. For example, the science fiction list includes new titles from award-winning authors Orson Scott Card, Michael Moorcock, and the autobiography of Isaac Asimov.

One of the best features at this site is called "Eyes and Editors." Eyes and Editors are actually two distinct notification services that send you email when a book that may be of interest to you is published. **Eyes** is an automated service that can be highly customized to your preferences. For example, if you want to know when the next Tom Clancy thriller is available in paperback, sign up and you'll get an email. (You can make your criteria much more specialized than this.) The **Editors** service is more general. A group of real people (not a computer) reviews new book releases and sends you email when new books of interest in a particular subject or genre are published.

Fig. 13.1
The main page at Amazon.com changes on a daily basis, so check in regularly to see what it has to offer.

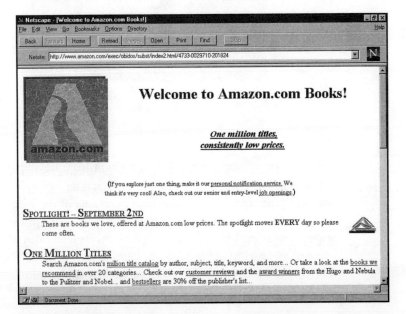

Time Inc.'s Pathfinder is a magazine rack on your computer

http://www.pathfinder.com

There's no doubt that Time's Pathfinder is one of the best sites on the Web. (It pains me to say this because the company I work for is owned by Viacom, one of Time's big competitors. But it's true!) This site is more than just a token effort at being on the Web. Time has content from dozens of major magazines on the Web including *Sports Illustrated*, *People*, *Life*, *Entertainment Weekly*, and *Fortune.* All of these are reviewed later in this chapter.

Fig. 13.2
The Pathfinder site features magazines from Time's large collection.

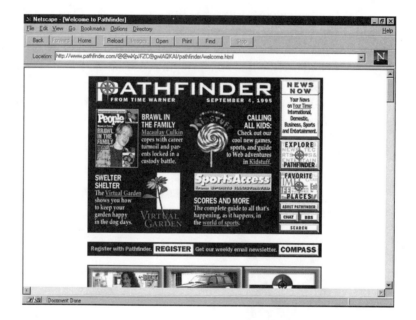

Time has done more than just toss content from the paper versions of the magazines onto the Web. You can search a huge online database and enjoy features that aren't available in paper editions of the magazines. For example, see *Entertainment Weekly*'s Critical Mass page (**http://www.pathfinder.com/ ew/critmass.cmi.html**). You can look up reviewers' grades for about 100 current and recent movies and then grade any of the movies yourself. There's also an interactive bulletin board service (if you're familiar with UseNet newsgroups, this bulletin board is similar to UseNet). This service enables you to participate in group discussions about entertainment, sports, politics, society, and dozens of other topics.

To get the most out of Pathfinder, you need to register. It doesn't cost anything (except a minute or two of your time) and it's well worth the effort.

Que leads the way in computer book publishing

http://www.mcp.com/que

Que Publishing has been publishing books that explain computer software and hardware since the early 80s. Its Web site is one of the largest sites specializing in information about personal computers and software.

Que's site features sample chapters from current and recent Que books. You'll also find short descriptions of the books, along with chapter-by-chapter tables of contents. With this information, you can find books that will help you with a specific computer program, read a sample to see if it is to your liking, and even order a copy.

Fig. 13.3
Choose from the various categories, a top ten list, and special events at the Que Publishing site.

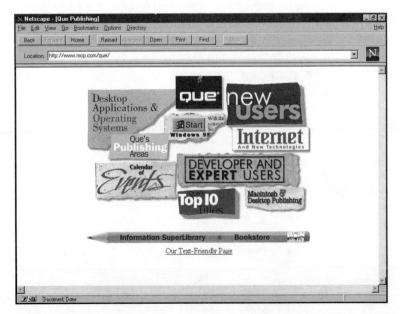

The Que books site is broken down into categories based on the type of book and computer savvy of the intended reader. Currently, the most content lies in the pages by the Internet and New Technologies group. In addition to reading about new and upcoming books for Internet users, you can express interest in reviewing books for technical accuracy or in writing books for Que. Here's your chance to break into technical editing or writing!

This site is part of Que's parent company site, the Macmillan Information SuperLibrary. The SuperLibrary is discussed in the Publishers section of this chapter.

Read computer magazines online at ZDNet

http://www.ziff.com

More than a dozen of the top computer magazines are published by Ziff-Davis. This site includes content from some old favorites such as *PCWeek* and *MacWeek*, as well as from new entries such as *Computer Life*.

So what does the site have to offer? The answer to this question varies depending on the magazine. Some magazines, such as *PCMagazine*, offer the entire editorial content of the publication online. *PCMagazine* presents its editorials, product reviews, and feature stories in hypertext for its standard edition as well as for its special edition for network gurus. You can use the included links to learn about the shareware utilities and software highlighted in the magazine. While this online version will never replace my printed copy, I've found that I use the online version to reference colleagues to information.

Computer Shopper takes a different approach than *PCMagazine*. Only some editorial content is presented on the Web. There are excerpts from reviews, a few features, and some of the cover stories. The real value of *Computer Shopper* is in the advertisements. The printed version of the magazine is the best resource there is for computer hardware and software advertisements. None of these ads are included online, although there are links to a handful of advertisers with Web sites. The Web site for this magazine has little to offer for devoted readers of the printed periodical.

Fig. 13.4
More than a dozen computer-related magazines are represented at the ZDNet Site.

Bookstores

There's nothing like bookstore browsing. Nothing can replace the unique pleasures of scanning the shelves, cracking open promising reads, leisurely reading book spines and jackets. Still, online bookstores are impressive and offer a different sort of experience that is, perhaps, no less pleasurable.

TIP **As with any product or service you order online, you have to pay** for it somehow. Keep in mind that no matter how "secure" a site or Web browser claims to be, there will always be a hole or a hacker that finds a way to break in. While I find the risk of someone stealing my credit card information over the Web fairly low (I think it's more likely that a salesperson in a department store is stealing credit card numbers from carbons), some people would rather not send this information over the Web. Make your own decision here. If you prefer, you can call; most of these bookstores will take orders over the phone.

Most online bookstores are more than just a place to order books. They offer reviews of the latest new books, online discussions with authors, and custom services to help you find books of special interest. And, there are times when you just don't want to make the long drive to the bookstore in bad weather. The bookstore proprietors also note that their online stores are very popular with customers outside the U.S. and with customers in rural parts of the U.S. Whatever your book-reading interests, one of the stores certainly has what you're looking for.

BookWeb

http://www.ambook.org:80/bookweb/

The American Booksellers Association put together this large Web site devoted to information about books, authors, and bookstores. There is a bookstore directory, along with links to bookstores on the Web. BookWeb also gives you news and information about the book industry and updates in specialty areas such as science fiction, scientific and technical writings, and others. The book news is updated weekly.

TGRS Publishing

http://www.netmart.com/tgrs

Books don't necessarily have to be written words printed on paper. This distributor specializes in audio books and original online publications. You can order from a catalog of the best-selling audio books (at a discount off list price) and order electronic publications all online.

Book Stacks Unlimited

http://www.books.com

If you're a book lover, you'll soon add this site to your bookmarks. From here, you can: order from a list of over 320,000 books; search books by author, title, or ISBN; and more. Check this site out on a regular basis so you won't miss any of the special sales. This site also has online author conferences and signings, reviews of current titles, and links to publishers' home pages. There's also a collection of electronic texts available online.

Virtual Book Shop

http://www.virtual.bookshop.com

Not your typical mall bookstore, this bookstore specializes in rare and collectible books. If you're looking for fine leather-bound editions of the classics, first printings from famous authors, or anything else out of the norm, this is a good place to search.

Booksite

http://www.booksite.com/

This site offers more than just volume (although it offers a list of 200,000 titles, which is probably more than you can read in a lifetime). Registered users (registration is currently free) get a 10 percent discount on all purchases for the first year. There is also a monthly guide to selected new books.

Online BookStore

http://www.obs-us.com/

This site includes "bookstore" in its name, but it's not as much of a bookstore in the traditional sense as some of the other sites listed in this section. The Online BookStore specializes in distributing electronic selections of books. You can find excerpts from an incredible variety of current books and order the printed editions of the books featured.

Fig. 13.5
The Online BookStore presents its Web site in four languages.

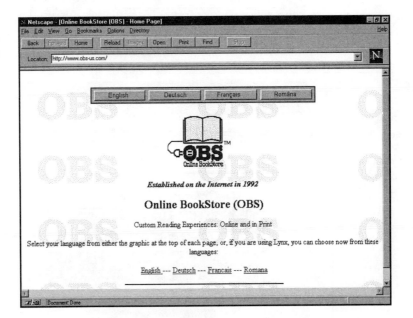

Publishers

Publishers are finding that the Web is a great way to get the news out about their new books. The publishers listed here post excerpts from their books so you can browse before buying. Some also host online conferences with their star authors and offer some way to order their books.

Most of these publishers also offer some general information about the types of books they publish, how to submit manuscripts, and a way to get in touch with the editors. There are a couple of sites listed here that aren't publishers' sites but which include links to more publishers or information about publishers.

Macmillan Publishing Information SuperLibrary

http://www.mcp.com/mcp

Macmillan Computer Publishing is the largest computer book publisher. This company is made up of several imprints (including Que, whose page is discussed in detail earlier in this chapter), all of which have Web sites within the SuperLibrary. The SuperLibrary offers samples and tables of contents from most Macmillan books published since the fall of 1994. In addition, many best-selling books from before that are featured with samples and tables of contents as well. You can order any of Macmillan's more than 1,000 computer books that are currently in print.

Fig. 13.6

The Information SuperLibrary features books from Que and from several other imprints that make up Macmillan Computer Publishing.

You can find special reference articles to help you solve tricky software and hardware problems, newsletters to keep you up-to-date on the computer industry, and software relating to Macmillan books. Watch for this site to grow as Macmillan's noncomputer imprints (publishers of library and reference materials) are brought online.

Aztec Books

http://world.std.com/~aztec

Aztec publishes books on all sorts of fun and interesting topics such as UFOs, ESP, paranormal and unexplained phenomena, ghosts, and more. Its Web site has a catalog you can browse. The site itself is fairly simple (the catalog is implemented through a **Gopher** menu) but the interesting subject matter makes it worth a visit.

 Plain English, please!

> **Gopher** is an Internet file system based on textual menus. Clicking a menu item opens either another menu with more choices or a file like a document or software program.

Bantam Doubleday Dell

http://www.bdd.com/

Bantam is a major paperback publisher. This site wasn't finished when I visited, but it showed some real promise. In addition to the standard publishing fare (descriptions of new releases and catalogs), you can enter a contest to write the ending for a new book. (This contest will have ended by the time you read this, but, hopefully, this is a taste of things to come and not just a onetime event.)

Wiley Publishing

http://www.wiley.com

This site includes information about Wiley's many publishing ventures, including academic and computer publishing. The computer publishing links include some sample chapters and software.

Random House

http://www.randomhouse.com/

Random House is just getting started with this site. At present, the best part of the site is from Random's Del Rey science fiction and fantasy imprint. Also included are sample chapters from several dozen books.

Publishers' Catalogs Home Page

http://www.lights.com/publisher

This comprehensive list of publishers includes links to publishers' pages and catalogs on the Web. The list is made up of a broad cross section of publishers from all over the world, with about two dozen countries represented.

Ventana Online

http://www.vmedia.com/home.html

Ventana is a small computer book publisher. Its Web site includes a catalog with online ordering options. Another feature is a visitor's center where Ventana customers can get software to accompany Ventana books and online support.

Thompson Publishing

http://www.thomson.com/

Thompson is a large publisher specializing in educational and reference texts. This site includes links to more than thirty individual publishing divisions that make up Thompson. You can also view these by topic area or audience levels. Most of the publishing divisions represented here include on their Web page an online catalog, technical support, and information about the company. Other offerings vary from publisher to publisher.

Bookwire

http://www.bookwire.com

This **meta-site** includes reference information about books (such as the *Publisher's Weekly* bestseller lists), a calendar of book events, and links to hundreds of publishers and bookstores online. A **meta-site** is a Web site that links together many other sites.

Paper Magazines on the Web

Many traditional printed magazines offer online selections from their publications. Some of the real giants in the magazine industry are represented in this group, as you'll see from the listings that follow.

Byte Magazine

http://www.byte.com/

Byte Magazine is renowned for its thorough testing and benchmarking of computer hardware. At this site, you can search the archives of the magazine's benchmarks and even download the software used to test and benchmark systems. This way, you can test your own hardware and compare its performance to that of systems reviewed in *Byte*.

Entertainment Weekly

http://www.timeinc.com/ew

Here's the place to look at the text of *Entertainment Weekly*'s cover stories. You can search back issues for items of interest and even vote for your favorite movies.

Fig 13.7
Entertainment Weekly's Web site is a must for entertainment junkies.

 TIP ***Entertainment Weekly, Time Magazine, Sports Illustrated, Life, People,*** *and* ***Fortune*** *are all part of Time Inc.'s Pathfinder Web site, which is reviewed earlier in this chapter.*

.net

http://www.futurenet.co.uk/netmag/net.html

Here's an online companion to a nifty British Internet magazine. It's not as bland (or hopelessly trendy) as most American magazines. The site features stories from the printed magazine, as well as extra content that's written especially for online readers and not available in print.

Time Magazine

http://www.timeinc.com/time

This site starts with the stories from the week's printed issue of *Time*. Beyond that, you'll find *Time Daily*, Time's Web-based news update of the major stories each day. The Time Daily page includes form boxes to help you search other issues of *Time* for related articles.

Fig. 13.8

Time's World Wide Web site offers up-to-date and in-depth coverage of all the major news stories in the U.S. and internationally.

Life Magazine

http://www.timeinc.com/Life

This site includes a "This Day in Life" feature that lists notable happenings from the current day in years past and a picture of the day, both of which are updated daily. You'll also find descriptions of the month's major stories, photo essays, and exclusive stories.

People Magazine

http://www.timeinc.com/people

From Tonya Harding to OJ to Jerry Garcia, *People* has featured them all. There's a daily update of "news" that will appeal to people who like to read about stories such as Ted Danson's wedding and a Robert De Niro fistfight. (It's interesting to compare the coverage in *People Daily* to that in *Time Daily*.) A photo gallery, and pages for special major current events of interest are also included.

Fortune

http://www.timeinc.com/fortune

Here, you can find links to the Fortune 500 list for U.S. companies and the Global 500 for the top 500 corporations around the world. You can search both lists and rank them according to criteria you select. You can download the lists in several presorted orders. For example, you can find the U.S. list sorted by state and by industry.

Sports Illustrated

http://www.timeinc.com/si

Sports Illustrated puts the cover story from the printed magazine on this site each week. An archive of stories from back issues dates back to Feb. 14, 1995. Other highlights change from time to time. At the moment, I'm looking at a tribute to Mickey Mantle and a baseball photo gallery. And, there's a good collection of up-to-the-minute sports stories and scores. These statistics aren't as up-to-date as those kept by ESPNet or Nando Sports (both reviewed in Chapter 18), but they're usually updated within a few hours of the games.

Mother Jones

http://www.mojones.com

Mother Jones was one of the first magazines to appear on the Web, appearing in November 1993. (Issues from as far back as January 1993 are available online.) The magazine bills itself as "progressive." Article headlines from recent issues blast Newt Gingrich and the Christian Coalition. I don't stand with the writers politically, but I'll be the first to compliment them on a well-done Web site.

HotWired

http://www.hotwired.com/

The online companion to the trendy *Wired* magazine is here. For those of you not familiar with the print version of *Wired*, it covers technology (not just computers but other high-tech areas such as satellite TV, genetic engineering, cellular phones, and personal digital assistants) and technology's impact on society. After spending some time at this site, you can answer the burning question: "Wired or Tired?"

Popular Mechanics

http://popularmechanics.com/

Popular Mechanics is a 93-year-old magazine, but there's nothing outdated about this site. *Popular Mechanics* has taken an interesting approach by combining a small amount of content from the printed magazine with a large amount of material made specially for (and about) the Web. Be sure to check out the collection of QuickTime movies here. Auto lovers will appreciate the PM Automotive section that has specifications on hundreds of current-model cars.

Adults Only!

If you're under 18 or offended by nudity, please don't read this! (If you have children using the Internet, do take precautions to see that they stay away from these sites.) Yes, it's true there are a few adult magazines on the Web. For the most part, they offer a small selection of the photos from the paper publications, a couple of photos you won't find printed, text of some of the articles, and opportunities to buy things, such as subscriptions and videos. If you're looking for this sort of magazine, here are a few of the most recognizable ones:

Playboy **http://www.playboy.com**

Hustler **http://hustler.onprod.com**

Penthouse **http://www.penthousemag.com**

(Sorry, ladies, I haven't seen *PlayGirl* online.) Be forewarned that these sites are some of the most popular and heavily trafficked on the Web. You will most likely experience delays getting connected.

If you're interested in software that will block access to this type of site, you should see the listings for SurfWatch and NetNanny in Chapter 11.

Web Week

http://www.mecklerweb.com/mags/ww/

This relatively new magazine focuses on issues for Web developers. Topics include software for creating Web pages, Web server software and hardware, software for analyzing traffic at a Web site, security issues, and anything else related to Web site management. (I'm not sure I understand the name of the magazine because it's published *monthly*, but there are online updates every week.)

Macworld Online

http://www.macworld.com/

In addition to good articles and links to software, this site occasionally sponsors contests for free goodies such as computers and software.

NetGuide

http://techweb.cmp.com/net/current/

NetGuide is a monthly Internet magazine aimed mainly at individuals using the Internet for personal use. The electronic version is updated daily. It includes a calendar of Net events and special features, such as its tribute to Jerry Garcia that was featured soon after his death.

TIP *NetGuide* **is one of 16 CMP periodicals with a home on the Web.** Most of the other publications (including *Interactive Age*, which is listed under "Zines" in this chapter) are geared toward business and information technology users. You can find the main home page for CMP, Techweb, at **http://techweb.cmp.com/techweb**.

Family World

http://family.com/homepage.html

Family World is a joint effort by more than 40 monthly parenting magazines and newsletters to bring parenting information to the Internet. The site features a large calendar section broken down by geographic region. The calendar lists upcoming parenting and family events and is updated daily. Typical events include entertainment and parenting seminars about education for children. You can also read feature stories from the publications at this site.

Zines

The Internet and Web have brought a new form of electronic magazine. Most of these Web-zines are new publications that offer publishing opportunities for writers missed by the traditional paper magazines. Some of them represent a new breath of life for paper magazines that couldn't survive financially in the traditional magazine marketplace.

Most of these zines offer cutting-edge commentary and writing geared toward very focused audiences. The views represented in these works are often outside the confines of what traditional magazines find appropriate (or salable). Thanks to the Web, another medium has been developed that continues to expand freedom of the press.

Word

http://www.word.com

This zine offers a combination of social and cultural commentary, along with original fiction and prose. To get involved, register and you can read and post in its discussion groups.

Fig. 13.9
Word's features and articles have a sense of immediacy and impact.

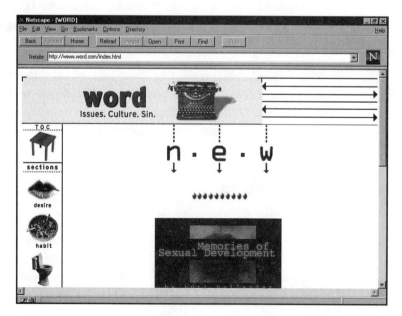

Hip

http://www.hip.com

Like many zines, *Hip* features cutting-edge commentary on music, social issues, gender issues, and human sexuality. You can "subscribe" by filling in a form so that *Hip* can send you email announcing new issues.

Cyberkind

http://sunsite.unc.edu/shannon/ckind/title.html

This zine is an excellent collection of original nonfiction (mostly about the human and computer interaction), fiction, poetry, and art. *Cyberkind* is more like a growing work-in-progress than a regularly "published" periodical. Look here on a monthly basis to see the new material.

Buzznet

http://www.hooked.net/buzznet

In addition to music reviews and original poetry and fiction, this zine features discussions about some good underground comics.

CyberKids

http://www.mtlake.com/cyberkids/

It's hard to find a safe place for your kids to play online. This zine provides stories, artwork, games, and puzzles for kids.

Interactive Age

http://techweb.cmp.com/techweb/ia/current/

Interactive Age began its life as a printed publication and recently switched over to Web-only distribution. The focus is on business applications and issues on the Internet.

Electronic texts

This collection of sites represents one of the best uses of the Web. All these sites have put many classic literary, religious, and philosophical works online. The works include a wide variety of writings from many cultures.

The range includes *The Acharnians* by Aristophanes to *Zen and the Art of the Internet* by Brendan Kehoe. All these works are in the public domain (the copyright has expired or they never were copyrighted) and, as far as I can tell, no one is making any money by putting them online. It's purely a charitable act by these organizations to ensure the widespread availability of these writings.

 TIP If you have some time on your hands and want to help put more books online in electronic form, many of the groups that maintain these sites need volunteers. See the sites for more information.

Wonderland—Written Works

http://www.wonderland.org/Works/

This site includes a wide variety of classic literature online. The authors represented here include Edgar Rice Burroughs (several of his Tarzan works are here), Lewis Carroll (the site name is Wonderland—it's only fitting to find this), Charles Darwin, and Mary Shelley. About half a dozen authors are here now with another dozen or so under construction. The Webmaster has done a nice job integrating some of the drawings from these books into the Web pages.

Project Gutenberg

http://jg.cso.uiuc.edu/pg/pg_home.html

Project Gutenberg was one of the pioneering groups on the Internet to make numerous books available online. Its large collection of texts is divided into three main areas: light literature, which includes works such as *Alice in Wonderland*, *Peter Pan*, and *Aesop's Fables*; heavy literature, which consists of religion-inspired literature, such as *Paradise Lost*, and large novels, such as *Moby Dick*; and reference works including a thesaurus, a dictionary, and encyclopedias.

ETEXT Archives

http://www.etext.org

All sorts of electronic texts are linked at this site. You'll find links to many online books, as well as political and religious documents, legal essays, and e-texts in several other categories.

Online Books Page

http://www.cs.cmu.edu/Web/books.html

This electronic book repository currently includes more than 850 English works in text and HTML formats. The collection is growing almost daily. Links here include pointers to books online at other sites. (But does it really matter to you whether the book is on its computer or another one? All you have to do is click the link and, through the magic of the Web, the book appears, regardless of its origin.)

 TIP If you don't want somebody else telling you what you should read, look at **http://www.cs.cmu.edu/Web/People/spok/banned-books.html** to see the Banned Books Online page. This list includes the text of several books that various groups have attempted to ban.

Internet Book Information Center

http://sunsite.unc.edu/ibic/IBIC-homepage.html

This site includes many well-written book reviews (updated regularly) and links to other book-related sites.

The Bookplex

http://www.gigaplex.com/wow/books/index.htm

This site features excerpts from recent books by popular authors such as Anne Rice. You can also read interviews with some of the authors. The site also includes coverage of movies and screenwriters.

The Hacker Crackdown

http://ice-www.larc.nasa.gov/ICE/papers/hacker-crackdown.html

This is the electronic version of Bruce Sterling's now classic treatise on law and disorder on the electronic frontier. Anyone spending serious time (or money) online should read this.

Authors

Many pages on the Web are devoted to individual authors. Enthusiastic fans generate and maintain most of these pages. Many of these fans are university students and faculty, so their Web pages may come and go as they graduate or move. For that reason, I've only listed a few pages as a sampler.

TIP If you're looking for a Web page devoted to your favorite author, start with the lists at **http://www.yahoo.com/Entertainment/Books/Authors/** or **http://www.li.net/~scharf/author.html**.

Edgar Allan Poe

http://www.et.byu.edu:80/~conradt/poepage.html

The complete works of Poe are available in an alphabetical listing here.

Shakespeare

http://the-tech.mit.edu/Shakespeare/works.html

This site is special for several reasons. First, it's complete. You'll find all of Shakey's plays and poetry here. Second, the text is in hypertext. So, if you're reading *All's Well That Ends Well* and come across the word "ward," you can click the link and see that "ward" is a prison in this context. It's a great way to not only read these classics, but also to understand them more easily. Finally, this site includes a host of special features such as a complete glossary, a searchable index that helps you find any line in any work with a given word, and a list of familiar quotations.

J.R.R. Tolkien

http://www.lights.com/tolkien/rootpage.html

This page is one of the best pages I've seen that is dedicated to an author. It includes dozens of links to lists, such as FAQs, book lists, societies dedicated to Tolkien, games, and Internet mailing lists. There are links to the major search engines so that you can perform searches for Tolkien material. (See Chapter 7 for details on Yahoo and Lycos, two popular search engines.) These links have all of the search fields for searching filled in and ready to go. You'll also find links to online games, MUDs, newsgroups, and more—all dedicated to Tolkien.

Fig. 13.10
The complete works of William Shakespeare will take you some time to read, but you'll find them all here for your pleasure.

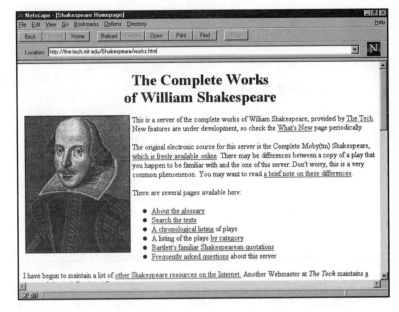

Robert A. Heinlein

http://www.clark.net/pub/ahasuer/heinlein/heinlein.html

This page includes a good collection of information about Heinlein and his science fiction classics including *The Cat Who Walks Through Walls* and *Stranger in a Strange Land*. There's a complete bibliography and a hypertext FAQ.

Isaac Asimov

http://www.clark.net/pub/edseiler/WWW/asimov_FAQ.html

This page is a huge hypertext FAQ about Asimov. You can click links to jump to lists of books, biographies, audio clips, and much more.

Comic Books

Comic books are becoming as popular on the Web as they are in paper. Traditional paper comic book publishers and stores are showing off their wares on the Web and new publishers are creating new comics exclusively on the Web. The major comic publishers have been slow to move to this new format, but you can find some exciting pages about some lesser known comics and some enterprising individuals have put up good Web pages about their favorite comics.

Comic Book Depot

http://www.insv.com/comxdepo

If you're looking for any type of information about comic books on the Web, start here. Several major comic publishers have Web pages within this site. The pages include contests, information about new and upcoming comics, and catalogs. There's a lot to explore here.

X-Men

http://www.santarosa.edu/~sthoemke/x.html

This site is the most comprehensive X-Men site I've seen. Here you can find dozens of links to information about X-Men comics. There are character FAQs and facts, graphics, links to other mutant-related pages, and much more.

Fig. 13.11
Read up on all of your favorite members of the Marvel mutant family.

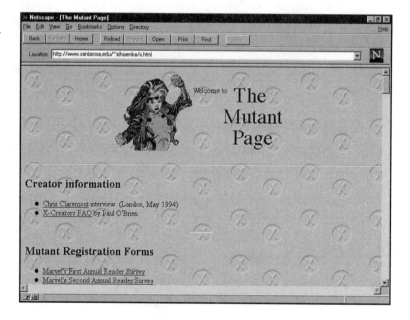

FalconStar

http://www.infi.net/falconstar/

This superhero comic is published exclusively on the Web. Watch this site as the action develops page-by-page in the comic.

New Comic Book Releases

http://www.mnsinc.com/hyworth/comics/new.html

Keep on top of the latest events in the comic book world with this page. Every Tuesday, there's a list of new comics to be released for sale that week. The list includes issue number and price.

Galaxy Heroes

http://www.galaxymedia.com/protectr.html

The home page for this Web-only comic describes it as a tongue-in-cheek superhero series. Issues are released in serial fashion, with several new pages added every two weeks. Each "page" of the comic is presented as a single large image in JPEG or GIF format. The JPEG files are smaller (so they download faster), but there isn't much difference in image quality between the two.

14

Religion

● In this chapter:

- **Visit some of the most inclusive spiritual sites, spanning several religions**

- **What religious publications appear online?**

- **See sites dedicated to specific faiths, including Christianity, Buddhism, Islam, Judaism, Hinduism, and the New Age**

- **Study religious history from several perspectives**

Faiths from every point on the spectrum are using the Internet to educate, organize, and link their followers . . . . ▶

Religion is as much a part of many people's lives as work, socializing, and recreation. Though the secular side of the Web gets lots of press, it should come as no surprise that religion thrives in the virtual congregation of the World Wide Web.

Even religions that normally reject technological convenience have embraced the flexibility and power of the World Wide Web to help spread their messages.

 TIP Several of the sites presented here are "clearing houses" with ever-changing lists of links to related resources. Because these sites are usually the first to know about new Web developments, you'll probably want to check them frequently.

Faith has always drawn out the best in artists, and that apparently includes Webmasters as well. Many of the religious sites in this chapter show a refreshing depth and attention to detail that less "inspired" sites lack.

Even in this field of stars, though, a few sites stand out as exemplary. They cross the boundaries of their specific congregations, offering something to people of all beliefs. Before you read the sections dedicated to specific religions, take a look at some of these sites that have broad appeal.

From the caves to the Web: The Dead Sea Scrolls

http://sunsite.unc.edu/expo/deadsea.scrolls.exhibit/intro.html

The Dead Sea Scrolls exhibit from the Library of Congress is a marvel. It gives a complete history of the controversial documents, from their discovery in Qumran through the near-Herculean task of deciphering them. Most pages on this well-designed site include photos of scrolls or fragments with translations—sometimes multiple possible translations for the same fragment. In addition to translations, various interpretations are presented from a variety of perspectives.

Fig. 14.1

The Library of Congress's Dead Sea Scrolls exhibit explores the history of the oldest surviving religious manuscripts.

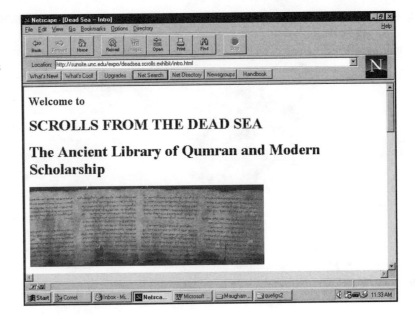

The Vatican

http://www.christusrex.org/www1/vaticano/0-Musei.html

As home to one of the largest art collections in the world, the Vatican is very attuned to aesthetics, and its Web site is no exception. Not only does it include downloadable pictures of a healthy number of the Vatican's art collections, but also messages from the church councils and the Pope. The Pope's travels are also covered, with reports on recent and upcoming trips around the world.

Fig. 14.2
The Vatican's Web is inspiring from several perspectives.

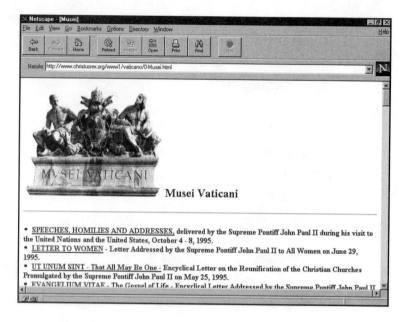

Vedic (Hindu) Astrology

http://www.fairfield.com/jyotish/index.html

This site is simple and fun, with an attention to detail you'll have to admire. It tells the story of the world's oldest known system of divination, on which much of modern astrology and biorhythm studies are based. The reason the site is so popular, though, is its personalized astrology chart feature. You tell it the date, time, and place you were born and it sends you an email with your Vedic Astrological chart. The information is more personalized than you might guess—it's based on much more detailed information than just your birthday. In fact, you'll probably have to get out your atlas to accurately fill out the form—it asks for the longitude and latitude of your birthplace.

Fig. 14.3
Find out what the world's oldest divination technique has to say about your future on the Vedic Astrology site.

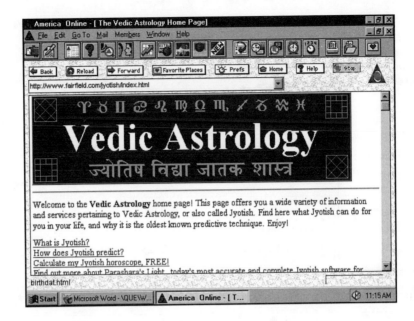

The Mennonite Central Committee

http://www.mennonitecc.ca/mcc/

The Mennonite Central Committee site is one of the most complete and ambitious religious sites on the Web. It reports on each of the church's missions around the world, history, and news. But it also takes an extra step beyond reporting. When you visit the site, you are positively struck by the feeling that the church is working to help all visitors, regardless of their faith. It provides resources to help with issues like domestic abuse and AIDS, and global issues like refugees and famine relief.

As you tour religious sites (in the real world and on the Web), you'll be hard-pressed to find a group that deals more openly, honestly, and compassionately with touchy and sometimes unpopular issues of modern society.

Fig. 14.4

The Mennonite Central Committee site is a model site for spiritual presentation.

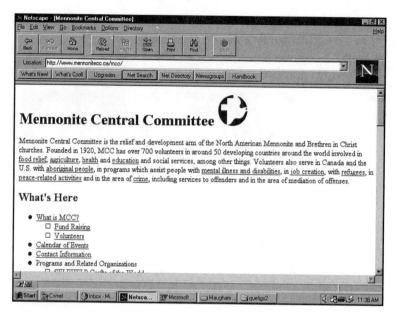

Comparing Bible versions with the Bible Gateway

http://www.gospelcom.net/bible

One of the joys of studying the Bible—regardless of your personal beliefs—is comparing different translations of the ancient Hebrew and Greek texts. Gospelcom's Bible Gateway site makes it easy (and fun) to compare five English versions of the Bible, as well as versions in German, Swedish, Latin, French, Spanish, and Tagalog. You can search for all the occurrences of a word in each version of the Bible, or look for a particular verse.

To use the Bible Gateway, enter information in the form at the bottom of the welcome page. In that form, you can specify the books to search, the words to look for, the verses to find, and the number of search matches ("hits") to return. Click the Lookup button, and you'll get a list of matching verses. Click the one you want to see.

TIP   **You can also view the whole text of a chapter without searching** for anything. Just click the hyperlinked name of the version you want on the welcome page, and select the chapter that interests you. You can read the chapters in sequence this way, too, without using the index, by clicking the "Next chapter" hyperlink at the bottom of each chapter page.

Fig. 14.5
The Bible Gateway welcome page—entryway to a dozen Bible versions.

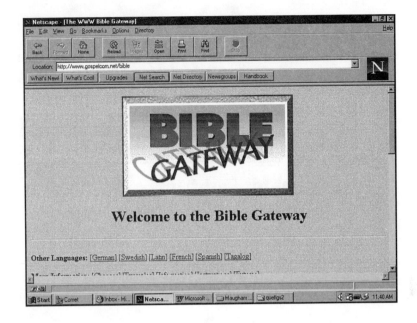

Christianity

Christianity is probably the best-represented group of religions on the World Wide Web. You can find Christian advice and information on everything from archaeology to zoology, with a healthy dose of business, politics, and relationships in the middle. Christian businesses thrive on the Web, with bookstores carrying what is probably the biggest share of the bandwidth.

A note of caution: if you're a devout follower of one belief system or another within Christianity's diverse congregation, you'll probably find a host of sites with views at odds with your own. Take them however you will, and remember that you won't have to search far to find people who share your views.

Billy Graham's Training Center at the Cove

http://www.asheville.com/cove.html

Meet the foremost teachers in the Christian community at Billy Graham's resident training center. The site provides a very detailed overview of the courses offered, with scriptural cross-references. Unlike most professional seminars, the rates are very reasonable and the material seems practical.

MorningStar

http://www.MorningStar.org/

This is something you don't see very often in the technological market-place—a nonprofit company. MorningStar is dedicated to helping Christians use technology to share information and grow in their faith. MorningStar produces Web pages and offers training and on-site consulting of all kinds. Its Web site has a good selection of links to other Christian sites.

Internet for Christians

http://www.gospelcom.net/ifc/newsletter.html

Author Quentin J. Schultze presents this biweekly electronic newsletter, featuring new Web sites and newsgroups. Some of the highlights include the Web oddities of the "Huh?" section (subtitled "Proof that we're lost in the cosmos") and a continually-updated index of Christian sites on the Net.

The best-selling Christian books list

http://www.christwh.com/cw/top_books.html

Christian Warehouse presents the weekly bestselling Christian books list, compiled from Christian bookstores across the country. The lists don't include reviews, but you should be able to find some in the List of Cool Christian Links.

The Jesus Fellowship ("The Jesus Army")

http://www.tecc.co.uk/jesusa/

The Jesus Fellowship (The Jesus Army) presents this exceptionally upbeat Christian site. With an intriguing combination of in-your-face pleas to repent and laid-back stories of the fallen who've cast off the shackles of crime and drugs, this site's not one to miss. Even if you see nothing else, check out Streetpaper, a magazine "for sinners and saints, seekers and surfers."

Baker Books

http://www.bakerbooks.com/ccc/

One of the best starting points for Christian Web-surfers has to be Baker Books. The Christian Internet Directory on the home page is very thorough;

it includes online bibles, education, politics, home study, theology, and many other resources. Of course, Baker also offers contemporary Christian literature and nonfiction books.

The Evangelical Lutheran Church in America

http://www.elca.org/

This is the official home page of the Evangelical Lutheran Church in America (there are several unofficial ELCA sites). While the site is still under construction as of this writing, it already boasts an impressive collection of links to other Lutheran resources, as well as definitive reports on church beliefs and history.

The Religious Society of Friends WWW Site

http://www.quaker.org/

There's nothing frilly about this site—it's just a bunch of hyperlinks to resources of particular interest to Quakers. Still, this site has some good resources, including links to the Friends Committee on National Legislation, which concerns itself mainly with pacifist issues. There's also a link to a Quaker book list— a good way to get information about the Quaker way of life.

Anglicans Online

http://infomatch.com/~haibeck/anglican.html

This site embodies superior design, a great deal of information, and a slight sense of humor. The Anglicans aren't trying to proselytize here, but they tell you what their church believes about a lot of things, and they provide a list of resources of interest to Anglicans and other Christians (including some of the sites in this chapter).

Buddhism

Many of the Buddhist sites on the Web are unique in their visual presentation. A common thread seems to be the elegant use of graphics without the giant in-your-face headlines you find on so many Web pages.

In addition to being visually striking, most Buddhist online presentations seem to offer a great number of differing perspectives, sometimes linking to sites that espouse totally opposite views.

The Journal for Buddhist Ethics

http://www.psu.edu/jbe/resource.html

The Journal for Buddhist Ethics' Global Resources for Buddhism page is full of links not only to other Buddhist sites, but also to art, literature, and even music sites. It is a very inclusive and easy-to-use site.

DharmaNet Electronic Files Archive

http://sunsite.unc.edu/dharma/defa.html

DharmaNet Electronic Files Archive (DEFA) maintains a page with Buddhist events, links to many Buddhist sites, magazines, and "The Dharma Marketplace," which offers commercial services and products for Buddhists. A definite high point is Gassho, the (currently text-only) electronic journal of DEFA.

Hinduism

In addition to the sites listed in this section, take a look at the Vedic Astrology site covered earlier in this chapter.

A beautiful online Bhagavad Gita

http://www.cc.gatech.edu/gvu/people/Phd/Rakesh.Mullick/gita/gita.html

This online version of the Bhagavad Gita is not to be missed. It includes intricate artworks, English translations from the Sanskrit, and an excerpt from a book on interpreting the Bhagavad Gita (which the site erroneously calls the "Bhagvad Gita"). The downloadable chapters are in PostScript, so if you don't have a PostScript printer, you'll need to get a PostScript viewer (like GhostView) before you download them.

Hinduism Today

http://zeta.cs.adfa.oz.au/Spirit/Veda/HT/

Hinduism Today is a monthly Hindu newsletter, published in seven editions for each of the languages spoken by the largest groups of Hindu worshippers (including English). Its focus is much more on human interest stories than hard news, and its news stories examine the news from a strongly Hindu point of view. All in all, *Hinduism Today* is a fascinating read.

Fig. 14.6
Several back issues of the popular *Hinduism Today* are available online.

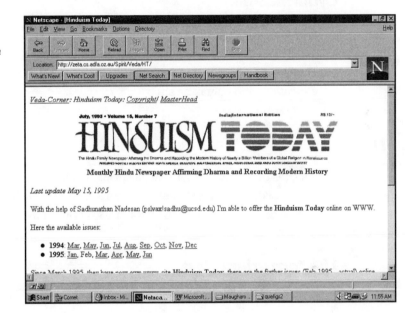

Islam

Islamic faiths have a very strong presence on the Web, with close to 100 large sites currently active.

Islamic Links

http://mars.superlink.net/user/tashour/islamlnk.html

Islamic Links is one of the best places to start. Updated frequently, it has links to educational, religious, and government pages around the world. You can even follow links to the entire text of the Qu'ran, presented in English or Arabic.

The Mosque of the Internet

http://www.nmia.com/~mosque/

The Mosque of the Internet includes much information about Muslim life, work, and faith, including a Mecca and Madina database. The site frequently overloads, either because of heavy traffic or insufficient computing power, so you'll probably have to try several times to get in.

CyberMuslim

http://www.uoknor.edu/cybermuslim/

Selim the CyberMuslim is your guide on this entertaining and very useful site. It includes a search function for Muslim activism and many links to Islamic art, education, and magazine sites.

Judaism

Jewish sites on the World Wide Web spring up almost daily, so make sure you check out a good site list for new additions. *The Jewish Bulletin of Northern California* and ANJY (both covered in this section) have continually updated site lists.

The Jerusalem Post

http://www.jpost.co.il/

The Jerusalem Post includes selected articles and columns from its daily printed newspaper online. It's all the best of traditional newspapers—the news is fresh and professional, and the editorial content is hard-hitting and very opinionated. For the non-political, check out the People and Places section, with a rich variety of features. "Dear Ruthie" ranks with the best-of-the-Web advice columns, providing recommendations on everything from home economics to relationships.

Torah Fax in Cyberspace

http://www.netaxis.qc.ca/torahfax/

Torah Fax in Cyberspace is a bite-sized chunk of learning presented in a very easy-to-digest manner. Rabbi Zalmen Marozov revises this entertaining and very informative page daily (except Sunday and Shabbat). It lists the importance of each day's date in Jewish history, and usually includes extra bits of trivia and fun. The Rabbi has an intriguing sense of humor, calling his *USA Today*-style briefing "Torah on the spot for inTORAHnet people on the go!" Back issues are available online.

Fig. 14.7
Torah Fax is fun and informative—but watch out for Rabbi Marozov's bad puns.

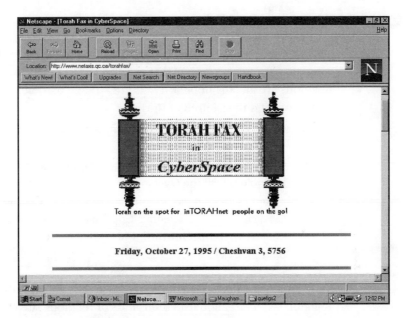

The Jewish Bulletin of Northern California

http://www.jewish.com/

The Jewish Bulletin of Northern California is an electronic magazine with much, much more than theology—it's also brimming with politics, entertainment, and personal ads. The tantalizing cooking section is also well worth a look.

A Network for Jewish Youth (ANJY)

http://www.ort.org/anjy/

A Network for Jewish Youth (ANJY) presents a fun and very useful site for the faithful of all ages. Check out the pen-pal service to meet Jewish youth around the world. The site is based in the UK; even though its event schedules are almost exclusively British, most of the material is useful for anyone. The A-to-Z of Jewish and Israel related resources is especially handy, with a very easy interface that allows you to add new links.

Other spiritual sites

The Internet boasts representatives from just about every "real-world" religion, plus some religions that are specific to the virtual world. Cyber-Religions are gaining popularity, as are strange parodies of religion like McChurch and the Church of the Sub-Genius.

 Plain English, please!

CyberReligion is a religion that, usually, merges principles of science and technology with the teachings of one or more traditional religions, and promotes itself on the Internet. An example of CyberReligion is the First Cyberchurch of the Scientific God (**http://pages.prodigy.com/CA/church/firstchurch.html**), which combines Christianity with scientific principles. **99**

To get a feel for the alternatives, take a look at your favorite Web searcher's Religion section. Yahoo lists thousands of religious sites under dozens of broad groupings. You can also look at the religious studies and guide sites covered in this section.

Lysator religious archives

http://www.lysator.liu.se/religion/index.html

This site is dedicated to religion in general, with nods to most major religious groups (including worship of "adversary deities" in Satanism). This site includes pointers to newsgroup archives for many faiths. The owner describes herself as a neo-Pagan, and many of the site's resources lean toward that end of the spectrum.

New Age Web Works

http://www.newageinfo.com/

New Age Web Works is something of a clearing house for New Age products, publications, and organizations. It is not just a list of links, though. It also includes its own archive of articles, poems, and editorials. The "Fun" section includes Pagan WAV files and New Age software.

Religious Atheism

http://www.chattanooga.net/~tpkunesh/atheism.f/relaths.htm

Most of the other sites in this chapter celebrate the existence of one or more deities—supernatural entities worthy of reverence. The Religious Atheism provides lots of resources of use to Atheists and those who want to know what Atheists do—and do not—believe. Be sure to look at the section on modern Western stories that allegedly are parables for atheism—some of these interpretations may surprise you.

Hell: The Online Guide to Satanism

http://www.marshall.edu/~allen12/index.html

Regardless of what you think of Satanism, this site is seriously good-looking. The black backgrounds compliment the blue and red graphics well, and the layout's really good. What's at the site? Well, a guide to Satanic churches, and an online bookstore that sells books about summoning demons. Also, take a look at the alt.satanism newsgroup FAQ, which explains a lot about this religion.

Taoism

http://www.ii.uib.no/~arnemo/tao/tao.html

Technically not a religion, in the Western sense of the word, Taoism derives a way of life from the teachings of Lao Tse, an ancient Chinese philosopher. In fact, "Tao" translates loosely to "the Way." This site offers hyperlinks to online editions of Lao Tse's works, as well as information about Taoism and other Eastern belief systems.

The ULC Church of Amazement

http://www.kaiwan.com/~amaze/

What can I say about a site that opens with the sentences, "This Page is UNDER CONSTRUCTION. Watch for falling dogma."? The Church of Amazement page has links to all kinds of Pagan-interest resources, including the World Pagan Network and a Los Angeles-area Pagan events calendar.

CyberQueer Lounge Spirituality Page

http://www.cyberzine.org/html/GLAIDS/Spirituality/
spiritualitypage.html

This portion of the CyberQueer Lounge deals with the problems faced by gays, lesbians, and bisexuals who want to be active in religions that, in many cases, reject their ways of life. This site offers hyperlinks to information-exchange groups, as well as sites that organize campaigns against the most vocal anti-gay evangelists.

The Bertrand Russell Society

http://freenet.buffalo.edu/~bk553/

This site promotes the work and memory of Bertrand Russell, an agnostic philosopher, among other things. At this site, you can become a member of the society, or learn what other members have been doing. Unfortunately, there's no Russell FAQ that I could find, so it's hard to get a basic understanding of Russell's beliefs.

15

Recreation and Hobbies

● **In this chapter:**

- **Get expert advice on your favorite pastime**

- **Learn how to care for your pets, plants, and possessions**

- **Pick up a new hobby**

- **Get connected with others who pursue the same recreational activities as you**

- **Find out how to have fun on the Net!**

The Web isn't the exclusive domain of computer geeks anymore. There are sites on the Web for every conceivable interest, from automobiles to zymurgy . . . . ➤

The World Wide Web is bringing about a revolution in the way people spend their free time. And it's not just about spending weekends cruising the Net; in fact, the Web is helping people to better enjoy their time away from the computer, too.

With the advent of the Web, the Internet is easier to use than ever before—and that means it's no longer the exclusive province of computer experts and nerds. Nor are its uses limited to work-related research and communication. In fact, ordinary people are getting online and exchanging opinions, information, and advice about hobbies, pastimes, and favorite sports. The Web is fast becoming a major resource for ideas and information about all kinds of recreations. From fish to flowers, from mountain bikes to macramé, just about any recreational topic you can imagine is covered in great depth somewhere on the Web.

To be sure, many special-interest groups have been on the Internet for a long time, in the form of UseNet newsgroups devoted to particular interests or hobbies. These discussion forums still exist, and they can be a good place to turn for quick answers. But one of the most valuable products of UseNet has been the many FAQ (Frequently Asked Questions) files produced by the various newsgroups. There are literally hundreds of FAQ files, covering every imaginable topic, and most of them are treasure troves of information, embodying the collective knowledge of many people. Fortunately, many of these files are available on the Web. These files are usually the best place to start looking for answers to your questions about a topic.

In the pages that follow, you'll learn about some of the Web's best special-interest and recreational sites. Automobiles, Outdoor Recreation, Home & Garden, Games, Pets, and Crafts & Collections are the categories I've divided these sites into. If your hobby matches one of the interests covered here, you owe it to yourself to check out the relevant sites. It's like discovering a club or user's group with a well-stocked library—and no membership fees! Even if you don't spend your time pursuing one of the activities listed here, stop by some of the sites. You'll find material there that will entertain and intrigue you, and you might even pick up a new hobby.

Travel the world and learn photography at photo.net

http://swissnet.ai.mit.edu/photo/

One of the best ways to learn something is to watch someone who really knows what they are doing and listen to his advice. If you want to learn something about photography, you can do no better than to spend some time at photographer and Web pioneer Philip Greenspun's feet. He's a masterful photographer and an excellent travel writer. His site will not only educate you about the practice and appreciation of photography, it will also entertain and move you.

Fig. 15.1
Learn how to take snapshots like the pros.

When you visit this site, you'll find a generous collection of travel and action photos available. Under the Photo Exhibits heading, you'll find stunning examples of nature and sports photography, as well as Greenspun's travel-ogues. These entirely Web-based books feature Greenspun's thoughtful and well-crafted (if somewhat long-winded) writings, and they're beautifully illustrated with full-color JPEGs and GIFs. Be sure you don't miss "Travels with Samantha," an award-winning Web "book" that chronicles Greenspun's journeys across the U.S. and Canada.

But there's more to **photo.net** than simply a gallery of beautiful photos. This site is also packed with technical information and advice for beginners and expert photographers alike. There's an article that gives practical advice on what camera to buy if you're just starting out in photography. There are reviews of various kinds of cameras, from the point-and-shoot variety to large-format cameras. There are even reviews of color printers.

Turn to the Technique and How-To sections for advice on taking better pictures, getting the most out of your equipment, and getting film developed and photographs framed. The first how-to section covers the ins and outs of traditional film-based photography. The second section deals with the intricacies and idiosyncrasies of digital photography—scanning, software editing, and color printing.

All in all, this is a beautifully crafted, very useful site. Whether you're a novice photographer, an experienced hobbyist, or a professional, you'll want to see what photo.net has to offer you. Even if you're not interested in photography, you'll want to stop by just for the travelogues.

Create your own Web Newspaper with CRAYON

http://www.eg.bucknell.edu/~boulter/crayon/

The Web has more news sources than you can shake a stick at, but the problem is that they're not all in the same place. It's hard enough to find all the news sources you like and add them to your bookmark list. But once you find them, you still have to jump from one to another. You could spend half a morning reading news stories at one site, and then navigating over to another site for sports, and so on.

CRAYON comes to the rescue with a create-your-own Web newspaper that incorporates news from a variety of sources and puts all the news on one page where you can read it quickly and conveniently. What's more, CRAYON—an acronym for CReAte Your Own Newspaper—lets you pick the news sources you want, organize them by category, and even give your personal "paper" a name of its own.

To create your newspaper, first navigate to the CRAYON Web site, listed above. There are plenty of instructions on how to use the service, so if you need help at any point, just return to the top of the home page and click one of the instructional headings.

To begin creating your paper, follow these simple steps.

1 Scroll down this page until you reach the form section. Enter the name you want your paper to have.

2 Decide if you want graphics, such as cartoons and weather maps, to appear as inline images in your newspaper, or as links only. If you choose the latter, you'll need to click the links to see the pictures, but your newspaper will download more quickly. Unless you're sure you want to look at those pictures every time you open the paper, pick the second option, Show Graphics as Links.

3 Scroll down the list of news sources and pick the ones you want to appear in your paper. There are dozens of possibilities, organized by categories: U.S. News, World News, Weather, Business Reports, Information and Technology, Editorials, Arts and Entertainment, Sports, the Funny Pages, the Tabloid Page, and a section devoted to New and Hot Web sites. The choices here are many, so pick as many or as few as you want.

4 Pick the order you want the sections to appear in, using the drop-down boxes at the bottom of the form.

5 Finally, when you've set everything up, click the Make Me a Paper! button to create your paper.

 TIP **You don't have to return to the CRAYON site to read your news-** paper. Once you've set up your paper at the CRAYON site, your paper will appear on-screen. Save that page as an HTML file on your hard disk. From now on, when you want to view your paper, open the file on your hard disk using your Web browser. You don't need to go back to the CRAYON site unless you want to make a new paper—all the links you'll need are contained in the file you saved.

Fig. 15.2
Crayon lets you
become the reporter,
editor, and publisher of
your own newspaper.

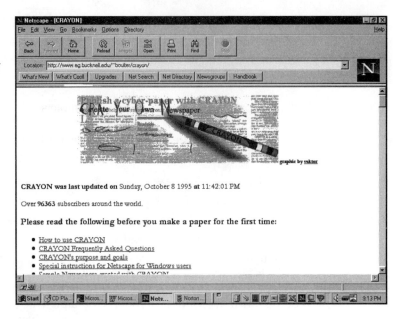

To see the news, weather, or other items you selected, just click the links and your browser will take you to the sites for the items you requested. It's that simple—a customized newspaper that shows only what you want to see, and in the order you want!

Discover Nature in the Internet through *Outside Online*

http://outside.starwave.com/outside/online/

The definitive publication for outdoor activity enthusiasts, *Outside Magazine* brings the great outdoors to the World Wide Web with its online site. More than just an electronic version of the printed magazine, this site has a character and content all its own. In the words of the site's designers, "It just might be the best new piece of gear out there."

Interested in hiking? Mountain biking? Camping? The Ironman triathlon? You'll find information on all these topics and more in *Outside Online*. There's news, human interest stories, how-to's, equipment reviews, and travel guides within the Web pages here.

Fig. 15.3

Discover the nation's premier hiking spots right from your desktop using *Outside Online*.

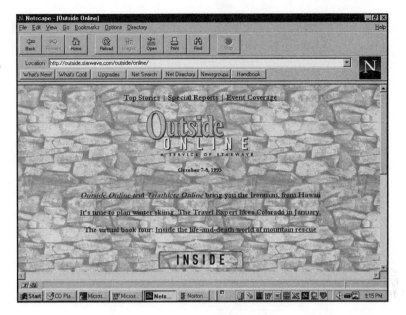

Outside Online is divided into several categories. News & Views gives you the scoop about the world of nature and outdoor sports. Stories are collected from various news wires and the *Outside Online* staff, and are presented with verve and a pro-environment attitude. Check out the Going Places section for trip planning advice, including where to go, what to pack, and how to get there. Need to buy some new gear? Stop in at the *Outside* Store for reviews of the latest and greatest camping, hiking, biking, and skiing equipment.

Outside Online's Activities department gives you in-depth information about a variety of outdoor activities, and the searchable Events calendar is the place to turn when you want to find out about upcoming competitions, races, festivals, and other events.

Finally, the "Trailhead to the Internet" leads you down the path to other Web sites and Internet resources of interest to nature enthusiasts.

This site is part of Starwave's extensive Web site, which also hosts Mr. Showbiz (see Chapter 19, "Television and Movies").

Get technical with the *Popular Mechanics* Zone

http://popularmechanics.com/

Now over 90 years old, *Popular Mechanics* has been rendering complex technical subjects easily understandable for generations. It should be no surprise that when the magazine came onto the Web, it took the same no-nonsense, practical, get-the-job-done attitude to the Internet as it took to its previous topics. As a result, this site is easy to use, provides a lot of useful material you can't find anywhere else, and serves as a good starting point for Web explorers as well as home improvers.

Fig. 15.4

Get to the nuts and bolts of any problem through *Popular Mechanics'* PM Online.

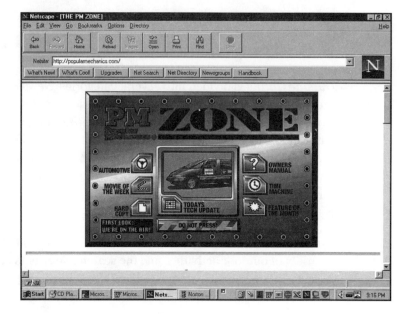

The material in the PM Zone falls into two categories: Web-related material and more traditional *Popular Mechanics* topics, such as repairs around the home. The Web-related topics are where this site really shines. If you're looking to add a QuickTime movie viewer to your Web browser, this is the place to come to download the files you'll need. Unlike other sites, PM Zone includes clear, explicit directions on how to install the viewer. The PM Zone also provides technical support, bug fixes, and tips for PC, Mac, and Internet users.

The second category of features in the *Popular Mechanics* Web site are those devoted to home repair and DIY projects. If you're having problems fixing something around the house, you're wondering what the different kinds of pliers are used for, or if you're just looking for some ideas for home improvement projects, this is the place to look.

Want to find out about the cutting edge of technology and industry? Click the Tech Updates button to read a short illustrated piece on some aspect of new technology. There's a new Tech Update every weekday. You can also read intriguing pieces about where the cutting edge was decades ago, and how long ago certain "modern inventions" were developed.

The PM Zone is a great place for anyone fascinated with technology or simply looking for a few home improvement tips and tricks. The past meets the future in this unique online site.

The world according to GORP—the Great Outdoor Recreation Pages

http://www.gorp.com/

Outdoors enthusiasts may know "gorp" as the nutritious peanut-and-raisin snack packed by many hikers on their wilderness expeditions for quick energy on the trail. On the Web, GORP provides information rather than energy— a quick dose of advice on outdoors topics from A to Z.

The Great Outdoor Recreation Pages site is more comprehensive but not as slick-looking as the *Outside Online* site profiled earlier. An independently-run site, you'll find less attitude here than at the heavily-designed corporate sites, but more straight facts. The site boasts hundreds of text files, from park descriptions to FAQs to resource lists. In many cases, GORP simply provides a convenient way to access files that are normally spread all over the place— in the rec.backcountry newsgroup and various FTP sites, for example. In other cases, the GORP editors have added value to the files. For instance, the extensive national park guides are taken from National Park Service publications, but they're updated and corrected based on the combined experiences of the GORP staff.

Fig. 15.5
GORP's comprehensive coverage of the outside will make it a favorite site for all outdoor enthusiasts.

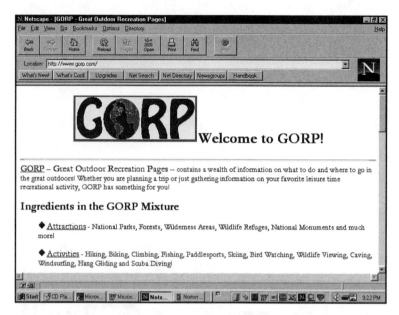

The Attractions and Locations sections of the GORP site are where you'll find guides to parks in the U.S. and around the world. It's a good source of detailed information, from the history of the region or park in question to descriptions of the attractions there to a list of activities.

Look under the Activities heading for hundreds of links to outdoors-related Web sites, organized by activity. Whether it's water-skiing, hiking, boating, biking, or anything else, this is a good place to find lots of Internet resources for your hobby.

GORP also gives you access to online bookstores specializing in travel and outdoor activities, online gear shops, and online tour agencies. Finally, at the bottom of the home page, you'll find a bunch of additional material, from "Traveler's Tales" to a newsstand and cartoon gallery. From top to bottom, GORP is a no-nonsense outdoors guide that should be indispensable to outdoors enthusiasts. It's a serious source of information.

Domesticating the Web: the HomeArts On-Line Network

http://homearts.com/

This site proves that nostalgia is alive and well, even on the Web. The HomeArts Network gives you a heavy dose of the "traditional country living" theme. With its decorative backgrounds and quaint illustrations, it hearkens back to a time of innocence and good living. But it's not just nostalgia you'll find here; the HomeArts site is also a rich source of housekeeping, cooking, home maintenance, and health and beauty information. As the site's designers put it, it's "a place where high tech meets common sense."

Fig. 15.6
HomeArts puts more than 1,200 informative pages at your fingertips.

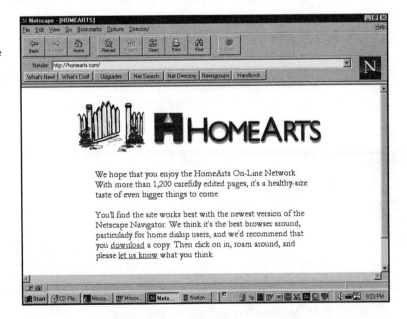

The backbone of this site is the content it derives from four magazines: *Redbook, Good Housekeeping, Country Living,* and *Popular Mechanics.* You can go directly to these magazines' Web sites from here. Each one is listed towards the bottom of the HomeArts home page.

But the site also lets you access general information without your having to look through each magazine. For example, click the Answer Desk to search through the HomeArts files on food, health, gardening, and more. When you click the Food button, you get a clever search engine that lets you sort through the recipe library—you can specify not only the ingredients you're interested in, but also the preparation time involved and the calories per serving.

Other sections of the HomeArts site organize articles from the four magazines by topic. Interested in health issues? Turn to the Health section. Home and Garden contains articles from the four magazines that tell you how to improve your house, grow a better garden, and the like.

 TIP **The HomeArts pages have lots of graphical content, so make sure** you've got a fast connection—at least 9600 or 14,400 baud—before trying to visit this site.

HomeArts is a convenient source of household, health, and beauty information. If you don't mind the heavy dose of nostalgia and "traditional values," this is a great place for useful tips and advice on a variety of topics.

Automobiles and motorcycles

From sites sponsored by car companies to independent Web sites run by car and motorcycle enthusiasts, the Web is teeming with information about the vehicles you rely on and have come to love. Of course, you can shop for a car on the Web in any number of interactive "showrooms." But if you want to go a little deeper, and get more in-depth coverage of the newest models and the most enduring classics, you should turn to the sites listed below.

BMW Automobile Information

http://cbsgi1.bu.edu/bmw/bmw.html

In the 1980's, BMWs became the yuppie status symbol of choice. And no wonder—their precision German engineering, Autobahn-ready performance, and classic European good looks give them a deservedly great reputation. For information about BMW cars, events, auto clubs, and books, this page can't be beat. It's also loaded with FAQs from UseNet and links to other sources of information on BMWs.

Chrysler

http://www.chryslercorp.com/

Here's where you'll find the Chrysler Corporation's full complement of Internet services, from sneak peeks at the latest technology and cutting-edge concept cars, to the current offerings, and even a look at the upper echelons of Chrysler management. There's even a library, where you can get the latest news from the car company or read about the history of Chrysler cars.

Shop for a car online

If you're shopping for a new or used car, you've probably visited many dealer showrooms and car lots, browsed the newspaper ads, and made plenty of phone calls. But have you considered using the World Wide Web to shop for a car? Why not?

Many regional dealers have Web sites where they show their wares and often give special discounts to Internet users. Not only that, but the Web boasts huge, national and international "virtual showrooms" where you can access dealers all around the world. If you're really serious about shopping for a good deal, this may be the place to start.

Of course, with current Web technology, you can't simply purchase a car online and expect it to be delivered to your door. Electronic cash and electronic check transactions simply aren't secure enough to handle a major purchase like this. Besides, Web technology doesn't provide a way for you to test-drive a car online. But if you shop on the Web first, you can walk onto the car lot already knowing what you're looking for, and what the dealer has.

Check out the following virtual car showrooms:

- AutoWeb Interactive
  http://www.autoweb.com/

- DealerNet's Virtual Showrooms
  http://www.dealernet.com/

- The International Auto Mall
  **http://www.mindspring.com/~mikea
  dealer.html**

- AutoMallUSA
  http://www.automallusa.net/

If these sites don't have what you're looking for, check out Yahoo's extensive Dealers page. Many of the dealers listed there are regional, so you'll have to live nearby to take advantage of their services. But as they say, there's no charge to look. Yahoo's Dealers page can be found at:

**http://www.yahoo.com/
Business_and_Economy/
Companies/Automotive/Dealers/**

The Saturn Site

http://www.saturncars.com/

Saturn's commercials promise that it's a "different kind of car company." Maybe you'll find out why at its Web site. The main feature of this site is detailed information on its latest line of cars, with lots of photos from different angles and a complete rundown of features, options, and accessories. There's also a sampling of Saturn news items, and a US/Canada map you can use to find the nearest Saturn dealer.

Ford Worldwide Connection

http://www.ford.com/

This site is home to the Ford Motor Corporation. It's a good place to find out about Ford, Lincoln, Mercury, and even Jaguar cars (both the latest models and the more vintage models). There's historical information, as well as current news. The site also provides links to Ford's extensive customer credit programs. You can even join Ford's Web-based focus group and give your feedback on upcoming models and products.

Fig. 15.7

Find all about new and old Fords, Lincolns, and Mercurys at the Ford Worldwide Web Site.

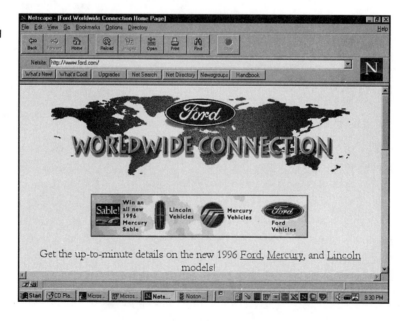

FerrariNet

http://pscinfo.psc.edu/~rsnodgra/Ferrari/

FerrariNet is an excellent Internet resource for Ferrari lovers. This site includes graphics, historical information, and a newsletter focusing on the ins and outs of purchasing Ferraris. It's maintained by a Ferrari fan, not the car company itself, so its coverage is a little more impartial.

BikeNet

http://www.bikenet.co.uk/

The place for motorcycle enthusiasts on the Web, this site contains many stories and articles on the subject of motorcycles. You'll find news, motor-cycle reviews, notices of upcoming events, coverage of races, and biker lifestyle columns, along with a good selection of links to other motorcycling Web sites. Although it's a British site that focuses on news and events in England and Europe, there's a lot here to interest American motorcyclists as well. Conveniently, this site has a text-only menu for those accessing the Web with narrower bandwidth.

Outdoor recreation

In addition to the sites mentioned earlier (Outside Online and GORP), the Web is home to many outdoors-related organizations. Maybe you like skiing, or perhaps birdwatching is more your speed—in either case, there's some-thing on the Web for you. You may find, as others have, that a little time spent on the Web can leave you better prepared for your excursions out-of-doors, wherever they may take you.

Hiking and Walking Homepage

http://www.teleport.com/~walking/hiking.html

This low-key page has lots of useful resources for avid or casual hikers, walkers, and ramblers. There's information on hiking gear (boots, mostly) and destinations, as well as links to many Internet-based and real-world hiking organizations. A little bit of hiking philosophy completes the mix of this useful and interesting page. It's updated weekly with new material, so there's always something fresh here.

The Birding Home Page

http://www.zender.com/birder/

The definitive source for birding information on the Web, this site has links to dozens of international birding sites, along with lots of pictures, information, and checklists for different parts of the world. Chat with other birders around the world and find out how to spot the most elusive species!

Boating and sailing: MarineNet

http://www.gsn.com/

MarineNet is a huge commercial site where you can connect with boating and sailing companies of all descriptions. If you're thinking of buying a boat, the Buyer's Guides and the classifieds will certainly help—there are over 15,000 boats for sale here. The Destinations department will help you find a safe harbor anywhere in the U.S.; its harbor descriptions are taken from the M.P.C. Boaters' Directory. You'll also find a discussion forum, plenty of additional information, and lots of boating equipment vendors at this site. Anchors aweigh!

Fig. 15.8
Find all about boating products and then purchase them directly on MarineNet.

To get to MarineNet, you must first go to the Global Shopping Network at the URL shown above. Once you get to the GSN, select MarineNet and choose text or graphics mode. Then click the Guest Entrance button.

Note that like the Pathfinder site, this URL maps to a much longer one. The one I've included above is the shortened one. The long notation version is: **http://www.gsn.com/bin/fishing.exe?/sports/boating/ marinenet.htm&graphics&guest**

Fishing at Anglers Online

http://www.inetmkt.com/fishpage/index.html

If you or someone you know is a fishin' fool, direct your Web browser to this page for one of the most comprehensive sources of fishing information around. Anglers Online features a large classified ad section where you can buy, sell, or swap fishing equipment. The Fishing Report gives you up-to-date reports on fishing conditions around the world. And the Internet Fishpages section connects you to other fishing sites across the World Wide Web. In addition to these valuable resources, there are also files of information on fly fishing, fishing equipment dealers, news, and even weather reports.

Hyperski

http://www.hyperski.com/index.htm

Hyperski—it's not some new Finnish brand of vodka, it's the latest hip skiing and snowboarding site on the Web. This online magazine concentrates on interesting feature stories and cool photos without excluding useful information; for example, there's a guide to ski resorts throughout the world, but primarily in North America. Still a work-in-progress when I visited, this promises to remain an exciting and fresh site for skiers.

Caving with the Speleology Server

http://speleology.cs.yale.edu/

Spelunking is the sport of climbing and crawling through underground caves, and speleology is the study of and exploration of caves. If you're interested in caves and caving, this is the Web site for you. Everything you ever wanted to know about caves is here, and there are practical guides to spelunking and caving sites and equipment as well. Maybe you're not ready to wander into an uncharted cave yourself, but just want to see what it's like—this site also brings you photos and descriptions. And, of course, there are many links to other caving sites on the Web.

Home and Garden

Before the Web, homeowners had two choices when they needed an answer to a gardening, cooking, or maintenance question: go to the library and wade through dozens of how-to books, or write a letter to a newspaper columnist like Hints from Heloise, wait a few weeks, and hope that the answer would get printed. No more. Now you can go to the Web and find answers to all your household questions within minutes. If the answer isn't already there, many sites feature their own Q&A columns and public bulletin boards, so your wait for an answer could be measured in hours rather than weeks.

By browsing the Web, you're connecting to a powerful source of collective knowledge about all the problems and issues that crop up in the home and garden, from aphids to zucchini. It's like having a backyard fence that runs around the world!

 TIP   **If you're interested in gardening, household hints, and other** domestic issues, don't miss the HomeArts On-Line Network profiled earlier. It's a rich source of advice, tips and tricks culled from a number of household magazines.

The Virtual Garden

http://www.pathfinder.com/vg/

Time Inc.'s Virtual Garden is an invaluable reference for gardeners of all descriptions. Whether you're trying to get your broccoli to grow, planting marigolds, or building a backyard pleasure garden, this site is sure to have the information you need. One of the most valuable resources is the Time Life Electronic Encyclopedia, found in the Gardening Library; it's a searchable database of over 3,000 plant species, with pictures, climate recommendations, and detailed care instructions.

GardenNet

http://www.olympus.net/gardens/welcome.htm

More than just an information resource, GardenNet aims to facilitate networking among serious gardeners and garden aficionados. This site features helpful how-to articles, guides to professional gardens around the country, and many links to other gardening sites on the Internet. The Ardent Gardener is a question-and-answer columnist who solves a variety of gardening problems. If you have a question that isn't answered here, you can post a question to the Ardent Gardener using an HTML form. GardenNet is a little friendlier and less commercial than the Virtual Garden (mentioned previously), but together the two sites make a formidable addition to any gardener's bookmark list.

The WWW Virtual Library for Landscape Architecture

http://www.clr.toronto.edu:1080/VIRTUALLIB/larch.html

Are you thinking of landscaping your lawn? Perhaps you just want to plant a tree or two, or make some changes to the shrubbery. Whether you're undertaking a major landscaping project or simply caring for your lawn, this site is an unbeatable source of information. It gathers in one place a vast number of Internet sites for landscape architecture, and includes a powerful search tool so you can zero in on just what you want. In addition to landscaping resources, there are also categories for environmental issues, architecture, the earth sciences, and other related fields. Homeowners and landscape architects alike will find plenty of material in this truly comprehensive site.

The WWW Virtual Library for Furniture & Interior Design

http://www.i3.se/furniture.html

Locating Web sites on furniture and interior design can be difficult. That's why the Virtual Library is so useful; it collects disparate sites from around the world here. From Finnish and Swedish furniture designers to San Francisco-based interior redecorators, it's all here. There are also links to academic sites, at schools of interior design, and a list of museums and related special exhibits. This site tends to focus more on furniture than interior design, but the latter category is also fairly well-represented here.

Mama's Cucina

http://www.eat.com/

This is Ragu's Web home page, but don't turn away just because it's a corporate site. This just happens to be one of the most entertaining, well-designed, and useful food-related sites on the Web. A strong dose of Italian-style grandmothering makes this site feel homey. It's also a good place to learn about Italy and see some pictures of famous Italian architecture. There's even a glossary of Italian terms, along with sound clips so you can get the pronunciation right! But what's really useful is the cookbook; it has lots of great Italian recipes, many of which are very easy to prepare. If you know what you're looking for, use the search feature to skip right to it, or just browse the cookbook until something tasty catches your eye. *Mangia bene!*

Fig. 15.9
Ragu's home page can help you prepare a delicious Italian feast.

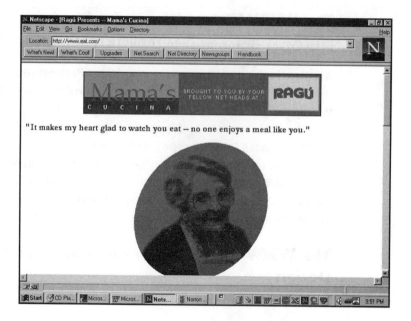

Games

What's your game? Cards, role-playing games, and even some new, Internet-only games are all represented on the Web. If you're looking for rulebooks, reviews of new games, or partners for play-by-mail games, you can find them here. Let the games begin!

The Game Cabinet

http://web.kaleida.com/u/tidwell/GameCabinet.html

This site collects together reviews of new games, official rules for traditional games, and lots of other information relating to card games and board games. As the title suggests, this site is a bit like a cabinet or shelf full of games— slightly disorganized, but lots of fun to root around in. One plus for international users is that rule sheets and reviews are available in French or German as well as English; also, many of the new games reviewed are from European game companies. All together, this site packs plenty of fun and it's a good gamer's reference as well!

The House of Cards

http://www.sky.net/~rrasa/hoc.htm

This site is a valuable resource for card-players of all descriptions. While its primary focus is solitaire (in its many variations), you can find information here on pretty much any card game, traditional or non-traditional. There are links to Bridge, Poker, Hearts, and other sites around the Internet. This site's strengths are downloadable shareware card games, and links to specialized card-game sites on the Internet.

Role-Playing Game Internet Resource Guide

http://www.common.net/~shadow/rpg_index/

This is a great source of information, files, and Web links relating to role-playing games of all kinds. The site's keeper seems more familiar with Advanced Dungeons & Dragons than any other role-playing gaming system, but due to TSR Inc.'s copyright policies, the Web resources for this particular game are fairly limited. Still, players of AD&D and of other games will find lots of useful information and suggestions on this site. The resources are sorted by game manufacturer and by genre. Near the top of the home page, you'll find some links to "mega-archives" on the Web that contain huge quantities of files and data for dedicated gamers.

The Strategic Simulation Gaming Home Page

http://world.std.com/~ctate/strategy.html

Strategic simulation games, wargames, and historical gaming with miniatures are all covered on this page. It's a good collection of rules, tips, and links to other sites. There's even a section where you can look up real-world historical information, to make your historical recreations that much more realistic. Add to this game reviews, play-by-mail services, and a gaming events calendar—this site has plenty to keep you interested and informed.

Computer Gaming World Online

http://www.gamingworld.ziff.com/~gaming/

Computer Gaming World is one of today's premiere computer game magazines. Its Web site features slick, futuristic graphics and is packed with information for serious computer gamers. There are reviews of new games, hints and strategy tips, and a big library of downloadable shareware games and demos. The eclectic collection of Web links here features some fascinating and hard-to-find Web pages gamers won't want to miss.

The Billiard Congress of America

http://www.netins.net/showcase/bcahome/

Pool-players will want to check out this Web page, home to the Billiard Congress of America, an organization devoted to popularizing the game of billiards, sponsoring competitions and events, and commemorating the champions. If you're looking for a place to play pool, click the News, Publications and Information button and then select the Billiard Rooms link for a list of pool halls around the U.S. and Canada. This page is also where you'll find tips on improving your game and official billiards regulations.

Warpig Paintball Home Page

http://warpig.cati.csufresno.edu/paintball/paintball.html

In paintball, players are armed with guns that fire paint-filled capsules. They stalk around the woods, trying to shoot each other without getting shot themselves. It's a fast-paced, high-adrenaline adventure for weekend warriors. Find out all about the sport at the Warpig home page, one of the first paintball-related sites on the Web. In addition to rules, you'll find descriptions of a variety of paintball guns, and an image gallery showing some of the lengths paintball players go to in pursuit of their game.

Interactive Fiction at Hyperizons

http://www.duke.edu/~mshumate/hyperfic.html

The Web is spawning a new kind of literature—interactive fiction. This genre includes non-linear stories where the reader makes decisions that affect the course of the plot; it also includes, collaborative stories that are created on the Web by many people at once. For a glimpse of this fascinating new phenomenon, part literature and part entertainment, stop by the Hyperizons Hypertext Fiction page. It's a compendium of the many interactive and hypertext works of fiction you can read and take part in on the Web.

Web games with Sprawl

http://sensemedia.net/sprawl

First, there were MUDs (Multi-User Dungeons) and MOOs (Object-Oriented MUDs)—text-based interactive games on the Internet. Users would log in, assume an identity, and begin exploring a virtual world unto itself. Along the way, you could interact with other players, create and move objects, and help build the world.

Now, at the Sprawl, MOOs are taken to the next level. With the addition of a Web interface, it's easier than ever to explore the virtual world of the MOOs here. Plus, MOO players are no longer limited to plain text—they can use all the graphical and formatting power of the Web to create complex documents that enrich the MOO experience. Check it out!

Pets

The sites listed here can help you pick a pet, decide on a breed, and learn how to take care of your animal companion once you have one. Generally, these sites are maintained by pet owners who are committed to one particular kind of pet, and the sites often reflect these owners' particular preferences. But what better place to turn for expert advice than to someone who loves the same kind of pet as you do?

Doggy Information on the Web

http://www.io.com/~wilf/dogs/index.html

Despite the cutesy title, Doggy Information on the Web is a formidable resource for dog owners and prospective dog owners. It consolidates a lot of facts not easily available elsewhere. The Breed FAQs page assembles lengthy and informative FAQs on dozens of breeds from Airedale Terriers to Vizslas. There's also a wealth of information on keeping dogs and taking care of them, pictures of many dogs, and some links to merchants providing dog accessories and equipment. Plus, check out the links to dogs' home pages around the Web.

Feline Information Page

http://www.best.com/~sirlou/cat.shtml

Cat fanciers will want to start their Web-browsing at this nicely organized page. It's a useful collection of practical, historical, and philosophical information on cats from a real cat lover. Articles on care and nutrition will be of help to current cat owners, and an article on the various breeds might help you make up your mind if you're thinking of buying a cat. The page also has links to cat FAQs, newsgroups, and home pages featuring cats.

Aquarium and Fish Stuff

http://rampages.onramp.net/~clawson/fish/

There's no original content on this site, but a heckuva lot of links to fish and aquarium pages around the Web. It makes sense to start here if you're looking for info on freshwater or saltwater aquaria, fish species, and the care and feeding of pet fish. It may be the biggest collection of fish links on the Web.

Fig. 15.10
Fish aficionados can investigate exactly what their tank dwellers are up to on the Aquarium and Fish Stuff page.

The Hamster Page

http://www.tela.bc.ca/hamster/

Hamsters make cute and convenient pets for people who don't have a lot of room or big yards. They're also the first pet many kids own. So why is it so hard to find hamster information on the Internet? It isn't if you turn to the Hamster Page. The maintainer of this site has divided the links into Useful Hamster-Related Resources, including FAQs, breed information, care, and more; and Useless Hamster-Related Resources, which are mostly pages featuring pictures of pet hamsters. Still, even the useless links can be fun!

Paulson's Rabbit World

http://pages.prodigy.com/CA/timp/rabbit.html

Maybe you haven't considered rabbits as pets, but why not? They're smart, lovable, and—believe it or not—very trainable. Find out all about these furry pets at Paulson's Rabbit World page, which includes recommendations on where to keep rabbits, what to feed them, and how to keep them healthy and happy.

Iguanas: Dupree's Home Page

http://iguana.images.com/dupree/

Dupree is an iguana, and the star of the "IguanaCam," a page featuring a live picture (it's updated every few minutes during daylight hours, Pacific time) of this pet iguana. The IguanaCam page is part of this site, but you'll also find useful information on the care and feeding of iguanas here. Check out "Dupree's tips for obtaining an iguana and keeping it happy" and, for links to other iguana resources on the Internet, "Iguana stuff on the Internet."

Collectibles

These sites deal with collections and collectible objects. Turn to these sites for historical background, catalogues, and buyer's guides, as well as links to dealers around the world.

Antiques

http://www.ic.mankato.mn.us/antiques/Antiques.html

Directed at the beginning collector, the Antiques & Collectibles site has two key parts. The first is an Antiques Index—a list of collectible things, many with links to further information on collecting this type of item. The second is a guide to buying antiques, including pointers for choosing and negotiating with an antiques dealer. Friendly and helpful, this site should be on any collector's hot list.

Stamp Universe

http://www.stampworld.com/index.html

This site aims to be a complete resource for stamp collectors, amateur and professional. It's got lists of dealers and upcoming stamp shows, so you can find a place to buy and sell your stamps. There's also a dictionary of philately (stamp-collecting) terms, and several other useful Web pages for stamp collectors.

Rockhounds Information Page

http://www.rahul.net/infodyn/rockhounds/rockhounds.html

This is a big page that gathers information for rockhounds and mineral and gem collectors. Among other things, it gives you access to rock and mineral shops, pictures of and articles about various collectible rocks, and general earth science and paleontology information. Finally, there's a software library and links to the personal home pages of a number of rockhounds.

Crafts and Other Pursuits

Some hobbies require years of study to truly master. The following sites cover these harder-to-learn crafts and skills. When you use the Web, you may be able to accelerate your learning process—after all, why reinvent the wheel?

Origami

http://www.usis.com/~barber/origami/

If you've ever wanted to learn how to fold paper sculptures, now's the time to do it. Alex Barber, a graphic artist, maintains this easy-to-use site that contains lots of origami diagrams, with instructions. The diagrams are in PDF format, so you'll need Adobe's Acrobat document viewer to look at or print them, but the viewer is free; Barber provides a link so you can download the viewer right from this page. Very nice! It's hard to imagine a simpler way to learn origami online.

WoodWeb

http://www.woodweb.com/woodweb.html

This information-rich site is aimed at professional woodworkers and the woodworking industry, but hobbyists will also find it useful. Concentrating on providing lots of textual information rather than splashy graphics, the pages here will load quickly even if you don't have a fast connection. Among the resources here are the "Wood Doctor" who answers tough woodworking questions, an industry index listing suppliers of materials and equipment, and articles from a couple of woodworking magazines.

Paper Airplane of the month

http://pchelp.inc.net/paper_ac.htm

Every month, this site features a new paper airplane design, complete with directions, diagrams, and a picture of what it will look like when finished. It's a nifty site to send your kids to, or go there yourself before you take that stack of paper to the recycling bin!

Ham Radio: The Amateur Radio Web Server

http://www.acs.ncsu.edu/HamRadio/

Before the Web, Ham Radio was the primary way people from around the world could "virtually" meet, talk, and share information. You'd think that the advent of the Internet would spell the demise of ham radio. Not so! In fact, computers and ham radio go together quite well. Here's where you'll find information about amateur radio, learn how to get a license, get the latest news from the world of ham radio, and find lots of technical information that will help you improve your transmission and reception.

Ballroom Dancing: the Dancescape home page

http://wchat.on.ca/dance/pages/dscape.htm

Dancescape is where you'll find information about the sport of competitive ballroom dancing. Upcoming events and competitions are listed here, along with organizations you may want to contact if you'd like to get involved. If you're looking to learn how to do ballroom dances, go to the section titled The World of Ballroom Dancing and read the articles there; then follow the links to other ballroom dancing sites on the Web.

16

Science

● **In this chapter:**

- Examine other planets and take a ride on the space shuttle

- Would you like to visit all the Smithsonian museums and galleries?

- Virtually dissect a frog or check for current earthquake activity

- What can you do to save the environment?

- Discover sites that involve the whole family in science education

Einstein said that imagination is more important than knowledge. On the World Wide Web both traits are put to use because weighty subjects are presented in imaginative pages. ⊳

Science and technology sites have popped up all over the World Wide Web. You can find information for all the major fields, as well as some lesser known and unusual fields. Many of the science sites aren't as trendy as the less technical sites, but they are just as informative, if not more so.

The more "trendy" science sites are simply wonderful. The NASA site is full of great graphics and you could spend days digging through all the information at its home page, as well as all the NASA space centers. By the same token, you could spend a month exploring the vast museums and galleries of the Smithsonian Institution. Only on the World Wide Web can you see the Hope Diamond, Apollo 11, and African Artifacts without leaving the comfort of your home.

You can also examine the evolution of organisms from their respective taxa or time period at the Museum of Paleontology. If you prefer the leading edge of technology, you'll love to visit the Fermi National Accelerator Laboratory.

On the World Wide Web, you can also chase a tornado, see a comet strike Jupiter, study the human heart, or familiarize yourself with endangered species. You will also find environmental tips, and ideas for involving your whole family in science knowledge.

Explore the universe at NASA

http//www.gsfc.nasa.gov/NASA_homepage.html

NASA (National Aeronautics and Space Administration) is not only a great science site, but also one of the most extensive and entertaining pages on the Web. Space lovers will really enjoy this site.

Even if you're familiar with NASA and all its missions, you will still find many interesting facts, statistics, and history at the NASA Web site. A good place to start is with the time line that includes pre-NASA information as early as 1915. You can also find biographies of NASA directors, astronauts, and other personnel. Although it made my head spin, I enjoyed reading the National

Aeronautics and Space Act of 1958. The information on the space missions is my favorite by far. At **http://www.gsfc.nasa.gov/hqpao/history.html**, the documentation from the Apollo 13 mission had me spellbound. The other Apollo missions are just as fascinating and don't forget Gemini, Mercury, Skylab, Apollo-Soyuz, and, of course, the space shuttles. There's also in-depth information about the unmanned missions. All missions include incredible images and some include movies and sound.

 Most of the sites in this chapter are graphic intensive. If you watch your online time, as I do, I suggest you set your Web browser so it won't load images automatically. I prefer this to selecting a text representation of the page (which is an option) because I can choose whether or not to view any particular graphics. Choosing the text-only option will make many of the graphics unavailable.

The space shuttle site, **http://shuttle.nasa.gov**, is worth a visit because the pictures, background, layout, and content are fantastic. The amount of information available is astounding. You can find out all that's involved in a countdown, launch, orbit, and landing including the current status and plans. You can explore the USML-2, United States Microgravity Laboratory, and send in questions to be answered by the shuttle or ground crew. No problem. You'll find the crew's pictures and biographies and even their meal schedule right at your fingertips. The NASA TV and Tracking images are updated every few minutes and allow you to watch what is currently happening and to track the shuttle. Current photos and videos are also available. If you want information on previous flights, you can search the archives.

 The archives at the shuttle page only back up to STS-69. If you want information from earlier shuttle trips, you need to return to the NASA history site in the previous section. Specifically, all previous shuttle missions are archived at **http://www.ksc.nasa.gov/shuttle/missions/ missions.html**. If you're looking for information on the tragic Challenger launch, it was mission 51-l and its archive is **http://www.ksc.nasa.gov/ shuttle/missions/51-l/mission-51-l.html**.

Fig. 16.1
Follow a shuttle mission from count-down to landing at the space shuttle site.

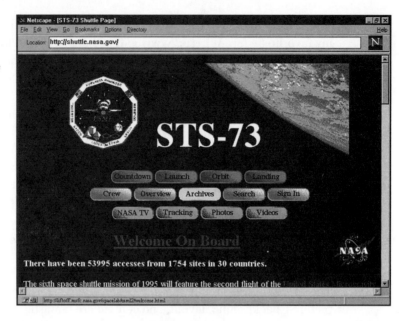

Many people think of Kennedy Space Center in Florida or Johnson Space Center in Houston when they think about NASA. The Headquarters are actually in Washington D.C., and NASA has centers and research laboratories throughout the country. You can find a complete list of all the NASA sites by looking under NASA Centers or jumping to **http://www.nasa.gov/nasa/ nasa_centers.html**. Each center has its own home page. Kennedy Space Center is my favorite of the 13 sites because it contains the space shuttle information, an extensive FAQ (Frequently Asked Questions), and links to other KSC servers, as well as other cool sites. I also enjoyed the Jet Propulsion Laboratory in California. Although its name is rather dry, the site is a bevy of planet images, facts, and even a basic explanation of how missions operate. The Ames research site could keep you busy for hours since the site's detailed home page images change every minute or so. The Goddard Institute for Space Studies is also a colorful site with information on global climate modeling, climate impact, bio-geo-chemical cycles, the earth, and other planetary facts. All the sites are inviting and enlightening.

Fig. 16.2
You'll be captivated by the incredible images of planets and stars at the Jet Propulsion Laboratory.

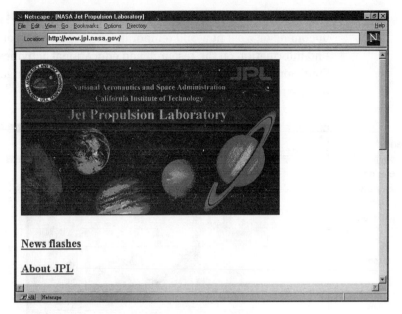

Visit the Smithsonian

http://www.si.edu/start.htm

I have always wanted to explore the vast museums and galleries at the Smithsonian. This isn't a problem since the Smithsonian is online at the World Wide Web. The Smithsonian is not a single place, rather it contains nine museums/galleries at the National Mall in Washington D.C., five more museums/galleries elsewhere in Washington D.C., two museums in New York, the National Zoo in Washington D.C., and research facilities around the world. The Smithsonian has millions (139 million) of items for display ranging from early artifacts to current spaceships.

The quickest way to investigate each Smithsonian site is to read through the overview. It will let you know each museum or gallery's theme and highlights. Sometimes you can view some of the attractions. For example, you can look at the Hope Diamond at the Museum of Natural History or the Foucault Pendulum at the Museum of American History. If you visit any museum, gallery, or the National Zoo, you can see what events and activities are upcoming or what new and temporary exhibits are available. You can also find information on the research and educational activities. From the Smithsonian Places page, for any individual museum or gallery, click its picture for a serious exploration of the individual site.

Fig. 16.3
You can spend days browsing through millions of items on display in one of the Smithsonian's many museums or galleries.

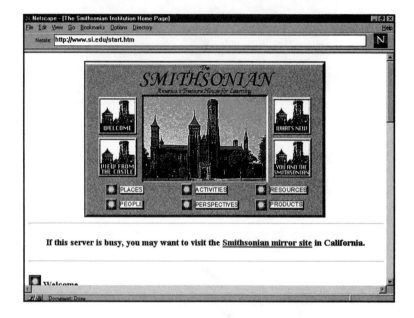

TIP **You can take an automated "tour" of the Smithsonian from the** overview site. The tour, however, consists of the same pictures displayed with each museum/gallery's description and doesn't allow you to jump to the museum's information.

As mentioned in the previous section, the overview will take you to a Smithsonian Places page for each individual museum or gallery. To visit that individual museum or gallery and examine all the exhibits and resources, simply click the site's picture. Each and every museum or gallery is worth stopping by. Just like the real Smithsonian, it's hard to cover everything in a short period of time. One nice thing about visiting the museums and galleries through the Web is that you don't have traffic and you don't have to wait for that large group to move out of the way to see your favorite exhibit.

The National Air and Space Museum is a definite must see. You will find man's journey from an earthbound creature to space explorer chronologized at the National Air and Space Museum. You can see the Wright brothers' plane, the Spirit of St. Louis, Apollo 11, and other milestone aircraft and spacecraft at the center of the museum. Throughout the museum, you will find sections for other early aircraft, World War I and II planes and radar, space and moon facts, jet aviation, the Einstein planetarium, and much more.

The Earth itself is as unknown and uncharted as space. This fact is supported by the incredible exhibits at the National Museum of Natural History. If you look at the museum layout, you'll see dinosaurs, tombs, gems and minerals, and much more. Be sure to visit the Ocean Planet for a look at some truly uncharted territory.

The National Zoo has what you would expect at any zoo, great animals and beautiful settings. The National Zoo also used some innovative ideas. Rather than just a wildlife zoo, it has evolved and is evolving into a "BioPark." It integrates wildlife with natural history, aquariums, gardens, and art to "illustrate the splendor of all living things."

Although you can't see every exhibit, you can see and read about some of the most commonly sought after items. The Smithsonian Encyclopedia attempts to answer some of the most common requests. This includes information on a Stradivarius violin, the Titanic, a World War I carrier pigeon, and other miscellaneous facts. You will also find advice on preserving antique quilts and silks, information on rare or endangered animals, and even coverage of the Loch Ness Monster.

Investigate the past

http://ucmp1.berkeley.edu/welcome.html

The Museum of Paleontology has all sorts of prehistoric facts and exhibits. If you think that paleontology is simply the study of fossils, you're wrong. Paleontology combines knowledge from many fields, like biology or anthropology, to define the origin, evolution, and sometimes the destruction of organisms. You can find information about this science as well as research documents, publications, and other facts at the Museum.

Smithsonian museums and galleries

Since this is the science chapter, I didn't mention many of the museums and galleries at the Smithsonian. However, all are worth a glance.

- Anacostia Museum

  http://www.si.edu/organiza/museums/anacost/homepage/anachome.htm

- Arthur M. Sackler Gallery Freer Gallery of Art

  http://www.si.edu/organiza/museums/freer/homepage/start.htm

- Arts and Industries Building

  http://www.si.edu/organiza/museums/artsind/homepage/artsind.htm

- Cooper–Hewitt, National Design Museum

  http://www.si.edu/organiza/museums/design/homepage/ndm.htm

- Hirshhorn Museum and Sculpture Garden

  http://www.si.edu/organiza/museums/hirsh/homepage/start.htm

- National Museum of African Artifacts

  http://www.si.edu/organiza/museums/africart/homepage/nmafa.htm

- National Museum of American Art

  http://www.nmaa.si.edu

- National Museum of American History

  http://www.si.edu/organiza/museums/nmah/homepage/nmah.htm

- National Museum of the American Indian

  http://www.si.edu/organiza/museums/amerind/nmai/start.htm

- National Portrait Gallery

  http://www.si.edu/organiza/museums/portgal/homepage/portgal.htm

- National Postal Museum

  http://www.si.edu/organiza/museums/postal/homepage/start.htm

Fig. 16.4

Explore the creation and evolution of organisms from the ancient era through today at the Museum of Paleontology.

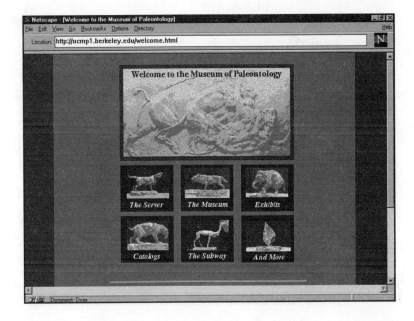

I usually take the museum's "Web Lift," a utility provided at this site, to find interesting exhibits. Information is sorted by taxon and geological period. If you're unfamiliar with a lot of the terms, you may want to take the Web lift to Any Topic for a listing of terms and their definitions.

Choose any taxon and you will find a thorough definition, a fossil record, and the taxon's life history and ecology. A taxon morphology can be interesting. This section covers a taxon's formation and evolution in great detail.

You will find fossils and their locations for each time period, Paleozoic, Mesozoic, and Cenozoic. The facts provided for each time period also include current land formations, ecological conditions, and other relevant data.

Although the Museum provides incredibly detailed information on all forms of life and time periods, everyone loves the dinosaurs. If you want to hop there quickly, its URL is **http://ucmp1.berkeley.edu/diapsids/ dinosaur.html**. This page attempts to dispel some dinosaur myths and replace them with factual data. Of course, the site wouldn't be complete without pictures of the different dinosaurs, and you'll find many pictures at the museum.

Fig. 16.5
At the Museum of Paleontology you can view images of dinosaur bones so vivid you think you can almost touch them.

A Quarky site

http://fnnews.fnal.gov

The Fermi National Accelerator Laboratory, a leading high energy physics facility, contains the Tevatron, the most powerful particle accelerator in the world. I know, why would you want to hurl particles at such incredibly high speeds?

If you're asking the question above, you need to read the overview of high energy physics. The results of the research in this site may benefit the medical and power industries and probably many others. To further understand what the FermiLab is about, you can also read the Beginner's Guide to FermiLab physics. The information in this guide builds a foundation that enables you to better understand the different functions of the lab.

You can find out what research is currently being conducted, the FermiLab's mission, and other interesting tidbits. I, however, like the tour the best. I find it amazing that you need a facility so big to study the laws of nature.

You'll also find job postings, schedules, and general laboratory information at the site. Oh, and don't forget to read about the discovery of the Top Quark. I didn't even know it was missing.

Fig. 16.6
Particles are accelerated to incredible speeds thanks to the Tevatron at the Fermi National Accelerator Laboratory.

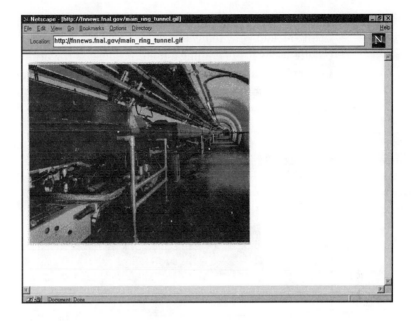

What's it like outside?

http://www.infi.net/weather

If you're planning a trip or picnic, you may want to check the current weather conditions at The Weather Channel. In the Weather section, you'll find the current forecast as well as tomorrow morning's and tomorrow afternoon's forecast. Currently, you only get national Weather maps for a broad overview. If you can't read all those symbols, you can simply check the predicted highs and precipitation. If you are planning to travel any distance, you may want to review some of the Traveler's Reports that detail the future locations of fog, storms, and other nasty weather.

Although the section was under construction at publication, The Weather Channel will soon provide any individual location's forecast. In the meantime, you can use some of the links provided under Weather and jump to a local site for forecasts. If you have any weather-related questions, you can email them to The Weather Channel. Many questions are answered in a week. The questions and answers are published on the page for all to read, but you may submit your questions anonymously.

The Weather Channel provides more than just forecasts. It provides the channel's history, meteorologist's biographies, and programming guides.

Under the Cool Stuff, you can enter current sweepstakes, preview a CD-ROM, and view many awesome video clips. You can also explore the requirements for becoming a meteorologist and working for The Weather Channel. Oh, and don't forget to look in the Weather Tool Box. It contains many useful items such as a heat index, weather term list, and weather-related shareware.

Fig. 16.7
Visit The Weather Channel for current conditions and other meteorological information.

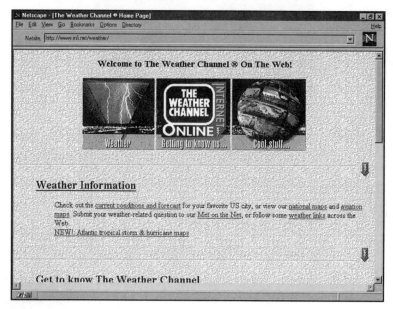

Storm Chasers

http://taiga.geog.niu.edu/chaser/chaser2.html

While some of us may hide under the covers at the first crack of thunder, others grab a camera, hop in a car, and head out to the heart of the storm. If you're a storm chaser, you should hook up with other storm chasers on the World Wide Web. If you don't chase storms, you should stop by anyway and read some of the harrowing stories and see some wonderful pictures. Check out the FAQ if you're curious as to what storm chasing is about.

Although there are other storm chaser sites on the Web, I like the graphics and content at the Storm Chaser home page the best. An obvious must for storm chasers is weather reports. At this site, you'll find current weather and forecasts, including the latest satellite and radar images.

Chasers and non-chasers will enjoy the eyewitness accounts. Some of these people are much braver than I would ever be. The pictures in the photo gallery are astounding also. There are pictures of tornados, thunder clouds, lightening, and other violent skies. One of the pictures has a note that states that the light poles weren't actually shaking—the camera man was!

If you do chase storms, you should read the storm chaser's documents, the tornado talk information, and the Weather Service Interface Guide. You may also want to check out the other news and documents. If you're looking for a partner, you can find one at this site.

The whole big universe

NASA is certainly my top site for space exploration and information, but there are plenty of other sites on the World Wide Web that provide additional facts and images from space.

Hubble Space Telescope

http://www.stsci.edu/pubinfo/BestOfHST95.html

The pictures taken by the Hubble Space Telescope (HST) are truly incredible. Lots of sites have information on HST, but if you're interested in the best pictures, you should visit the HST's Hits 1990-1995. You can see a Supernova explosion, the birth places of new stars and maybe solar systems, a suspected black hole, and much more. These are just the "best" pictures. You can also find additional pictures and close-up shots by clicking an individual topic, like Saturn Storm, or by checking the archives.

Fig. 16.8
The HST captured a
Supernova explosion in
detail. You can find
this and other images
at the HST's Hits
1990–1995.

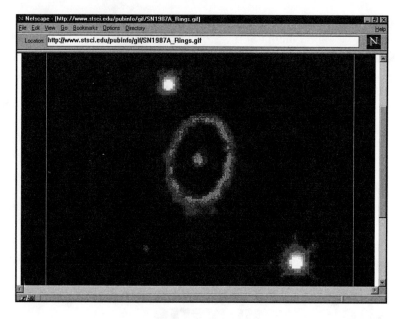

The other solar system members

http://www.virtualrome.com/virtualrome/parth.html

The planetarium offers great images and information about our neighboring planets, comets, the sun, asteroids, and just about anything else floating around. You'll find pictures from UFO reports that have yet to be explained, as well as a link to a UFO page. If that isn't enough, this site also provides several interesting asides. It has an interactive Astrology Chart, a weekly horoscope, alien games, and, of course, a Star Trek archive.

Will your next home be in space?

http://issa-www.jsc.nasa.gov/ss/SpaceStation_homepage.html

Well maybe not *your* next, but an international team is working on a space station. Stop by the International Space Station and be stunned by the incredible view. While you're there, you can read the documents on why we want a space station, commonly asked questions, specific health issues, and research plans. You'll also find a lot of interesting technical information and reference material. If you have any questions or comments, feel free to submit them.

What on Earth?

Space exploration is fascinating, but studying our very own planet provides plenty of intrigue. You can find Web sites for all of the basic Earth sciences like biology, geology, ecology, energy, and others.

How well do you know your own mind or heart?

http://www1.biostr.washington.edu/DigitalAnatomist.html

Well, the pictures are great, but the tests are impossible. The digital anatomist is a program from the University of Washington. The atlases are incredibly detailed. You can see actual cross sections of the brain and heart. However, I suggest you look through the labeled versions before attempting the interactive tests. I failed one miserably; I didn't realize the brain had so many parts.

The Virtual Frog dissection kit

http://george.lbl.gov/vfrog

Thanks to the World Wide Web, frogs aren't as nervous as they used to be. The virtual frog dissection kit is an interactive program that walks you through a frog dissection. After you have completed the dissection, you can then test your knowledge with the frog builder game. If you're having difficulty, check out the tutorial. I personally like this site because it's a pioneer in alternative teaching methods. Plus, it didn't smell nearly as bad as the frog I dissected in eighth grade.

Can we engineer people?

http://www.er.doe.gov/production/oher/hug_top.html

Although genetic engineering raises many ethical questions, genetical engineers continue to learn about how human characteristics are fundamentally written. The Human Genome Program is a national program to understand and determine the complete structure of DNA (deoxyribonucleic acid). To find out what this all means, what is being done, and what the future plans are, you need to stop by the program page at the Department of Energy.

The National Geophysical Data Center

http://www.ngdc.noaa.gov

Find out what's happening in the world of geophysics. Of course, that could be solid earth geophysics, solar terrestrial geophysics, marine geophysics, paleoclimate geophysics, and a couple other sections. The National Geophysical Data Center is a comprehensive site for environmental data in each of the previously mentioned fields. You can find a topographical map of your state, learn about the ionosphere, or see hurricane images provided by the Defense Meteorological Satellite Program.

The National Earthquake Information Center

http://gldfs.cr.usgs.gov

You can find current seismic maps for the entire world at the National Earthquake Information Center. You'll also find maps of the largest earthquakes and earthquake facts, like the most destructive or deadliest earthquakes. You can also jump to other earthquake home pages for additional information.

The Ecology Channel

http://www.ecology.com

The Ecology Channel is a page of current ecological events. You can read that wolves are back in Yellowstone park or learn about the campaign to rescue chimps from central Africa. I like the information about the Bears of the World and the Endangered Species. You should also read through the Earth Journal and the Home Planet Earth Gallery.

Join the American Solar Energy Society

http://www.engr.wisc.edu/centers/sel/ases/ases2.html

I have difficulty imagining the world without enough energy resources like coal, oil, and hydraulic dams. Someday, however, this might be reality. One great alternative is solar energy. The American Solar Energy Society facilitates the exchange of information concerning solar energy, distributes educational materials, and promotes solar energy technologies. You can read through the educational publications, press releases, and other resources to learn more about implementing solar power in the future.

Office of Fusion Energy

http://wwwofe.er.doe.gov

Nuclear fusion power is another alternate way of producing electricity, but many concerns arise with this type of power. The Office of Fusion Energy provides some insight into this controversial issue. You can read the current program overview, informational documents, and visit fusion research centers around the country.

A trip to the zoo

http://netvet.wustl.edu/e-zoo.htm

I have to drive over a hundred miles to the nearest zoo and some people are even further away than that. Using the World Wide Web, however, you can visit the Electronic Zoo without driving a mile. You can see reptiles, rodents, farm animals, primates, exotics animals, aquatic creates, and even fictional animals at the Electronic Zoo. You can also find veterinary news and laws, other zoo-related publications, and Internet sites. I'll admit, however, that I go to see the animals.

Fig. 16.9
Regardless of age, you should enjoy the many animal displays and exhibits at the Electronic Zoo.

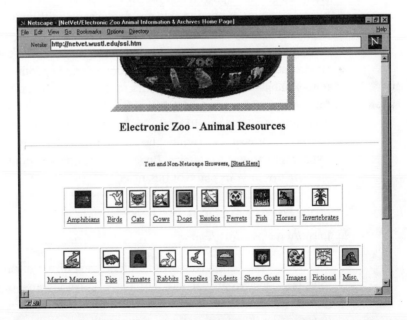

The Oceanography Society

http://www.tos.org

The oceans are another vastly unexplored region of our planet. To find out what is being done in the realm of Oceanography, you should visit The Oceanography Society's home page. You'll find many interesting articles in the magazine "Oceanography" as well as general society information. You can check into future conferences, gather information from the news system, or download related documents from the FTP sites.

Taking care of the planet

One of the hottest topics today is the environment. The World Wide Web provides advice and information on preserving the Earth.

40 Green Tips

http://www.ncb.gov.sg/jkj/env/greentips.html

Here are 40 easy tips you can follow to help save the environment. These are not a collection of boycott this and protest that, although those methods can be effective, but rather simple tasks you can do everyday. Take tip 9, which suggests using real towels instead of paper towels. That's easy, and it reduces waste and tree usage. If you do that, don't forget to follow tip 11 and wait until you have a full load of laundry to do any wash. Some tips you should follow regardless; the fact that it helps the environment is an added bonus. An example of this would be tip 15, which suggests keeping tires inflated to the proper pressure to reduce the amount of gas. You need to do that anyway to prevent damage to the tire. Be sure to encourage some of the work-specific tips at your place of business.

Rainforest Action Network

http://www.ran.org/ran

The Rainforest Action Network is full of great information, ideas, and opinions. It's also a great Web site with lots of great layouts, organization, and graphics. Examine the impact the rainforests have on global weather and the dangers that they face. You can also research ways you can get involved and the current RAN (Rainforest Action Network) campaigns. I also like this site because it has a kid's corner where kids can learn about the environment and the roles they can play.

Fig. 16.10
Drop by the RAN Web site to discover what impact the rainforests have on the earth and the dangers they currently face.

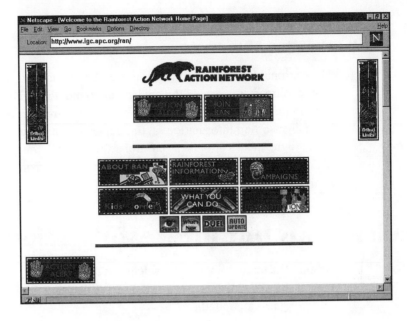

The original Sierra Club

http://www.sierraclub.org

Founded in 1892, the Sierra Club is one of the oldest organizations dedicated to preserving the environment. At its home page, you can find out what the organization is all about and locate your local chapter. You can also read through current publications, reports, and documents. Use the keyword search utility to find specific information. Request outing brochures and find a family vacation that will be fun, educational, and environmentally sound. You should also browse through the bookstore for some interesting selections.

Use Linkages to join the environmental movement

http://www.mbnet.mb.ca/linkages

Linkages is an international site for environmental and developmental issues. Check into the Convention on Biological Diversity, the Global Forest Policy, the Conventions to Combat Desertation and Drought, and many others. This site also provides information on developmental issues, such as child care, women's rights, and general social structures.

Environmental issues and your health

http://www.niehs.nih.gov

The National Institute of Environmental Health Science (NIEHS) has extensive resources concerning the environment and health issues. You can access current publications, as well as a library, and search the NIEHS databases. You can also find information on the Superfund, an ongoing research project to study the health effects of harmful substances in the environment. The National Toxicology Program is a hop away, as are many other related sources.

Miscellaneous but interesting science sites

Despite the many "ologies" for science, a few sites don't really fit into any typical science category. These sites are still interesting and provide some intriguing insight and ideas.

Get your children involved in science

http://www.npac.syr.edu/textbook/kidsweb

This is a terrific site no matter what your age, but kids will especially love it. The science sections includes topics like Astronomy and Space, Chemistry, Computers, Biology, Weather and Meteorology, and many more. All the information is easy to understand, and the site contains lots of wonderful pictures to maintain interest. You'll find links to those Hubble Space Telescope shots and the Virtual Frog. You'll also find neat experiments and intriguing facts. Don't forget to peruse the non-science sections.

Get the whole family involved in science

http://www.parentsplace.com/readroom/explorer/index.html

The Family Explorer catalogs simple clever activities that demonstrate scientific principles or facts. For example, you can demonstrate that if the polar caps melted, the sea level would change. All you need is a cup of water and some ice cubes. This is just one of the many interesting activities available at the family explorer. This would be a great site for science teachers, as well as parents. Even if you're neither, I'm pretty sure you'll still learn something at this site.

Sheer chaos

http://www.prairienet.org/business/ptech/

Yep, scientists have even documented Chaos. Chaos is actually a broad technology that was originally dubbed in a book by James Gleick, *Chaos: Making a New Science*. Chaos describes complex systems that, in a way, are unpredictable, yet stable. Fractals are popular changing images that would fall into the chaos realm. To understand, you'll just have to visit the Chaos network, or maybe you can't understand and that's the point.

Finding more science sites

There are tons of sites that deal with science and technology on the World Wide Web. Many aren't as entertaining as other sites for business or shopping. The information, however, is still excellent. To locate additional sites, you can visit the Yahoo Directory on science at **http://www.yahoo.com/ Science**. You can also use any of the search engines, such as WebCrawler (**http://webcrawler.com**) or Lycos (**http://lycos.cs.cmu.edu**).

17

Shopping

● **In this chapter:**

● **Browse through mega malls or small shopping centers from the comfort of your computer chair**

● **Pick up a Netscape server or an Internet inspired T-shirt**

● **Seafood, steaks, wine, coffee, and other tasty treats are at your fingertips on the World Wide Web**

● **Buy an environmentally sound product, find your dream home, or grab some diapers at specialty shops littered throughout the World Wide Web**

The World Wide Web has spanned the 100 miles between me and my favorite chocolatier and eliminated my fear of ordering flowers by phone. Merchants are utilizing the World Wide Web as a new means of reaching customers and business is booming. . . . . ➤

I don't think I'll ever have to fight the mall crowd or drive all over town for that one item again. The vast amount of products and services available on the World Wide Web makes shopping at home fun and simple.

For convenience, malls have sprung up all over the Information Superhighway. You can always find music shops, computer stores, fashion merchants, food courts, and flower/gift shops at these malls. In addition, you can often find financial services, travel agencies, Web page designers, and other services at the malls.

But not everything can be found at the mall. You'll also find plenty of unique, one-of-a-kind, out-of-the-way shops on the Web.

So grab your credit cards and let's shop!

Explore a consumer's future at Shopping2000

http://www.shopping2000.com

Wow, I think Shopping2000 has more shops and services than my local mall. As with any mall, just browsing is fun. Enjoy looking through the different books available at Barnes and Noble, the professional kitchen equipment at Chef's Catalog, and the antique signs at Politically Incorrect signs. Don't forget the food and wine section where you can pick up an entire meal: a steak, some wine, and for dessert, coffee and cake. To work off all those calories, you can think about ordering a Nordic Track.

 TIP **If you want to order direct from your PC screen, Shopping2000** isn't the place for you. You can order by phone, fax, or mail because Shopping2000 does provide 800 numbers, fax numbers, and addresses for the merchants. The quantity and quality of the products offered make it worth your time.

Fig. 17.1
Shopping2000 has enough stores with enough variety to keep the whole family entertained.

You also find lots of interesting gift stores including one of my mall favorites, the San Francisco Music Box Company. Not only can you look at the different boxes, you can listen to the tunes they play. Marshall Field's has lovely collectibles from Waterford, Spode, Wedgewood, and don't forget the Frango chocolates. For exclusive collectibles not sold in stores or galleries, visit the New England Collectors Society. To wrap and send all these gifts, run into Current and pick up the paper, cards, and stationary you need.

You don't have to drive to Donneckers, Pennsylvania to visit all of the town's cozy shops. You'll find the entire town right at Shopping2000. Besides the lovely gifts and knickknacks at Donneckers, this site prompted my interest enough that I inspected the guest houses and restaurants. Shopping2000 has plenty of other sites that make me want to travel. Delta DREAM vacation is a great place to check if you are wanting to visit the Disney gang. Besides the beautiful sounds, bird feeders, and nature trinkets that I could buy, the National Wildlife Federation made me want to put on a pair of hiking boots (which I would have to buy first) and head for the hills.

If you don't like shopping for music boxes, Shopping2000 still has plenty to offer. Besides the office and electronic equipment, Shopping2000 has an entire sports section. You can get shoes, equipment, or workout clothes. If you stop by Upper Deck Authenticated, you can pick up an item signed by your favorite sports heroes. Once you are tired of sports, you can check out the home and motorist section. Besides tracking down a car, you can get stuff like car covers at Beverly Hills Motoring accessories and even check into joining the Allstate Motor Club.

Children aren't to be left in the car at Shopping2000. The Museum of Fine Arts offers some wonderfully imaginative products for children as does the Right Start. Of course, all kids and adults love to stop in the pet store, and Shopping2000 wouldn't be a complete mall without the Pet Warehouse. Oh, and all those educational programs from the Discovery channel can be found at the mall also.

For great computer products and other gifts, visit ISN, Internet Shopping Network

http://www6.internet.net/cgi-bin

Found on the Netscape cool site list, the Internet Shopping Network is a terrific place to shop. This mall specializes in computer specific offers. You can always find great hardware and software bargains in the great deal list, and other reasonably priced computer merchandise is listed. You must be a member of the ISN to order any products, but membership is free and can be done right before you place any orders. The membership and order forms are all carried over a secure link, but if you're still uncomfortable, you can call in your order.

 TIP   http://home.netscape.com/home/whats-cool.html

Netscape has a team that compiles a list of sites that are "cool." These sites may contain in-depth information, unique products, great graphics, or they may just be flat-out fun. Many sites are or have been a cool site at one point or another but if you are looking for a good place to start your Web journey, you may want to jump here first.

Even if the computer deals aren't enough to hook you, ISN has plenty of other attractions. The Global Plaza is a mall within itself. You can find everything from books to watches. You can pick up a truck phone for your father-in-law, a pair of sunglasses for your boss, and a pearl necklace for yourself or wife. In addition to having an interesting name, Hammacher Schlemmer also has interesting merchandise: unique gidgets and gadgets like a natural wake-up-to-light alarm, sonic toothbrush, car phone holder, folding guest bed, and many other goods.

Fig. 17.2
Hammacher Schlemmer offers some great gifts for under $50 including this penny shooting bank.

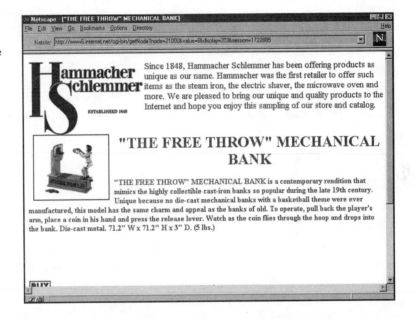

Internet security, let the buyer beware

Often when you're on the World Wide Web, a third party can access any information that you transmit. This means that if you submit personal information, someone might be able to read it. To prevent this, many shops and information services provide a **secure link**. This means only you and the person to whom you are sending information can see the information.

You can set your browser to notify you of security changes. You may have several security options. I

suggest that you at least configure your browser to warn you if you submit a form insecurely. Then, any time you try to submit information with a nonsecure link, you will be warned beforehand.

You may also want to check into ecash and/or netcash. These are payment methods especially designed for the Internet. For information on ecash, go to **http://www.digicash.com/ecash**. For information on net cash, go to **http://www.teleport.com/~netcash/index.html**.

TIP   **As you move around at the Internet Shopping Network you may** notice confusing numbers at the end of each URL. These numbers let the Web server keep track of sessions and who is doing what. You don't need to worry about them because the server will take care of assigning sessions and keep track of the numbers.

Unlike Shopping2000 you can order your Omaha International Steaks right through your PC at ISN. If you're interested in food, you should also check out the gift baskets and treats at Hilyard and Hilquist.

Although computer products are the ISN staple, you can also find other electronics. Check out the deals on phones, VCRs, stereos, and electronic organizers.

Welcome to the Super Mall

http://supermall.com/director.html

The Super Mall does not provide on-site ordering but it does have many services uncommon to real or virtual malls. The Super Mall is geared to selling the Internet. It showcases useful sites, Internet products, and Internet services. It has several opinion polls, such as "Favorite Web Browser" or "Baseball Strike." It also has current sports, weather (very current), news, and entertainment pages. But we came here to shop, so let's see what's for sale.

Who knows what you'll find in the special offers section. It may be anything from personal defense videos for kids to cuddly clip art. Sometimes the special offers may be an upcoming conference or interesting publication. You just won't know unless you look yourself.

Food, food, and more food. If you're here to check out food manufacturers on the Web, you'll find a great list at the Super Mall. Make sure you pop over to Ben & Jerry's home page, it is very entertaining. At the Super Mall, you can also get a one day diet, find survival foods, learn to cook Chinese food, and gather some cool online coupons.

If you own a business and are considering making an entrance onto the World Wide Web, you may want to hire one of the design experts listed in the Super Mall's Internet services. Check to see if the free Online Marketing

Strategy is still an available newsletter. You can also find suggestions on how to start and what kind of small business to choose. The Super Mall also lists different seminars and conferences that could be useful to businesses as well as others that are useful to the general population.

Besides the expected array of computer equipment, hardware, software, and electronic equipment, the Super Mall has some unusual listings. Cars and motorcycles are not too surprising, but what about dating? Yes, you can use the Super Mall to find your ideal mate or just a fun date. You will also find services to help you locate a new job or a new house.

Stroll through Downtown Anywhere

http://awa.com

If you prefer to stroll down a street and peek into windows, you'll love Downtown Anywhere. As you stroll—oops, I mean scroll—through the shops and read each shop's description, you get that lazy afternoon shopping experience.

The first stop is Main Street where the bulk of the stores are located. You'll find many familiar sites, but many unique stores also. Make sure you go into the Doomsday Brunette where you can use your browser to read a book. The shop offers Internet browsable books of science fiction, humor, or mystery. If you like fractals, don't miss the San Francisco Fractal Factory. In addition, there are plenty of computer stores, several book and video stores, music stores, shoe and clothing stores, a fishing equipment store, a Mexican pottery store, other specialty shops, and, if all else fails, you can visit the Five and Dime.

You also find some wonderful services on Main Street. Several computer support specialists are available along with some Internet training groups. The National Association of the Self Employed and International Writers Electronic Syndication Agency also have homes on Main Street. You'll also find several print services and a secretarial service.

The only problem with the products on Main Street is that you can only see what's available. You cannot order a product or service right then and there.

However, turn the corner at 5th Street and discover the developing online ordering district. When I last visited, only a few shops like MarcoArt Tee

Shirts, CyberShoes, the Speak to Me Catalog, and a souvenir shop were open. Many stores had opening soon signs posted, so I would suggest you check to see how many are doing business now.

Of course, any downtown has more than just shops and Downtown Anywhere also provides some of these other fun spots. Stop by the library or newsstand and read current publications, check out references on the U.S. Constitution, find interesting novels, and much more. You may need more than a day downtown if you plan to visit all the museums and galleries. The Smithsonian is in Downtown Anywhere as are the Australian National Botanical Gardens! I spent hours in these wonderful places and didn't buy a thing.

Fig. 17.3
Downtown Anywhere offers more than shopping. You can visit museums and art galleries, run by the Post Office, pick up the latest stock quotes from your financial advisor's office, find a great book at the library, and much more.

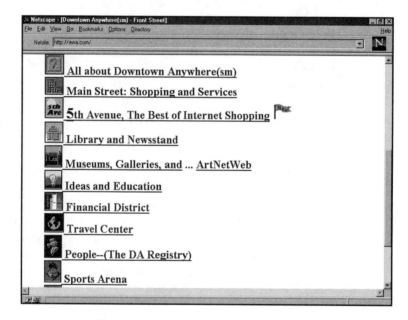

The Financial District is full of stock prices, business news, Morningstar's mutual fund analysis, currency rates, and lots of financial advice. If you need graphs, no problem, check out the colorful graphs for the S & P 500, Dow Jones Industrial average, and other performance reports for NASDAQ and individual stocks. Downtown Anywhere's Financial District is one of my favorite business-related sites. For more business information and sites, read Chapter 6, "Business and Employment."

A bargain hunters paradise is at Good Stuff Cheap

http://www.onramp.net/goodstuff

All you bargain hunters haven't been left out in the cold—Welcome to Good Stuff Cheap. This is a great mall with great products at incredible prices.

Fig. 17.4
GSC, or Good Stuff Cheap, lives up to its name. You can find some great deals and it's a lot of fun to use.

As all bargain hunters know, good deals don't last. For that reason, the list of products is updated daily. The products are always at least half off and usually much more than that. Pictures, descriptions, and retail and discount prices are provided for each product. If a product sells out, it is marked as such and removed the next day.

Many of you don't have time to stop by the GSC mall every day, but you're still interested in a good deal. What you need is a personal shopping agent. Someone or something to watch the bargains and email you when a bargain that interests you is available. GSC has such an agent. Simply check the categories that interest you, supply your email address and click the button. Any time something is offered in a chosen category, your agent will email you. If you're looking for something that doesn't fit one of the 24 categories, you can create a special agent. Simply type in your own category, click the Create button, and you have an agent that will watch for products in your personal category. Good deals disappear quickly, which makes agents an excellent tool because you get the information 24 hours before the product is listed on the Internet.

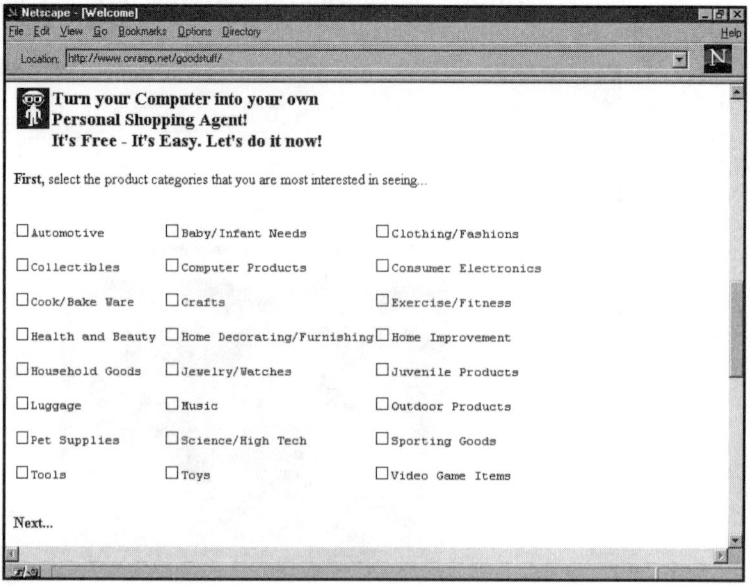

Fig. 17.5
Create your own personal agent to watch for and inform you of excellent discounts in the areas of your choice.

Explore the vast Empire Mall

http://empire.na.com

Another mall you may want to visit often is the Empire Mall. It has a large number of stores, an enjoyable interface, and fun monthly contests.

I love the Einstein "Imagination is more important than knowledge" shirt at America's T-shirt Catalog. If you prefer tie-dyed shirts you need to stop by DeBray Enterprises Inc. (You'll find some neat mouse pads and other accessories at DeBray as well.) Crazy Moon fashion has some torn Levis to go with your tie-dyed shirt and, while you're at it, why not pick up some Manic Power hair color in Vampire Red or Green Envy.

Why not pick up some new jewelry to go with your new wardrobe? Find quality diamonds already set or loose at Diamonds by Van-Daaz. You can find additional stones at the Gem Hut and check out the cool aquatic critters at Robert L. Straight Marine Jewelry.

Climb down to Bub's Bargain Basement and buy that helicopter you have always wanted. If a helicopter doesn't interest you, check all the other great deals on electronic equipment, old tapes, and Sega games. You can find other computer products and/or electronic equipment at Brooklyn North Software Works, Net Shop, or the Cyber Warehouse.

If all this shopping has made you hungry, Omaha Steaks International is at the Empire Mall also. I enjoyed the shop Salsa Express for great party dips. You can also pick up a gourmet gift basket at Tailgate Picnic.

The Empire Mall has plenty of unique stores like Blue Planet Surf Gear, which carries its popular brand of surf gear. Browse through the Gallery of American Artisans for truly beautiful items. Pick up a new rain coat or CD case at Boston Slickers. Find all the Halloween accessories you need at Tombstone Productions. Cool gadgets at Hammacher Schlemmer and Carter Enterprises. Oh, and don't forget VISI-Tech for fog free mirrors.

Fig. 17.6
Pick up a ghoulish mask, your very own alien, or a complete costume at Tombstone Productions.

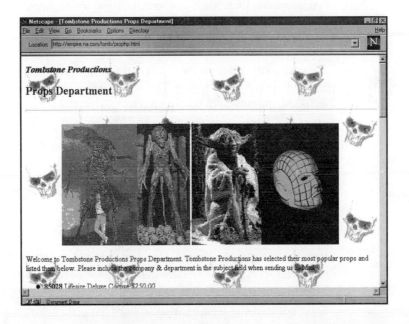

Don't forget to review all the services available at Empire Mall. You can find auto insurance, a good attorney, resumé experts, even jet aircraft consulting. In addition, Empire has online magazines, weather reports, and a dating service.

The Branch Mall, great products in a cozy environment

http://branch.com

Okay, there are many malls that you like to visit but you never actually buy anything. Then there are those other malls where you just can't help yourself. All I have to do is hear the words "The Branch Mall" and my hands start itching for the credit cards. I feel at home at this mall.

For one thing, I like the products. I can always find a great gift for myself or whoever I'm shopping for at a price that doesn't make me faint. For example, in the Gifts and Decorations sections, I recommend that everyone have their parents and/or grandparents fill out a Grandparent's book. It includes over 300 questions that, when answered, will allow future generations to share in the family history that is so often lost with the death of a loved one. You can find plenty of other great gifts at the Gift Connection or Gift World.

If you're looking for clothes, you can find everything from a Sputnik T-shirt to a tuxedo at the Branch Mall. I love the sweaters and casual wear at Stonewall partners, and if you're looking for NFL or collegiate wear this is definitely the place to be. If you eat breakfast in your car on the way to work, you may want to check into the clothing section for the commuter cover-up.

For true designer fragrances, visit the Fragrance source. You'll find not imitation fragrances but true designer perfumes, colognes, lotions, and potions at discount prices. You can also pick up other skin care products from Avalon, Louise Bianco, and others.

If you're hungry, the Branch Mall has the food to satisfy. I gained a pound just browsing. The Toucan Chocolates are great because part of the proceeds are used to save the rainforest, but the chocolate covered strawberries from Sophisticated Chocolates are also hard to pass by. You can order lobster from Nova Scotia or Maine. And if pet food is what you need, you'll find kitty and dog treats.

Fig. 17.7
A portion of the
proceeds from each
box of Toucan
Chocolates is used to
save the rainforests—
you aren't indulging,
you're helping a good
cause.

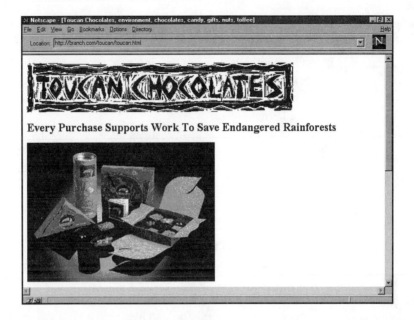

More and more malls

There are so many malls on the Web that I can't list them all. You can find links to several other malls at the Hall of Malls.

http://nsns.com/MouseTracks/ HallofMalls.html

In addition, here is a short list of some other great malls.

- Access Market Square
  http://www.icw.com/ams.html

- The Tarheel Mall
  http://netmar.com/mall

- marketplaceMCI
  http://www2.pcy.mci.net/ marketplace/index.html

- Cybershop
  http://cybershop.com

- Emall
  http://www.eMall.Com/Home.html

- Digimall
  http://digimall.com

- Avant Garde
  http://www.infoanalytic.com

Get your own Net products

If you suspect that you can buy Internet products on the Internet, you are correct. You can download free software, buy your own Web servers, find additional computer equipment, and grab a T-shirt or two advertising your Internet knowledge.

 TIP **For a really thorough list of the hardware, software, and other** computer products available on the Internet, read Chapter 7. While all the malls listed in this chapter have great computer sections, the Internet Shopping Network is my favorite stop for computer products.

Netscape Store

http://merchant.netscape.com/netstore/index.html

At the Netscape Store, you can pick up the latest Netscape navigators, handbooks, and servers. You can also find additional publications for setting up your own server, creating awesome Web pages, and programming guides. For those of you selling Netscape products, be sure to pick up some of the product literature. If you cannot find the answers you need in the handbooks, you may want to purchase one of the support packages offered by Netscape. Of course, all programmers know that after the initial product idea, the next step in writing an application is to design the T-shirt; and Netscape has many products, so you can get many Netscape T-shirts. Just hop on over to the Bazaar and pick up a shirt and maybe a coffee mug.

Assorted paraphernalia

http://www.icw.com/netsweat/netsweat.html

Net Sweats and Tees has some entertaining and fun clothes for Internet users. Even if you don't need a T-shirt or two, you should stop by anyway. The graphics and backgrounds are awesome and the captions are hilarious.

Fig. 17.8
Grab a cool T-shirt or two to advertise your Internet expertise.

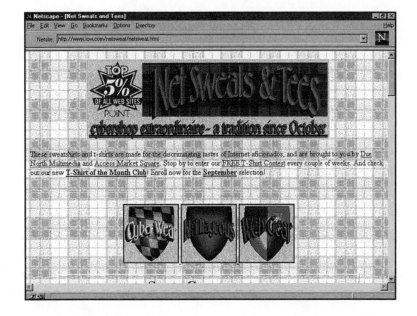

The Internet contains a vast variety of flowers and gifts

Some of the most prevalent products offered on the Web are flowers and shippable gift items. For example, the Branch Mall has nine stores dedicated to flowers and plants as well as other gift items the stores will deliver. But if you don't feel like going to a mall and looking for a flower/gift shop, the WWW gives you entrances other than the mall doors.

1-800-FLOWERS

http://www.shopping2000.com/shopping/teleway

I hate calling in flower orders. The salesperson asks, "How much would you like to spend?" I answer, "About $25." Then I give my credit card number and hope I haven't just bought $25 worth of rag weed. If you use 1-800-FLOWERS on the Net, you can actually see what you're ordering first. The salesperson doesn't haven't to interpret, "Something fun and humorous, but not flip."

Don't think you can only send flowers or plants. You can send balloons, cheesecakes, and even a steak!

Teleflora

http://www.shopping2000.com/shopping2000/teleflora

Another great place to look at flowers and gifts before you send them is Teleflora. You can send traditional flowers or plants, send flowers in a lovely gift, or choose a lovely gift basket.

PC Flowers and Gifts

http://www.pcgifts.ibm.com/index.html

You can send just about everything from PC Flowers and Gifts. Flowers are obvious, so how about a big fluffy bear instead? Maybe you'd prefer some jumbo shrimp or a fruit basket. You can send all these and more from PC Flowers and Gifts. If you hate elbowing everyone out of the way to find the card you want, then you'll love this shop. Browse through a large selection of cards from American greetings and have it sent right over.

Blooming Candy Bouquetzzz

http://www.marketnet.com/mktnet/bloom

Flowers are great but they die eventually. So if they're going to disappear, why not send a bouquet of…candy!! Blooming Candy Bouquetzzz offers products that are as tasty as they are beautiful.

Fig. 17.9
Looks like fresh flowers picked from a spring field, doesn't it? Look again, these flowers are really tasty pieces of candy and other delights. Stop at Blooming Candy Bouquetzzz and send an arrangement to a friend.

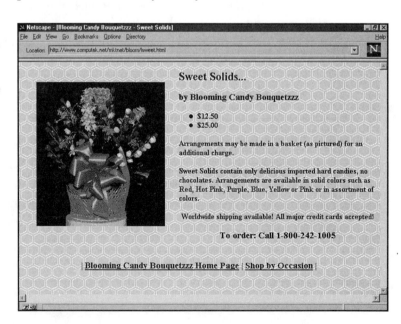

Discover a bounty of food and beverages

If you use any of the search engines on the World Wide Web to look up food, you are likely to get back a huge list. I like food, so I compiled a list of my favorite food sites.

Godiva

http://www.godiva.com

I know some true chocolate connoisseurs who think Godiva chocolate is just good, but I love it! Thank goodness they are on the Web because I have to drive 120 miles to get to a mall that carries these fine chocolates. Choose chocolates, caramels, gift boxes, truffles, and then order online. Don't forget to check the recipe section for some great desserts and treats.

Fig. 17.10
Test (and maybe fail) your willpower by visiting the Godiva Web site. It's hard to resist great chocolate.

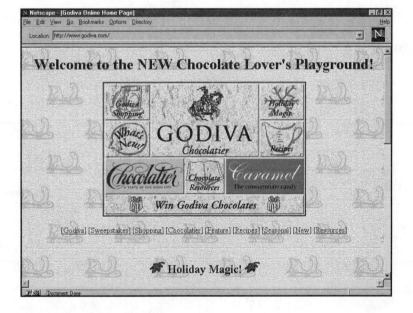

Gourmet Gift Net

http://www.aob.org/gift

For gourmet food, coffee, cookbooks, spices, and other products, visit Gourmet Gift Net. Besides great food and food ideas, you can also find designer dishes and trays for setting a grand table. If you need pots and pans for cooking delicious food you should stop by the Copper Kettle. If you're not shopping for yourself, you'll find an extensive variety of gift baskets and ideas.

American Coffee and Espresso

http://www.bid.com/bid/cima

I was impressed by the selection of coffees and teas at American Coffee and Espresso. You'll also find all the necessary accessories. You can pick up an espresso machine and the utensils to clean it. You'll also find creamers, filters, cups, decanters and more. If you own a company or just provide coffee to a large number of people, you'll appreciate the accessories in sizes and quantities suited to your needs.

Find that elusive product with some handy Internet tools

Finding exactly what you want on the World Wide Web can be tricky. Names are misleading, sites move, and it's hard to know where to even start looking.

- Fido: the Shopping Doggie
http://www.continuumsi.com/cgi-bin/ Fido/Welcome

When you are looking for a particular site, you might want to take advantage of Fido: the Shopping Doggie. Provided by Continuum Software, Inc., Fido will let you type in a product description, then Fido goes and retrieves it for you.

- Netscape Home page
http://home.netscape.com

When looking for shops or any other site, you can begin at the Netscape home page.

You can go to the Net Directory, which groups sites by subject or use one of the engines provided under Net Search.

- Point
http://www.pointcom.com

Another way you can search is to visit Point. Supported by Point Communications Corporation, Point reviews thousands of Web sites. When you use the search engine at Point, you get a list of sites just like any other engine. But the list links you to a review of the site. So before taking the time to wait for an entire site to transfer, you can read the review and decide if you really want to go to the site. You can save a lot of time that way.

Sam's Wine Warehouse

http://www.ravenna.com/sams

I loved Sam's Wine Warehouse when I was in Chicago and I was happy to see the same great selection of fine wines and spirits on the Web. You can trust the tasting notes and the prices are reasonable.

 TIP For a comprehensive listing of wine sites around the net, check out the Wine Page at **http://www.give.com/wine.html**

Specialty Sites

You can find an incredible variety of products on the World Wide Web. You can even find entire malls dedicated to a specific theme.

Earth Stewards

http://www.persimmon.com/earth

Visit Earth Stewards for products that are environmentally friendly. You'll find great books and records and some very innovative recycled products. It's amusing to see some of the tactless greetings you can send. Don't forget to read the environmental articles while you are there; they're free and informative.

Save the Earth Art Rock Auction

http://www.commerce.com/save_earth/auction/auction.html

Another site that lets you contribute to world betterment is the Art Rock Auction, where you bid on items donated by famous musicians. The proceeds go to the Save the Earth Foundation.

Spencer Gifts

https://www.spencergifts.com/spencer

A specialty shop itself, you can find some unusual and fun items at Spencer Gifts. Need a lava lamp, a neon Budweiser sign, or a Star Trek phone? Find these items and more when you drop in Spencer Gifts.

dotSpiegel

http://www.ravenna.com/sams

One of my favorite catalogs for fashion, home furnishings, and more is online on the World Wide Web. You'll find more than just the catalog online. You'll also find special deals, recipes, gardening advice, wardrobe advice, and more!

Burlington Coat Factory

http://www.coat.com/ burlington

Don't let the name fool you. While you can find great coats at Burlington Coat Factory, you can also find baby items, clothes, and linens. When I visited, the only products I could view were the baby products, but the site was under construction. You should see what's available now. Even if the site isn't finished, it includes a store locator so you can find a store near you.

Automobiles

Believe it or not, you can shop for a car over the Internet. Check out the following sites to learn more about it.

Dealer Net

http://www.dealernet.com/point

If you're in the market for a new car, stop by DealerNet. Find information on all types of cars, locate a dealer and make an appointment, and even read your credit report. You can also find information on used cars, special interest cars, RVs, and boats.

AutoMall

http://www.automall.net

Do you know what kind of car you want but now you just want to find the best deal? Before you buy, make sure you can't get a better deal at AutoMall. Simply submit your requirements and the nearest AutoMall Online dealer will send you a proposal. These proposals are supposed to be lower than any you'll find elsewhere. You can look for both new and used vehicles.

Auto-by-Tel

http://autobytel.com

Similar to AutoMall, you can submit your automobile request to Auto-by-Tel. Within 48 hours a registered Auto-by-Tel dealer will respond. Auto-by-Tel prices are supposed to be at wholesale prices.

Real Estate

If you're moving and want to buy a house, get an idea of price range and locale by visiting the following sites.

World Real Estate Network

http://www.wren.com

Home buyers, this is your site. Search for the perfect house around the globe with the World Real Estate Network. For U.S. listings, you click a state and then you search by city, county, price range, minimum number of bedrooms, and any combination thereof. You'll also find international listings, industrial sites, farms, and ranches.

Listing Link

http://198.147.75.21/index.htm

If you're looking for a new home, some acreage, or a commercial site for your new business, stop by Listing Link. You can search by city, price, and neighborhood.

International sites

No longer do you have to travel to visit shops in other countries. You can use the Web.

The London Mall

http://www.londonmall.co.uk/default.htm

Our friends across the Atlantic know how to build a mall. You find great stores like Eton Antiques, Mayor Sworder & Co. Ltd., or Callhaven PLC at the

London Mall. But you can also find a job, gather tourist information, learn about spread betting, and much more. If you are going to visit London make sure you check out Arthur's pub guide for great food and fun.

Fig. 17.11
Offering a little more than clothes, computers, and food, take a trip across the ocean and browse through the London Mall.

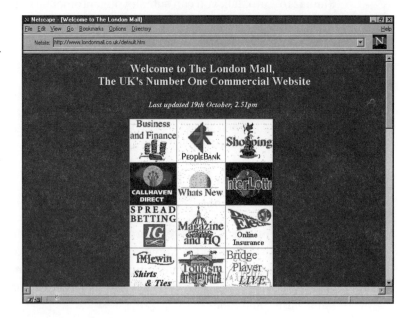

MexPlaza

http://mexplaza.udg.mx/Ingles

For more international flavor, visit MexPlaza. You'll find great shops, wares by Latin American artists, local job listings, real estate, and more. In addition, the graphics are great.

The South African Wine Express

http://www.aztec.co.za/biz/africa/wine.htm

South Africa may not be the first place you would look for fine wines, but you should explore the interesting selections at the South African Wine Express. You can find wines grouped by varietal (grape type) or producer. The prices shown are in South African Rands, but a converter is included.

Miscellaneous Shops

You'll find all kinds of shops via the World Wide Web. Here are a few that you may be interested in.

Parents Place.com

http://www.parentsplace.com/index.html

If you have or plan to have any children you should visit Parents Place.com. You can find baby food, diapers, books, toilet trainers, and many other great baby products. You can also talk with other parents, find support for children with learning disabilities, read parenting articles, and find out about the Nanny Tax.

Virtual Toys

http://www.halcyon.com/uncomyn/home.html

Hate fighting those Christmas crowds for toys? Well, you can either buy early or check out Virtual Toys. However, this is not your usual toy store. You'll find a Martian Popping Thing, Dragon Ball Z figures, and other oddities. This store offers some alternatives just in case all the X-men are gone again this year.

Star Shop

https://www.bendtech.com/marketplace/starshop/index.html

Do you like Star Trek or Star Wars? Then you need to run into the Star Shop and pick up some merchandise. You can find videos and books of your favorite movies or TV episodes, but you'll also find key chains, mugs, T-shirts, and much more memorabilia.

CD World

https://gate.cdworld.com

You can find almost as many music stores as computer stores on the World Wide Web. My favorite, however, is CD World. CD world has an incredible selection as well as great prices. Plus it's easy to find the items you want and it's a fun place to shop.

Online Sports

http://www.onlinesports.com

Just about every item you could possibly want concerning every sport and sports figure you can thing of is at Online Sports. You can find a jersey for some Toledo Mud Hens player named Moses Fleetwood Walker. You can look for items by distributor, sport, player, item, and team. In addition to all the great products, you can also sign up to receive a newsletter, look at current sports-related job listings, and access other sport resources.

Ben's Fish Food

http://www.halcyon.com/guppy/fishfood

I told you that you could find just about everything on the World Wide Web. If need some plankton or mosquito larvae for you aquatic friends, swing on by Ben's Fish Food. You'll find great prices (including delivery).

18

Sports

● In this chapter:

- **The best sites for news and information about any and every sport of major interest**

- **Where can you go for helmet-crunching NFL action?**

- **Get the latest on the boys of summer at some great baseball sites**

- **Check out the limited collection of NBA and NHL sites**

- **What else is out there for fans of other sports?**

The Web has all of the helmet-to-helmet football action; the high-flying slam dunking and three-point hoops; the boys of summer hitting tape measure dingers; and body-checking, hat-tricking action on the ice . . . . >

You know who you are. You'd rather watch Jerry Rice go deep than see David Hasselhoff (or Pamela Anderson Lee) in *Baywatch*. You prefer Chris Berman's nicknames and that familiar "da da da...da da da!" refrain to poetry or classical music. Admit it. You're a sports fan and there's no cure.

Sports fans of all ilks have flocked to the Web. And the major players in the sports business have come to join them. You'll find that most of the major leagues have set up shop on the Web, as have ESPN, *Sports Illustrated*, and some of the major broadcast networks.

This chapter focuses on sites that have broad coverage of a range of sports or a single sport. You won't find specific coverage of individual teams here; there are just too many to cover in a book like this and if you cover one, you have to cover them all to be fair to all fans. (You will find some pointers to lists of team sites though.) And if your sporting interests lean toward broomball, yachting, curling, or any of the other lesser known sports, use one of the search or directory pages listed in Chapter 11, "Internet and Web Information," to find sites of interest. I've stuck with sites that cover the most popular sports that will be of the broadest interest to most readers.

So snap on your chin strap, lace up your high-tops, step into the batter's box, or just pop open a cold one, and jump into the wide world of Web sports.

This is not the Deuce, it's ESPNET SportsZone

http://espnet.sportszone.com

If you're looking for an all-purpose general sports news and information site, ESPN takes the MVP award with ESPNET SportsZone. Who better to bring you up-to-date news and in-depth features than the most widely subscribed to cable TV channel? (Yes, more cable companies carry ESPN than any other cable channel, including MTV and CNN.)

Fig. 18.1

You'll feel like you're on the set of ESPN with Chris Berman at ESPNET.

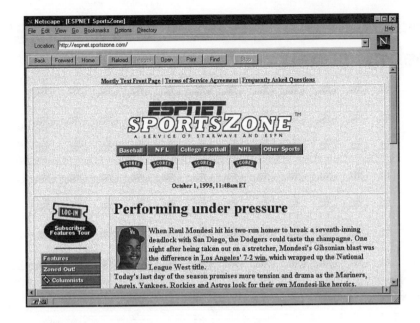

One layer of information here is the full sports news. You'll get all of the expected game summaries and statistics for all of the major sports. (If it's on ESPN, you'll find coverage of it on ESPNET.) What really adds value to this site though is the second layer of information. This is where you'll find in-depth feature stories from the games' leading analysts. Some of these stories are from ESPN broadcasts, others are on ESPNET only (not seen on TV). A link to the ESPN studios gives you access to familiar multimedia clips from the show (da da da…da da da!), a chance to send questions to the on-air personalities (which may get answered on air during special online segments of shows like *NFL Gameday*), and information on ESPN (and the Deuce) TV events.

As a final bonus, this site offers some special features for subscribers. For a low monthly or annual fee, subscribers get additional news and analysis. Some of the additional subscriber features include AP sports photos, enhanced sports coverage like depth charts and injury reports from *Pro Football Weekly*, and graphics depicting quarter-by-quarter shot attempts in NBA playoff games. As long as the price is right here, this is a real bargain for sports information. You'd pay much more than this for a fraction of the information in the form of printed sports magazines and journals.

This site will have you coming "back, back, back" (no apologies to Chris Berman) for more on a regular basis.

Catch baseball fever at Major League Baseball @BAT

http://www.majorleaguebaseball.com/mlb/

This is the official Major League Baseball site. During the season, you'll find box scores here as well as special stories updating you on pennant races, playoffs, and the World Series. Expanded box scores give you not just the inning-by-inning scores and summary players statistics, but also include a breakdown of hits (by singles, doubles, and so on), player's fielding statistics (put-outs and assists), a complete rundown of substitutions, errors, double plays, and other plays of note, and complete statistics for pitchers.

Fig. 18.2
Don't get pine tar on your mouse when visiting @BAT.

The MLB Photo Galley area highlights some of the leagues' biggest stars. It provides a photo and story about a player's major accomplishment for the year.

In addition to the news and highlights, watch for special events and contests. During the 1995 pennant race, for example, there was a 1995 Batter Up contest that gave away tickets to Game 4 of the World Series in 1995 for the winner of this online trivia contest. Don't expect patsy questions here. Tough questions like, "What is the last name of the tenth Oriole second baseman to play with Cal Ripken, Jr. since July 1, 1982?" are what stand between you and victory. (Give yourself 20 points if you know the answer is Juan Bonilla.)

Carrying the torch: 1996 Olympics

http://www.atlanta.olympic.org

Here is the official home of the 1996 Olympics. Prior to the games, you'll find ticket-ordering information, descriptions of the 26 sports and 37 disciplines featured at the 1996 Olympics (including video clips), and travel information for those planning to attend. During the games, look for the addition of scores and highlights.

Fig. 18.3
Check out news on 1996's Centennial Olympiad in Atlanta.

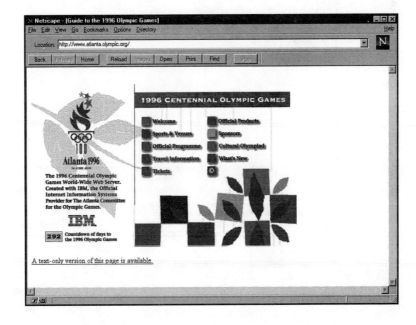

Check the set, bring the heat, watch them bail: Volleyball

http://www.volleyball.org/

Did you know that volleyball was developed over 100 years ago as an alternative to basketball for middle age men who needed exercise but wanted less physical contact than hoops? Maybe that explains my renewed interest in the game in the last few years. Worldwide, volleyball is played by over 800 million players, placing it second only to soccer in sports participation.

Fig. 18.4
Dig this! It's the best volleyball on the Web.

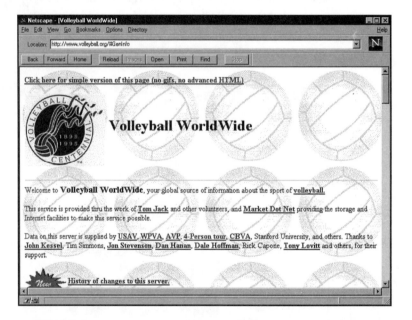

Other Olympic sites

The 1996 summer games aren't the only games in town and the official site isn't the only place to look for info. Here's a short list of other Olympic related sites:

• 1998 Winter Olympics

http://www.linc.or.jp/Nagano/index.html

• Atlanta Journal Constitution

http://www.ajc.com/

• NetLanta

http://www.intadv.com/olympic.html

At this large Web site, you'll find information about all of the professional volleyball tours, including the popular 2 man beach AVP tour and the Bud Light 4 on 4 women's and men's tours. There's also a wealth of information on collegiate and Olympic volleyball and the FIVB, which is the international tour sanctioning body. Beginning and advanced players will find useful information here from recommendations on balls and shoes to abridged versions of rules for referees and players.

General sports information and news

The sites covered in this section are the best places to look for information and news about all of the major sports. These news and information services generally feature stories and statistics that are updated regularly (some updated as often as every minute, others on an hourly or daily basis).

FoxSports

http://www.foxsports.com/sports/index.html

Regardless of where you stand on Fox's coup to win the contract for coverage of the NFC, you'll want to check out this Web site. In addition to NFL scores that are updated every two minutes during games, there are sports news, trivia contests, and fantasy football. Fox also has an NHL broadcast contract, so look for some hockey coverage during the NHL season.

Fig. 18.5
The NFL on Fox is just part of the story at the FoxSports Web site.

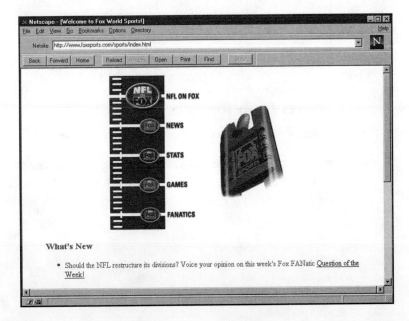

NandO

http://www.nando.net/SportServer

NandO's goal is to be the most complete source of sports information on the Web. You'll find coverage of all major sports and an online chat area. One unique special feature here is the SCORE (Specially Configured Online Readers Edition). Here you can customize your own personal sports page with the links and information you want. This makes it easy to get the information you're interested in without working your way through all of the information each time you visit.

Fig. 18.6
NandO has it all—
photos, stories, stats,
the SCORE, and more.

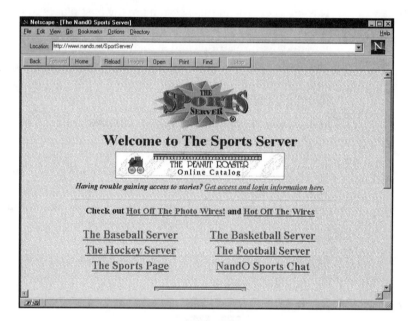

Sports from Reuters Online

http://www.yahoo.com/headlines/current/sports/

Reuters news service and Yahoo have teamed up here to give you an update summary of sports headlines. Stories are updated 24 hours a day, as breaking news hits. All major professional and college sports are represented here.

World Wide Web of Sports

http://www.tns.lcs.mit.edu/cgi-bin/sports

It looks as though the folks that maintain this site have not been taking good care of it lately. The links to highlights from "yesterday's" games for all sports are outdated and several of the links go to nonexistent pages. But, some of the archival information—like slam dunk photos—is worth seeing.

 CAUTION Unless you're running X-Windows, you won't be able to view the video clips from the NBA and MLB.

SportsLine USA

http://www.sportsline.com/

This site is for "serious" fans. The translation for "serious" means you need to be willing to pay to get access to most of the services here. Non-members can get a small sample of information such as sports news, odds from the major Vegas hotels, and memorabilia sales. Some special features include online chat with sports celebrities and contests.

Grandstand Sports Services

http://www.gstand.com/

This site offers sports news and statistics for major sports and fantasy sports leagues. You'll find some in-depth stats here that can't be found on other sports sites. This also serves as the official site for a couple of less prominent sports such as fencing and championship wrestling.

Sports Schedules

http://www.cs.rochester.edu/u/ferguson/schedules/

Use this site to get complete schedules for MLB, NFL, NHL, and other major sports leagues. Or, you can create your own custom sports schedule from any of these leagues.

Sportsworld.Line.Com

http://sportsworld.line.com/

This site features up-to-the-minute sports scores and news updates. There are also chat areas and discussion groups. You can even customize the view of the pages to suit your sports information desires.

Ultimate Sports Page

http://sportsone.radix.net/

Check here for sports headlines on most sports, games previews, and fantasy leagues. In the future, you'll be able to submit your own stories to this site.

CNN Sports

http://www.cnn.com/SPORTS/index.html

Not everybody has time for in-depth sports coverage. If you just need the quick scores and stats, this is a good site for you to visit.

USA Today

http://www.usatoday.com/sports/sfront.htm

This site features the top sports stories. You'll be pleasantly surprised to find better coverage and statistics here than in the *USA Today* paper.

Major League Baseball

The national pastime has struggled through some painful times recently. You'll find more than just statistics and scores at these baseball sites. The Web has become a very open and honest forum for discussion of the current state of the game and what fans are suggesting needs to happen to rejuvenate it.

TIP   **All of the major league teams and many of the minor leagues have** at least one official site, and sometimes several unofficial ones. For a list of sites devoted to specific major league teams, check out **http:// www.yahoo.com/Recreation/Sports/Baseball/ Major_League_Baseball/Teams/**. For the minors, the most complete list I've found is at **http://www.webcom.com/~rmd/baseball/ other_minors.html**.

Instant Sports

http://www.InstantSports.com/

During the 1995 baseball season, this service offered a play-by-play view of the baseball season. Its Web pages are updated to include descriptions of every play of a game. You can "watch" the game unfold on the Web. If you use a browser that supports automatic refresh (like Netscape 1.1 or later), the Web page will be automatically updated in your browser every minute during the game. This service was free to all users during the 1995 baseball season. For a small fee, you can receive this information via email instead of the Web. You have options for receiving updates after each play, every inning, or just a game survey.

While this site featured baseball only at the outset, look for it to add similar services for other sports in the future.

Dugout Magazine

http://www.io.org/~dugout/

This baseball magazine provides an index of its current and coming issue online. Selected stories are posted to the Web site. The stories and photos here have depth and appeal to the fans of the game; they're more than just box scores and summaries of current games. Real fans will want to subscribe to the printed version.

Baseball Hall of Fame

http://www.enews.com/bas_hall_fame/overview.html

I refuse to say anything nice about this site until Pete Rose is voted in. Until that happens, feel free to visit the "incomplete" display of baseball history and records on the Web. Get directions to Cooperstown, see a list of Mickey Mantle artifacts at the hall, and send your comments to the hall. (Be sure to let them know that you won't be there until Pete is!)

Fastball

http://www.fastball.com/

This site is home to batter-by-batter coverage of all major league games. There are hourly AP radio updates (which require Real Audio to listen to), and some very good chat areas. This site also has special in-depth coverage of a few teams. Currently, the extra coverage is limited to the Reds, Braves, and Rockies. This extra coverage includes audio updates from local broadcasters, stories from local sports writers, and other special features. (See the discussion of RealAudio in Chapter 11, "Internet and Web Information.")

Fig. 18.7
Baseball fans will appreciate the wide variety of services and information at Fastball.

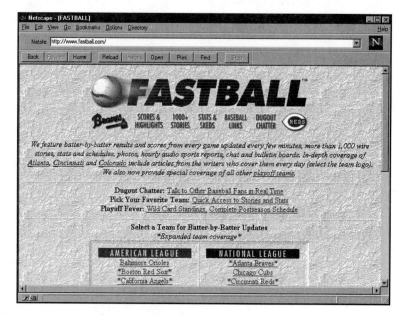

National Football League

You know what it's like on Sunday afternoons in the fall. You only get coverage of a couple of games on TV and you want all the news. You don't want to wait for Fox or NBC to update the scores every 15 or 20 minutes; you want to know the score now. And after the game, you want all the details of all the games, not just the 30-second summaries from the local news. You can find all this and more at these great Web sites.

Team NFL

http://nflhome.com

Here's the official page for the NFL and its teams. (Although you shouldn't be surprised if Jerry Jones signs a deal with American Express and Nike to put his official Dallas site elsewhere.) The contents of the main page here vary depending on what day of the week you visit. On game day, the first thing you'll see are current scores for all of the day's games. But there's much more here than current scores. The Team Talk area is a chat forum. (This forum is fairly active on game days, but it could be improved by adding some focused areas and having the entries show the time of the post, instead of just the day. Maybe it will be improved by the time you read this.) NFL personalities sometimes join in the chat. By the time you read this, the search function that helps you find player and team statistics, rosters, schedules, and records should be up and running too.

Fig. 18.8

That's grass growing in the background at Team NFL. Maybe some of the NFL stadiums should follow this lead and tear up the turf to plant real grass!

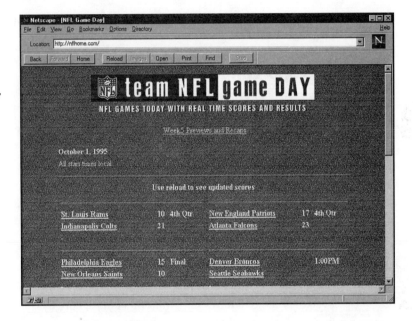

NFL Kids is just what the name implies: a special section with coverage aimed at youth. There's a chat area, bios of league stars in a question and answer, and, of course, there's coverage of the famous Punt, Pass, and Kick competition. Over 350,000 kids (including a female player who made it to the finals in her age group) participated in the 1994 competition. There's a list of famous NFL players who participated as kids, registration information, and tips from the pros for competitors.

SuperBowl Guide

http://www.imall.com/superbowl/superbowl.html

At last check, this was just some dated coverage of SuperBowl XXIX. Hopefully, you'll see an update here for SuperBowl XXX and beyond. If not, you can be sure that the Team NFL site will have extensive coverage.

The Pro Football Expert

http://www.he.tdl.com/~football/

What makes this site an expert? Read all about its handicapping software and football statistics database.

Professional Football Server

http://www.netgen.com/sis/NBA/NBA.html

Check here for an extensive list of statistics from current seasons and the past.

CBS Sports Radio

http://www.cbsradio.com/

Check out the NFL games broadcast on the Internet here using RealAudio. (See the discussion of RealAudio in Chapter 11, "Internet and Web Information.") You'll also find a schedule of games broadcast on "normal" radio by CBS Sports Radio and a list of affiliate stations by state and city. One neat feature is a set of links to weather forecasts for game day. This is available for most, but not all, NFL cities.

National Basketball Association

I've got some bad news for pro hoops fans: There's not much out there for you on the Web. Of course, you'll find good coverage of the NBA at ESPNET, NandO, and all of the other general sports sites, but there's no major NBA site at this point. In fact, I've even seen some personal Web pages for individual teams that have been shut down at the request of the NBA. What's the NBA thinking? That Web publicity is a bad thing? In any event, here are a couple of sites to get you started. Hopefully, there'll be more in the near future.

On Hoops

http://www.vidya.com/hoops/

This is mostly discussion and commentary on the players, teams, and NBA in general. There's a real wise-cracking and fun attitude to this place that fans will enjoy.

Fig. 18.9
If you take basketball too seriously, stay away from On Hoops. Fans with a sense of humor will like it.

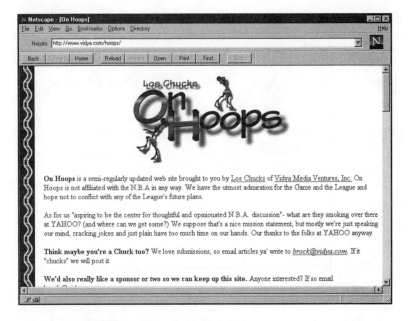

Professional Basketball Server

http://www.netgen.com/sis/NBA/NBA.html

This is a major archive of statistics from the current season as well as years past. From common statistics, like a list of all of the championship winners, to the obscure (winners of the Walter D. Kennedy Citizenship Award—don't look for Dennis Rodman's name here anytime soon), you'll find a wide variety of useful and useless statistics.

National Hockey League

As is the case with the NBA on the Web, good hockey sites are thin picking. But at least there are a couple of good officially sanctioned pages to get you off to a good start.

National Hockey League Players Association

http://www.nhlpa.com/

Check here for some interviews with players, get a bio and photo of a "player of the day," and play trivia.

Fig. 18.10
Get the inside scoop sponsored by the real insiders, the NHL Player's Associations.

NHL Open Net

http://www.nhl.com/

This is fairly typical for a league sponsored Web site. You'll find scores, statistics, merchandise (how would the pros survive without merchandise revenue?), history, and trivia.

Other sports sites

There's more to life than football, basketball, baseball, and hockey. Right? Sure! There's auto racing of all varieties, tennis, and volleyball just to name a few. And there's more than just the pro version. Plenty of good sites cover the college games. In addition, I've included some coverage of a few sports magazines and other odds-and-ends sites.

AutoRacing Archive

http://www.eng.hawaii.edu/Contribs/carina/ra.home.page.html

This site covers Formula 1, IndyCar, and NASCAR racing. There's a gallery of racing photos featuring all of the favorite drivers, race results and championship points standings, addresses, contact information for fan clubs and sanctioning organizations, and even some humor about the sports. Be sure to check out David Letterman's top ten reasons he should go to a NASCAR race or the top ten perks of winning the Indy 500.

Local Sports News

All of the sites listed in this chapter are great if you're looking for coverage of nationally (or internationally) known sporting teams and events. But where can you go to find coverage of your favorite local high school teams, small colleges, and other local events? You won't find these on the major sports servers. Your best bet is to look for a local newspaper, radio, or TV news station with an online edition that covers sports. Here are a few from selected cities:

- Indianapolis

  http://www.starnews.com/news/inddir.html

- Houston

  http://www.chron.com/fronts/chronicle/sports/index.html

- San Francisco

  http://www.sfgate.com/sports/

- Colorado Springs

  http://www.usa.net/gtwork/today/spt.html

- Huntsville, Alabama

  http://www.traveller.com/sports/

- Detroit

  http://www.detnews.com/

In the event that you don't live in one of these cities, check with your local paper, radio, and TV, your local service provider, or local friends on the Net to see if they know of sites in your area. (Most of the local TV station's Web pages I've checked out across the country haven't quite figured out this Web thing yet. Who cares about a picture of the sports anchor? We see his ugly mug every night! Give us sports news on the Web!)

American Racing Scene

http://www.racecar.com/

This site includes racing information for the NASCAR and IndyCar racing circuits. You'll find some excellent photos from recent races, schedules and results (including standings in championship point races), driver information, and fan club registration forms.

Fig. 18.11
You'll feel like you were there watching them go through the corners nose to tail when you see the pictures at American Racing Scene.

Gifts for Race Fans

Real race fans are easily spotted by their driving habits and race memorabilia. While a Web site won't do anything for the former, here are a couple of sites where race fans can add to their collection of race goodies:

- NASCAR

  http://www.netways.com/nascar/home.htm

- Formula 1

  http://www.compusmart.ab.ca/vtong/

SpeedNet

http://www.starnews.com/speednet/

From the motorsports capital of the world (also the home of Que Publishing), SpeedNet is run by the Indianapolis Star and News (Indianapolis' local papers). During May, this is the premier site for information on the Indianapolis 500, the greatest spectacle in racing. Throughout the rest of the year, you'll find information from many other motor racing venues. (The motto here reads, "If it's on four wheels, and moves very fast, we have it covered.") And of related interest, see the Indianapolis Motor Speedway's pages at **http://www.inetdirect.net/home/IMS.html**. These pages cover both the Brickyard 400 and the new Indy Racing League in infinite detail.

Competitor Sports Magazine

http://web.idirect.com/~compete/

This site promises more than just recycled scores and statistics. Check out its original in-depth feature articles that have a mostly Canadian twist. For example, to examine the effects of Mike Tyson's release from prison on the boxing community, one article interviewed kids learning boxing in Toronto gyms.

Sports Spectrum

http://www.gospelcom.net/rbc/ss/

Look for some feature sports articles that are about topics off the beaten path. Articles from the archives here profile Nebraska football coach Tom Osborne, former San Diego place kicker Rolf Benirschke, and LPGA golfer Barb Thomas. This is not your cookie-cutter Michael Jordan interview or Cal Ripken Jr. life history site.

SportZwired

http://www.sportz.com/~sportz/

This is a monthly sports zine. You can send in your email and recorded comments (in the wave file format) and see if they get published in next month's issue.

NBC Sports

http://www.nbc.com/sports/index.html

There's not much at this site yet. But, NBC covers the NBA and the NFL's AFC so watch for this site to grow. (Okay, there is some coverage of golf.) One interesting and unique part of the site are the pages about several nationwide participatory sports tours. Hoop It Up, Spike It Up, NFL Air It Out, and others give ordinary weekend warriors like us a chance to participate in major tournaments in cities across the country. The Air It Out final event (played by the tour winners against a few NFL stars) even got some TV coverage.

OverTheNet

http://www.imaginet.fr/~sdc/

This tennis site features news from the ATP and WTA tours. Look here for player info, tournament standings, and rankings.

Tennis Country

http://www.tenniscountry.com/

Look here for information about tennis clubs and tournaments around the world, tips to improve your game, and a junior tennis club. A Pro shop with apparel and equipment is in the works too.

Tennis Server

http://www.tennisserver.com/

This site features player pictures, official rules, a tennis FAQ, tips, and links to tennis equipment suppliers on the Web.

ATP Tour

http://atptour.com/

This is the official Web home of the ATP (Association of Tennis Professionals), which is the sanctioning body for men's tennis. This site has a wealth of tennis information. There are in-depth biographies and statistics for top players, descriptions of the "Super Nine" tournaments, a Pro shop, and descriptions of special events at tournaments for fans.

Volleynerd

http://volleynerd.saic.com/4man/

Here's a site featuring coverage of both the men's and women's Bud Light 4-on-4 tour. Schedules, results, TV coverage, and more are available.

Women's Sports

http://fiat.gslis.utexas.edu/~lewisa/womsprt.html

This site is acknowledged as the definitive collection of links to information about women's sports. While women's sports are under-represented on the Web (as they are everywhere), you'll be sure to find something of interest in women's athletics here.

College Football Hall of Fame

http://collegefootball.org/

At this site you can tour the College Football Hall of Fame (without traveling to scenic South Bend, Indiana) and play some college football trivia. The tour consists of text describing the hall and a few photos. If you really want to see the hall of fame, you'll probably have to go to South Bend after all.

GolfWeb

http://www.golfweb.com/

Find out what's new in golf and see what's happening on the pro tours here. There are also links to the many golf courses that have Web sites.

Online Sports

http://www.onlinesports.com/

The main focus of this site is an online sports catalog. Sports equipment, apparel, and memorabilia from several dozen companies are on sale here. There's also a job listing and resumé bank for sports careers.

Planet Reebok

http://planetreebok.com/

There may be something here of lasting value. If you find it, let me know. Otherwise, this looks like just a thinly veiled Web-based commercial. It's neat for a quick visit, but there's not much here to bring you back.

Spalding Sports Worldwide

http://www.spalding.com/

Spalding's site is focused mainly on golf balls and other golf products. You'll also find some limited information about other sporting goods. There is a search form to help you find information about products for the sport of your choice.

Sports Illustrated

http://www.timeinc.com/si/simagazine.html

Sports Illustrated puts the cover story from the printed magazine up on this site each week. There's an archive of stories from issues dating back to February 14, 1995. Other highlights change from time to time depending on the current hot sporting events. There's a good collection of recent sports stories and scores. It also has a photo gallery, early Olympic coverage, and *Sports Illustrated for Kids*, an online version of the kids' sports magazine. (The SI Web folks could learn something from SI for Kids. The kids' version is top notch!)

Fig. 18.12
The writers here really knocked themselves out to come up with that catchy Sox Appeal headline.

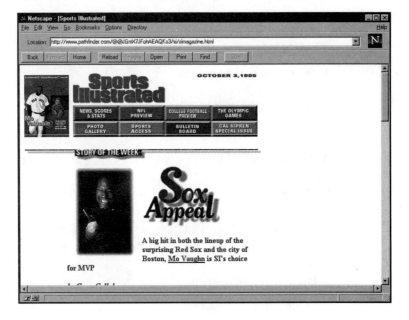

Sports Tours, Inc.

http://www.travelsource.com/sports/sti/

Watching the big game on TV is one thing, but being there is the real thing. Use this Web page to access a travel agency that specializes in sports road trips. Football, baseball, and major special events, like the Kentucky Derby and Indianapolis 500, are on its menu.

Lizard's College Basketball

http://bronze.ucs.indiana.edu/~rdannenb/bball.html

The NCAA hasn't wised up and created an official basketball Web site. Until it does, this site will fill that need nicely. This is the place to look for the most comprehensive set of links to individual team home pages (go Hoosiers!), conference home pages, statistics, standings, polls, and much more. If it happens on the college hardwood, you'll find a link to it here.

Logo Sports

http://virtumall.com/Logo/main.html

You can shop here for all of your authentic league sports apparel and collectibles needs. Well, maybe not all, but there is official merchandise for MBL, minor league baseball, NBA, NHL, NASCAR, and much more.

GNN Sports

http://gnn.com/gnn/meta/sports/index.html

This is mostly a list of links to other sports sites. But you'll also find some original content here covering the major sports.

College Sports Internet Channel

http://www.xcscx.com/colsport/

This site maintains a master list of Division 1a college sports sites on the Web. The sites are organized by sport (football or basketball), conference, or geographical region.

Minor Leagues, Major Dreams

http://www.deltanet.com/minorleagues/

Check out this site to order sports apparel from your favorite minor league team. Minor league baseball and hockey are represented here, as are other non-major leagues, like the CBA and Arena football.

Professional Bowler Association

http://www.pba.org/

This page opens with an audio clip of a bowling ball going down the alley. (It could just be cheap speakers on my PC but it sounded like a gutter ball to me.). The site has tour schedules for PBA events, a chat area, and links to other bowling sites.

19

Television and Movies

● **In this chapter:**

● **Search comprehensive, hyperlinked databases of movies, actors, directors, and more**

● **Read film and TV reviews from television shows, newspapers, magazines, and the Internet**

● **Get current television lineups and schedules**

● **Find out the latest Hollywood gossip, get the scoop on your favorite stars, and read exclusive celebrity interviews**

You'll quickly see why the Web is fast becoming a powerful resource for anyone who watches TV or movies. When you get tired of clicking the channel changer, grab your mouse and start clicking on the Web! . . . . ▶

magine a database of film information and reviews so complete that it lists every film ever made, along with the complete cast and credits, plot summaries, and even lists of bloopers that made it past the editors. Impossible? Not really—it already exists on the Web, and you can connect to it today. What about movie reviews, television schedules, and celebrity news? All this and more is available on the Web, usually in a searchable format so you can get directly to what you want. Even better, with hyperlinks, you can move quickly from a movie to its star to all the other movies that star appeared in.

One thing about film buffs is that they often collect vast amounts of information about their favorite movies, directors, or actors. The same goes for favorite TV shows—some folks just love to make lists of every Brady Bunch episode, or every episode of the X-Files, and to collect trivia and other facts about these episodes and their stars. The Web makes it easy for these people to make their information public, and to link it up with the databases of other film and TV buffs. Of course, you get the benefit anytime you want to know something about a rerun you just saw or a film you're considering going to.

The best sites in this chapter have been created and maintained by people who do it for the sheer love of TV and film, and as a result they're often a little quirky or downright unusual. These sites are rich repositories of information unmatched anywhere, online or in print.

Add to this all the self-promoting sites created by networks, TV shows, and movies, and you'll see why the Web is fast becoming a powerful resource for anyone who watches TV or movies. In fact, the Web is a natural fit with the many fan clubs, so it's not surprising to find not just one, but three, four, or more sites dedicated to a popular show or star. There's a kind of synergy between these sites, too, so you'll find that many of them list additional Web resources covering the same or related topics.

Find it all with the Internet Movie Database

http://www.msstate.edu/Movies/

Everyone has at least one friend who seems to know all there is to know about a particular movie star or director, or who has watched *Jurassic Park* 25 times and can recite the entire script line-by-line. When you want to know something about Cary Grant, you go to your Cary Grant expert friend, right? Now imagine you knew someone who had the same amount of knowledge about every movie ever made, about every actor or actress who ever appeared on-screen. You'd probably turn to him every time you went to the movies, right?

Fig. 19.1
Want to look up a movie or star? You can be sure to find it on the Internet Movie Database.

The Internet Movie Database is that friend. Its vast archives contain files on nearly 60,000 films, from the earliest silent films to the latest releases. Want to know about the career of an actor, director, cinematographer, or costume designer? The database has over 700,000 filmographies, with detailed information on individuals you never knew existed, as well as more prominent stars. The Internet Movie Database is a collective effort, spawned in UseNet's rec.arts.movies discussion, so it continues to grow as more and more people use it and contribute additional information.

Everything in the database is hyperlinked, so you can move quickly from, for example, *Pulp Fiction* to the Quentin Tarantino filmography to *Desperado* to Antonio Banderas to *Women on the Verge of a Nervous Breakdown*. Plus, the database features a lot of information you'll never find in a printed movie guide: selected quotes, lists of goofs (factual and continuity errors in the movie), links to reviews from UseNet, and multimedia clips (video, sound, and still pictures). Of course, everything is searchable, so if you want to know who said "I'll be back" and in what movies, it's a snap.

Of course, plot summaries are also readily available for most movies in the database. The Internet Movie Database even features a rating system based on the votes cast by database users. If you've seen the movie whose filecard you're reading, scroll down to the bottom of the form to vote on how good you think it is. The votes are automatically tallied and averaged to create a one-to-ten-star rating that appears at the top of each file.

It's hard to imagine a more comprehensive film resource anywhere, and best of all, it's totally free. If you're looking for film information, this site belongs at the top of your hot list.

The Web site for couch potatoes: TV Net

http://tvnet.com/TVnet.html

Think *TV Guide* on steroids. Think all-in-one Web and television resource center. Think combination television industry newsletter, job bulletin, and reference database. Think TV Net—probably the most exhaustive locus of television-related information available anywhere, let alone on the Internet.

Fig. 19.2
TV Net is the most comprehensive television database anywhere.

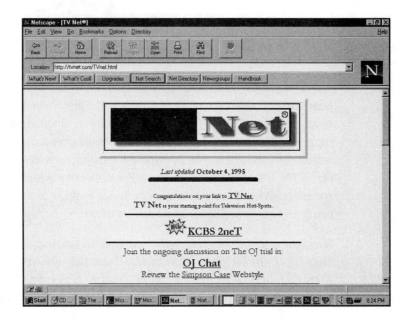

Okay, so it doesn't have the most attractive or well-organized screens to be found on the Web. But if you take the time to sort through the clutter, you'll find more than enough information here to satisfy even the most avid of couch potatoes. And television industry executives and employees will find plenty of ideas for new shows here.

TV Net's Ultimate TV List is an exhaustive roll-call of almost all television shows known to humankind, complete with short descriptions and links to show-related resources on the Internet (Web pages, UseNet newsgroups, FAQs, and mailing lists). There are also connections to the Web pages of many local and international stations and networks, and TV Net provides contact information where Web pages aren't available.

Finally, if you're in the television business, check out the TV Net classifieds for job listings, to post your resumé, or simply to scroll through the lists of equipment for sale.

TV Net is definitely a work-in-progress, and while it's far from complete, there is still a wealth of material to be found here. If you're an avid screen-watcher, turn to TV Net for those times when you can't find a good channel on the tube.

Get the showbiz skinny from Mr. Showbiz

http://web3.starwave.com/showbiz/

One of the sassiest and liveliest film sites around, Mr. Showbiz provides a unique mix of film reviews, Hollywood gossip, interviews, and star biographies. If you're interested in current cinematic culture, don't miss Mr. Showbiz.

The Mr. Showbiz site is divided into several sections, each with its own type of information. The Daily Dose tells you who was born and what happened in show business on today's date in history; it also has a vocabulary builder, which features a new piece of oh-so-trendy vocab every day. Scoop features, you guessed it, entertainment news, but it also has interviews and other timely features. Think of it as the Mr. Showbiz newspaper, with breaking news articles as well as longer features. When I was there, Scoop was commemorating the anniversary of James Dean's death with a thoughtful, picture-packed story.

Fig. 19.3

For a sassy glimpse into the entertainment industry, Mr. Showbiz can't be beat.

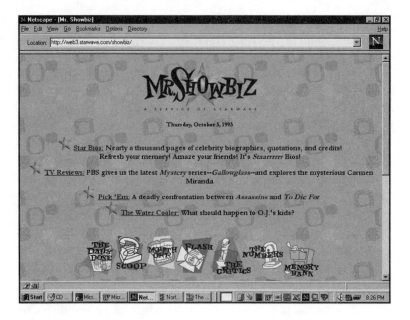

The Flash section also features news and interviews, but it also has amply illustrated celebrity profiles and a sampling of tabloid headlines from around the world. You'll also find a guide to what the "terminally chic" are wearing nowadays, and other frequently-updated items.

Of course, Mr. Showbiz has reviews a-plenty, with critical appraisals of the latest movies, TV shows, and music. Opinionated but always detailed and well-written, these reviews are fun to read even if you disagree with them. Forget the traditional one-to-five star rating system; Mr. Showbiz uses a thermometer or meter that goes from zero to 100. Just click on the scale to see an explanation of how it works—for example, the movies scale was illustrated with a listing of all of Spike Lee's movies, from the worst (*Crooklyn* rated only a 4) to the best (*Clockers*, which scored 96). This sample meter changes from time to time, so check back in to see who's targeted this week. For reviews of new movies and shows, click on the Critics icon.

As if all that isn't enough, Mr. Showbiz also features a smattering of columnists and a wide selection of message boards under the Mouth Off icon. If you disagree with a review, don't just sit there—stop by the message boards and let the writer know what you think! Finally, stop by The Numbers to see this week's lists of top-grossing films, highest-rated TV shows, best-selling books, and to check out Billboard's top albums and songs.

Best of all, Mr. Showbiz is free and doesn't require any registration. Just stop by any time and get the lowdown on the high and mighty!

If it's movie-related and it's on the Web, it's in Cinema Sites

http://www.webcom.com/~davidaug/Movie_Sites.html

Although it's not one of the more glitzy film sites on the Web, Cinema Sites is one of the best-organized meta-sites for film information. Find your way quickly and easily to any of the hundreds of movie-related Web sites using Cinema Sites' easy-to-understand outline format.

If it's movie databases you're seeking, Cinema Sites offers links to some of the best databases on the Web. Reviews? There are links to newspaper and movie reviews, as well as reviews that originate in cyberspace or on TV. Cinema Sites also gives you connections to film-related organizations, news sources, newsletters, and film festival information from around the world.

Fig. 19.4
Links to major newspaper's movie reviews make Cinema Sites a must-have for cinemaniacs.

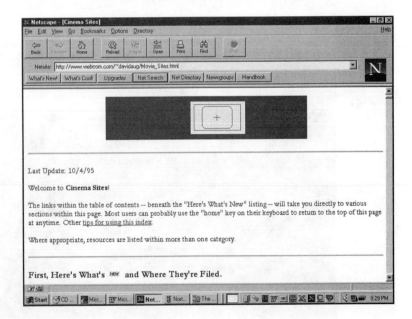

One nice feature of the Cinema Sites collection of links is that it provides not only mere links, but also short descriptions of most of the resources referenced. You can generally see at a glance whether a particular site is one you want to visit.

Cinema Sites uses an almost totally text-based screen that users with slower Net connections will appreciate. While it doesn't provide much information or graphics in and of itself, Cinema Sites is an invaluable link to the many rich sources of information that can be found on the Web.

Turn to the CNN Showbiz Main Page for news & reviews

http://www2.cnn.com/SHOWBIZ/index.html

Sometimes you don't want a vast database of information—you just want an authority you respect to tell you a few pertinent and interesting things. CNN's Showbiz page is perfect for that. It narrows the vast film and entertainment industry down a bit by focusing on the latest releases and hits, with a few art-house movies and lesser celebrities thrown in for balance.

Fig. 19.5
CNN's Showbiz site is excellent for keeping tabs on the entertainment industry.

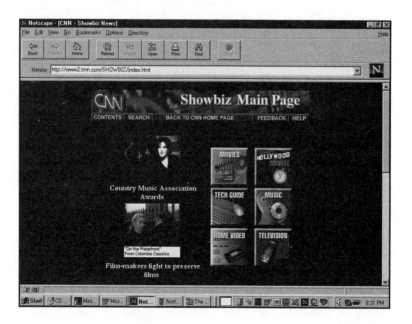

This site includes material from CNN's showbiz-related programs, such as Showbiz Today and the Hollywood Minute, which gives compressed summaries of up-to-date happenings in the world of music, television, and film. But there are also unique items to be found here. Click on Reviews for a respectable list of movie reviews, each one written with the level and direct style that made CNN famous. Click the Tech Guide icon to see reviews and stories on recent developments in the world of technology, including the Internet, video games, and movie animation.

The Music department provides news of the music world, along with some reviews, while Home Video lets you know about the movies most recently released on video. Finally, click the Television icon to catch up on your favorite shows.

The CNN site may not be the most comprehensive of showbiz sites, but it's certainly well-organized and readable. Instead of burying you in information, it feeds you a carefully-filtered and nicely presented set of stories. And if you still hunger for more, follow the links that CNN provides—an unusual feature in a corporate site like this one.

A diversity of opinions rages at film.com

http://www.film.com/

The problem with movie reviews is, well, movie reviewers—how can you tell whether you agree with the reviewer until you see the movie? But at this site, you can read *several* reviews. Then you can get a range of opinions and a better sense of whether you want to shell out seven bucks to see the film. That's the idea behind film.com, which never gives you just one movie review, but at least three at a time.

Want to see what the hype is around the latest box-office smash? Click on the movie title on film.com's home page, and you'll be taken directly to a short review. At least two (and sometimes more) other reviews are just a click away from this one, so you can start comparing opinions right away. If you've seen the movie, and you want to add your opinion to the mix, click on 2 Cents to post your own thoughts to one of the many bulletin boards.

Fig. 19.6

Film.com's claim to fame is that it provides several reviews of a single movie.

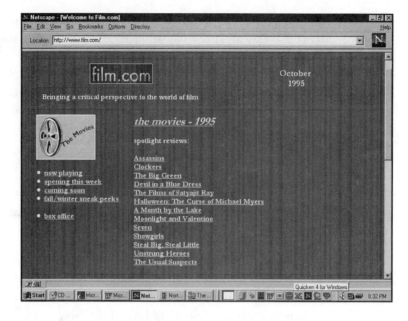

The top of the home page also gives you information on what movies are being released this month, and how the current crop of films are doing at the box office. Click on Now Playing to see all the movies that are currently showing in theaters—although finding a theater showing some of these movies is up to you!

Scroll down the page a little further for several more valuable departments, including a video/videodisc guide (with links to video store databases and a calendar of when movies are going to appear on video), a guide to film festivals around the world, and Cinecism, a collections of columns, essays, interviews, gossip, and more.

Down at the bottom of film.com's home page is some miscellany including the site's archives, a search tool, and hot links to other film-related sites. Some of these items are among the most useful tools on the site, so don't miss them—be sure to scroll down and check them out!

Overall, the quality of the reviews and information at film.com is quite high. The services here are free, and no registration is required, other than entering your zip code, which is optional.

Hollyweb Online provides useful, easy-to-access film information

http://www.ingress.com/users/spease/hw/hollyweb.html

While it's still a work in progress, Hollyweb Online already ranks among the slickest and most usable film-related Web sites. And its links to movie reviews are among the best the Web has to offer.

Fig. 19.7

Hollyweb aims to be the online film Mecca.

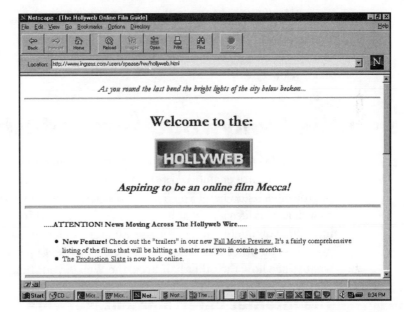

The Movie Preview and the Production Slate are both simple listings of movies about to be released or currently in production. Unfortunately, in some cases, there isn't much detail other than who stars in them and who's directing, plus when they're expected to appear in theaters.

The Hollyweb Cafe is where you can turn for informal ratings and reviews of current films, and where you can post your own reviews. It's worth a look if you're considering seeing a movie, but haven't made up your mind yet—you might find some useful advice among the postings here.

How many Steven Spielberg films do you think are in the list of the top 10 grossing movies of all time? The answer may surprise you. Stop by the All-Time Blockbusters department to find out. It lists not just the top ten, but all the movies that have grossed $100 million or more—a select bunch!

But probably the most useful part of Hollyweb Online is the searchable reviews index. Most searches will turn up dozens of reviews from a variety of sources, making this one of the Net's most valuable resources for film mavens. You can also get direct access to the movie review search engine at:

http://www.cinema.pgh.pa.us/movie/reviews

For an easy-to-use and not overwhelming Web movie guide, stop by Hollyweb Online. While it's not as complete as some other Web sites, you may find it's more your style.

More on the Hollywood film industry

Hollywood is almost synonymous with moviemaking in America. If you, like many people, are enamored of this fascinating and glamorous town, check out the sites listed here. You'll find information relating to the film industry, as well as services aimed at helping make you a star! If you're trying to break into film, you might want to make your start online, where many talent agencies and other film-related companies have set up shop. Or, if you just want to see how the other half lives, the Web is your ticket to ride.

The Internet Entertainment Network

http://hollywoodnetwork.com/

Most of this vast and intricate site is dedicated to Hollywood in all its consumerist glory. This site offers a variety of products and services for sale to movie fans as well as aspiring actors, screenwriters, and directors. Its organization is a bit confusing, and the home page is simply enormous, so it can be difficult to find what you want. But if you live in Hollywood, or want to, you owe it to yourself to see this site. But what's with those peach-colored backgrounds?

Hollywood Online

http://www.hollywood.com/

Hollywood Online is a good source for multimedia files—sound and video clips—from recently released movies. You can even download entire movie trailers (previews) here! You should have a fast Internet connection before surfing to this site, however; even the basic graphics take a while to download, and the multimedia files can be several megabytes in size.

Fig. 19.8
For movie clips and sounds bytes, visit Hollywood Online.

 TIP Most movies on the Internet are in a special format called QuickTime. See Chapter 2 for advice on installing and configuring QuickTime with your Internet browser.

Hollywood Spy-Cam

http://www.rfx.com/holly.html

This Web page is linked to a digital camera that takes pictures of the famous hillside Hollywood sign at regular intervals, and then uploads them to the

Internet. If you don't live within sight of the Hollywood sign, but wish that you did, make this page your Web browser's home page and you'll catch a glimpse of Hollywood every day. You can choose between a larger, 54K picture and a smaller, 14K one, or download a movie made up of all the pictures taken in the last 24 hours. Not all that useful, but fun!

 TIP   **See a site that you want to make your home page? In Netscape,** select Options, General, check the box that says Home Page Location, and type the name of the page you want to call home. Click OK, and the next time you start Netscape, you'll be taken directly to your new home page.

The Hollywood Mall

http://www.HollywoodMall.com/

If you're considering a move to Hollywood to break into the movie business, check out this virtual mall first. Stop by the talent agencies to see who's listed or to sign up yourself. Don't have a promo photo? Drop in on the film bureaus and photographers. When your portfolio is set, be sure to check out the listings of casting calls. The site includes everything the aspiring actor, actress, or model could want.

Cinema and movie reviews

The databases mentioned above aren't the only source of cinematic information and reviews. Some commercial sites also provide respectable collections of reviews, and you won't want to miss the ones listed here. Whether you're trying to find a review or looking for a theater to see your favorite movie in, you'll find it in one of these sites!

MovieLink

http://www.777film.com/?TP:National

Hello, and thank you for calling MovieFone! This site provides current theaters and showtimes for any movie you'd like to see, or tells you what's showing at any given theater. You have to live in one of the metropolitan areas served by MovieLink (about 20 nationally), but within those areas, the coverage is complete. And it's free—all you have to do is put up with the ads. It even links you to downloadable clips, trailers, or movie posters to help you browse and make up your mind.

Fig. 19.9
MovieLink shows you what's playing and where in your neighborhood.

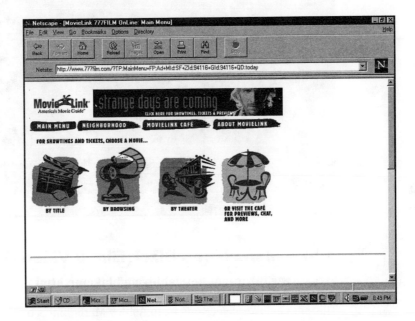

CineMedia

http://www.gu.edu.au/gwis/cinemedia/CineMedia.home.html

CineMedia is a good meta-site with lots of links to Web-based resources in the fields of Radio, Film, Television, and New Media. Its flashy, graphical interface is pleasant to look at, but sometimes the things you're looking for can be many levels down in the site, so be patient, and keep clicking. Everything is well-organized, so it's easy to find your way to what you want. However, there's not much original content here; it's mostly a collection of Web links.

Fig. 19.10
For a cornucopia of entertainment coverage, CineMedia can't be beat.

Ashley Marcelline's Black Film & Video Guide

http://www.inforamp.net/ashleyma/blakcine.html

This site features selections from Ashley Marcelline's book, which compiles information and capsule reviews on films that have Black stars, writers, or directors, or which contain themes relating to Black experiences or aspects of Black life. Unfortunately, this information isn't very comprehensive, so you still have to go out and buy the book. More useful are the many links to other sites relating to Black cinema, ethnicity and film, and related topics.

Science Fiction Film Archive

http://www.primenet.com/~laurus/scifi/scifi.htm

This home page is a quirky, bizarre collection of science fiction movie reviews and links to other science-fiction related sites on the Web. For film buffs, its most interesting resource is to be found on pages 2, 3, and 4—a lengthy list of SF movies with capsule reviews and a rating system that goes from 10 (epically good) to –10 (epically bad). The creators of this site clearly spend too much time watching strange science fiction films—but hey, that's why it's so interesting!

Fig. 19.11
The Science Fiction Film Archive contains a bizarre assortment of reviews and links to other sci-fi sites.

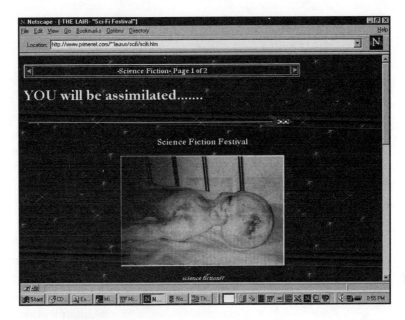

HBO Home Video Online

http://hbohomevideo.com/options.html

This site doesn't seem to have much of a connection to the cable channel of the same name. Instead, it's a useful reference for information and reviews of movies on video. It tells you what's coming soon, what's just been released on video, and what's in stores now. While it's not a comprehensive archive of movie reviews, each video review is formatted magazine-style, with lots of pictures and plenty of audio and video clips sprinkled throughout. It's a convenient way to learn more about a movie without having to read through a lot of text.

Teen Movie Critic

http://www.skypoint.com/members/magic/roger/teencritic.html

Roger Davidson is a sixteen-year-old movie critic who writes primarily for a teenage audience, though adults may find his reviews interesting as well! He's a thoughtful and unpretentious reviewer. Roger generally covers four movies per week: two new films and two classics. A good site to check out every week to see what he's added to the list!

Guide to Film and Video Resources

http://http2.sils.umich.edu/Public/fvl/film.html

This resource is maintained by a library student at the University of Michigan, and sometimes shows a preference for library- and librarian-related resources. Still, it's an important stop on the Internet movie highway. While many of its resources aren't Web pages, but rather Gophers, FTP sites, and UseNet newsgroups, they contain lots of information not available anywhere else.

MovieNet

http://www.movienet.com/movienet/

MovieNet gives theater locations and showtimes for Goldwyn/Landmark movie theaters. If you live in a city with one of these theaters (and you can find out from this site), this can be a convenient way to find out what's showing. There is also a smattering of movie reviews and promotional material. Not as comprehensive as MovieLink (mentioned earlier), but still useful.

Network television

Almost every one of the television networks has a Web site where you can get information about the network and its shows. In addition, there are sites listed here for PBS and for some other special-interest channels you can find on the airwaves.

Most of the network sites tend to be rather one-sided promotional devices, with little original content of their own. Still, if you're interested in the network's shows, this can be a good source of additional information, pictures, and biographies. Some sites also have bulletin boards where you can chat with others about your favorite sitcoms. For independent opinions, you'll have to turn to one of the review-oriented sites listed above.

CBS Television Home Page

http://www.cbs.com/

Here's where to turn for information on current CBS shows, including *60 Minutes*, *Murphy Brown*, and the *Late Show with David Letterman* as well as newer features like *Central Park West* and *American Gothic*. The site has promotional graphics and lots of information about each show, which fans may find interesting. Check out the David Letterman site, which features a complete archive of the daily Top Ten lists, right up to the most recent. There's also the "Eyeware Gallery," which features photos of the various shows' cast members.

Fig. 19.12
Visit the CBS Web site to find out what's hot on this network channel.

Welcome to Fox!

http://www.foxnetwork.com/

Stop by this slick site for an entertaining glimpse at the online wing of today's hippest network—the creator of the *Simpsons*, the *X-Files*, *Melrose Place*, and *Cops*. Sure, it's shameless self-promotion from Fox, but it's a fun site to visit anyway. Some of the sites are really involved; you can spend a fair amount of time just exploring them. And while you're there, pick up the latest schedule and find out what the stars of your favorite shows are up to.

NBC httv

http://www.nbc.com/index.html

NBC's home page features the usual network material: series descriptions, pictures, schedules, and more. It's also got biographies of all the actors and actresses appearing in NBC shows. Stop by Peacock Park before you leave for some novel items, such as a downloadable NBC screen saver and an NBC pachinko game. Be forewarned that this site, like the other network sites, is fairly graphics-intensive, so you'll want to have a fast Web connection if you don't want to spend all day waiting for the pictures to download.

Mind Extension University

http://www.meu.edu/meu/meu.html

Mind Extension University offers home-study courses for college credit, and even has accredited degree programs. Many of their course lectures can be found on the ME/U channel, where anyone can watch them. Stop by here to find out what courses are showing when, and to learn more about ME/U's course offerings and policies. Although the Web site isn't a fully developed educational site on its own, it shows promise.

PBS Online

http://www.pbs.org/

PBS has recently been targeted for Congressional budget cuts. Direct your Web browser to this site to scan the shows that might feel the ax—there are more than you might think! The PBS Online site is a thorough, well-organized companion to the many educational and informative public television shows airing on TV. It's more than just *Masterpiece Theater* and *McNeil-Lehrer*; there are a lot of fascinating and trend-setting shows covered here.

Fig. 19.13
The PBS site offers an advance look at a year's worth of programming.

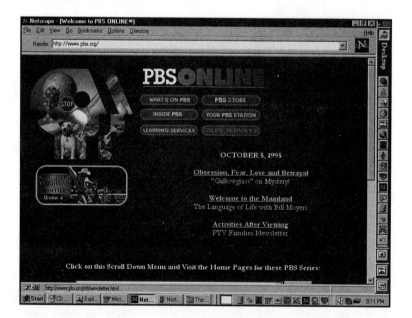

TV Episode Guide

gopher://wiretap.spies.com/11/Library/Media/Tv

Ever wanted to know about all the episodes of *Alf* or the *Brady Bunch*? Here's the site for you. This Gopher features plot summaries for every episode of dozens of series, from the silly to the sublime. Why? Maybe you're trying to complete your videotape archive of a particular series. Maybe you're nostalgic, or just curious. In any event, this link is a must for serious TV fans.

United Paramount Network

http://www.cdsnet.net/vidiot/UPN/upn.html

This is the unofficial UPN site, dedicated to UPN's new shows, among them *Star Trek: Voyager* and the quirky, groundbreaking *Live Shot*. There's lots of information on each show, beginning with a general summary and continuing with detailed information about cast, production, and more. The site also has information about UPN executives and affiliates, and provides detailed (and sometimes unflattering) ratings reports that would never show up on the official home pages of the established networks!

Cable television

Cable TV is home to a vast profusion of channels, shows, and markets. Many cable channels aren't limited by the same mass-market constraints as are the big networks, so their shows are often more innovative or experimental. Naturally, this attitude often meshes well with forays into the new medium of the Web. The experimental approach of a successful upstart cable channel may translate very well into a Web site that is both entertaining and inventive.

The sites listed below will help guide you through the increasing number of cable channels and will provide you with a wealth of information about your favorite channels once you've found the ones you like. These sites show how well the online medium complements the television medium.

VH1

http://here.viacom.com/vh1/

Nowadays, VH1 comes closer than anything else to being a dedicated music channel. Its Web site proves that VH1 hasn't (yet) wandered off into the twilight of nearly nonstop twenty-something game shows, "reality" TV, and animation filmfests. The focus here is music, and the artists who make it. From sound samples to video clips to exhaustive biographies, this site has plenty to interest the music video fan who really wants to watch music videos.

Fig. 19.14

See how your favorite stars on doing on the charts on the VH1 page.

SciFi Channel

http://www.scifi.com/

This is one of the few TV-channel sites that features more than just the channel's programming. While you'll find that here—complete listings of SciFi channel specials, theme weeks, and more—there are also links to SciFi-related magazines, Internet resources, and more. This is a lively and creative site. If you're interested in science fiction, you'll certainly want to click around here. Be warned that the opening screen, with its blinking- and scrolling-text animations, may take awhile to download, and probably will display best in Netscape Navigator.

Comedy Central's Totally Free Web Site

http://www.comcentral.com/com-menu.htm

Lotsa laffs! The Comedy Central is home to a number of hilarious shows (and, of course, some less-than-inspired humor) and its lineups often don't find their way into the newspaper's TV listings. Check out this site for the skinny on your favorite Comedy Central shows, like the over-the-top British sitcom *Absolutely Fabulous*, or Bill Maher's irreverent talk show *Politically Incorrect*. The site also offers goodies like downloadable clips, an online store where you can order Comedy Central merchandise, and a bulletin board of sorts, which features some of the more outrageous email sent to Comedy Central.

Fig. 19.15
The Comedy Central Web page is advertised as totally free. It's also totally funny.

Discovery Channel Online

http://www.discovery.com

This is truly one of the most innovative educational Web sites around. It's more than just the usual interactive schedule and show list; it's an educational tool in its own right. The Discovery Channel Online folks have created interactive "stories" with intriguing layouts and beautiful illustrations that teach you about a topic as you click through them. It's all done with the same flair and quality you see on the Discovery Channel on TV. This is one site you'll want to return to again and again. If you've got kids of your own or if you're a teacher, you'll be doing your kids or students a big favor by directing them here.

Letterboxed Movie TV Schedule

http://www.metronet.com/~martin/lbx.html

If you prefer watching wide-screen movies on TV in those narrow, black-margined "letterboxes" that preserve the original aspect ratio and show the whole screen, then this is the site for you. It lists only movies shown in this wide-but-short format. The site lists dates and showtimes for movies on the American Movie Classics Channel, Turner Classic Movies, the SciFi channel, and others. Plus, each movie is linked to the Internet Movie Database for complete, crosslisted descriptions (see the description of the Movie Database earlier). This site is an aficionado's movie-watching companion.

Film school and filmmaking

With today's computer technology, it's possible to make a movie on your desktop PC and upload it to the Web. Unfortunately, these movies are still unsatisfying; they tend to produce large files, so they take a long time to download, and the video quality is still largely unsatisfying: choppy motion in a small window.

But there are other ways an aspiring filmmaker can make use of the Internet. Check out the sites below for some concrete, practical advice about the business of making movies. There's even an online film school, where you can take courses and attend virtual "classes" without leaving your computer screen. Whether you seek help identifying financial backers or help loading film into your camera, the Web has sites to answer your needs.

Cyber Film School

http://www.io.org/~cincan/cfs.htm

An experiment in online education, this site features lectures, educational documents, and other resources designed to help you learn how to make movies. They cover all aspects of filmmaking from A to Z. There is even an Online Artist in Residence program featuring the contributions of an established filmmaker, and online Film Workshops where you can get real-time training and assistance through interactive Web pages and IRC (Internet Relay Chat) discussions. This virtual film school is a product of Cinema

Canada Online, whose site also features Action!, a newsletter filled with tips and information for filmmakers, and a directory of the Canadian film and TV industry. If Hollywood won't take your film ideas, maybe Toronto will!

Film School Confidential

http://wavenet.com/~tomedgar/fsc/fsc.html

This site posts several useful chapters from as-yet-unpublished books about film schools. It covers many topics an aspiring film student ought to know before filling out those applications: the relationships between the big-name film schools and Hollywood studios, how to apply, what to do once you get into film school, and so forth. This site is mostly text, but it's well-written and contains worthy advice. Check it out if you're looking for some level-headed, well-informed advice about film school in the real world, not just online.

The Indy Cine Filmmaker's Page

http://www.indycine.com/st/

As this page puts it, being an independent filmmaker means doing everything from raising the money for a film to buying the supplies and equipment to managing the personnel to getting the film distributed and sold. It's a big job, but luckily this page collects a number of useful resources in one place. If you're serious about making films, come here for links to equipment and supply stores, talent agencies where you can hire actors and actresses, guilds and organizations to help you out, and even some moral support from various other film- and production-related sites. It's all there for you—now all you have to do is make the film!

Hot TV shows

If you're a devoted fan of *Melrose Place, Mystery Science Theater 3000*, or another TV show, the following sites are right up your alley. The Web is home to a large number of TV show fan clubs and informational pages, and often these sites boast an almost unbelievable quantity of information about their respective programs.

Some of the sites listed below are run by the companies that produce these shows—for instance, Letterman's home page can be found in the CBS site. Others, like the MST 3000 page, are independent productions, acts of love created by people who are devoted to their shows or who simply have nothing better to do. Often the independent sites have better and more impartial information, but if you're a fan, you shouldn't miss the corporate-sponsored sites either.

Melrose Place Update

http://www.speakeasy.org/~dbrick/Melrose/melrose.html

Turn to this unofficial site for updates about Fox's prime-time twenty-something soap opera. If you missed an episode, here's the place to find out who did what to whom. The site also has links to other unofficial *Melrose Place* sites as well as the official-sanctioned one at **http://melroseplace.com/**. Between the official and the unofficial sites, you'll find out more than you ever wanted to know about the twists and turns of the show's plots and the questionable doings of its characters.

The Late Show with David Letterman

http://www.cbs.com/lateshow/

This home page is featured in the CBS site (above). It's the place to turn for the goofy CBS talk show host's Top Ten Lists, photos of Dave and of *Late Show* guests, or for tonight's guest list. There's even information on the *Late Late Show with Tom Snyder*, which airs after Letterman's show. But don't look here for information from Letterman's NBC days—this site covers the CBS version of Letterman only.

Lois and Clark—The Web Server

http://www.webcom.com/~lnc/index.html

Lois and Clark: The New Adventures of Superman is ABC's romantic adventure comedy based on the familiar story of Superman (a.k.a. Clark Kent) and Lois Lane. If you're a fan of this show, starring Teri Hatcher and Dean Cain, stop by this site for links to some Internet resources that will interest you. There are also some pictures and other information you'll want to check out.

Jay Leno

http://www.nbctonightshow.com/

After Johnny Carson left the *Tonight Show*, comedian Jay Leno took the helm. It was rocky at first, but now Leno has established himself among the pantheon of late-night talk-show hosts. This site, maintained by NBC, provides all the information you could want about the *Tonight Show*, including guest lists for the coming week, jokes from the show, funny headlines from around the country, and more. Best of all, the site is updated daily with video clips from the previous night's show. If you missed the *Tonight Show*, mouse over here to download some of the highlights.

ER

http://www.nbc.com/entertainment/shows/er/index.html

The official NBC site for the award-winning show about a big-city hospital's emergency room and its harried staff. Click here to find out more about the show's cast members, to read a summary of the show's premises, and to read up on the creators of the show, including author and one-time medical student Michael Crichton.

Matt's *Mystery Science Theater 3000* Page

http://cybercom.net/~fringe/mst3k.html

Mystery Science Theater 3000 has, in just a few years, achieved cult status for its send-ups of really awful movies. This page is brought to the Web by Matt Duhan, MST 3000 fan and keeper of several MST 3000 FAQ files. The site also features an episode list, song lyrics, and links to some of the many Internet sites devoted to this popular and wacky show.

Fig. 19.16
The MST Web page is every bit as quirky as the cult TV show.

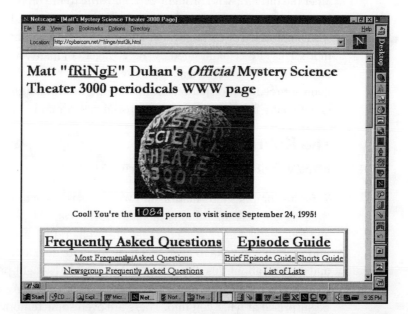

You Can't Do That On Television!

http://cctr.umkc.edu/user/rbarrow/ycdtotv.html

You Can't Do That On Television was one of Nickelodeon's most popular kids' shows—you know, the one where guests kept getting "slimed." You might be surprised to learn that the show ran for almost ten years—enough to support a large site on the Web here. This site boasts that it contains "over 3 megabytes of information," including FAQ files, images, and a bulletin board. There should be more than enough silliness here to entertain you for hours.

Directors

Just as the Web is home to fan clubs for actors and actresses, there are also many sites devoted to movie directors. These are the definitive sources of information on moviemakers, both classic and recent. Stop by to find out more about these geniuses behind the camera.

Orson Welles

http://www.voyagerco.com/CC/gh/welles/intro.html

Meet the director who brought *Citizen Kane* to life on the silver screen. This site presents some beautiful, carefully-chosen photos and movie stills along with summaries of *Citizen Kane* and other movies, in-depth essays, and more. This site is maintained by the Voyager company, which sells laserdiscs, so much of the material leads directly to Voyager order forms. Still, it's a good source for information about Welles. You will definitely want to see this site if you're interested in this directorial mastermind.

The Kubrick Page

http://www.lehigh.edu/~pjl2/kubrick.html

This site compiles information and Web links relating to the director Stanley Kubrick and his films, among them *2001: A Space Odyssey*, *Dr. Strangelove*, and *Full Metal Jacket*. It's a detailed and well-crafted site with enough information and links to keep you busy for quite awhile looking at pictures and reading about this director's fascinating and thought-provoking films. Even if you're not yet a fan of Kubrick's work, check this site out—you might be surprised at what you find. There are even some tempting rumors about Kubrick's next movie. You heard it here first!

Fig. 19.17
Learn how Kubrick directed his master-pieces on the Kubrick page.

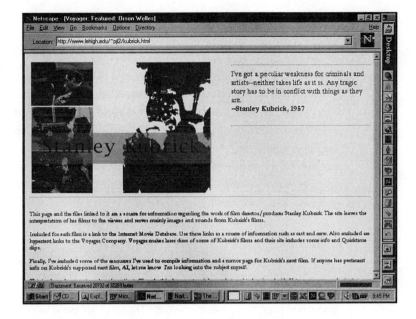

Woody Allen

http://www.idt.unit.no/~torp/woody/

This site proclaims itself as the source for "Everything you always wanted to know about Woody," and it might just live up to that claim. It's got a complete listing of Woody Allen's many films, and also includes references to Allen's books and essays. Finally, there are lots of links to other Internet resources of interest to fans of the world's most famous neurotic New Yorker.

The Hitchcock Page

http://www.primenet.com/~mwc/

Alfred Hitchcock practically invented the suspense movie genre with such classics as *Psycho* and *Vertigo*. Relive these films and find out more about them at the Hitchcock page. This site is a well-organized repository of Alfred Hitchcock memorabilia and trivia, from his biography to his filmography to coverage of the many awards he received during his career. There's even a section devoted to Hitchcock's work for television, which connoisseurs won't want to miss, especially the *Alfred Hitchcock Presents* series which aired in the early 1960s.

Akira Kurosawa

http://www.voyagerco.com/CC/gh/graphics/kurosawa.html

Turn to this page to find out more about the film director the Japanese call "The Emperor." Kurosawa's epic, cinematically breathtaking films include *The Seven Samurai, Ran* and *Yojimbo*. Now advanced in years, Kurosawa continues to create introspective, sweeping films with the eye of a painter and visual storyteller. This site is the place to learn more about this fascinating and brilliant director. Like the Orson Welles site described earlier, this page is maintained by the Voyager laserdisc company, so you can also order laserdiscs of Kurosawa films here.

John Woo Central

http://underground.net/~koganuts/Galleries/jw.main.html

If you like Hong Kong movies, kung fu movies, or any kind of action films, you'll love the work of John Woo. Director of such bone-crunching action films as *Bullet in the Head* and *Hard Target* (starring Jean-Claude Van Damme), Woo has made a name for himself as the purveyor of a unique style of gritty, pull-no-punches violence and black humor. This site presents a partial filmography and lots of pictures of the director, plus some movie stills. It also has links to Web sites covering other Hong Kong-produced movies.

Quentin Tarantino Central

http://underground.net/~koganuts/Galleries/qt.main.html

Quentin Tarantino has been redefining American cinema, first with the shocking violence of *Reservoir Dogs* and most recently with the smash hit *Pulp Fiction*. Click over to this page to see some pictures of Tarantino and stills from a few of his films. Plus, there are lots of links to the growing number of Tarantino-related Web sites, so this is a good first stop for anyone on the Tarantino trail.

20

Travel

● **In this chapter:**

- Browse the mind-boggling array of travel options with travel-specific link collections

- Take virtual tours of possible destinations and find out how you can fill your days and nights

- Once you've found your destination, hook up with online travel agencies for air, sea, train, or other transportation

- Locate the most comfortable (or cost-conscious) accommodations

Surfing, cruising, and trekking on the Web helps you surf, cruise, and trek in the real world . . . .

Would you like to ski the #1 rated ski resort in the world? How about diving in the coral reefs and caves around a private island in the Pacific? Maybe you want to feel the wind burning your face as your horse charges after a stray calf in a real cattle drive? Whatever your travel tastes, the first place to start trekking is the World Wide Web.

The Web holds a treasure of online travel brochures, virtual tours through exotic sites, and travel consultants who can book your trip—usually saving you a good chunk of money in the process. Some online travel agencies even let you book your trips with their interactive pages, showing you exactly what your options are and how to get the best rates, often giving you a discount for taking the real-world travel agent out of the picture.

TravelSource

http://www.travelsource.com/

TravelSource (voted one of the top five percent WWW sites) is a great starting point for any online travel planning. Though it doesn't list many options outside of its advertisers, it offers a fine cross-section of travel options. Some of its advertisers have full-featured Web sites, including excellent photography and maps. For those without Web sites, you can get electronic brochures through TravelSource's email system or printed brochures in regular mail.

The TravelSource welcome page features the Travel Store, an imagemap that leads to information about everything from trekking to wine tours. Click the subject that interests you, and you'll see links to information about (or the Web sites of) TravelSource advertisers who specialize in that field. Make TravelSource an early stop in any trip-planning effort.

Fig. 20.1
See travel pictures that will really whet your appetite on TravelSource.

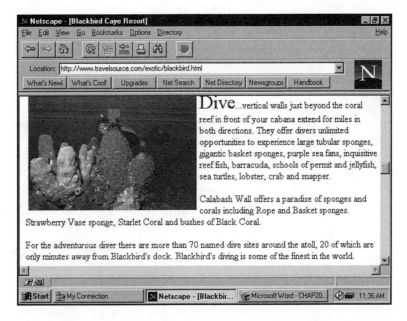

Information for travelers and would-be travelers: Lonely Planet

http://www.lonelyplanet.com.au/

Lonely Planet is an Australian online travel magazine with several twists. Its layout is noticeably more professional than most online magazines, putting it in a category with *National Geographic* and *Condé Nast*. Some of the articles read more like encyclopedia entries, but the information is never dull. The visual index (a world map with hotspots for several remote locations) is extremely intuitive and well-designed.

Furthermore, real travel buffs put this site together—who else would include the slogan "Get off your butt, get a guidebook, get a ticket and get a life!!!"? The affection the site's creators have for their subject is evident in the information you access with the Destinations search engine—into which you enter a city, country, or other subject, and from which you get informative articles in return.

CAUTION   **Because the information comes from Australia, look for some** trans-Pacific delays if you're in North America. Instances of slightly corrupted text (a few words replaced with garbage characters) are not uncommon.

Fig. 20.2
Lonely Planet looks as much like an encyclopedia as a travel brochure.

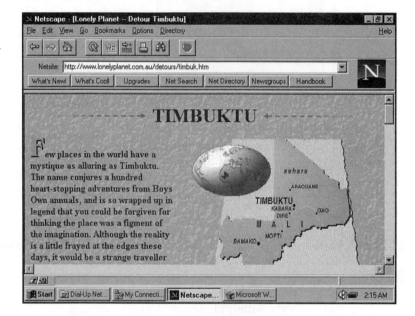

Fig. 20.3
The Destinations search engine allows you to get useful and current information about travel destinations worldwide.

Everything that's going on at your destination: City Net

http://www.city.net/

City Net is probably the most thorough resource on the world's cities. Whatever you want to know about your destination, City Net's probably got it. You'll find links for everything—currency exchange, government information, tourism, travel, and even weather.

To use City Net, click the region of the world that interests you on the welcome page—Germany, say. Then, on the Germany page, click the hyperlinked name of a city, such as Freiburg. The city page includes links to resources about that city, and offers you the chance to submit more via email.

TIP **You can bypass the multiple levels of organization by clicking the** Search hyperlink on the welcome page and entering the city that interests you in the text box.

Fig. 20.4
City Net offers easy access to resources about hundreds of world cities.

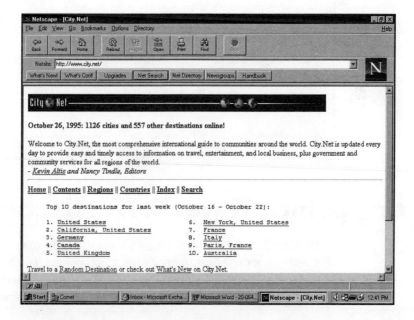

The Digital Retreat: Bed and Breakfasts on the Web

http://www.webcom.com/~neatstuf/bb/home.html

Webcom's Bed and Breakfasts on the Web page (one of the top five percent of Web sites) lists B&Bs by state, with direct contacts to many B&B-only travel advisors (usually called "RSOs"). While you're there, check out the Resorts on the Web page.

Use this site by clicking the link that leads to the Location Index—a list of B&Bs organized by state. First, select the state you want, then click one of the hyperlinks for an RSO or an independent B&B operator. Usually, the B&B and RSO pages have information about rates and availability.

Fig. 20.5
Bed and Breakfast on the WWW lets you find a rustic B&B on the decidedly un-rustic Web.

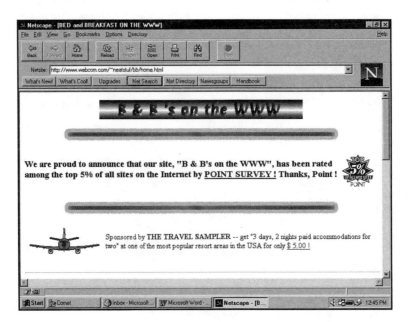

Starting points: Travel link collections

Even if you know exactly where you want to catch rays (or catch fish, for that matter), it can't hurt to check out your options. The Web has several sites that specialize in just that—options. These link collections are invaluable in guiding you through the jungle of online travel sites.

The sites usually include searchable databases, so you can cut the thousands of links down to a more manageable size. Even the ones without search features break the links down into areas of interest—like cruise ships, skiing, and hiking—or by location.

Hotel Anywhere

http://opendoor.com/rentals/homepage.html

Hotel Anywhere says it's "the Yahoo of travel," and it's pretty close. With what may be the largest list of travel-related links on the Web, it has something for every traveler. Its links include over 500 travel agencies, 50+ travel magazines, and hundreds of airlines, hotels, and cruise lines. You can also search its database by location, type of travel, and several other options.

TravelWeb

http://www.travelweb.com/

TravelWeb is another fine starting point for planning a trip. Though its interests are primarily hotels, you'll find plenty of links to other travel-related sites to round out the vacation. It offers a searchable database of member hotels.

Teleportal—for international travelers

http://teleportal.com/

Teleport Travel is one of the Web's best *international* travel agencies. You can purchase packages and tickets with your credit card through its very easy-to-use system.

GNN Travel Resource Center

http://gnn.com/gnn/meta/travel/index.html

GNN is a publisher of travel books and brochures, and its site reflects a good understanding of travel needs, desires, and woes. It includes savvy articles, a catalog of books, and much more information. It lists links to many other Web sites, including an electronic version of Fodor's Worldview Destinations (it chooses one per month and publishes it free, but you can order others).

Travel Hub

http://www.travelhub.com/

Travel Hub is something of a travelers' club, with a network of travel agencies to help you plan and save money on your trip. Its resource list goes beyond most others, including not only cruises, tours, and resorts, but things like subway maps to most of the world's cities and classified ads.

TravelEZ

http://www.travelez.com/

TravelEZ has another nice collection of links, including a better selection of off-beat services and locales than you find most other places. Its site also has a treasure hunt, where one person per month digs up a secret hotspot and gets a free vacation.

Get the knowledge for the voyage: Virtual tours, magazines, and more

Online travel magazines help you prepare for your journey, with personal accounts of trips by travel experts and enthusiasts.

Getting to an exotic locale is only part of the equation—you can't just sit in front of the TV in Cancun. This section shows you how to find some of the best ways to spend your travel time.

Condé Nast Traveler

http://www.cntraveler.com/

Condé Nast Traveler is the elite in travel magazines. True experts in hospitality, transportation, and tourism report on all aspects of the travel industry. The photography alone (much of which is available online) is enough to send many people to their travel agent. Don't miss its unique ability to sniff out the very best of any location.

Fig. 20.6
One of the most sought–after travel magazines, *Condé Nast Traveler*.

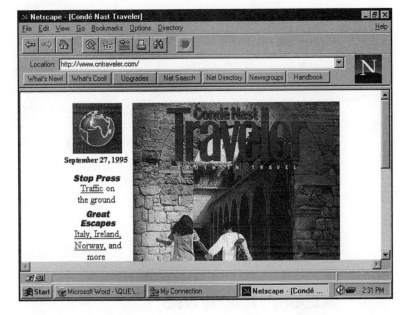

CEO Traveler

http://www.ceotraveler.com/

CEO Traveler is a quarterly online magazine for the upper crust of business travelers. Written mostly by the publisher and editor (two folks who must have permanent jet lag), it offers intricately detailed reviews of business trips around the world. It tells you where to stay, what to buy, where to exchange your money, and which rooftop revolving restaurants to patronize.

21st Century Adventures

http://www.10e-design.com/centadv/

Adventure travel is becoming big business. Formerly restricted to safaris, diving, and mountain climbing, adventure travel now includes fantasy camps (race cars, combat, cattle drives), dangerous remote research, and other hair-raising scenarios. 21st Century Adventures explores adventure travel every month, with a perfect mix of well-done photography and heart-pounding narrative. Even if your concept of adventure is trekking through Old World villages without a translator, you'll find plenty of interesting articles and photos in 21st Century Adventures.

Hawaii Net

http://www.hawaii.net/

If Hawaii is your destination, check out this home page first. It's mostly a list of links to other Hawaiian resources, but what a list. You'll find a visitors magazine (**http://www.thisweek.com**), a virtual tour of Hawaii (**http://www.cyber-hawaii.com/vacation**), and a fascinating page from the University of Hawaii's world-renowned aquarium (**http://www.mic.hawaii.edu/aquarium/**).

Biztravel.com

http://www.biztravel.com/guide/

Biztravel.com is an exceptional online magazine for business travelers. It includes stories from all over the world, opinions, and executive getaways.

Kilgore's Ranch Web

http://www.ranchweb.com/

If you prefer your fondue on a pitchfork, Kilgore's Ranch Web might be for you. Some of the site is geared to ranch operators (you can buy your own dude ranch through the Kilgore Real Estate Network), but you'll also find tips on attending a modern-day roundup.

Go Green Ecotourism Magazine

http://www.peg.apc.org/~tasol/gogreen.html

Go Green Ecotourism Magazine is an Australian/Canadian collaboration with environmentally friendly tourism news and first-person accounts of ecotours. Many of the articles have an eco-political slant, but they're much more humorous and insightful than heavy-handed.

Green Arrow Guide to Central America

http://www.greenarrow.com/welcome.htm

The *Green Arrow Guide to Central America* is an ecotourism guide of amazing proportions. It includes complete information on all Central American countries, including national parks and forests, nature conservatories, and educational expeditions.

Fig. 20.7
Green Arrow provides one of the most comprehensive guides to Central America available anywhere.

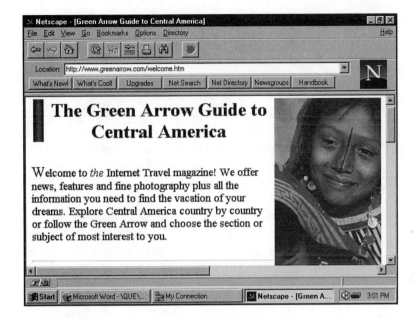

Whistler Resort—the #1 ski resort

http://www.whistler.net/

Whistler Resort is the bee's knees in ski resorts. Just ask the folks at *SKI* and *Snow Country* magazines, who rank Whistler the number one ski lodge. The Web site is very cool (no pun intended), with interactive tours of many Whistler facilities, stories from satisfied visitors, and links to other ski-related sites. You can even win a free dream ski trip in its interactive contest.

Club Med

http://www.clubmed.com/cm/pages/homepage

Club Med's home page takes you to the ultimate beach party (which now includes cruises and ski resorts). It's one of the most multimedia-rich sites on the Web, with videos, an audio welcome, and even a graphical weather report. You can make your reservations online, or just read the history, features, and stories of the world's most famous resort collection. See Club Med sites from Cancun to Colorado, including the Club Med 1 cruise liner.

Timberland Lodge

http://www.teleport.com/~timlodge/

The famous Timberland Lodge in Portland, Oregon takes its place in history seriously. As one of the most ambitious projects of the government's WPA (which put many people to work during the Great Depression), it stands as a monument to the craftspeople who built it. Dedicated in 1937, it has become an official National Monument—not to mention one of the finest ski resorts in the American west. The lodge sits near the 6000 foot mark on Mt. Hood, one of the best skiing mountains in the country.

The site features an intuitive interface to information about Timberland: an imagemap of books on a shelf. Click the Maps book to see maps of the slopes and the area surrounding Timberland. Click the Special Events book to see what's happening at Timerland, or click the The Hotel book to learn about accommodations at Timberland.

Fig. 20.8
Timberline is firmly rooted in U.S. history, and it's a thriving modern ski resort.

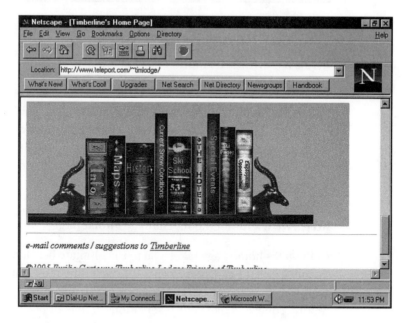

Outrigger resorts

http://www.outrigger.com/infoweb/

This site features almost 30 Hawaiian resorts and hotels, dining, and shopping favorites. You can book your reservations through the Web site, and you get a discount if you mention the site when you make telephone reservations.

Fig. 20.9
Outrigger brings Hawaii
to your desktop.

Can't leave your WWW access behind? Try an Internet cruise

http://www.centrum.is/com/vinland.html

Vinland Limited offers adventure cruises of the North Atlantic, including cold-water angling and Arctic photo safaris. One of the most interesting features of some of its ships (to a techie like myself, at least) is on-board Internet access. Now you don't have to leave your email behind when you go whale-watching.

infoGuide Florida

http://infoguide.com/

infoGuide is a Florida-only site with thousands of hotels and restaurants in a searchable database. It's very nicely done, but it's graphics-intensive so you may want to try the text mode on slower connections.

Travel Weekly

http://fenris.novalink.com:80/travel/

Travel Weekly knows the business. It's one of the leading magazines for the travel industry, but the Web site is aimed at travel consumers. In addition to hundreds of industry links, you'll find informative articles from Travel

Weekly's archives. This is one of the only online travel publications to include a deep industry perspective, making it a first-rate choice for seasoned travelers and beginners who want to know the secrets of the pros.

Destinations Magazine

http://www.travelersguide.com/destinations/destcovr.htm

Though still in its infancy, *Destinations Magazine* is a great example of an online publication. Articles are nicely illustrated, but not overdone (you won't wait a week while your browser loads the articles). The writing entertains and informs. When I visited the Destinations site, articles about fall in New England and driving camps for adults populated the site, and both offered valuable information for trip-planners.

Travel Assist

http://travelassist.com/mag/mag_home.html

Travel Assist is a monthly electronic magazine for travelers. It's nicely done, with pictures and well-written reviews of various U.S. and international locations. Its lodging directory is worth checking out. You can even take advantage of special travel discounts through *Travel Assist*.

Jamaica Tourism Board

http://www.jamaica-tours.com/Jamaica/

This is a fine virtual tour of Jamaica's hotspots by the Jamaica Tourism Board and Changes in L'attitudes Travel Agency. The tour is visually spectacular, with information and history about many of Jamaica's cities. You'll learn about golf, fishing, and diving activities, and even special Jamaican marriage trips.

Dive Travel Magazine

http://www.cruzio.com/~divetrav/

Dive Travel Magazine highlights exotic undersea destinations. Loaded with stunning photography and savvy travelers' information (even for your non-diving companions), this site is well worth a look.

Fig. 20.10
Check out the best places to sink around the world in *Dive Travel Magazine*.

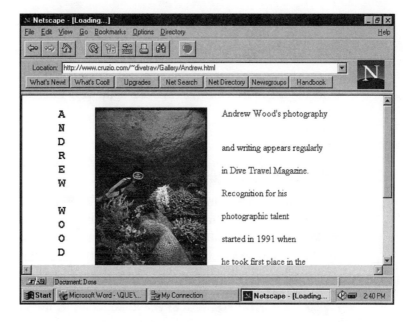

Getting there's half the work: Travel agencies

Travel agents have always been the best way to book trips. Their services, until recently, were traditionally free to the traveler. A recent commission cutback by major airlines has forced some agencies to charge nominal fees, but you'll still probably save more with an agent than you would on your own. Many agents (especially larger agents and corporate travel specialists) belong to groups that can get discounts not offered to the public.

PCTravel

http://www.nando.net/pctravel.html

PCTravel is a real travel agency, where you can book entire trips, even purchase airline tickets, on the Web. Fill out your password-protected travel profile—including seats and meal preferences, frequent flyer numbers, and any other special requests—and then book your trips. There doesn't seem to be a hotel function, but there are plenty of hotel companies in this chapter.

Access 2 Travel

http://www.kaiwan.com/~travel/index.html

Access 2 Travel is a list of online **travel agencies, grouped** by their specialties. It includes contests for free trips **and some very** interesting and unusual links.

AmeriTel

http://www.directions.ca/

AmeriTel is a Canadian travel agency. Once you register, you can book entire trips online. Its interface isn't quite up to the level of some others, but it makes up for it in depth. AmeriTel features more than simple point-to-point bookings, adding special events and promotions you'll want to check out before booking with anyone else.

 TIP   **AmeriTel, because of the demand on its Internet resources, makes** you choose among its five servers at its welcome page. There's no way to tell which server has a high load and which has a low load, so pick one at random and try another if the one you choose doesn't respond.

Cruise Vacations

http://www.cruise-vacations.com/

Cruise Vacations, a travel agency specializing in water trips, maintains a Web site with Carnival Cruise Lines trips. This is not the official Carnival Cruise Lines page, but it may as well be for the amount of information you'll find. You can't book trips online, but you can fill out the interactive form to obtain an email or telephone quote on the cruise of your dreams.

Amtrak

http://www.amtrak.com/

Train travel is convenient and cheap, and it keeps you close enough to the ground to see the sites you pass. Amtrak's site has maps, tips, and contests, but no schedules. Thankfully, railroad devotees keep an active list of Amtrak schedules on another site (**http://www.libertynet.org:80/~dvarp/amtrak/**).

Rosenbluth

http://www.rosenbluth.com/

One of the largest travel agencies in the world, Rosenbluth offers expertly-designed packages and individual trips. The reason to visit this site *after* you've tried others is that you'll find decent discounts on options most other agencies can't offer. Rosenbluth can even find discounts on some discount airlines—and that's practically unheard of. The package trips reflect the company's 100-year history of experience in worldwide travel.

Travel Discounts

http://www.traveldiscounts.com/discount/index.html

Travel Discounts offers (no surprise) travel discounts on airlines, lodging, car rentals, and cruises. For a fairly reasonable membership fee, you can gain access to the club's negotiated rates on almost every aspect of travel.

Sea & See Travel—for divers only

http://www.batnet.com:80/shicho/see%26sea/

See & Sea Travel is the world's largest divers-only travel agency, and its Web site is breathtaking (again, no pun intended). As if the site weren't enough of a draw for the underwater set, it offers a five percent discount if you book your trip through the Web. The photo album has a host of amazing shots of sea scenery, sea life, and sharks—See & Sea Travel is very proud of its shark collection.

Hotels

Most large hotel chains and some resort-type hotels now have Web sites with online booking and information. Most of those without online booking have toll-free telephone numbers, so you can check out the facilities on the Web and call in your reservation.

Westin

http://www.westin.com/

Westin's home page includes brochures, golf course layouts, and other information in downloadable Adobe Acrobat files. This site also has a link to download Adobe's acrobat reader, if you don't already have it.

Radisson

http://www2.pcy.mci.net/marketplace/radisson/

This is Radisson Hotels' Worldwide directory. Explore one of the industry's fastest-growing mid-luxury chains on this impressive multi-lingual Web site.

Hilton

http://www.hilton.com

Hilton's online guide includes a searchable database of locations and a great deal of information about each location. The online robotic concierge is an interesting touch.

Marriott

http://www.marriott.com/

The Marriott site offers information about Marriott hotels, Courtyard Inns, Residence Inns, and Fairfield Inns. In addition to the standard features (database searches of all locations, online booking, etc.), this site includes handy detailed maps to most of the locations.

Promus

http://www.promus.com/

Promus is home to Embassy Suites, Homewood Suites, and Hampton Inns, hotels tailored mostly to business travelers. This site provides you with information about each of Promus' hotel chains, and allows you to make reservations at any of them with a simple form.

Hotel Choice 2001

http://www.hotelchoice.com/

Comfort, Sleep Inn, Quality, Clarion, Friendship Inn, Econo Lodge, and Rodeway Inn share this site. It includes a searchable database and a good amount of information about each location.

San Francisco Reservations

http://www.hotelres.com/

Agencies and discount clubs that focus on one geographic area are often able to negotiate discounts with hotels and other travel-related businesses. San

Francisco Reservations is a fine example, offering negotiated discounts with many San Francisco hotels.

Florence's classic hotels

http://www.dada.it/

The Pendini Hotel and Hotel Brunelleschi in Florence have very nice online brochures, with photos and online booking. Hotel Brunelleschi is a 6th-century building with modern conveniences and classic touches, including a private museum.

Holiday Inn

http://www.holiday-inn.com/w_main.html

While not as fancy as some of the other hotels with Web sites, Holiday Inns (and their affiliated Express, Garden Court, SunSpree Resort, and Select variations) offer rooms all over the world. You're very likely to be able to locate a Holiday Inn in whatever city you're visiting, particularly if it's in the United States or Canada. This site allows you to make reservations at any of Holiday Inn's hotels.

Fig. 20.11
The Holiday Inn welcome page leads to information about hotels all over the world.

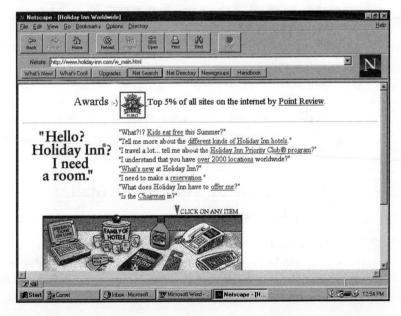

Bed and Breakfasts

"B&Bs" are rapidly gaining popularity among travelers. They are typically large (sometimes historic) houses with private bedrooms, a common area for dining, and shared bathrooms. Almost universally quaint and quiet, they are perfect for those of us who don't want to risk being woken up at 3 a.m. by rowdy conventioneers in the hallway.

B&Bs can be expensive, but smaller ones are remarkably reasonable. Even in the higher-end B&Bs, though, the cost is justified by the personal service, atmosphere, and accommodations.

The Internet Guide to Bed and Breakfast Inns

http://www.traveldata.com/biz/inns/

The Internet Guide to Bed and Breakfast Inns lists thousands of U.S. B&Bs. When you do a database search, it lists its members as "featured propertied" with other matching B&Bs in a separate section. The listings usually include a price range to help you match your needs with your means.

Time shares and long-term options

If you prefer a little luxury but you're not the type to have someone else cook your meals, you may want to check out the options in condominium time shares or travel apartments.

 TIP **Some hotels are geared to long-term stays, including all the** convenience of apartment living. The Residence Inn (**http://www.marriott.com/**) is a good example.

The Worldwide Time Share Mall

http://timesharemall.com/

For a site with not only listings but advice and articles on timeshares, the Worldwide Time Share Mall is hard to beat. It includes worldwide listings, contests, and even resort employment listings.

Global Travel Apartments

http://www.globaltrvlapt.com/gta/

Global Travel Apartments finds furnished apartments for business and leisure travelers worldwide. Its database includes quite a bit in Canada, the U.S., and Europe, with a few prime locations in the rest of the world. Online booking is free. Most of the apartment management companies offer extra services (secretarial, fax, and computing) for business travelers.

CyberRentals

http://opendoor.com/rentals/homepage.html

CyberRentals lists vacation homes for rent across America and around the world. All properties includes rates and facilities, but since most are independent, quality is likely to vary widely.

Home exchanges

Why would you put your valuables in storage and open your home to a traveler's family? Many people around the world do it. They're not (necessarily) crazy—they're saving money. With home exchange, you trade your home for someone else's for a time, rent free. This is not only one of the most economical lodging options, it's one of the most convenient. You'll get full kitchen facilities (which come at a premium at most hotels), plus you'll have contact with someone who really knows the area you're visiting. In some cases, you can even use the family car while the family is away. It's a bit more work than dialing a toll-free number and reciting your credit card number, but it's well worth it.

The International Home Exchange Network

http://www.magicnet.net/homexchange/

The International Home Exchange Network makes it easier to trade accommodations with new friends around the world. The listings here are mostly U.S.-based, but there are a few interesting international listings (most of whom seem to think "America" and "New York City" are the same thing). This site also includes a nice list of student postings.

The Internet Home Exchange

http://www.gorge.net/exchange/

The Internet Home Exchange (not to be confused with the above) is another home listing service. The site is under construction as of this review, but it has potential. Eventually, you may have a better chance at finding an international exchange here, as the site thoughtfully accommodates people who speak French, German, and Spanish.

Index

Complete and Return this Card for a *FREE* Computer Book Catalog

Thank you for purchasing this book! You have purchased a superior computer book written expressly for your needs. To continue to provide the kind of up-to-date, pertinent coverage you've come to expect from us, we need to hear from you. Please take a minute to complete and return this self-addressed, postage-paid form. In return, we'll send you a free catalog of all our computer books on topics ranging from word processing to programming and the internet.

Mr. ☐ Mrs. ☐ Ms. ☐ Dr. ☐

Name (first) ☐☐☐☐☐☐☐☐☐☐☐ (M.I.) ☐ (last) ☐☐☐☐☐☐☐☐☐☐☐☐☐☐☐

Address ☐☐☐☐☐☐☐☐☐☐☐☐☐☐☐☐☐☐☐☐☐☐☐☐☐☐☐☐☐☐☐☐☐

☐☐☐☐☐☐☐☐☐☐☐☐☐☐☐☐☐☐☐☐☐☐☐☐☐☐☐☐☐☐☐☐☐

City ☐☐☐☐☐☐☐☐☐☐☐☐☐☐☐ State ☐☐ Zip ☐☐☐☐☐ ☐☐☐☐

Phone ☐☐☐ ☐☐☐ ☐☐☐☐ Fax ☐☐☐ ☐☐☐ ☐☐☐☐

Company Name ☐☐☐☐☐☐☐☐☐☐☐☐☐☐☐☐☐☐☐☐☐☐☐☐☐

E-mail address ☐☐☐☐☐☐☐☐☐☐☐☐☐☐☐☐☐☐☐☐☐☐☐☐☐

1. Please check at least (3) influencing factors for purchasing this book.

Front or back cover information on book .... ☐
Special approach to the content .... ☐
Completeness of content .... ☐
Author's reputation .... ☐
Publisher's reputation .... ☐
Book cover design or layout .... ☐
Index or table of contents of book .... ☐
Price of book .... ☐
Special effects, graphics, illustrations .... ☐
Other (Please specify): _____ ☐

2. How did you first learn about this book?

Saw in Macmillan Computer Publishing catalog .... ☐
Recommended by store personnel .... ☐
Saw the book on bookshelf at store .... ☐
Recommended by a friend .... ☐
Received advertisement in the mail .... ☐
Saw an advertisement in: _____ ☐
Read book review in: _____ ☐
Other (Please specify): _____ ☐

3. How many computer books have you purchased in the last six months?

This book only .... ☐   3 to 5 books .... ☐
2 books .... ☐   More than 5 .... ☐

4. Where did you purchase this book?

Bookstore .... ☐
Computer Store .... ☐
Consumer Electronics Store .... ☐
Department Store .... ☐
Office Club .... ☐
Warehouse Club .... ☐
Mail Order .... ☐
Direct from Publisher .... ☐
Internet site .... ☐
Other (Please specify): _____ ☐

5. How long have you been using a computer?

☐ Less than 6 months   ☐ 6 months to a year
☐ 1 to 3 years   ☐ More than 3 years

6. What is your level of experience with personal computers and with the subject of this book?

	With PCs	With subject of book
New	☐	☐
Casual	☐	☐
Accomplished	☐	☐
Expert	☐	☐

Source Code ISBN: 0-7897-0645-8

7. Which of the following best describes your job title?

Administrative Assistant .... ☐
Coordinator .... ☐
Manager/Supervisor .... ☐
Director .... ☐
Vice President .... ☐
President/CEO/COO .... ☐
Lawyer/Doctor/Medical Professional .... ☐
Teacher/Educator/Trainer .... ☐
Engineer/Technician .... ☐
Consultant .... ☐
Not employed/Student/Retired .... ☐
Other (Please specify): _____ ☐

8. Which of the following best describes the area of the company your job title falls under?

Accounting .... ☐
Engineering .... ☐
Manufacturing .... ☐
Operations .... ☐
Marketing .... ☐
Sales .... ☐
Other (Please specify): _____ ☐

9. What is your age?

Under 20 .... ☐
21-29 .... ☐
30-39 .... ☐
40-49 .... ☐
50-59 .... ☐
60-over .... ☐

10. Are you:

Male .... ☐
Female .... ☐

11. Which computer publications do you read regularly? (Please list)

_____
_____
_____
_____
_____
_____
_____
_____
_____
_____

Comments: _____
_____
_____

Fold here and scotch-tape to mail.